THE FATAL CRUISE OF THE ARGUS

The Fatal Cruise
of the *Argus*

Two Captains in the War of 1812

Ira Dye

Naval Institute Press
Annapolis, Maryland

Library of Congress Cataloging-in-Publication Data

Dye, Ira.

The fatal cruise of the *Argus:* two captains in the war of 1812 / Ira Dye.

p.   cm.

Includes bibliographical references (p.) and index.

ISBN 1-55750-175-0 (acid-free paper)

1. United States—History—War of 1812—Naval operations.

2. Privateering—United States—History—19th century.

3. Argus (Ship)   4. Allen, William Henry, 1784–1813.   5. Maples, John Fordyce.   I. Title.

E360.D94   1995

973.5'2—dc20   94-17810

Printed in the United States of America on acid-free paper ∞

3 5 7 9 8 6 4 2

First printing

This book is for Evelyn.

Contents

Acknowledgments

THIS BOOK WOULD NOT HAVE BEEN WRITTEN without the help and encouragement of many persons over many years. I am especially grateful to four friends: First, Dr. Christopher McKee of Grinnell College for advice and support over these years, and for the sharing of his research on the officers and men of the early U.S. Navy. Then to Dr. J. Worth Estes, M.D., of the Boston University School of Medicine, for much information on early naval medicine and especially for his sound advice to me after reading a previous version of the manuscript; to Dr. W. M. P. Dunne for sharing his Resource Data Files for Henry Allen's ships and for providing his expert advice on naval architecture and other arcane matters; and to Mr. F. M. Chamberlain of the staff of Her Majesty's Prison at Dartmoor for giving much information on the history of the prison and for digging out facts on early-nineteenth-century Plymouth.

Because this project has been several years in the writing and almost fifty years in the research, two who provided significant help are now dead: Commander W. E. May, RN (Ret.) and Mr. Mahlon Janney, the great-grandson of Midshipman William Jamesson.

Beyond these, I am very grateful to many others: To Elisabeth Null for sharing her research on Commodore James Barron and Admiral G. C. Berkeley; to Virginia Steele Wood for materials from the Library of Congress; to Count Godwin Spani for the use of a copy of the portrait of John Maples; to

Rob Salzar for finding sources in the Alderman Library, University of Virginia; to Anthony F. Chiffolo for his skillful editing of the manuscript; to Robert Richardson for preparing the index; and to Anne White for timely help in copying the manuscript.

My debt to the librarians and curators of many libraries and archives for their assistance is enormous, but I must particularly mention Miss J. Milan, formerly at the Library of the National Maritime Museum, Greenwich; Miss Margaret Cook of the Earl Gregg Swem Library at the College of William and Mary; and not least, the several librarians at the oceanfront branch of the Virginia Beach Public Library for their skill and patience in obtaining many difficult-to-find resources through the Inter-Library Loan Program.

Introduction

THIS BOOK IS THE RESULT OF A VISIT I MADE in 1945, near the end of World War II, to Saint Andrew's Church in Plymouth, England, then a bombed-out shell. At the side of the churchyard a tombstone marked the grave of two American naval officers killed in battle in an earlier war, the War of 1812. Here, among headstones carrying the soft Devon names of many generations of the residents of Plymouth, were buried Lieutenant William Henry Allen, the twenty-eight-year-old captain of the U.S. Brig *Argus,* and eighteen-year-old Midshipman Richard Delphey, one of his officers.

My curiosity aroused, I wanted to know what chain of events had brought them to this resting place in a foreign land. A brief look in Mahan's history of that war gave the short answer. The *Argus,* in the midst of a highly successful commerce-destroying cruise in the English Channel, was defeated in a quick, hot battle by His Majesty's Brig *Pelican,* Commander John Fordyce Maples. Allen, Delphey, and several others on both sides were killed.

After World War II ended, I began to search more deeply into the history of the *Argus* and *Pelican* and found that it was more significant than Mahan's brief description implied. First, the cruise of the *Argus* was an important tactical breakthrough: Henry Allen and his crew proved that a small, nimble American warship, handled with daring and ingenuity, could create havoc in British home waters, right under the nose of the Admiralty and the then-all-powerful British Navy. Although American privateers operated successfully in

British waters, a real warship like the *Argus* was another thing entirely: she carried gun power much greater than any privateer and was committed to destruction rather than capture for profit, captures that were often retaken.

In a three-week rampage the *Argus* destroyed or captured twenty merchant vessels, drove up insurance rates by more than 25 percent, and threw mighty Britain off balance. Henry Allen's deft, bold strikes into the enemy's own bays and channels showed the American public and the navy the way to effectively attack this powerful adversary.

The U.S. Navy sent other ships to try to repeat the exploits of the *Argus,* but none came near her success. The feats of the *Argus* were not duplicated until World War II, when long-range American submarines operated with terrible effectiveness in enemy home waters.

In the process of learning the story of the *Argus,* I began to appreciate Henry Allen himself as an important, engaging, and complex person. Henry Allen was a paradigm of the new navy of the new United States. He and the other young officers of those times *created* the navy, often in the face of opposition from the political greats of the nation. The brash, hotheaded personalities of these young officers put an indelible stamp on the navy's esprit. Their bold, impetuous actions became the navy's traditions and set the service on the path of honor, valor, and mastery of the sea that it still follows.

Henry Allen was one of the most enterprising, spirited, and charismatic young officers in the early U.S. Navy. Handsome and candid, he held the loyalty of the sailors and officers that served under him, and he gave his full loyalty, sometimes too uncritically, to those above him. He was driven by an ardent sense of personal honor, sometimes carried to excess, sometimes verging on arrogance. Like a character in an Aeschylus drama, Allen's excessive sense of honor was his flaw. When it grew to hubris, it took him to his death.

Henry Allen himself participated in nearly every important action of this small, intrepid navy: the Quasi-War with France, the Barbary Wars, the *Chesapeake-Leopard* Affair, and two of the most important battles at sea in the War of 1812. He often had a central role in these events, a rare thing for a young lieutenant.

His adversary on that fatal August day in 1813, Commander John Fordyce Maples, Royal Navy, was Henry Allen's diametric opposite. John Maples was mature, cool-brained, and competent. He was an immensely experienced officer who had entered the British Navy two years before Henry Allen was born, and in 1813 at age forty-three had twenty years of war under his belt, including action in two of the major sea battles of the age, Copenhagen and Trafalgar.

John Maples exemplified the mainstay, the solid backbone, of the officer corps of the British Navy during this golden age of warfare under sail. This central strength of the Royal Navy was not made up of dashing, smartly turned out young aristocrats, as is often told in fiction, but of resourceful, courageous men drawn to the sea as boys from the great emerging middle class of British society. This was an immensely capable and powerful navy: highly organized, self-confident, proud of its history and hard-won traditions. It was arguably the best navy that has ever existed. John Maples contributed to, and was shaped by, its excellence.

This book tracks the colorful and exciting lives of these two very different men as their separate paths take unexpected twists and turns in the eventful times between the end of the American Revolution and the closing of the Age of Napoleon. The exploits of Henry Allen and John Maples, men who lived the adventures of that time, have more bite and immediacy than fiction. Their stories, the true stories of two important actors in an era of decisive battles and pivotal events, provide us with an extraordinary historical drama.

There is another dimension to this narrative: As I began to dig into the history of the *Argus* and *Pelican,* and the portraits of Henry Allen, John Maples, and their men began to take shape and color, I found that whenever I went to look for some needed fact or key record, perhaps the physical appearance, or the tattoos, or even the life story of some long-forgotten sailor, the wished-for item was almost always there, ready to be picked up and fitted into the puzzle. This is highly unusual in historical research, even for a period as well documented as the Napoleonic Era. I was fortunate to be able to draw together a huge amount of material about the *Argus* and *Pelican,* the two captains, their men, and the events they helped to shape. There were letters and journals, logs and prisoner-of-war lists, and more. All helped delineate an accurate, exciting picture of that age.

These two captains, and the men that sailed with them, and the others whose lives became entwined with theirs or touched by the cruise of the *Argus,* played their assigned roles in the great events of those times. Their story is the story of the age, told here from the viewpoint of these lesser players, rather than from the usual perspective of the Great Men who directed the events.

So here they are, Henry Allen and John Maples, their men and their ships. And here are the others in the story: poet Joel Barlow; Commodores William Bainbridge, John Rodgers, James Barron, and Stephen Decatur; Georgia Senator William Crawford; Admirals Sir Hyde Parker and the Earl of St. Vincent; flogging captains William Henry Ricketts and Hugh Pigot; the immortal Nelson; and Napoleon himself.

THE FATAL CRUISE OF THE *ARGUS*

PART ONE

WILLIAM HENRY ALLEN, U.S. NAVY

CHAPTER ONE

Midshipman to
Mediterranean Man

THE HARVESTED FIELDS SLOPED DOWN to the blue-black, white-capped water of Narragansett Bay. The wood lots, behind their stone fences, were brilliant with the yellow of hickories and the scarlet of maples. The day was 21 October 1784, and in the town of Providence a baby was born to Sarah Allen and her husband, Major William Allen. Coming into a growing family, this was a welcome child, especially for being the first son. He was christened William Henry and joined two older sisters, Elizabeth, eight years old, and Sarah, just barely two.[1]

The Allen's were distinguished and respectable in Providence society. William Allen had joined Hitchcock's Regiment less than a month after Lexington and Concord, had served through the entire Revolution, and had been in every action in which the Rhode Island forces were engaged. He had witnessed Burgoyne's surrender at Saratoga and been present at the British defeat at Yorktown, standing in front of his company to watch Cornwallis's troops march out of their lines.[2]

He had retired from active service in late 1783 with the brevet rank of major but with his health permanently damaged.[3] Later, in 1799, he was appointed as brigadier general of Rhode Island's militia forces and elected as sheriff of Providence County.[4]

He had married Sarah Jones of Newport on 24 January 1776. The press of events had hastened the marriage: their oldest daughter, Elizabeth, had been born just three months later.[5] The second daughter, Sarah Bowen Allen, had followed in October 1782. When William Henry was born in 1784, his father, now thirty-two, had been out of the army for less than a year.

Other children arrived later: Julia Ann in 1787, Thomas in 1788, Harriet in 1793, and Frederick Augustus in 1795, but only Sarah, William Henry, and Thomas survived into adulthood.

Both parents wanted Henry to follow a civilian career: Major William Allen's wartime experiences had taught him the "hardships, the dangers and the horrours of a military life," and he had no wish to "encounter them again in the person of his son."[6] So Henry's schooling was aimed at preparing him for a liberal education at one of the colleges in New England, and it was expected that he would follow a life of peaceful pursuits.

No information has survived concerning what preparatory school he attended or just how far he advanced. His later journals and letters show that he learned grammar and logic, although he had some trouble with spelling. He learned mathematics well: the summarized navigation work in his journals is thorough and neatly laid out from the very beginning of his career at sea. He also became a skilled penman, writing letters that are still easy to read. He was a more than passable artist, often creating well-executed sketches in blank spaces in his journals. Henry Allen himself probably drew the only surviving picture of him, a portrait in profile.[7]

In 1797, when Henry was twelve, his mother died. Major William Allen remarried in September 1798 to Mary Nichols of Stratford, Connecticut. She was a loving stepmother to the Allen children for all of her and their lives. The new marriage produced four more children: three baby girls, all named Mary, who all died before their second birthdays, and a son, George Nichols Allen, Henry's half-brother, who survived to become an adult.

At about this time Henry began to "pant . . . for a more active life" than was planned for him and became eager to enter the navy. His father's service in the Revolution gave him a precedent, and his maternal uncle, William Jones, a Newport merchant and politician, had been a captain of marines aboard the Continental Navy Frigate *Providence*.[8]

It is also likely that Henry's decision for a life in the navy was influenced by the excitement of the undeclared naval war with France, the Quasi-War, which in 1798 was in full blaze, with French privateers capturing American merchant vessels off the coast of the United States. The Quasi-War occupied much of the attention of John Adams's administration from 1797 onward. President Adams strongly favored the development of a navy to keep the United States from becoming entirely dependent on England for protection against the French, and the embryo American Navy was hastily expanded. But in spite of heroic events like the capture of the French Frigate *Insurgente* by Captain

Thomas Truxtun in the U.S. Frigate *Constellation,* the "pressing remonstrances" of his father kept Henry in school for the time being.[9]

At last, in early 1800, William Allen and his new wife gave in to Henry's pleadings, and through the influence of Senator Ray Greene of Rhode Island Henry was appointed a midshipman by a warrant dated 28 April 1800.[10]

Henry Allen was fifteen years old when he entered the navy. From this time forward his tie with his family was mostly through letters—only rarely was he able to get home to Providence. He was an excellent correspondent, writing particularly to his father and his older sister, Sarah. His father and sister kept their letters from him, and more than fifty of them survive today, in spite of gaps of some years.[11] The record is one-sided: none of their letters to him survive.

Young Midshipman William Henry Allen reported aboard his first ship in late May 1800 at Newport, Rhode Island. His earliest letter to his father was written on 30 May and datelined "On board the Frigate *Washington.*" His reception aboard the *George Washington* gave him an enthusiasm for the navy that rarely waned during his career: he was "immediately introduced into the Cabin" and to the senior officer then aboard, Lieutenant Phillips. Later he met Lieutenant John Warner and Sailing Master Augustus Hallowell, who became friends and mentors to him, and Lieutenant Wilson Jacobs, the ship's first lieutenant, who was temporarily in command. Henry immediately decided that he "like[d] the situation very well."[12]

The *George Washington,* a converted merchant ship, was far from being a genuine, effective frigate. She had been purchased into the navy in late 1798 along with several other merchantmen as a response to the depredations of French privateers and, although well-built, was a slow sailer. Large for a merchant vessel, she was small for a frigate—only 108 feet long on the keel and about 600 tons—compared with the big American frigates like the *Constitution* or the *United States* that were about 175 feet long and more than 1,500 tons. She was rated as a twenty-four–gun ship and was fitted with twenty-four 9-pounders and eight 6-pounders—very light armament for a frigate.[13]

Henry was thrown right into the duties of the ship. The midshipmen—there were nine of them on board, and there would soon be seventeen—stood two-hour watches in port after 8 P.M.[14] After asking his father to send his "coarse Cloathes, Hatt & Shoes," he closed his first letter, "It now being almost ten O'Clock [it is time for] my next watch. . . ."[15] School, home, and the easy times of boyhood were now behind him.

Henry Allen's first cruise in the navy was a short one: the ship left Newport on 14 June to run around to Philadelphia. By early 1800 the war with France was winding down; the American diplomats of the Ellsworth Mission were in Paris, discussing peace with Talleyrand; and Napoleon's plans called for a period of friendship with the United States. At this time he was incubating, in some secrecy, a grand scheme for a maritime alliance of neutrals against England in which he hoped to enlist the United States. This was to be followed by the establishment of a French empire in Louisiana and the American West.[16]

But information about these larger affairs was not available on board the *George Washington,* and the French were still seen as an enemy. So this short trip was made with all guns loaded and, even so, with some trepidation: only about one-third of the crew was on board, all of them new to the ship.

Just southeast of Cape May, at 10 A.M. on the second day out, the *George Washington* sighted a "large sail" and, though short-handed, sent the crew to their quarters, ready for battle should she prove to be French. The stranger was a warship, and her course was taking her across the *George Washington's* bow. Henry Allen, trying out his new nautical vocabulary, said that she was "standing ath[w]ort our fore foot." At noon the stranger tacked and began to close. The *George Washington* "hoisted the stars and stripes," and the stranger immediately ran up "St. George's Cross" and then broke away without speaking them.[17] She was a thirty-six–gun English frigate, Henry Allen's first contact with the British Navy.

The *George Washington* made her way up the Delaware River, and as the stream narrowed she passed through rural prospects of fields and farms, past Stony Point, Penn's Neck, Wilmington, and Marcus Hook, and on the seventeenth, in the early evening, anchored abreast of the navy yard, on the southern edge of Philadelphia. In the morning the ship was moored to two anchors, and the officers and crew settled down for a stay.

A few days later Captain William Bainbridge took command of the ship.[18] Bainbridge was twenty-six, a young, newly made captain, and was on his way to becoming one of the most famous men of the early U.S. Navy. Tall and muscular, he was a hard driver and strict in his discipline. During past voyages as a merchant skipper he had put down two mutinies with his fists and will power—a useful skill in early–nineteenth-century seafaring.[19]

His regime aboard the *George Washington* quickly became the opposite of what the men in the crew had experienced under the easy-going temporary command of Lieutenant Jacobs. Bainbridge told one of the crew who tried to approach him with a request, "I don't allow a sailor to speak to me at all," and he normally addressed the sailors as "you damned rascals"—hardly a morale-building approach.[20]

Bainbridge's reputation preceded him aboard, and nineteen sailors, including four petty officers, deserted shortly after he arrived.[21] John Rea, a sailor-chronicler of events on board the *George Washington* and something of a professional malcontent, gave highly critical glimpses of Bainbridge from below-decks. Rea told of his shackling sailors hand-and-foot in irons and hitting them with his fists or the flat of his sword. But although he was apparently quick to strike, he was not a flogging captain: over his long career he had one of the lightest punishment records in the navy.[22]

With his officers, Bainbridge was a more tolerant person, and in Henry Allen's fifteen-year-old eyes he "appear[ed] to be a fine man, much the Gentleman and is reckoned a good seaman."[23] The trait of "gentleman" in the makeup of an officer was important to Henry Allen, even from his first days in the navy.

Bainbridge immediately won over his midshipmen. A couple of days after coming aboard he called all of them into his cabin for a first meeting. They found that he knew their names, personally recognizing each of them in turn. After some discussion of shipboard duties, Captain Bainbridge gave the midshipmen the address of his house in Philadelphia and, as written home by Henry Allen, "desired us when we came on shore to call and refresh ourselves as we would do at our fathers'."[24]

The portrait of eager, clean, well-scrubbed youths entering on their country's service is probably a reasonably accurate picture. But John Rea saw the midshipmen on board differently, describing them, no doubt including Henry Allen, as "brats of boys, twelve or fifteen years old . . . strutting in livery about [the] decks, damning . . . old experienced sailors."[25]

These two pictures are not inconsistent: the view from below is not the same as the view from on top, and Rea's bias toward the mids was the traditional view from the lower deck. For each midshipman it was a necessary but difficult task to earn the respect of the sailors. Later events show that Henry Allen had the open personality and easy manner that made him very good at this.

Shortly after taking command, Captain Bainbridge tightened up the ship's watch schedule, organizing it into two watch sections, starboard and larboard. Henry told his father, "I am now called upon to do my tour of duty upon deck four hours, on and off."[26]

Bainbridge would need all of his short experience plus a keen sense of judgment and a good deal of tact to handle the delicate mission that the *George Washington* was to undertake: to carry the American tribute to Algiers.

The petty Moslem states along the Barbary Coast of North Africa—Morocco, Algiers, Tunis, and Tripoli—had for centuries enriched themselves by capturing European ships, enslaving the crews and looting the cargoes. The recently independent United States was no longer protected by British treaty arrangements with the Barbary powers, and these corsairs viewed American merchant ships as particularly easy game, to be had merely for the hunting.

Wars, even small ones, are highly expensive, and nearly all of the European nations had long since found it cheaper to bribe the Barbary princedoms with tribute and pay ransom rather than fight. The great French admiral, Count D'Estaing, said that bombarding the Barbary pirate towns was "like breaking windows with [gold] Guineas." The Barbary princes well understood this, and after one heavy bombardment by the French in the seventeenth century the dey of Algiers, informed of the cost of the effort, said that for "half the sum, he would have burnt down the whole city" himself.[27]

Because in the 1790s there was no other way for the weak and distant United States to solve this infuriating problem, a treaty was worked out with Algiers, the strongest and most aggressive of the Barbary States. This treaty was signed on 5 September 1795 by the dey Hassan Bashaw and Joseph Donaldson Jr., a diplomat sent over for the purpose, and approved by the Senate in March of 1796.

This treaty called for payment to the dey of Algiers a large ransom, $525,500, for the 115 American sailors he was already holding as slaves, plus presents and commissions that brought the total up to $642,500, an immense sum for the struggling new American government. Then there were also annual payments of tribute in the form of naval stores and other merchandise, as well as a 538-ton frigate to be built and delivered. For these bribes he was expected to leave American ships and sailors alone in the future.[28] This would all prove quite expensive: before the situation was finally cleared up in 1815, the United States would pay tribute to the deys of Algiers for seventeen years, as well as building several vessels for them.

As things stood in 1800, the United States was three years behind in the treaty commitments to Algiers, and the Adams administration decided to send the tribute. The *George Washington* was assigned to carry it.

Early in the evening of 23 June she unmoored from her river anchorage and was hauled in to a wharf in the navy yard. There her hold was cleared, and most of the iron ballast along her keel removed to allow for the weight of the tribute cargo.[29] Born as a merchant ship, the *George Washington* was more roomy in her hold than most warships, and she was apparently selected for this reason. But as a fighting ship, she needed enough freeboard to keep her gun deck well above the water and, therefore, could not be loaded so deeply as during her former career as a merchant vessel.[30]

Not only did she need most of her capacity for the expensive tribute cargo, but in addition the Navy Department had given Captain Bainbridge permission "to take an adventure with him," although "the size of the adventure must not interfere with the cargo."[31] This was a profitable opportunity indeed: Bainbridge could carry some cargo of his own to sell and trade for his own account, in Algiers or wherever else the ship might go. How much was left to his own sense of judgment and restraint.

Henry Allen recorded in his journal the rich variety of the shipload of tribute: coffee, tea, fish in barrels, cloves and pepper, mahogany planks, looking glass and tin, gunpowder and nails, and much more.[32] Of course, in addition to the tribute, the crew had to find space to stow their own water casks, food for 130 men, all of their boatswain's, carpenter's, gunner's, and purser's stores, and their powder and shot.

The ship completed loading at the wharf by about 3 or 4 August, got a Delaware River and Bay pilot aboard, then moved back out into the stream and downriver to the mouth of the bay and there anchored to wait for favorable weather.

This was to be Henry Allen's first real cruise, and in his last letter to his father before the ship's departure he was excited and a bit homesick, but conscious of the drama of his situation, aware that sea voyages were dangerous and uncertain: "We . . . shall sail by God's Blessing day after tomorrow on a voyage to Algiers . . . [with] sundry articles for the Dey. . . . I now bid you a short adieu, but should it be the last, you shall have the satisfaction to hear of my good conduct . . . as an Officer and a Gentlemen. . . ." Henry Allen had a strong interest in his personal honor, even as a fifteen-year-old midshipman.[33]

At midnight on 8 August 1800, with "moderate breezes and fair weather," the *George Washington* got up her anchor and "made sail for sea." Henry Allen was rapidly picking up the sea lingo, the vocabulary of his new profession. At 1 A.M. the ship dropped the pilot, and at two o'clock the crew could see the light at Cape Henlopen some nine miles to the north and west.

It was now time for a new midshipman to begin his practical training in navigation, and Henry Allen noted in his journal, ". . . from [Cape Henlopen Light] I take my departure, it lying in the Latitude of 38°—46'N, Longitude 75°—5'W."

The entries in his journal show that Henry Allen's first days at sea were much taken up with learning the science and art of navigation. This early training was under the guidance of Sailing Master Hallowell, who helped him over the rough spots and let Henry use the tiny desk in his stateroom as a quiet place to work up his calculations.[34] It would be some time before Henry became deft and skilled enough to handle his "day's work" as a navigator with only a few hours' effort.

Perhaps a third of a navigator's daily work in those days was "dead reckoning": keeping track of the compass course being steered and measuring the ship's speed by casting the log over the stern and counting the knots run out on the log line during one turning of a one-half-minute sand glass. The courses and speeds were recorded on the traverse board, and once during each watch the course made good and the distance run were laid out in pencil on the ship's chart.

But the navigator's real work was in the domain of nautical astronomy and celestial navigation: only by measurement of the sun, moon, and stars could the ship's position be accurately fixed. And this required, every day, several periods of a few minutes for taking sextant observations of the sun, stars, or moon, intermixed with hours of tedious calculations by hand, with pencil and paper, using the sextant data together with numbers extracted from the *Nautical Almanac* and its companion volume, the *Requisite Tables*.[35]

The most difficult problem in navigation was determining the longitude accurately. For a ship carrying a chronometer, a recently developed, extremely accurate clock sturdy enough to be carried on shipboard, this problem was much simplified. But chronometers were difficult to make and were scarce in 1800, even on naval ships. There is no indication that the *George Washington* carried one on her voyage to Algiers, although she probably carried one or more normal, not-too-accurate, wind-up clocks.

For ships lacking chronometers, the usual way to get the longitude was by lunar distances. This was an intricate, difficult process that required measuring the fast-changing angles between the moon and the sun, or the moon and one of six particular stars, then matching the readings with tabulated angles in the *Nautical Almanac*.

In comparison, determining the latitude was easy: the altitude of the sun as it crossed the ship's meridian at noon, or the altitude of one of the navigational stars crossing the ship's meridian during morning or evening twilight, when the horizon could be seen, or the altitude of Polaris, the North Star, each gave an accurate latitude after some fatiguing calculations.

So Henry Allen's days as a tyro navigator were full. In midafternoon, if the sun and moon were both visible and high enough, fifteen degrees or so, to allow accurate observations, he took his sextant in hand and measured the sun's lunar distance, and after an hour or so of calculation had the ship's longitude. After running his noon position forward on the chart to the new longitude, he was free until sunset, when he measured the bearing of the setting sun to get a correction for the ship's compasses. Then during evening twilight, while the horizon was still bright enough to see, he took his sextant in hand again to get the altitude of one of the navigational stars as it crossed the ship's meridian, or to measure the altitude of Polaris. After perhaps an hour of mathematics, he had an accurate latitude to put on the chart and to cross with his longitude.

In the morning Henry Allen was up before twilight to catch a morning star for latitude, or to take the lunar distance of a star to get the longitude, hoping to have his computations finished by breakfast. Then at noon local time, as the sun reached its highest point and crossed the ship's meridian, he shot a noon sight for latitude and brought his earlier positions forward to noon.

At that point, the exact time that the sun crossed the ship's meridian, a new day began aboard the *George Washington,* as on other ships of those times. The officer of the deck informed the captain that it was twelve o'clock meridian and requested permission to strike eight bells to signal the new sea day. Following the time-honored custom, the captain gave the order to "make it so," and the bell was struck, the sand glass turned, the first watch of the new day begun, the wind-up clocks reset, and the calendar changed. Those few aboard with pocket watches set them ahead the ten minutes or so required to make their watches conform to the new local time for that day and location, as they sailed east.

Henry Allen learned his navigation quickly. When the positions he recorded in his journal are plotted on a chart of the Atlantic Ocean, it is clear that he learned immediately how to observe and compute the latitude but that getting a correct longitude took him more practice. During the early part of the voyage across his longitudes were often wildly off, although the latitudes look to be correct. After a few days he seems to have gotten the knack of it, and his positions track well.

There was much more than navigation for a young midshipman to learn. The daily routine was full of sail handling as squally weather with "sharp lightning" called for reefed topsails, and then soon after, with pleasant weather, the ship bowled along "under all sail." Nearly every day at four o'clock in the afternoon all hands were called to quarters to "exercise the great guns and small arms." Passing ships kept monotony away. Early in the voyage the *George Washington* spoke the British sloop-of-war *Pheasant,* which was "bound on a cruise," and later, on one of his first ventures into the rigging, Henry saw, from the fore-topgallant masthead, a schooner in the distance to the east.[36]

Busy as he was, there are indications that fifteen-year-old Henry Allen was homesick or, at the least, thought a lot about those he had left behind. In the blank pages in the front of his journal are two well-executed sketches of a woman. Not a young, pretty girl but a mature, motherly woman wearing a mobcap, perhaps his dead mother: One sketch shows her bust and head in profile, with a long, straight nose, much resembling Henry Allen's own appearance as shown in his only surviving portrait. The other sketch shows the same woman looking out of a window, a very specific window, perhaps taken from the Allen house, with a "nine-over-nine" colonial-style sash, the curtains drawn back, and a lintel with a keystone over the top.[37] There is no surprise here. For all of his short life Henry Allen filled his letters with inquiries about his family and friends, with love and regards to all, and with requests for more frequent letters from those at home.

About a week out, the lookouts sighted a ship and a schooner to leeward that "had the appearance of French Cruisers." The *George Washington* went after the strangers with "all sail set in chace," but she was a dull sailer, and the quarry easily left her well behind, the schooner showing American colors to confuse Bainbridge as she pulled away.[38]

The voyage dragged on into its second and third weeks, with only a random ship to now and then break the line of the empty horizon. Any event was seized on as news, and there was great excitement with the ship's company crowding the rail when they "saw a whale, turtle and several porpoises" on the calm Sunday morning of 24 August. Then a couple of days later Bainbridge spoke the merchant brig *South Carolina,* bound from Hamburg to Charleston. She had been chased by a ship and a schooner, possibly the "French Cruisers" that the *George Washington* had been unable to catch some days before.[39]

The ship was now due to make a landfall on the Azores Islands. Most men who follow the sea never get over the uplift that they feel each time a new land comes into view, and of all of the experiences that come to a new, young seafarer like Henry Allen, the first sighting of land after a long passage across the open ocean is one of the most enriching. Henry was on deck as daylight came on 28 August. His navigation told him that the land should be there, and by 5 A.M. he could pick out the tops of the islands of Fayal and Pico to the east and a little south. First there was a small hazy place on the horizon ahead, gray like a distant cloud, which soon became more solid. Then the land itself began to rise out of the sea and take on the shape and color of green hills.

With light winds and under all sail, the *George Washington* moved closer, to pass along the southern coasts of the islands, and at about four in the afternoon she was twenty miles south of Fayal. She passed Pico during the night. By 10 A.M. the next day she was south and west of São Miguel, the last island in the group, and early the next morning she rounded it to the east. Here Henry Allen entered in his journal, "The East point of St. Michael . . . from which I take my departure . . . [is] in Latitude 37°—47.8', Longitude 25°—48'." The *George Washington* was now on a course for Gibraltar.

As the ship entered European waters, the mood aboard was tense: Seaman John Rea described the fatigue of the crew from being repeatedly "called to quarters" as they approached the coast.[40] England was at war with France and Spain, the United States was still at least somewhat at war with France, and all concerned tended to attack first and find out later at whom they were shooting. The French still had a large and heavyweight (although out of practice) navy, but fortunately for the arriving Americans, it was tightly blockaded into its ports at this time by the British.

The United States was at peace with England, and although the relationship between the two navies during this brief period of the Quasi-War with France tended to be cooperative, the British were still stopping American merchant vessels and impressing sailors.[41] Most British sea officers "disliked and half despised" the Americans and considered the U.S. Navy an irrelevancy.[42] American naval officers, for their part, resented the arrogance of the British officers but viewed the British Navy with mixed envy and admiration and copied it in nearly everything, from styles of uniforms to the printed administrative forms used for logs and muster lists.

The officers of the tiny American squadron in the Mediterranean, frequently operating in the same waters as a fleet of British battleships, or anchored in port with them in Gibraltar or Malta, tried to uphold American honor by showing "personal courage, skill and correctness of discipline" and by having the most tautly run, freshly painted, and highly holystoned ships that the world had ever seen.[43] Young Henry Allen was learning all these things early in his career.

Henry Allen had his first look at Europe early on the squally, rainy evening of 6 September. He saw Cape Saint Vincent, at the southwestern corner of Portugal, to the east as the ship worked her way south around it. Later that evening, during the long twilight, the lookouts saw a cluster of eight sail, merchant vessels, ahead of them, closer in to the coast. Captain Bainbridge must have thought that they were pirates or French, and he "made all sail and gave chase," but again the ship was too slow: Bainbridge fired six shots at his quarry, to try to bring them to, but the intended victims didn't stop, instead running in close to the land, leaving the *George Washington* well behind, and were soon lost to sight.

Early the next morning the situation was reversed. As daylight came, there were several large British warships in sight. Soon after, Henry Allen noted, one of them "gave chace to us." The *George Washington* turned away and made sail, with the British ship in full cry after her. The British vessel was a ship-of-the-line—a battleship—and a normal frigate would have outrun her easily. But the *George Washington,* a slow ex-Indiaman, was gradually overtaken.

Henry Allen's excitement at these events comes through in his journal: The battleship "fired a gun to leeward and hoisted the English Ensign ... [the *George Washington*] answered her [with a gun] and hoisted the American Ensign." The Briton then fired a loaded gun in the *George Washington*'s direction to bring her to—an arrogant gesture, and illegal as well: the British had no right to stop the warship of a friendly nation. The *George Washington* crowded on "all sail" to get away, and the battleship fired another shot, but she was still too far away to do any harm. After a seven-hour chase, she finally got close enough to have the American frigate in range, and as Henry Allen watched these events, probably with strong feelings of resentment, the battleship "fired a shot close on board of us." At this, honor was served: under the guns of overwhelming force, Captain Bainbridge hove to. The pursuer came within hail, and the Americans "spoke her, she being the British Ship of War *Dragon* of 74 Guns, Captain Campbell."[44] It was the kind of minor humiliation that the American Navy often received in those early days but never got used to.

The long chase by the *Dragon* gave the *George Washington* another problem: she had been forced to run well to the south of her previous course and in the process had lost track of her position. The course changes and distractions of the chase had made dead reckoning difficult, and for some reason, perhaps because the weather was getting stormy, Henry Allen didn't shoot the sun at all. His journal records no navigational information for that day, Sunday, 7 September.

By midnight the ship was experiencing "fresh gales," and it soon began to rain. At 2 A.M. the lookouts sighted land ahead, and uncertain of his position, Captain Bainbridge hove to and waited for daylight. While waiting, he had the anchor cables roused up and bent to the anchors, to be ready for whatever eventuality daylight might bring.

At half past four in the morning he saw that the ship was north of Cape Spartel, the northwestern corner of Africa, about forty miles west of Gibraltar. With gale-force winds from the west, the *George Washington* bowled along under courses, topsails, and jib and arrived in Gibraltar harbor, on a rainy day, at eight-thirty in the morning.

The ship had hardly anchored when a boat carrying an official from the port came alongside, and Captain Bainbridge was told that no one could go ashore until the ship had undergone quarantine, and that he had to hoist the yellow flag. He had planned to stay for only a few hours, and the quarantine meant that there would be no contact at all with the shore. So Henry Allen spent his first day in Europe, sitting at anchor in "fresh gales and plenty of rain," looking across the harbor at the town and the famous Rock, having a long-glass liberty.

During that day in Gibraltar, Henry Allen learned that the British Navy was not infallible—an important lesson. Two British frigates also anchored in the harbor parted their anchor cables in the gale-force winds and were "laying in distress," drifting in toward the shore and destruction. They signaled for help, firing several guns, and "hoisted the English Ensign, Union down." One of them, in the nick of time, got out her boats and towed the ship clear. Henry Allen didn't record what happened to the other.

The weather moderated during the night, and the *George Washington* got under way at seven the next morning and started up the Mediterranean. It was one of those good days at sea. The weather was pleasant, and she ran with all sail set, with the wind from astern, and was pushed along by more than a half knot of current setting to the east. Birds and fish could be seen around the ship—always a good omen. When a day or two later a man fell overboard while the crew were tacking the ship, even this incident had a happy ending: they "hove [the sails] aback and caught him again."[45] This was not the usual outcome of such an event.

At 10 P.M. on Monday, 15 September, the lookouts saw the light at Algiers to the southeast. The *George Washington* stayed well off the coast until the morning of the seventeenth, and then with pleasant weather and under all sail headed in toward the land. First, the coast took shape and the Bay of Algiers became visible, with Cape Matafore at the eastern end on the left, and the city at the western side to the right. Closer in, the city of Algiers itself was plainly visible, the dazzling white jumble of houses and the walls and buildings of the Casbah stretching up the hill. At the harbor front was the citadel, a formidable stronghold, although "in a poor state of repair," mounting 16-, 24-, and 36-pounder cannon, all fine brass guns.[46]

By four in the afternoon the *George Washington* was off the harbor, and the American consul general, Richard O'Brien, came out in a boat to meet the ship, along with the Algerian captain of the port himself, who was to pilot the frigate in. Captain Bainbridge, feeling that his mission "entitled him to the hospitalities of the Dey," allowed the pilot to take the ship inside the Mole, close to the citadel and under its guns. Bainbridge may have had some misgivings as this was going on, but if so, he took no action to get himself a safer, more remote anchorage and even allowed the sails to be unbent and removed from the yards for repairs. This lack of caution was to have its consequences. However, at the time no one aboard seems to have been alarmed. Henry Allen in his journal simply said, "Moored ship and got everything snug."

On the next day, 18 September, Henry Allen noted that "the American and British Consuls visited our ship," and with some gusto he told his journal that the ship had received a "great plenty of fine fruit such as Grapes, Green Figs, Oranges, Almonds, pomegranates and Prickly Pears," all great luxuries at home in Providence.[47]

But also on the eighteenth Consul O'Brien took Captain Bainbridge to meet the dey, Baba Mustapha, who had replaced Hassan, the signer of the treaty.[48] This was not a pleasant meeting. The dey was described by other sources as "insolent," likely to "fly into a passion . . . give way to rage . . . and [indulge in] personal violence."[49] He was also given to "gnashing" his teeth.

At their meeting Bainbridge learned that Mustapha wanted him to carry the Algerian prime minister, his harem, his official family, all his slaves and servants, plus a menagerie of wild animals and some tonnage of presents to Constantinople to pay honor to the sultan of the Ottoman Empire. The sultan, styled the Grand Seigneur of the Sublime Porte, was the dey's overlord, Mustapha being only a bashaw, or regent. The presents were intended to mollify the sultan, who was unhappy with the dey for making a treaty with France, with whom the sultan was at war.[50]

The dey threatened war with the United States unless the *George Washington* made the journey, and given Mustapha's violent and erratic temperament, this was not likely to be mere bluff. The consequences of war would be the capture of more American merchant vessels, the enslavement of more sailors, and the loss of the benefits, small though they were, of the 1796 Treaty. War just now was something to be averted if possible.

Bainbridge protested that such a voyage was far and away outside his orders and that he was supposed to return immediately to the United States. He and Consul O'Brien argued with Mustapha, but the dey would not be moved. However, there were some powerful reasons in favor of making the voyage, particularly the matter that war was to be avoided at all but dire costs. And there may also have been the glimmer of a thought in Bainbridge's mind that a trip to Constantinople, famous as a great entrepôt of trade, might not be so bad. Even with the ship full of Algerines and wild animals, there would be ample room for him to carry a personal trading "adventure," for which he already had the blessing of the secretary of the navy. Seaman John Rea's account gives this possibility some credence, and a different, rather sinister twist. Rea stopped just short of accusing Bainbridge of receiving "—rich— very rich presents, and a lucrative trade between Algiers, Constantinople and America" as a quid pro quo for voluntarily agreeing to make the trip.[51] This interesting and rather mysterious insinuation was never cleared up.

In any event, Bainbridge decided to make the voyage. Whether this was under the duress of a credible threat of war and the destruction of the *George Washington,* which was sitting immobilized under the guns of the citadel (the accepted version), or whether there was something of a voluntary dimension to his decision in consideration of "rich presents and a lucrative trade," is unknowable.

Mustapha may well have evinced some surprise at Bainbridge's objections: there was a past and continuing precedent for such voyages by European warships when requested by the Barbary princes. The British consul offered to send H.M. Sloop-of-War *Termagant,* soon to arrive in Algiers, in lieu of the *George Washington* (the dey refused, viewing her as not commodious enough), and in 1806 the British allowed the dey to dispatch H.M. Frigate *Unite* to Constantinople on a mission almost identical to that of the *George Washington.*[52] Then there was Article XIV of the 1796 Treaty, which stated that "should the dey want to freight any American vessel that may be in the regency, or Turkey . . . he expects to have the preference given him." While this was obviously intended to apply to merchant vessels, there was some shadow of applicability to the present case.[53]

With all these nuances, the exact circumstances surrounding Captain Bainbridge's decision to make the run to Constantinople are not clear in the historical record. Most indications are that he and O'Brien sincerely and strenuously tried to get out of the task. But whatever the level of sincerity, although he knew on 18 September that he had been told to go or have a war and had apparently decided to go, Bainbridge didn't put out the information on board the ship until three weeks later, and his actions during that interval led everyone to assume that the ship would be going home. Sailors have sensitive antennae for such things, however, and John Rea mentioned that there were some rumors running around the lower deck of the impending voyage to the east.[54]

So the ship's company remained ignorant of the coming events, and on Friday, 19 September, the day after the meeting and two days after their arrival, the crew started the long job of discharging the cargo of tribute, pulling it piecemeal from the corners where it was stowed. On Sunday the work stopped, and some of the officers went on shore for a bit of sightseeing. For most of the next two weeks, including Sunday, up through Wednesday, 1 October, all hands were busy unloading.

Starting on 29 September the ship began receiving lighters of sand ballast, as well as continuing to unload the tribute, and then began getting her water aboard to be ready to go to sea, and home to America. The last of the tribute was unloaded on 1 October, and the next day the dey sent a present of three oxen and nine sheep, plus several bags of bread. The sheep may have been less than a bargain: John Rea described them as being small, all bones, and sickly, "unable to walk" to their slaughter.

On 4 October Henry Allen was free enough from his duties to visit the fortifications ashore, admiring "some Beautiful Spanish guns," but giving no indication that the citadel was considered to be a threat to the ship. During the following three days the crew continued to get ready for sea, watering and ballasting, and getting the sails back on the yards to be able to move again.

Then on 9 October the blow fell: the bitter news was announced on board that the ship was not going home as planned. Henry Allen's journal records that "this day we were big with the expectation of returning to the land of Liberty—Had everything prepared for the voyage. At this instant of Anticipated pleasure we receive a positive command from a Despotic Dey of Algiers that we must be the porters of savage Tygers and more savage Algerine Ambassadors ... to ... Constantinople."[55]

That afternoon of 9 October at 2 P.M. Captain Bainbridge, Consul O'Brien, and the "Dey's Executive Juncto" came on board, and a disgraceful event took place. The "pendant of the United States was struck and the red Algerine

Flag hoisted at the Main top gallant Royal Masthead." Then the *George Washington* fired a seven-gun salute to the new flag, which the citadel returned. Henry Allen noted that "some tears fell at this instant of National Humility." These tears were probably his own. The events of that day remained with Henry Allen all his life and without doubt helped to form his rigid sense of personal honor and his determination to be ready to fight rather than face disgrace.

The next day "begins dark and gloomy," Henry Allen told his journal, describing in one phrase the weather and the general attitude aboard the *George Washington*. The crew opened the hold and began, laboriously, to dig out the ballast that over the last days they had, laboriously, gotten aboard and put in place. This hard, dirty job took three days. While this was going on the carpenter and his mates began "fitting our decks for the wild beasts" and "putting up partitions for the passengers" in the living spaces.

Perhaps a hundred slaves were expected to come aboard, and the plan was very likely for them to be in the hold. With much of the hold space needed for the slaves, and with the added high-up weight of all the partitions and animal cages being built on the upper decks, the ship now needed denser ballast than sand or stones to keep her stable at sea. So Mustapha lent the *George Washington* forty old cannon, which were brought aboard and stowed in the bottom of the hold, along the keel, on 12 and 13 October.[56] These junk cannon were later to be important.

With the ballast in place, the crew finished bending the sails to the yards and started packing away the cargo, taking in baggage, trunks, water, and no doubt strange and wonderful foods. Then later the animals came aboard: 4 lions, 4 tigers, 5 antelope, 2 ostriches, 20 parrots, and—to give the menagerie a more domestic, barnyard flavor—4 horses, 25 "horned cattle," and 150 sheep.[57]

On 18 October, Algiers time, the ambassador's party came aboard, "20 gentlemen, 100 negro Turks, 60 Turkish women. . . ."[58] This entourage, plus the animals, more than doubled the number of souls on board, and the crowding and the strange smells must have been close to insupportable. Henry Allen didn't tell where he ended up sleeping during this cruise, but the midshipmen were certainly displaced into hammocks in some corner of the ship to make way for some of the "20 gentlemen."

The next day at twelve meridian, the start of the sea day of 20 October, the *George Washington* got under way. She fired a signal gun, "for sailing," and the fort answered with a shotted gun, something only done "on Extraordinary Occasions." The Algerian prime minister and general of marines came on board at 2 P.M., and the ship made sail. At 6 P.M. she was just out of the bay, and Henry Allen told his journal that the *George Washington* was "bound for Constantinople with a cargo to deliver to the Grand Seignior."[59] Captain

Bainbridge, to his credit, brought down the Algerine flag and hoisted the American as soon as he was out of range of the guns of the citadel.

Along with the crowded living conditions and the extra work that came with having this huge group of passengers on board, the ship's company got another shock: their rum allowance was cut in half. The reason possibly was that there was not enough to last through the voyage if full rations were issued and that no rum, or anything alcoholic, could be obtained in strictly Arab-Moslem Algiers; the captain was probably unsure about Turkish-Moslem Constantinople. Whatever the reason, this must have been close to the last straw for those overworked sailors. The day that this happened was 21 October 1800, which was also Henry Allen's birthday. He was now sixteen.

So, lions, tigers, sailors, harem ladies, and all, the ship headed eastward up the Mediterranean, at first in pleasant weather. Then a few days into the voyage the ship met "fresh gales and squally [weather] with rain," which quickly turned much worse, and she was soon scudding along under close-reefed mainsail, main topsail, and fore topsail, with the storm driving from astern. After twenty-four hours of strong gales, rain, and heavy seas, the storm blew itself out, and the *George Washington* was again in pleasant weather, well along on her course in the Malta Channel, with the island itself in sight to the south. The storm had been a stomach-wrenching experience for the passengers and perhaps the menagerie: the next day the crew "cleansed the ship fore and aft."[60]

Passing the southeastern corner of Sicily, Henry Allen noted in his journal one of the spectacular sights waiting for a first-time Mediterranean sailor: "The mountain of Ætna . . . distant thirty leagues," rearing up 10,000 feet, a perfect snow-tipped cone, hanging like a ghost in the sky. It was one of those brilliantly clear days at sea, with bright blue water and the horizon sharp as a knife.

The ship was soon off the coast of Greece, passing first the Island of Zante, then Cape Matapan at the southern tip of the Peloponnesus, then through that forest of islands, the Cyclades.

Late in the evening of 6 November the *George Washington* hove to off the windward side of the Island of Milos to get a pilot for the passage through the islands and up the Aegean Sea. Bainbridge fired a gun and "lighted the top lanthorn." Getting no response, he moved in closer. But coming in to a strange lee shore at night in those days was a risky matter, and at 3 A.M. Bainbridge brought the ship to again and waited for daylight. At 4:30 he headed in for land, hoisted the Algerine flag, and fired several guns. This got results, and at 8 A.M. off Milos harbor the pilot came aboard, and the ship headed north. She skirted the northwestern side of the Cyclades, Henry Allen noting that there were nine islands in sight.

The *George Washington* slipped through the Oro Channel between Euboea and Andros, then north into the Aegean Sea, and at 9 A.M. on 9 November was off the Island of Tenedos, about fifteen miles south of the entrance to the Hellespont, or Dardanelles, where she dropped the Aegean pilot and took on a Turkish pilot to guide her through the Straits and up to Constantinople. By noon she was turning northeast "between the castles at the entrance of the Hellespont," one in Europe and the other in Asia, appearing to Henry Allen as "very strong, having three tiers of guns, the lowest at the water's edge."[61]

As the frigate started up the Hellespont, she met a "strong current against [her]," a new experience for these navigators. The rivers of Eastern Europe and the western slopes of the Caucasus Mountains drain into the Black Sea, which in turn drains through the Bosporus into the Sea of Marmora, past Constantinople, down the Hellespont, and into the Aegean—a continuous, sometimes strong, sometimes weak, but never-ceasing, never-reversing flow of water. Sailing ships entering the Hellespont tried to be assured of a steady, strong breeze from the west or southwest to enable them to overcome this relentless current. The *George Washington* was fortunate that day to have favorable "fresh breezes."

A few miles up the Hellespont, at Çanakkale, are the Straits, the narrowest point in the passage, a little over a mile wide. In those years there were at this location two more forts, one on each side. Here Turkish law required that vessels present their passports before being allowed to proceed on up to Constantinople. Henry Allen didn't mention passports and said merely that the ship "saluted the Castles with three guns and was answered with two."[62]

James Fenimore Cooper, who wrote an account of this voyage at a time when he could have interviewed some of the survivors, gave an anecdote of Captain Bainbridge's ingenious handling of the moment of passing these forts. He didn't have a firman, which was a passport or grant of privileges from the sultan's court and would have been the most correct document. He apparently didn't even have a similar paper from the dey. The Algerine flag, or the fact that he was on a mission for Baba Mustapha, seems to have given his ship no standing, possibly because the sultan had not yet been propitiated with the presents the *George Washington* was now carrying.

Bainbridge, learning from the Algerines on board that the most threatening guns in these forts were really fixed, immovable mortars set to fire large stone balls at a single area in the center of the channel, shortened sail when within range and pretended to anchor, at the same time firing a salute of three guns, filling the area with smoke. The forts answered with two, temporarily obscuring their view, and the *George Washington* immediately made sail and was out of range before the smoke cleared and the surprise wore off.[63]

By early the next morning the frigate was abreast the Island of Marmora and being favored by a good strong breeze and a clear day. At noon Henry Allen recorded that "Mount Olympus bore SE x S, [the] top . . . covered with eternal snow." This was the Olympus of ancient Phrygia in Asia Minor. By early afternoon the lookouts had "the Spires of Constantinople in sight," and the trip had become an adventure for even the oldest salt on board, let alone young Henry Allen: no ship of the U.S. Navy had ever been in these waters, and few American sailors had ever seen these exotic sights. This was the first true City of the World that Henry Allen had ever seen, and he described it as "beautifully situated on the sides of seven hills gently ascending from the sea, making a most beautiful appearance from the sea."

A more articulate observer, a British architect arriving in Constantinople just a few years after Henry Allen's visit, gave a more vivid picture:

> We approached Constantinople as the sun rose, and as it shone on its glorious piles of mosques and minarets, golden points and crescents, painted houses, kiosks and gardens, our Turks pulled harder at their oars, shouting "*Stamboul, guzel azem Stamboul!*" The scene grew more and more brilliant as we drew nearer, till it became overwhelming as we entered the crowded port. . . .[64]

Constantinople, 'Stamboul, or Istanbul, it was then and is today one of the most impressive panoramas that an approaching seafarer can experience. First there is a glimpse of the seven-towered castle and the old Byzantine walls at the southwestern corner of the city. Then as a ship skirts the southern face of the great metropolis the vista gradually opens to show the Blue Mosque of Ahmed, the great Mosque of Suleiman, and the dome of that marvelous architectural gift from an earlier millennium, the *Hagia Sophia*. The overall impression is of the sun-reflecting domes of many mosques and almost a forest of minarets.

To the right, as the peninsula of the city rounds up toward the harbor of the Golden Horn, is the Seraglio Palace, dominating the foreshore from its acropolis. Today it is a museum, but when Henry Allen saw it from the deck of the *George Washington* it was still a lived-in palace.

The ship anchored off the southern part of the city early in the evening of 10 November, unannounced because of the way she had passed the forts in the Straits. A boat soon came out, carrying a Turkish official who asked to know "under what flag they sailed." He was told that the frigate was from the United States of America and upon receiving this information took his boat and went ashore. He returned later to say that his government had never heard of the United States and asked for a better answer. This time Captain Bainbridge told him that they were from the "New World." This was satisfactory, and the ship was welcomed and told to move around the end of the peninsula and into the harbor of the Golden Horn.

It was getting too dark to move that evening, but at seven the next morning the *George Washington* got up her anchor and made sail. Now lacking a good wind and facing the current, the frigate needed four hours to make this short three-mile move. Bainbridge anchored "opposite the Grand Seigneur's Barracks," at a point near where the old Byzantine chain had crossed in earlier times, near where the Galata Bridge stands today. All boats were put in the water, and no doubt with great relief the crew began to disgorge the varied and exotic cargo, that day "deliver[ing] the four horses and sundry articles of baggage belonging to the Algerines."

This was still going on the next morning when the rest of the menagerie—lions, tigers, antelopes, ostriches, parrots, and all—was sent ashore. That afternoon, 12 November, the Algerine prime minister and general of marines departed in the smoke of a seven-gun salute and was followed by "a large number of Algerines."[65]

So, now, that small adventure was over. Looking back on the voyage, the officers and the ship's company of the *George Washington* probably didn't view it as too bad an affair. It was surely crowded and uncomfortable, but every minute had brought a new and interesting experience, and they had done something that no one else in the American Navy had done. They now had wonderful material for a thousand and one sea stories, and messes all over the navy would in future years revel in tales of the lions and tigers and the harem the frigate had carried to Constantinople.

Early the next morning, life aboard reverted to reality as Captain Bainbridge began to convert his floating zoo back into a warship. Henry Allen noted, at "break of day all hands employed in washing decks," and then with hardly a pause for breath, "all hands [were] employed in scraping the gun and berth deck[s]." This went on from 4 A.M. until 9 P.M., by candlelight. The easy-going days were over: Captain Bainbridge stopped the crew's grog because some liquor had been smuggled aboard, had one man flogged and then ironed hand and foot for the next six weeks, and put the boatswain, Augustine Serra, in irons for a month for telling a "troublesome brat of a Midshipman" to "kiss his arse."[66]

The cleaning and scraping went on for three days, then the *George Washington* moved about a mile up the Golden Horn and moored. It was not a good choice of position: her moorings were barely established when a Turkish fifty-gun ship ran into her and, bouncing off, carried away the flying jibboom. One lesson was enough, and the Americans moved closer inshore and moored again. It was a wise move: that same afternoon another Turkish warship, this time a seventy-four–gun battleship, skimmed close by, but without harm.[67]

Once the frigate was cleaned up, the ship's company settled down to an in-port routine, probably with the officers and some of the more trusted of the crew going ashore to see the strange and interesting sights of the city and to barter for fascinating and unusual things in the great covered bazaar. Captain Bainbridge made official calls on the British ambassador, Lord Elgin, he of the Parthenon Marbles, and on the Danish ambassador, one Baron de Husleck.

A sailor on a British frigate that was sent to Constantinople a few years later on a mission similar to the *George Washington*'s spoke of the officers' giving a ball on board for the consuls of some of the European nations, so perhaps Captain Bainbridge put on something of this sort.[68] He certainly made a good impression on the Grand Seigneur and his court for the United States, his ship, and himself: just before the ship left, the very powerful Capudan Pasha, head of the sultan's navy, gave Bainbridge a "Firman of Protection," a document of great power and authority throughout the Ottoman world.[69] This was later to be highly useful.

Henry Allen didn't tell much of what went on in Constantinople: there is a gap in his journal from 19 November, just after the ship was cleaned up, until 30 December 1800, the day of departure. Why did the *George Washington* stay there for almost six weeks? There doesn't seem to be any good explanation. It could hardly have been just for the sightseeing. John Rea spoke of cold weather during this time, with snow on the deck and a lack of winter clothing.[70] Is there a slight possibility that it took Captain Bainbridge that long to profitably handle his trading "adventure"? The ship's official log, which might have shed some more light on the visit, has been lost.

Early on 30 December Bainbridge loosed the fore-topsail and fired a gun as a signal for sailing. Four Turks came aboard as passengers for Malta, plus apparently some Algerines heading home, then the ship was under way, sailing down the Golden Horn and firing a salute of twenty-one guns to the Turkish nation and seven to the Grand Seigneur. As the *George Washington* rounded the peninsula of the city and headed into the Sea of Marmora, seven guns from the Seraglio answered.

Going back through the Hellespont and down the Aegean was relatively smooth sailing. The winds were usually good, the current was from behind, and the landmarks and navigation were now familiar. Coming out into the Aegean, Henry Allen in his journal made much of the sites of the classical Greek myths, familiar from his schooling back home in Providence. The frigate passed Tenedos, "opposite which stood famous Troy," in the distance was "Mount Ida . . . where the Gods assembled to view the Battle" and "Lemnos, where Vulcan lit when he fell from Heaven and established his forge."[71]

The ship's company began to get back into their warship routine, and Bainbridge began gun drills for the first time since before passing Gibraltar. The frigate made a brief stop at Malta to off-load the Turkish passengers and their baggage and then was under way again. Six days later there was a disturbing development: some of the crew, probably infected in Constantinople, came down with smallpox, and one, Abel Hubbard, died at 6 P.M. and was "committed to the deep" at midnight.[72] Given the potential for disaster in this, it is surprising that the matter didn't get more attention. Henry Allen merely mentioned the incident in passing, and apparently the disease, although violently contagious, didn't spread widely among the ship's company. When the *George Washington* arrived at Algiers four days later, on 21 January, there was no mention of the outbreak—at least the ship was not quarantined. On the contrary, she received a twenty-one–gun salute.

The winter rains had nourished the dry hills around Algiers, and Henry Allen noted that the countryside was covered with green grass and that the fruit trees were in full bloom. Oranges were now in season and available "in great plenty."[73]

Captain Bainbridge was more cautious this time and anchored in Algiers Bay, outside the harbor, well out of the range of the guns of the citadel. Consul O'Brien came out, bringing news of the end of the undeclared Quasi-War between the United States and France: the Convention of Môrtefontaine had been signed in early October 1800. This agreement not only ended the Quasi-War but, by setting out principles for relations at sea between neutrals and belligerents that were highly favorable to France, also served Napoleon's broader purposes in his struggle against Britain.

But Consul O'Brien and Captain Bainbridge had more immediate problems: the dey wanted the ship to make another trip to Constantinople. Bainbridge refused, and as the ship was outside Mustapha's gun range, there wasn't much he could do except growl and gnash.

But the crafty dey had another card to play: he now said that he wanted back the forty old cannon that Captain Bainbridge had borrowed to use as ballast during the trip to Constantinople. Bainbridge asked for lighters to come outside to the ship to unload this junk iron, but the dey refused, at the same time insisting that he wanted his guns back or he would declare war. Early the next day Captain Bainbridge went ashore, apparently with a view to settling the matter with Mustapha.

It is not clear whether or not Bainbridge realized at this time that he held the ace of trumps. His audience with the dey started off badly, Mustapha going "into such a rage as to threaten personal violence."[74] But when Bainbridge brought out the firman from the Capudan Pasha and presented it, an astonishing change came over the dey; his anger and ferocity evaporated and were replaced by "expressions of friendship and offers of service." All problems were now easy of solution, and being given a credible promise that he would not be molested, Captain Bainbridge brought the *George Washington* into the harbor, unloaded twenty-four of Mustapha's old guns, apparently keeping the rest, and reballasted with sand.[75] The dey, now all smiles, sent down a present of four bullocks and ten sheep, with fresh bread and greens.

Using the newfound power of his firman, Captain Bainbridge then performed a truly humanitarian act. The dey had some weeks earlier declared war on France, in line with the policy of the Grand Seigneur, and had seized and enslaved the French consul and all the French citizens in the area that he could get his hands on. With the Quasi-War between the United States and France now over, Bainbridge was free to ask the dey to release these unfortunates and let them leave the country aboard the *George Washington*. Under the pressure of the firman, Mustapha consented, and at 1 P.M. on 31 January "the French Consul, five ladies and thirty gentlemen came on board."[76] Bainbridge immediately weighed anchor and made sail and by 5 P.M. was out of the harbor, almost out of the bay, with Algiers behind him.

The *George Washington* sailed north across to the coast of Spain and on 6 February landed the grateful French passengers at the port of Alicant. The American consul there delivered a sheaf of American newspapers, some as recent as 1 December 1800, and everyone caught up on the news.

There had been major happenings in the world, but not all of them were in the public prints: on 1 October 1800 the Second Treaty of San Ildefonso was signed at the king of Spain's summer palace, in an ambiance of some secrecy, transferring Louisiana from Spain back to France, which had originally claimed it by discovery in the seventeenth century.

This was a matter of great consequence and sinister implications for the United States: just less than a year before the coup d'état of *18 Brumaire* had overthrown the Directory and brought Napoleon Bonaparte to power in France as first consul. Napoleon was much more ambitious than the Directory to use Saint-Domingue as a base and stepping-stone to establish an empire in North America, in Louisiana and the American West. With the Second Treaty of San Ildefonso, Napoleon's plan for a North American empire moved another long step forward.

From Alicant the *George Washington* coasted around to Gibraltar and after waiting several days for a favorable wind left on 28 February, accompanied by four small American merchantmen that the frigate convoyed until well out to sea to protect them from roving Barbary corsairs. Then it was off for home. Henry Allen headed the next page of his journal, "From Gibraltar to America," and at 6 P.M. on 1 March 1801 he took a bearing off Cape Spartel, the last contact with the continents of the Old World, and from it "took [his] departure."

He was now, at age sixteen, an experienced Mediterranean Man who had seen more of that sea, "the school of our naval officers," than all but a handful of the men in his profession. He had learned much of the arcane knowledge of the seafarer and was rapidly maturing into a skilled and capable officer.

He had also learned what it meant to be humiliated by superior force, and his sense of personal honor was hardening. He never wanted to find himself, like Captain Bainbridge, forced to back down, whether by the citadel guns of a petty corsair prince or by an overbearing British battleship.

Leaving Gibraltar, the *George Washington* headed southwest to catch the northeast trades, the best winds for crossing the Atlantic. The ship dipped as far south as latitude 23° north and on 12 March crossed the tropic of Cancer. It was the ancient privilege of all crews crossing the tropic or the equator to have a day of misrule, when all discipline was relaxed and King Neptune alone controlled the ship. Captain Bainbridge gave his permission, and the traditional sea ceremonies for crossing the tropic were staged aboard the *George Washington*. No doubt Neptune, or "Old Tropicus," came aboard, and the neophytes and pollywogs were lathered with a foul mixture of soft soap, tar, and hen-coop scrapings, shaved with a rough razor, and ducked by Neptune's crew.[77] Then they promised never in the future to seduce another sailor's wife and pledged to run the ceremony for all greenhorns when next crossing the tropic or the equator. This was Henry Allen's only encounter with this ancient custom.

After a sometimes stormy passage of forty-nine days, the frigate sighted Henlopen Light early on 19 April. She passed the buoy on Brown Shoal at 9 A.M. and by late afternoon was anchored off Grub's Landing south of Philadelphia. Henry Allen's first cruise was over. His journal kept aboard the *George Washington* ended on that day.[78] Within a few days he left the *George Washington* but in the future kept up a warm relationship with Lieutenant Warner and Sailing Master Hallowell.

The navy was being reduced in size at this time, and many young officers were being let go, but Henry Allen was among the ones retained. He had hoped to have a short leave to visit his family in Providence, but eight days after leaving the *George Washington,* he was assigned to the frigate *Philadelphia,* Captain Samuel Barron, bound back to the Mediterranean.

The events at Algiers and the forced voyage to Constantinople caused a great deal of public excitement in the United States and left Captain Bainbridge with an uncertain reputation among his officer-colleagues. Many felt that he should have taken a bolder and more heroic stand, even at the risk of war with Algiers and the loss of his ship. President Jefferson, however, approved of Bainbridge's actions, and the incident contributed to firming the usually anti-navy Jefferson's views in favor of building up the navy to be able to take a strong line against the depredations of the Barbary princes.

Henry Allen's Mediterranean cruise aboard the *Philadelphia* was uneventful, even though the United States was now formally at war with the pirates: the bashaw of Tripoli had ceremoniously declared war against the United

States on 14 May 1801 by cutting down the flagpole in front of the American consulate.

Something about this cruise gave Henry Allen second thoughts about his choice of a career in the navy. Very likely part of the problem was that the *Philadelphia* saw no action. She spent most of her time stationed just inside the Strait, sailing back and forth off Gibraltar, blockading two Tripolitan cruisers that the American squadron found there upon arriving in Europe. One of these, the twenty-six–gun *Meshouda,* Henry Allen would meet again. But there was also the matter that Captain Samuel Barron was inconsistent in his discipline, being at most times kind and too easy-going, but then suddenly tightening things up. The result was that the midshipmen became unruly and were slovenly about their watch standing. Only with difficulty and after some confrontation was Barron able to get the worst of them under control.[79] This apparently disgusted Henry Allen and disillusioned him to some extent. Whatever the reason, the moment the ship arrived home on 27 June 1802 and anchored off Newcastle, Delaware, Henry wrote to his father, asking, "How is trade in Providence, and what B[e]rth could a young man get on board an Europ[e]an or India Ship If tolerably active."[80] The feeling apparently passed quickly, and the possibility of leaving the navy wasn't mentioned again until much later.

Henry Allen now finally got the furlough he had waited for and was able to spend three months at home with his family. He had left as a boy of fifteen and now returned as a man of seventeen, a salt-cured sea officer. His family's pride in him was beyond describing. The society of Providence, particularly a girl named Mary—a shadowy figure in Henry Allen's life—would have listened with amazement to his descriptions of Algiers, the barbaric dey, the voyage with the lions and tigers and the harem, and the mysterious cosmopolis of Constantinople.

In October he was back to duty, now aboard the frigate *John Adams,* bound again for the Mediterranean. His captain this time was John Rodgers, who although only twenty-eight was one of the more senior officers in the navy and undoubtedly the most difficult of all to deal with. Modern historians describe him as "an unpleasant man," "sullen and choleric," who "brooded and blustered," continually concerned about exerting his "masculinity."[81] A contemporary officer described Rodgers as one whose "reputation as a fighting man has originated . . . in his black looks, his insufferable arrogance, and the frequent and unmerited assaults he has made on poor and inoffensive citizens."[82] Like Bainbridge, Rodgers had received his training in the merchant service, and his approach to managing his crews was heavy-handed: in the frigate *Congress* he knocked down Warrant Officer George Painter with his fists, and when he got up, knocked him down again. Later, as told by Painter,

Rodgers seized "hold of my mouth and nose together with his hand and made me bleed a stream."[83]

All in all, Rodgers was not the type of man that most officers would enjoy serving with. He was very different from young Henry Allen, who at this time was an impressionable, seventeen-year-old midshipman. Henry was an attractive person, tall, handsome, open in his personality, and he had a certain charisma—during all of his short professional life senior officers asked for him, and men were willing to follow him from ship to ship. He was very hard working and enjoyed the challenge of being given a job that stretched his abilities. Even a man with Rodgers's difficult personality could like Henry Allen, and of course, all senior naval officers want to have ambitious, hard-working juniors under them.

Henry Allen, for his part, liked being able to get along with this demanding and complex captain and apparently admired what he saw in Rodgers as a strong sense of personal honor, but what others saw as hollow bluster and arrogance. In any event, they got along well: after only a few days aboard the *John Adams,* Henry Allen wrote to his father of his satisfaction in "being placed under the command of Gentlemen."[84] There are indications that he later had second thoughts and tried, although not openly, to get out from under Rodgers's command.

So Henry Allen, now fairly senior as a midshipman, was off to the Mediterranean for the third time. But he was still a boy away from home: his last letter before leaving on this cruise was full of terms of endearment for his family, and he asked them for letters to be sent to the Mediterranean—he seems never to have gotten enough letters from them. In a postscript he remembered the family's new baby with "give the Little cherub a Kiss for me."[85] Mary Nichols Allen was only five months old and would live but three more months.

The *John Adams* left Hampton Roads on 22 October, and although Henry Allen's first letter from Europe described the trip only as "a fine passage of 25 days," he gave more detail in his journal. The ship's surgeon, Doctor William Turner, died at 7 A.M. on the twenty-seventh, five days out. Henry noted that "at 5 [P.M.] all hands were called [—] Funeral service read & committed his body to the Deep."[86] Then in mid-November, near the Azores, the *John Adams* spoke a dismasted and leaking Portuguese merchant ship that "being entirely disabled and making 4 feet of water an hour induced Captain Rodgers to take her in tow." But the towline parted the next day, and Rodgers apparently let her go her own way—at least nothing more about her appeared in Henry's journal.

The *John Adams* arrived in Gibraltar on 18 November, then after a two-day stay went on to Malaga, Spain, which was at that time used as a replenishment and repair port by the American squadron in the Mediterranean. The commodore at this time was Captain Richard Valentine Morris, the least active, least effective of all the officers who commanded the American forces during the Barbary Wars. He had been appointed by Navy Secretary Robert Smith suddenly, without much consideration of his abilities, after Captain Thomas Truxtun refused the job.

In spite of the poor leadership, some ships of the squadron were finding action: when the *John Adams* arrived in Malaga in late November, the *Constellation* and *Enterprize* were there, recently returned from Tripoli, where they had enjoyed "a slight cannonade with the Batteries and Gun Boats," causing some damage and killing "several of the rascals." But Henry Allen himself was apparently finding time heavy on his hands: he wrote to his father, asking him to "send . . . all the Debates of Congress as I am a great *Politician!!!*"[87]

A little later the *John Adams* set out for Malta, towing the American merchant brig *Boston*. Henry Allen left a beautiful ink sketch of the *Boston* on the page of his journal for 19 December and another sketch of a "lateen boat" that his ship had chased the day before. The arrival at Malta provided a memorable lesson in shiphandling for Henry Allen and the other midshipmen. With a pilot on board and in full sight of an anchored British squadron, the wind took the *John Adams* aback, and she went aground on the foreshore of the castle, probably scattering and terrifying dozens of the fishing boats that normally clustered there. The crew ran a hawser to the opposite shore and took it to the capstan, and with this and the help of the boats of the British squadron—a humiliating thing—they got the frigate off. It is too bad that Henry Allen didn't record what the always irascible John Rodgers said to the sailing master about this incident.[88]

The entire small American squadron was assembled for a rendezvous at Malta during nearly all of January 1803, and Tripoli was left unguarded. Ten Tripolitan cruisers promptly "sailed in Quest of prey," some of them planning to get out into the Atlantic, where the eastbound trade from America funneled into the Strait of Gibraltar.[89] But the Tripolitans returned to port without having captured anything—a result of luck rather than any skill or activity on the part of the American squadron.

It was beginning to appear as though the rest of this cruise would be no more productive of action and opportunities for honor than his tour on the *Philadelphia*. Henry wrote home of sightseeing in Malta but sent no reports of battle, in spite of the ongoing war. Then in late January Commodore Morris made plans to appear off Tripoli with the squadron, then to call at Tunis. The squadron left Valetta on the thirty-first and immediately faced strong westerly gales. Sailing due south to Tripoli was difficult, and after arriving off North Africa thirty-five miles east of Tripoli, Commodore Morris decided that it was too rough to do anything useful on that exposed coast and returned to Malta ten days later, the squadron bruised by the experience.

In late February 1803 there was a little more excitement. The squadron made the long-planned visit to Tunis, and it turned into a humiliating disaster. On the twenty-sixth Commodore Morris, together with Captain John Rodgers and "other officers and diplomats," went ashore to meet with the bey. A couple of heated and disagreeable conversations took place, first between Morris and William Eaton, the American consul at Tunis, then between these two mutual enemies and the bey. After these unpleasant exchanges Morris, Rodgers, and James Cathcart, the former U.S. consul at Tripoli, were clapped under arrest and held for $34,000 ransom, the bey claiming that he was owed this amount by Eaton. The three men were finally freed five days later after some negotiating by the French and Danish representatives at Tunis, the payment of $22,000 cash, and promises of the rest. It was another embarrassing experience.[90]

The incident ended with the bey's declaring William Eaton to be persona non grata, and Dr. George Davis, the squadron surgeon, had to be left in Tunis to give the United States some level of representation there. Eaton then went home to the United States, infuriated with Morris and full of tales of the commodore's incompetence.

In early May things got better for Henry Allen, John Rodgers, and the *John Adams.* In late April a gunpowder explosion aboard Morris's flagship, the *New York,* left that ship in Malta for repairs while the *John Adams* was sent alone to blockade Tripoli. This was more to John Rodgers's liking. The instant the frigate arrived at Tripoli, around noon on 9 May, Rodgers took the ship in close to the barrier rocks, a "half gunshot" from the gunboats anchored in the harbor, firing broadsides at the boats and then into the town, the batteries on the walls firing back.[91] Some of the shot from the *John Adams* went through the walls of the bashaw's palace, frightened his "favorite wife" into a faint, and created "confusion in the City" with much "running to and fro."[92] The frigate went back briefly the next day and had a long-range cannonade with the gunboats. Henry Allen noted in his journal that in the course of this adventure a man fell overboard. John Rodgers quickly threw him an oar to hold on to, then backed the main and mizzen topsails, lowered a boat, and retrieved him—a neat bit of seamanship.

Then on the thirteenth the *John Adams* had the best luck so far of this cruise. She was about fifteen miles northeast of Tripoli when the lookouts saw a sail to the southeast headed toward the port. As the frigate closed her they realized that she was the *Meshouda,* the Tripolitan flagship that had been blockaded for so long in Gibraltar. Earlier, Commodore Morris had released her and turned her over to the emperor of Morocco with the provisos that she not carry contraband and not go into Tripoli. Now she was doing both of these forbidden things. The *John Adams* intercepted and captured her, took out her crew of fifty-eight, and put a prize crew aboard. Two days later the frigate left the blockading station off Tripoli and took the prize to Malta, towing her most of the way.[93] Off Malta, Henry Allen saw a sight to impress and raise envy in any American officer, a British Navy "squadron of twelve ships . . . eight of the line."

Her prize safe in Malta, the *John Adams*, together with the *New York* and *Enterprize*, returned to the blockade off Tripoli. During the following days the contrast between the recently viewed majesty of the British Navy at sea and the desultory pipsqueak actions of the American squadron must have been acutely obvious to all, even to eighteen-year-old Henry Allen. The *John Adams* and the others off Tripoli engaged themselves in powder-wasting exchanges of cannonading with the gunboats and shore batteries, never really coming to grips with them and accomplishing nothing useful. The war with Tripoli was going nowhere.

At the end of May Commodore Morris wrote to Mr. Nissen, the Danish consul at Tripoli, asking him to arrange for peace negotiations with the bashaw. This was done, although at this time the bashaw was not under much pressure to make peace: he had just received a large bribe of money from Sweden, and the actions of the American squadron were too ineffective to provide him with much incentive. For three days starting on the fifth of June white flags were hoisted on both sides, and some meetings, apparently rather at arm's length, took place. On the sixth Commodore Morris and John Rodgers, accompanied by Henry Allen acting as "aid," went into the town of Tripoli and met with the minister of war and the prime minister.[94] Henry Allen's letters to his family for most of 1803 are missing, depriving us of his personal account of these happenings.

The meetings all failed: the bashaw wanted a large amount of money, $200,000, plus future payments and reparations—conditions that were out of the question.[95] After this Morris sailed for Malta, leaving John Rodgers in command of the blockade, with the frigate *Adams* and schooner *Enterprize* in addition to the *John Adams*.

Then on 22 June Captain Rodgers, Henry Allen, and the *John Adams* had their best, most significant action of the cruise. The *John Adams* and the *Enterprize* managed to corner, close to the beach, a twenty-two–gun, three-masted, lateen-rigged Tripolitan "large poleacre ship," which they greatly outgunned. After a "smart cannonade" by both sides for about an hour, many of the Tripolitan crew abandoned their guns, jumped in the water, and swam or boated ashore. But before John Rodgers could take possession of her, a Tripolitan boat returned to the prize, and shortly thereafter the polacre blew up in a tremendous explosion, throwing two of her masts, with all of the rigging attached, high into the air.[96] Her own men may have destroyed her, although many of her crew were still on board, but she had as well taken enough of a pounding from the *John Adams* to account for the devastation.

This was all the *John Adams* accomplished. On the day before, 21 June, Secretary of the Navy Robert Smith, in Washington, wrote a letter ordering Commodore Morris home to explain his ineffective actions. The letter also told John Rodgers to relieve Morris as commodore of the Mediterranean squadron until the arrival of Captain Edward Preble, who would be the new commodore. Rodgers was to take command of the *New York,* and the captain of the *Adams* was to take over the *John Adams.* Morris was to come home in the *Adams.*

These orders began to take effect in mid-September when the letter and Preble arrived, together with the relieving ships from the United States. On 6 October John Rodgers left the *John Adams,* took command of the frigate *New York,* and temporarily hoisted his broad command pennant as commodore. Captain Hugh Campbell took command of the *John Adams.* John Rodgers was senior to Preble and went out of his way to irritate this delicate situation. But Preble swallowed hard and, for the short time that they would both be present, did his best to get along with Rodgers.

Then on 19 October Midshipman Henry Allen in the *John Adams* left Tangier together with the *New York.* After a difficult passage, during which "scurvy of the most malignant character" was rampant on board the *New York,* the ships arrived in the Chesapeake in early December and went up to Washington. There Henry Allen's cruise in the *John Adams* ended with a flourish: the ship received an official visit from President Jefferson, the members of the Cabinet, plus nearly the whole Congress. All hands worked to clean her up and make ready for this Great Occasion, and on the day appointed, 11 December 1803, the ship was dressed fore and aft with flags, the crew manned the yards, and as the August Party approached, salutes were fired and the band played "Hail Columbia, Happy Land."[97]

Then for Henry Allen it was off to Providence for another furlough, much anticipated. He wrote ahead, "I have a great quantity of news for you, but shall retain it as a subject of Winter evening Tales." These were less exciting tales than he would bring back from future cruises. His social life was apparently active, and in letters to his sister a few months later it is clear that he was taken, for the moment, with "the charming Anna." He sketched profile portraits of several of his family members and friends, telling Sarah that hers and Anna's were particularly good likenesses. He also found time to flirt with "Eliza," "May Sterry," the "miss Youngs," and lastly "Miss Dexter . . . I shall take particular care of her kisses."[98]

He was ordered back to Washington on 19 March 1804. There he learned that just after the *John Adams* and *New York* had left the Mediterranean the real action in the war with Tripoli had taken place, and both he and John Rodgers had missed the opportunities for glory that went instead to Preble, Decatur, and many others.

It happened that on 31 October 1803, twelve days after the *John Adams* and *New York* had left for home, Captain Bainbridge in the frigate *Philadelphia* was chasing a small vessel close inshore a few miles east of Tripoli. The *Philadelphia* got too close in and suddenly ran aground, sliding up high and dry on a reef. Bainbridge tried everything to get off, finally throwing most of the guns overboard and cutting away the foremast, but nothing helped. During all this some Tripolitan gunboats were watching, at first from a respectful distance. But then as the *Philadelphia's* predicament became obvious, the gunboats moved in and attacked, firing from positions that the frigate's remaining guns couldn't reach.

Finally Bainbridge decided that there was nothing to do but surrender, and for the second time in his Mediterranean career he brought down the Stars and Stripes. All 315 on board were taken prisoner, including 22 officers, and promptly locked up ashore in Tripoli, where they were to spend the next nineteen months and three days. It was not exactly a day of glory for the young U.S. Navy, and of course, having such a valuable group of captives gave the bashaw of Tripoli a big bargaining advantage during the future course of the war.

Bainbridge's surrender may have been a bit premature. Two days later, strong north winds piled the sea against the North African coast, and the Tripolitans then managed to refloat the *Philadelphia*. They fished her guns and other jettisoned equipment out of the shallow water and took her into Tripoli harbor, anchoring her about six hundred yards off the arsenal, with several gunboats nearby to protect her. They began to refit her, planning to turn her to piratical tasks as soon as the spring raiding season started in 1804 or to sell her to another Barbary state if the price was right.

While Commodore Preble and his officers were trying to figure out what to do about all this, Lieutenant Stephen Decatur, at this point a relatively unknown officer commanding the twelve-gun schooner *Enterprize,* had a piece of luck. Cruising at sea, he ran across a Tripolitan ketch, the *Mastico,* which was carrying a cargo of female slaves to Constantinople as a gift for the Sultan of the Sublime Porte, and captured it. What happened to the slave women was not recorded, but Decatur took the ketch back to Preble at Syracuse in Sicily, and after some discussion a plan was hatched to use the ketch *Mastico,* now renamed the *Intrepid,* to go into Tripoli harbor and destroy the *Philadelphia*. It was felt that there was no possibility of retaking her and bringing her out intact: letters smuggled out from Captain Bainbridge said that she still lacked her foremast, had no sails bent, had most of her yards lying on her gunwales, and was well guarded to boot.

So the ketch *Intrepid* was fitted out for the task and was to be commanded by Decatur, together with Lieutenants Lawrence and Bainbridge (the captured captain's brother), several midshipmen including Macdonough, Izard, Morris, and Rowe, a pilot, and sixty-two petty officers and sailors. The expedition took place on the night of 16 February 1804, and it was a smashing success. The *Philadelphia* was torched and completely destroyed, all performed heroic deeds, and the *Intrepid* got out safely. There was glory for all who were involved, Preble's reputation soared, Decatur was promoted from lieutenant to captain, and others were commensurately rewarded. But John Rodgers and Henry Allen, both of whom would have dearly loved the fame and honor, were far away, back home in the United States. The incident apparently put intense pressure on Rodgers to find some comparable path to glory before the war evaporated and his chance was gone. None of Henry Allen's surviving letters mentioned the *Philadelphia* incident at all, although he noted the earlier capture of the *Mastico* in a letter to his sister.[99]

When Henry Allen's furlough was over in late March of 1804, he found that there had been some shifts in commands during his absence. Captain Samuel Barron, Henry's old skipper in the *Philadelphia,* was taking command of the frigate *President* and going out as the commodore of the Mediterranean Squadron. Captain James Barron, his younger brother, was to command the frigate *United States.* Captain Isaac Chauncey was now to command the *John Adams,* and John Rodgers was to get the frigate *Congress.* All were to go to the Mediterranean together.

In New York on his way to Washington, Henry Allen ran into Captain Isaac Chauncey and was invited to dinner. Henry took the opportunity to tell Chauncey "how extremely happy [he] should be to go out with him in the *J[ohn] A[dams]*." Chauncey informed Henry that "nothing would give him greater pleasure," but that John Rodgers had put a prior claim on him, and that the information at the Navy Office was that Henry Allen was to go out as fourth lieutenant of the *Congress*.[100] Henry was elated at this news: he apparently had wanted to go with Chauncey to get out from under John Rodgers, but the prospect of this promotion overrode any such feelings.

But upon his arrival in Baltimore to join the *Congress,* he found that his promotion was not what he had expected and that he was appointed as a sailing master, not a lieutenant. He was deeply disappointed but swallowed hard and made the best of it, noting that there were officers with longer service than his who were still midshipmen. Henry blamed the change in his prospects on the "clamours" of midshipmen senior to him who were not being promoted at all.

Rodgers apparently assured Henry that he thought highly of him and would look out for his interests. So Henry was soon saying that the promotion was "very satisfactory," that the *Congress* was the "most beautifull ship in service," and that in any event experience as a sailing master would be of more use to him "should it be my intention of quitting the service on my return."[101]

Within a week after reporting aboard the *Congress,* Henry was too busy to think about anything but work. Captain Rodgers was taken up with matters on shore and rarely came aboard the ship. The first lieutenant received word that his father was dying and left the ship to attend to him, and all the other lieutenants were away at various ports, recruiting. This left Henry Allen as the senior officer on board, with the ship in the middle of a major refit. Henry liked this situation: he was proud and flattered to be trusted with the whole management of the ship and the 190 men then aboard and with "having charge of the fitting and rigging [of] a frigate." He told his father, "I assure you it is the means of making a seaman of me. . . ."[102] He had become very much a favorite and protégé of the difficult and choleric John Rodgers: Ashore one day, Rodgers was asked if, with his first lieutenant away, he didn't feel much confined to his ship. His answer was, "Not in the least, she is in good hands."

The squadron now being sent to the Mediterranean had the mission of finally bringing the war with Tripoli to a successful close "by energetic measures." One part of a rather ill-formed overall plan was for the ex-consul at Tunis, William Eaton, an adventurous man who had now cast himself in the role of soldier of fortune, to use the deposed brother of the bashaw of Tripoli to foment a revolt there, this to be coordinated with an attack by the squadron's marines and a naval bombardment. Henry Allen noted that the *Congress* loaded aboard five thousand 18-pound round shot, seven hundred canister and one thousand rounds of grapeshot, plus comparable amounts for the 12-pounders.[103]

The squadron left for the Mediterranean on 1 July. Henry Allen's duties as sailing master took him into the rigging much more than before, and on the trip across he had a close brush with death. The *Congress* was lying to in a "violent gale" but drifting downwind, bow first, very fast. Henry was well out on the fore yardarm, about seventy-five feet above the water, helping the topmen to take a reef in the foresail, when he lost his grip on the sail and fell off the footropes and the yard. He narrowly missed one of the anchors on the bows and plunged into the water alongside. By the time he got back to the surface the ship had almost drifted past him, but luck was with him and he came up close to the mizzen chains, where the mizzenmast rigging attaches to the side of the hull. He managed to catch hold and get back aboard—an extremely close call.[104]

The squadron, with Commodore Samuel Barron in command, arrived at Gibraltar on 13 August.[105] John Rodgers and the *Congress* were ordered to make a cruise along the Atlantic coast of Morocco before joining the rest of the ships off Tripoli. Barron took the rest of the squadron immediately up the Mediterranean to locate Preble and his group.

Henry Allen, John Rodgers, and the others in the arriving squadron could not know it, but most of the glory days for the navy in the war with Tripoli were already over. Preble's attacks on Tripoli harbor had taken place on 3, 7, and 24 August with much heroic hand-to-hand combat and making of Naval Tradition by Stephen Decatur, Richard Somers, and John Trippe and Midshipmen Thorn, Spence, and Macdonough.[106]

But while all of these efforts were clearly Glorious Adventures, they were just as clearly not doing much damage to the town of Tripoli or its arsenal and were of no effect whatsoever in getting Captain Bainbridge and his men released. The only positive effect of these Gallant Actions, an effect at this point unknown to the attacking Americans, was that the bashaw was beginning to weary of the harassment that his war had brought down upon him.

But there was one more Naval Adventure to come, and it happened while John Rodgers, Henry Allen, and the *Congress* were still at Gibraltar. Preble had for some time planned to try the use of fire ships and "infernals"—ships loaded with explosives—against the vessels in Tripoli harbor and the arsenal itself. It was either Preble himself or perhaps Lieutenant Richard Somers, Decatur's rival in heroics, who hatched the idea to fit the little ketch *Intrepid* as an infernal, a floating bomb. The *Intrepid* was still running errands for the squadron after serving as the vehicle for the burning of the *Philadelphia*. Now, filled with explosives, the ketch would, on a dark night, run into Tripoli harbor among the enemy's cruisers and be exploded, hopefully damaging some of them and even possibly causing some havoc in the town.[107]

A more harebrained scheme is hard to imagine, particularly as the squadron was growing short of powder, but Preble was desperate for results. A magazine was built in the forward hold of the little vessel, and as told by Henry Allen two months later, eighty barrels of gunpowder were loaded into it. On deck over the magazine were stacked 150 fused, explosive mortar shells. The explosion of the magazine was to throw the shells out in all directions, onto nearby vessels and over the wall into the arsenal and the town. After some experiments, two eleven-minute delayed-ignition devices were created by filling musket barrels with a fuse compound and placing them with their business ends in the magazine and their outer ends positioned to be ignited by a train of powder from the relative safety of the deck. Thus, as described by Henry Allen after the event, "a person had only to put his match down in either place, touch the [powder] train, and jump into his boat."[108] Once in the boat the *Intrepid*'s crew had eleven minutes, rowing frantically, to get out of range.

Lieutenant Somers was given the command of the Adventure, superseding Acting-Lieutenant Joseph Israel, the *Intrepid*'s normal skipper. Somers and his brave crew, thirteen men altogether, got the now highly inflammable *Intrepid* under way at 8 P.M. on 3 September 1804.

The night was as dark as the inside of a cat, but an officer of the *Nautilus* with a good night glass managed to keep the *Intrepid* in sight. Suddenly, two Tripolitan alarm guns were fired. Then fifteen minutes passed, but long before she could have reached her objective in the harbor, the *Intrepid* blew up with a mighty explosion and a flash that lit up the night.

What happened to her? There have been many theories, but to this day no one really knows. The condition of the bodies that were found indicated that the crew were still aboard when she went up. James Fenimore Cooper, who some years later probably talked to people who were present that night in the waiting ships, thought that the explosion was accidental.[109] Henry Allen, showing his biases toward excessive personal honor even at this early age, wrote his father two months later that it was generally believed that Somers had been boarded by the enemy and had intentionally blown up the ketch. There is no hard evidence to support this view, or any other.

Henry Allen, arriving in the squadron shortly after the event, drew a neat, probably accurate (he had seen her on earlier occasions), and certainly the most nearly contemporaneous picture of the forty-ton *Intrepid* as she appeared on the night of the big event (see the illustration in the photo section). In a later painting of the *Philadelphia* incident, the *Intrepid* looked much like Allen's sketch and could possibly have been copied from it.[110]

The *Intrepid* affair was the Last Hurrah of the naval war with Tripoli, and the next-to-last major event of the wars with the Barbary States. Two days later Preble sent all his squadron to Syracuse except the *Constitution, Argus,* and *Vixen,* ending his active operations against the bashaw. Cooper recorded that "not . . . another shot was fired at Tripoli."[111]

On 10 September 1804, sea time, Commodore Samuel Barron arrived off Tripoli in the *President,* accompanied by the *Constellation.* Barron and Preble stayed in company, turning over the details of the command, until the thirteenth, when Barron finally took over the squadron, relieving Preble. Preble left for Syracuse, then Malta, then home to the United States.

He left with much honor, in spite of the fact that his campaigns against Tripoli had not freed the crew of the *Philadelphia* or brought the bashaw to terms. He was replaced because, in the tiny U.S. Navy of that day, not enough captains junior to him were available to go to the Mediterranean. Preble himself was junior to both Samuel Barron and John Rodgers. He might have been willing to stay and serve with Barron but after an earlier set-to with Rodgers had no wish to serve with or under him.[112] So home he went. His time in command had been immensely successful in one long-lasting way: the traditions of bold, aggressive action, developed under his guidance by Decatur, Somers, and the others, have stayed with the navy for 190 years.

The frigate *Congress,* with John Rodgers and Henry Allen, arrived at the squadron in late September after having stopped in Algiers. By this time Commodore Samuel Barron had become ill with what was described as a liver ailment because he was yellow with jaundice, although his doctor called it "dropsy."[113] Samuel Barron was gradually becoming an invalid and was beginning to direct the operations of the squadron through his younger brother, James Barron, captain of the frigate *United States.* The Barron brothers were members of an old Virginia seafaring family from Hampton and like many officers in the early U.S. Navy were capable seamen first, rather than aggressive, fire-eating officers of the Decatur or Somers cut.

As Samuel Barron's illness worsened, John Rodgers, who was just one number junior to him and next in line to command the squadron, was savoring the pleasant prospect of taking over and then heroically battering Tripoli and the bashaw into submission. In November 1804 Rodgers had been detached from the thirty-eight–gun *Congress* and given command of the forty-four–gun *Constitution.* He had taken Henry Allen with him and promoted him to acting-lieutenant. John Rodgers was furious at Samuel Barron for not giving up the command of the squadron as soon as he had to take to his sickbed, and he was doubly furious at James Barron, who by this time was acting for his brother and, in all but title, commanding the squadron. John Rodgers and James Barron exchanged angry letters, and Rodgers called for settling their differences with pistols. But this matter had to be put off for the present.

In anticipation of his taking over the squadron and immediately going on the attack against the bashaw, Rodgers took Henry Allen, now his "favorite lieutenant," on a risky expedition in the *Constitution*'s gig, with muffled oars, to reconnoiter the harbor and fort at Tripoli and take some soundings inside the mole and close to the arsenal.[114] "Between one and two o'clock in the morning" of a Friday night they went in so close that Rodgers and Allen could hear voices ashore and were "in four feet of water, unperceived" as they observed the Tripolitan gunboats moored stern-to-the-beach, in the standard Mediterranean fashion, their guns pointing out "to act as a battery."[115] The adventure was carried off successfully, but the Americans almost lost it all when the weather turned bad as they were coming out of the harbor, and they nearly missed their rendezvous with the *Nautilus,* which was waiting for them.[116]

But John Rodgers's plans to sail into Tripoli with guns gloriously blazing went awry. It came about in this manner:

Samuel Barron had allowed William Eaton to proceed with his scheme to find the bashaw's deposed older brother, Hamet, who was theoretically the rightful bashaw, and to try to generate popular support for him in the countryside east of Tripoli. The hope was to overthrow the present bashaw, free the crew of the *Philadelphia,* and install a friendly ruler in Tripoli.

Eaton, who had styled himself general and donned Arab robes, was marching westward from Egypt, along the Mediterranean coast, with a force of some four hundred miscellaneous soldiers of fortune, accompanied by Marine Lieutenant Neville O'Bannon and Midshipman P. P. Peck.[117] At sea, to provide them some degree of support, was the U.S. Brig *Argus,* plus, from time to time, a couple of other small vessels. Eaton's force had about a thousand miles to march, and near the halfway point, at a town called Derne, it had its only success.

On 28 April 1805 Eaton and Hamet attacked Derne from the land side, while the eighteen-gun *Argus* and the tiny, seventy-one–ton, ten-gun *Hornet* bombarded the fort from the sea. Lieutenant O'Bannon led the handful of marines of the *Argus* in an attack that carried the fort, then hauled down the flag of Tripoli and ran up the Stars and Stripes. Rarely has so much been made of so little: the Marine Corps still sings about "the shores of Tripoli" from this incident.

Commodore Barron, ashore at Malta, had by this time partially recovered his health and was viewing Eaton's operation with some minimal optimism. But he had the common sense to see that it had no real chance of final success and that it indeed might endanger the lives of the men of the *Philadelphia* if the ruling bashaw actually began to feel personally threatened.

Also present in the area was one of the most effective American diplomats of the day, Tobias Lear, whose normal post was consul general at Algiers but who ranged the Barbary Coast. There had been some third-party conversations with Tripoli in late 1804, and Lear was convinced that the bashaw would negotiate an end to the war.

Now with Samuel Barron's support, Lear went to Tripoli. At about the same time, in late May 1805, Barron finally relinquished the command to John Rodgers. So while Rodgers would have liked to lead a Glorious Expedition to batter Tripoli into submission, his hands were tied while diplomacy was given a chance to work its magic. Rodgers also felt that he owed Lear some forbearance because of their friendship under dangerous and difficult circumstances in Saint-Domingue, in the West Indies, years before.[118]

The bashaw was indeed ready to parley, in part because of a false rumor that the American squadron had been greatly augmented, and the negotiations took Tobias Lear only a couple of weeks. On 4 June 1805 he and the bashaw signed a Treaty of Peace and Amity.[119] As a piece of diplomacy it was a great success: Article 1 restored peaceful relations and accorded "most favored nation" status to each. Article 2 released, finally, Captain Bainbridge and the men of the *Philadelphia*. The treaty wasn't exactly what President Jefferson had wanted because it included a payment of $60,000 to the bashaw, but it was better than continued war and the possible loss of some or all of the *Philadelphia*'s men. The $60,000 was included to even out the accounting of prisoners: the United States held about one hundred Tripolitan prisoners, and Tripoli held a few more than three hundred Americans. To the bashaw, these prisoners were cash in the bank, and he simply would not have understood an agreement in which those that he held, over and above an even exchange, were not somehow paid for.

In Article 3 of the treaty the United States promised to call off William Eaton's operation, and this was done, leaving Eaton in a rage and poor Hamet Karamanli in the lurch—perhaps the first, but far from the last, time that the United States remorselessly abandoned a small ally. There was also a shameful secret clause to the treaty in which the United States agreed that Hamet's wife and children, whom the bashaw was holding in Tripoli, could remain there for four more years as a guarantee that Hamet would not again try to take the throne.

The treaty ending the war with Tripoli seemed to foreclose any opportunity of military glory in Barbary for John Rodgers and Henry Allen. But within a few months Hamuda Bashaw, the bey of Tunis, was raising a clamor for the return of a Tunisian privateer he viewed as having been illegally seized off Tripoli: during the winter of 1804–1805, while blockading Tripoli, the *Constitution* had stopped and then confiscated a ten-gun Tunisian xebec, plus her two prizes just taken from the Italians.[120]

This capture had been one of the very few successes John Rodgers experienced during this cruise, and it undoubtedly incensed him that the piratical Tunisians wanted the vessels back. But more than that, the incident appeared to present a chance for the glory that had so far evaded him. Rodgers handled the situation beautifully. He unhurriedly proceeded to move his squadron to the Bay of Tunis to present Hamuda Bashaw with an ultimatum backed up by the reality of force.

This voyage took on the aspects of a gala event. The squadron left Malta at 6 A.M. on 23 July 1805—four frigates, a brig, two schooners, a sloop, and eight gunboats. The weather was clear and bright, with light breezes. Henry Allen noted that his wardroom mess on the *Constitution,* nine members, all "fine fellows," had "plenty to eat and drink": their dinner the first day out was "mutton soup, mutton boiled and roast, roast beef, vegetables various, a good rice pudding and plenty of wine"—hardly a diet to fight on.[121]

The squadron cruised leisurely, propelled by light breezes. North of the ships as they left Valetta was Sicily, and Henry Allen saw "Mount Etna, towering above, present[ing] its snowy top to the astonished and admiring eye." Consul Tobias Lear was along on the expedition, riding in the frigate *John Adams,* accompanied by his wife. The Lears were bound back to Algiers, but a revolt was in progress there, and Tobias was to first take part in the Tunis campaign, to provide a diplomatic gloss on the expected warlike events.

On Sunday, 28 July, the Lears visited aboard the *Constitution,* where the crew was mustered in white uniforms and, as customary for Sunday, the Articles of War were read. Consul Lear and his lady then took dinner in the wardroom with Henry Allen and his messmates: "Soup, roast and boiled fowls, roast Ducks, boiled ham, Tongues, Vegetables, Wine, Pudding, Porter and etc." According to Henry Allen's long letter describing the trip, this was how they ate every day. The navy has traditionally gone to war with white tablecloths, silver, fine china, and good food in its wardrooms. May it continue always to do so.

The squadron arrived in the Bay of Tunis on 31 July and the next day moored in a line across the entrance to the harbor, blocking all traffic coming and going.[122] Then the American consul presented an ultimatum offering peace or war to the bashaw while this convergence of power was in full view from the palace. Although Rodgers had hoped for war, the mere sight of the squadron finally overwhelmed Hamuda, who in any event was the most reasonable of the Barbary princes, and at the proper moment Tobias Lear went ashore to negotiate. A treaty was soon worked out, and the bashaw followed it up by sending to Washington an ambassador bearing "a present of Lions, Tigers, Ostriches, &C. . . ," to put forward his claim for the vessels that had initiated the incident.[123]

This ambassador, His Excellency Sidi Solyman Melimeli, and his suite arrived in Norfolk aboard the frigate *Congress* with Stephen Decatur on 4 November 1805. After impressing "the Mayor and . . . [the] respectable gentlemen of the town" with their "magnificent costume[s] in the true Turkish style," the Tunisians proceeded up to Washington in a small packet ship. No mention was made of the wild animals; perhaps they didn't survive the voyage, or maybe they didn't send them after all. But Melimeli did bring "four fine Arabian horses" to give as presents.[124]

For Henry Allen the Tunisian adventure ended in August of 1805, and in a letter to his father on the thirty-first Henry Allen was extravagant in his praise of John Rodgers. He spoke of the duty to his country that kept him in the Mediterranean but went on to describe a duty "still more powerfull" that he owed to Rodgers and for which he could offer only "assiduous attention, to any thing, that will contribute . . . to his interest."[125] Henry Allen seems at this time to have viewed John Rodgers as something like a surrogate father. For his part John Rodgers apparently accepted this filial bond.

The affair at Tunis ended for some years to come the U.S. Navy's involvement with the Barbary powers. The depredations on American merchant ships were greatly reduced but did not stop. Decatur, with Bainbridge close behind him, would be back in 1815 for another try at Algiers.

In 1816, after the Napoleonic Wars ended, the British finally took action against the Algerines, sending twenty ships under Admiral Lord Exmouth to level the place. In a six-hour bombardment the British ships threw in fifty-one thousand round shot plus one thousand explosive shells. This Mighty Raid quelled the enthusiasm of the Barbary powers for some time but did not totally stop the depredations, which continued sporadically.[126] In real terms, however, the Barbary Coast princes became irrelevant after the Great War ended in 1815 at Waterloo.

The whole range of events in the Barbary Wars was of immense value to the future of the U.S. Navy, providing the raw material of tradition and developing a cohesive and self-assured corps of officers, proud of their personal honor and ready for the challenges that were to come. Henry Allen had his twenty-first birthday on 21 October 1805, the day that Trafalgar was fought—a good omen for a naval officer. Henry was now a fully developed professional officer and seaman. Regrettably, he absorbed from his mentor, John Rodgers, a concept of personal honor that included an edge of arrogance.

After Tunis the *Constitution,* with John Rodgers and Henry Allen, moved to Syracuse, and the winter was spent in the ports of Sicily. There were no demands for warlike activity, and Henry Allen, in the company of John Rodgers, saw the wonders of antiquity at Pompeii and Herculaneum, and on another occasion climbed the southern slope of Etna and got lost on the way down. They were fortunately rescued by some Sicilian monks.[127]

In the spring of 1806 John Rodgers was ordered home. Most of the large squadron that had been sent over to subdue the Barbary States had already returned to the United States. The *Constitution* was to remain in the Mediterranean, so John Rodgers transferred to the small frigate *Essex,* taking Henry Allen with him, and in July 1806 the ship came home. Lieutenant Henry Allen then had several months with his family, on furlough in Providence.

CHAPTER TWO

The *Chesapeake* and the *Leopard*

HENRY ALLEN'S FURLOUGH LASTED until late January 1807, when on the twenty-sixth he was ordered to Washington to join the frigate *Chesapeake,* at that time fitting out in the Washington Navy Yard to be sent to the Mediterranean as the squadron flagship. The Senate had confirmed Henry's appointment as lieutenant on 8 January, and his date of rank was established as 17 February 1807. His beautifully engraved parchment commission bearing this date and signed by President Thomas Jefferson and Secretary of the Navy Robert Smith still exists in mint condition, stored in the archives of Great Britain.

The *Chesapeake* was to be commanded by Captain James Barron, the same man who had acquired the gratuitous enmity of John Rodgers during the recent events in the Mediterranean—an enmity that Rodgers wanted to settle with pistols.

James Barron was more than the skipper of the *Chesapeake.* He was to have the temporary rank of commodore, and his duties were to consist primarily of directing the operations and affairs of the Mediterranean squadron. The *Chesapeake* was also to have an officer with the title of captain but with the actual rank of master commandant, which was at that time the step between lieutenant and captain. This officer was to act as the captain of the ship, although the actual division of responsibility between the commodore and the captain for the affairs of a ship was not at that time entirely clear. Events were soon to bring more clarity to this issue. In any case, in early 1807 the duties of a captain when a commodore was aboard seem to have been more equivalent to those of the executive officer of a ship in today's U.S. Navy than to the total, unlimited responsibility held by a modern captain of a navy ship.

The *Chesapeake* was one of the original six frigates authorized on 27 March 1794 and intended to be powerful enough to "overmatch double-decked ships in blowing weather, handle any frigate, yet light enough to evade action in light winds."[1] The secretary of war managed the construction, as there was no Navy Department until 1798. The original design was highly successful and performed just as intended. However, only the *Constitution,* built at Boston, and the *United States* and *President,* built at Philadelphia and New York, were constructed to this design. The other three, the *Congress, Constellation,* and *Chesapeake,* were delayed, first because of a lack of funds and later because of material shortages, then were finally built to cut-down designs and were considerably smaller, about 152 feet in length on deck and with a 38-gun rating, as contrasted to 188 feet and 44 guns.

The *Chesapeake* was built at Gosport, now Portsmouth, Virginia, in a formerly private shipyard that was purchased for the purpose, and which over time came to be called the Norfolk Navy Yard. The shortage of materials—the live oak and cedar used in her had to be brought from Georgia—was eventually overcome, and she was finally completed and was launched on 3 December 1799. She was an unlucky ship from the beginning: The first attempt to launch her had to be aborted when she stuck on the ways because of cold tallow.[2] When she did go, a man was killed in the launching—always a bad omen. However, she was described as "both handsome and fast."[3] Although she had served in the West Indies (where she had a near mutiny in 1800) and in the Mediterranean (where she didn't fire a shot in anger), she had been laid up "in ordinary" at the Washington Navy Yard for four years when Henry Allen was ordered to her in February 1807 as third lieutenant.[4]

Even before reporting, Allen was sent to Philadelphia to recruit for the ship—a tough job, in part because the navy paid able seamen $12 per month even though they could get $18 to $28 on board merchant vessels.[5] The ship also had recruiters set out in New York and Norfolk.[6]

Allen's instructions were to ship up to 170 seamen, ordinary seamen, and boys and to somehow keep those that he managed to sign up together until there were enough to make it worthwhile to send them to Washington in a small merchant vessel that he was to charter when he needed it. After twenty-five days he had managed to sign up fifty-seven and was thoroughly exasperated, although obviously proud of having handled a tough job: ". . . my guardian genius, of good fortune certainly slumbered a little when she suffered me to be sent here. . . . think of 60 or 80 sailors, no doubt some of them wild

Irishmen, let loose in this city after you have advanced them from $18 to $70 each. . . . I have never had so much trouble with a pack of rascals in my life. . . ." Of the fifty-seven that he recruited, he released one because "his wife *overpersuaded* me." Two others were unfit, seven deserted with their cash advance—including a carpenter's mate, "as fine a man as I ever saw"—but the other forty-seven he managed to get on board "the packet" and on their way to the *Chesapeake* at about the end of March.[7]

The recruiters in Norfolk had had some early success in March, but by May "the scene [was] quite reversed."[8] By then sailors were scarce, the ship was still short handed, and recruiting continued in Norfolk right up to the time of departure. The crew was finally rounded out to about 340 men, some with sea experience, many with none, all of them new to one another—a far cry from a coherent, effective ship's company.

The officers presented another set of problems. The commodore, James Barron, was a Virginian, from Hampton, a small town north across Hampton Roads from Norfolk. He was thirty-nine at this time, a big man, over six feet tall and strongly built, but overweight, and he suffered from myopia, which made him habitually squint through narrowed eyes. He was good natured but worrisome and was too open and generous for his own good. Although an excellent seaman, he tended to be inactive and unaggressive. He was in most ways the opposite of the bold, dashing mold of naval officer admired by Henry Allen and the other young firebrands of that day.

Further, rumors were abroad that, out of fear, he was avoiding a duel, and his reputation was suffering as a result: he and John Rodgers were enemies as a result of the recent events in the Mediterranean, and it was thought that Barron was going to some lengths to avoid fighting him, although actually, behind the scenes, friends of both men were making efforts to defuse the quarrel.[9] This was not widely known, however, and Barron's reputation among his lieutenants was slowly turning to contempt.

For his part, Barron was horrified at the six lieutenants that had been assigned to the *Chesapeake,* all protégés of John Rodgers, and he later said that he viewed most of them as neither capable nor courageous.[10] Henry Allen in particular he greatly distrusted, knowing him to be a close friend and partisan of John Rodgers.

Nor was he encouraged by the officer assigned to be the captain of the *Chesapeake,* Master Commandant Charles Gordon, a young officer with fastidious tastes and a sardonic sense of humor.[11] Gordon came from an aristocratic Maryland Eastern Shore family with powerful connections in the Jefferson administration, his aunt being married to Secretary of the Treasury Albert Gallatin.[12] Gordon also had an uncle who was an influential member of Congress. Barron had known Gordon in the Mediterranean at an earlier time and thought him to be "much too addicted to pleasure . . . to bend his mind to business."[13] Upon hearing that Gordon was to be assigned, Barron protested strongly, but the secretary of the navy refused to cancel Gordon's orders.

At that time there was quite a heavy British presence in the Hampton Roads area. In mid-August of 1806 a severe hurricane, moving northward about three hundred miles south of Bermuda, had rolled over a squadron of the French Navy. Two French 74s, the *Patriote*, "in a very shattered condition, her topmasts gone and a number of her guns thrown overboard," followed by the *Eole*, in similar shape, entered the Chesapeake Bay about the first of September and went up to Annapolis, where they hoped to get repairs.[14] About the same time the *Cybele*, a French forty-four–gun frigate, dismasted in the same storm, arrived in Norfolk.

Within a few days a British force, after chasing the storm-damaged French 74 *Impetueux* ashore near Cape Charles and burning her, entered the Chesapeake Bay to blockade the three French ships. The British brought two seventy-four–gun ships—the *Bellona* and *Triumph*—the thirty-eight–gun frigate *Melampus*, the *Halifax*, a sixteen-gun ship-sloop, plus several tenders and a stores ship.[15] These ships settled down for a long stay and normally spent their time in Lynnhaven Bay, about four miles west of Cape Henry, just inside the Chesapeake Bay.

From the bay, Lynnhaven inlet led to the Lynnhaven River and a number of other waterways that threaded among the farms and plantations of Princess Anne County. The British squadron was a bonanza for the farmers, who immediately began to supply it with produce and livestock.

Twelve miles west of Lynnhaven Bay was the city of Norfolk and the open area of water north and west of it called Hampton Roads. The British ships often moved to Hampton Roads for a few days at a time, but even from Lynnhaven this was not a long sail in the ships' boats, or even too long a rowing distance for sturdy sailors, and the squadron officers soon became a fixture in the social life of the city. Of course, from Lynnhaven Bay the British could, and did, control traffic going in and out of Chesapeake Bay, stopping American and neutral vessels, going through their mail, searching them for contraband cargoes intended for the French, and occasionally impressing a sailor or two to make up for the continuous and debilitating losses from desertion.[16]

The British Navy, worldwide, suffered from a chronic shortage of manpower all during the long 1793–1815 wars with France. But the problem was particularly acute for the detached squadrons operating in American waters, where individual desertions occurred daily, and where occasionally the entire crew of a small British naval vessel would mutiny, run the ship in to the American coast, and desert en masse.[17]

The normal method of recruitment used when volunteers were in short supply—the usual situation—was impressment, a perfectly legal process of seizing British merchant seamen or watermen for an unlimited term of service in the navy. Naturally, this system worked best in the British home islands where there was a better, although not a plentiful, supply of British seafarers. In American waters, British officers quite often found bona fide British subjects sailing on board the American, and other, vessels that they illegally stopped and boarded, but where the officers didn't find British citizens they often took Americans, asserting them to be British, in spite of speech differences that by 1807 clearly delineated Americans, and in spite of "protection" certificates issued by U.S. collectors of customs and carried by nearly all American sailors.

Part of the problem was a conflict between the laws of the United States and those of Great Britain. U.S. law viewed as citizens not only those born in the United States and born elsewhere but living in the U.S.A. on 3 September 1783, when the Treaty of Paris ratified U.S. independence, but also "naturalized" citizens, those people who had lived in the United States for at least five years. British law recognized the first two classes of Americans but not those "naturalized," holding that a British subject could not of his own volition give up British citizenship.

As a result, British naval officers, particularly when in the process of impressing a couple of prime hands from an American merchant vessel, viewed all American protection certificates as hoaxes aimed at fraudulently covering British seafarers by giving them status as "instantly naturalized" Americans. In many cases this was true, but British officers often tore up perfectly legitimate "protections" and impressed their bearers who were bona fide, red-white-and-blue Americans. By way of example, the *Bellona,* the flagship of the British squadron, had at least seventeen impressed Americans in her crew, including fourteen-year-old John Hartsman.[18]

However, impressment was something that happened to merchant vessels, and there had not been any thought of trying to take sailors from a U.S. Navy ship, even among the most arrogant of the British, since the incident in 1798 between the British seventy-four–gun battleship *Carnatic* and the U.S. Sloop-of-War *Baltimore*. In connection with that affair, the British government did not assert that it had the right to search *national*—i.e., naval—vessels of another country to look for British sailors, and it appeared that this particular issue had been settled.[19]

Another result of the *Carnatic-Baltimore* incident was that the secretary of the navy issued an order to all commanders of U.S. armed vessels that, "overpowered by superior force, you are to strike your flag, and thus yield your vessel as well as your men, but never your men without your vessel."[20]

The American Navy had manpower problems too but depended on volunteers to fill its ships. Impressment was anathema to the American seafaring community, the memories of British press gangs operating legally in American ports during colonial times being fresh in all minds. It had been a big enough issue in late colonial days that impressment has its own paragraph in the Declaration of Independence.

So both navies got their men where they could and took what they could get. Sometimes what they could get was of appalling quality. Rarely could either fill a ship with sailors of its own nationality, and both the British and American Navies had many men of the other nationality on board. Henry Allen had remarked, earlier in 1807, "More than half the seamen in the United States Navy are foreigners, many of them British or Irish. They are the best seamen we have."[21] Henry was not far off the mark: a census of foreign seamen in the U.S. Navy, undertaken in 1808 as a result of the *Chesapeake-Leopard* affair, showed that something around 51 percent were foreigners, even by U.S. legal standards, and that about 75 percent of these were British.[22] On the British side, the number of Americans serving in the Royal Navy, willingly or unwillingly, was much smaller: a review of muster lists shows that a typical British crew of those times included about 5 percent Americans.[23]

Desertion was thus a major problem for the British Navy. It was bad enough in England where the law-enforcement system, rudimentary as it was, might bring back reluctant sailors. In American waters, desertion became a hemorrhage, with the population on shore usually ready to welcome and protect the deserters, and a new life in the new land to be had for the taking.

One evening in February 1807, while H.M. Frigate *Melampus* was anchored in Hampton Roads, her officers held a party on board for some of their gentleman and lady friends from Norfolk. The party apparently distracted the attention of the sentries normally posted to prevent desertions, and five men—John Little, Daniel Martin, John Strachan, William Ware, and Ambrose Watts—took the captain's gig, luckily for them the only boat in the water, and started for the beach. When noticed from the deck of the *Melampus* and hailed, they replied that they were "going ashore" and rowed like demons, in spite of "a brisk fire of musquetry" from the ship. They landed at Sewell's Point, carefully and neatly pulled the boat up on the strand, "gave three cheers and moved up the country."[24]

John Little and Ambrose Watts disappear from history, but the other three, probably short of money, showed up at the *Chesapeake*'s rendezvous in Norfolk within a few days. This recruiting post was performing in Norfolk the same service as Henry Allen in Philadelphia—locating the scarce and elusive sailorman and enlisting him for the *Chesapeake*. The Norfolk post was run by Arthur Sinclair, a newly promoted lieutenant who was not one of the *Chesapeake*'s own officers, and who therefore was not faced with the sobering prospect of serving on shipboard with those he signed up. This may well have made him a bit casual when it came to the quality and antecedents of potential recruits, but after all, there wasn't very much good material to be had, "owing to the scarcity of sailors at present in Norfolk."[25]

The three swore to being American, and Sinclair signed them up. These men—Daniel Martin, John Strachan, and William Ware—actually were Americans. Martin was "a coloured man" from Westport, Massachusetts, and had been impressed from an American merchant ship something over a year earlier. Strachan was a white man from the Eastern Shore of Maryland, who had been impressed out of "an English Guineaman." Ware, also from Maryland, was "an Indian looking man." He had served with Barron some years before in the U.S. Navy. There are differing versions of how they came to be in the British Navy in the first place, but in any event they were not English.[26]

A short time later, on 7 March, there was another desertion episode, and this one had a harder edge to it. H.M. Sloop-of-War *Halifax,* a small, three-masted ship, was anchored in Hampton Roads. She had earlier streamed a kedge anchor from the stern to swing the ship, a maneuver frequently done to check the compass or to bring a ship broadside to the breeze for better ventilation.

At six that evening the *Halifax* sent her jolly boat, with five men under Midshipman Robert Turner, to lift the kedge anchor and bring it back to the ship. It was twilight, the weather was squally, and while the boat was over the anchor it began to rain very hard. In the working party with Midshipman Turner were Henry Saunders, a boatswain's mate; Richard Hubert, a sailmaker; George North, a seaman and the captain of the maintop; William Hill, a seaman; and Jenkin Ratford, an ordinary seaman and sailmaker's helper. All were British-born except Hill, an American from Philadelphia.[27]

While the rain hid them from the view of the watch on the deck of the *Halifax,* the four seamen mutinied, apparently led by Hill, cut the boat free from the anchor, and started rowing for shore. Midshipman Turner shouted to the ship, trying to get someone's attention, until told by Hill that he would knock his brains out and throw him overboard if he didn't stop. Poor Saunders, the boatswain's mate, sat in the stern sheets with Turner, trying to stay out of trouble. The ship finally noticed the escape and fired muskets and even one great gun at the jolly boat, but it was already nearly lost in the dusk. The boat landed safely at Sewell's Point, where the mutineers jumped out. Saunders reluctantly accompanied them after being threatened with having his brains knocked out if he didn't. Midshipman Turner was left in the boat, and as one of the men had cut the painter, the boat started to drift off the beach. Turner, probably not wanting to drift around Hampton Roads on a rainy night or possibly be carried out to sea by the tide and current, jumped out into water up to his waist and, wading ashore, made the best of his way down to Norfolk.[28]

Two days later, on Monday, Lieutenant Marsters of the *Halifax* was ashore in Norfolk and encountered the deserters with a group of U.S. Navy enlistees who were carrying an American flag through the streets of Norfolk to attract more recruits, and he learned that they had all five signed on for the U.S.S. *Chesapeake*.[29] The next day he reported this to the captain of the *Halifax,* who was the Right Honorable Lord James Townshend, not only a member of the peerage of England but also a scion of one of the most politically powerful families in the realm. He decided to go ashore and himself try to get the American Navy recruiters to turn the men back over to him.

With Midshipman Turner in tow, Townshend went to the sailors' boarding house where he had been informed that the men were staying. Standing in the street, he sent in for Boatswain's Mate Saunders, who soon came out followed by Jenkin Ratford. Townshend asked Saunders why he had deserted and promised him that if he returned to the ship, all would be forgiven and forgotten. Saunders had been pulled into this situation against his better judgment, and the invitation to return was welcome. But as he started to walk away with Lord Townshend, Jenkin Ratford threatened to get some other sailors and "cut his bloody guts out" if he attempted to go back. Ratford then proceeded to tell off Lord Townshend, using "very abusive," undoubtedly unprintable, language, ending up that he would "be damned if he [would] return to the ship . . . he was in the Land of Liberty."[30]

Jenkin Ratford was a short, stocky man, a former tailor from London, with his full name tattooed on his left arm. He was thirty-four years old at this time, an ordinary seaman who now applied his tailoring skill as a sailmaker's helper.[31]

Like many sailors of the time, he apparently had difficulty visualizing the future consequences of his actions: for a British sailor, even an almost ex-British sailor, to use bad language to a British Navy captain was certain to bring him into trouble. Almost worse, persons of Ratford's social class could not throw insults at a Right Honorable Lord without making serious problems for themselves. However, there was nothing that Lord Townshend could do at the moment, and further, a hostile-looking crowd was beginning to gather, so he left.

Making his way next toward the *Chesapeake*'s recruiting rendezvous, he ran into Lieutenant Sinclair in the street. The two were "personally acquainted," and Lord Townshend, in some dudgeon, stopped Sinclair and asked him "if [he] had not enlisted his boat's crew." Townshend had learned the false names that the men had enlisted under—Jenkin Ratford was now called John Wilson—and asked for them by these names, giving Sinclair personal descriptions of the men. Sinclair readily admitted that he had recruited men like those described, and had known they were British, but denied knowing that they were deserters from the British Navy.

Sinclair then told Townshend that he did not have the authority to release the men, and neither did the local magistracy, but that the Navy Department could and probably would do so. Townshend's attitude then changed. He said that "they were not worth the trouble," and if he could get back Saunders, the boatswain's mate, who was "a favorite," and one of the others, so "that he might hang him as an example," he would be perfectly satisfied.[32]

Lord Townshend then called on Stephen Decatur, who was the commander of the Norfolk Navy Yard and the most senior American naval officer in the area. Decatur told him that it wasn't in his jurisdiction, in spite of what Sinclair had said. Lord Townshend was not accustomed to getting this sort of runaround. In British eyes, the *Chesapeake* was becoming "a kind of fly-paper for picking up deserters and other wandering British seamen."[33]

Townshend, probably by this time in a steaming rage, next sought out Mr. Hamilton, the British consul in Norfolk, and between them they wrote letters reporting the incident to David Erskine, the British minister in Washington, and to the Honorable George Cranfield Berkeley, M.P., Vice-Admiral of the White, and Commander-in-Chief, who from Halifax, Nova Scotia, ruled all the British naval forces in North American waters.

In Washington, Erskine protested formally to Madison, who through the bureaucracy asked Barron to look into the problem. Barron and the *Chesapeake* were across town at the Washington Navy Yard.

Meanwhile, the *Melampus* and *Halifax* deserters, along with some other recruits, were put on a small vessel and sent from Norfolk up to the *Chesapeake*. When this draft of men arrived alongside the *Chesapeake,* Barron sent for the ex-*Melampus* men. After hearing that two of them claimed to be Marylanders, one from the Eastern Shore, he asked Captain Gordon, born on the Eastern Shore, to talk to them. Gordon reported that he was convinced that they were telling the truth and were impressed Americans. Barron reported this and the details about the men to Secretary Madison. Unfortunately, Barron was totally unaware that he also had on board the *Chesapeake* Jenkin Ratford and the other *Halifax* deserters.[34]

At this time Erskine met with Secretary of State Madison and Secretary of the Navy Smith to discuss the matter. The result was confusion. Whether or not Barron was actually at the meeting is not clear, but his understanding of the outcome was that Erskine, on behalf of the British government, had consented to waive all claim to the deserters.[35] This was a serious misunderstanding. Erskine stated later that he was not asked for his view on the subject, that he had not been shown any proof that the men were Americans, and that, in any event, he left all decisions about sailors to Admiral Berkeley.

So this high-level meeting that was supposed to have cleared up the matter of the *Melampus* and *Halifax* deserters instead left things dangerously ambiguous:

Madison told Barron that the ex-*Melampus* sailors were Americans, that had he given them up he would have been in trouble, and that the British had now relinquished any claim to them.[36] Admiral Berkeley, on the other hand, was convinced that a high level of the American government had been unable to prove that his deserters were U.S. citizens and that they were still very much British sailors.

James Barron thought that his problems with British deserters were over with and that the whole matter had been amicably resolved. But there were clear indications that it had not: at about this time Henry Allen heard a rumor that the British intended to take back their deserters. Gordon also heard that the captain of the *Melampus,* talking openly in a tavern, threatened to take his deserters back by force. The ex-*Melampus* men, sensitive to the fact that the British often hung deserters when they got their hands on them, came to Captain Gordon and told him that they had doubts as to whether or not they would be protected if the British came after them. Gordon and Barron, aware of the rumors, had previously discussed this question, and Gordon assured them that they would be protected. Some of those aboard were apparently not convinced: shortly thereafter, four of the five *Halifax* deserters deserted from the *Chesapeake,* leaving aboard only Jenkin Ratford, or, as he was carried on the ship's books, John Wilson.[37]

At about this time James Barron faced another predicament: he found that the *Chesapeake*'s gunpowder was all bad, apparently not completely unusable but at least "not fit for service." When he informed the Navy Department of this and asked for "good powder," he was told that there was none to be had and that he should get his present powder "remanufactured" at Malta, after reaching the Mediterranean.[38] Barron complained bitterly, but nothing could be done, and he had to accept that in this important respect his ship was not ready to fight.

With this mélange of problems on board, the *Chesapeake* finally completed as much of her refitting as she could at the navy yard and prepared to head back down to Hampton Roads. By now Commodore Barron had gone back to his home in Hampton, leaving Captain Gordon in charge of the ship. Whether or not some lack of competence on Gordon's part contributed to the problems that followed is not clear, but certainly the incessant string of mishaps that dogged the ship during this short, two hundred–mile trip set some kind of a record for seafaring misfortune.

Early on 9 May the *Chesapeake* received a pilot and hauled off from the wharf at the navy yard. The ship had taken no guns on board at the yard, to keep the draft light enough to get over the bar at the mouth of the Eastern Branch of the Potomac. But in spite of this, by 9 A.M. the ship had run aground on Greenleaf Point, and it took the remainder of the day to heave her off using anchors and capstan. After getting off, the crew spent the next day in belatedly unloading most of their provisions and shot into a tender to further lighten the ship.[39]

So it took two days to drop four miles down the Potomac to Alexandria. Here the river was a little deeper, and Gordon took on twelve main-battery 18-pounders to aid in trimming the ship. Twelve was all that she could have aboard and still pass over the shoals lower in the river. The *Chesapeake* remained for several days in Alexandria while the carpenters and joiners from the navy yard fitted the half-ports to the guns in the cabin area.[40]

At this point the *Chesapeake*'s woes had just begun. The crew was about sixty men short, those that were aboard were mostly raw, and even the experienced men were totally new to the ship. In Alexandria, while they were bringing down some of the upper yards, an improperly tied rope caused the foreyard—a massive, seventy-five-foot-long piece of timber—to suddenly lurch, tumbling three men down forty or so feet to the deck below. Two were killed and the other badly injured.[41]

As if this were not enough, some serious illness was rampant in the ship's company, keeping 60 to 85 men, more than 20 percent of those aboard, on the sick list during the entire trip.[42]

Upon passing Mount Vernon, the *Chesapeake* rendered the customary salute to George Washington, firing sixteen guns. Henry Allen was in charge of the saluting and found that most of the wads and about half of the cartridges, flannel bags to be filled with black powder and calibrated to slide into the muzzles of the guns, were the wrong size. The carelessness or incompetence of the gunner, William Hook, had allowed these to be accepted from the navy yard, and Gordon had him arrested and kept on board for later trial.[43] Then, to top off the bad luck for that day, Seaman Gideon Winslow fell overboard and drowned.

Just below Mount Vernon, on 23 May, naval surgeon Dr. John Bullus, his wife, three children, a servant girl, and a black boy came aboard, together with all their baggage and some crated furniture and household goods. The doctor, a personal friend of Thomas Jefferson, with ties to the administration, was to be the navy agent in the Mediterranean and U.S. consul in Minorca. He and his family were to travel over aboard the *Chesapeake*. Also boarding at this time was the *Chesapeake*'s senior marine officer, Captain Hall, and his new bride.[44] Hall, a politically well connected officer, had also been given permission for his wife to travel over with him.

While the ship was becalmed the next day, still in the Potomac, and at anchor off Indian Head, Maryland, a seaman managed to desert from a boat's crew. Then one of the sick, Seaman William Barret, "departed this life" at 1 P.M. and at 5 was taken ashore for burial, the river being too shallow for a proper commitment to the deep.[45]

Even with only twelve guns aboard, the frigate had trouble getting over some of the shoals. Sailing vessels the size of the *Chesapeake* were normally trimmed so as to have a foot or so greater draft at the stern than at the bow. To pass the Mattawoman shoals, Henry Allen was ordered to move the guns far enough forward to bring the ship to a level keel. The effort was to no avail: the ship went aground, and with great difficulty the crew managed to heave her over the shoal with the anchors and capstan, parting a hawser in the process.[46] Then the *Chesapeake* made some brief progress, about fifteen miles, before trouble set in again.

Still in the Potomac after twenty-two days, only forty miles downriver from the navy yard, the frigate anchored off Maryland Point. Here eight men took the cutter and deserted. Captain Gordon sent Midshipman FitzHenry Babbit and some marines to track them down and sent another party to look for the cutter, which was found abandoned about five miles away on the Maryland shore. Babbit and the marines came back the next day, empty-handed. Then, while the jolly boat was away from the ship, her four-man crew mutinied on the boat officer and deserted, taking the boat with them. Again, Mr. Babbit was sent in pursuit.

Finally, on 3 June the *Chesapeake* sailed out of the river and into the Chesapeake Bay. Two of the sick men died that day, and now that the ship was in deeper, tidal waters, the bodies were "committed . . . to the deep with the usual sea ceremonies." In the middle of that night the wind came around to the north, fair for the trip down the bay, and late the next afternoon the frigate at last anchored in Hampton Roads and began to take aboard the stores for the cruise.[47]

Dr. Bullus and his entourage and Mrs. Hall left the ship and set themselves up temporarily ashore. On the sixth, the *Chesapeake* received the rest of her 18-pounder long guns, shot, and extra spars, brought down from Washington on the *Spitfire* ketch. Also on that day Commodore Barron came aboard and, curiously, again went through the ceremony of assuming command, having his blue, one-starred broad command pennant hoisted. Then after looking around below decks as much as he could, given the cluttered state of things, he went ashore in the early afternoon, leaving the preparations for the voyage in the hands of Captain Gordon and the lieutenants, and was not seen again until just before departure.[48]

There was a great deal to be done to make the ship ready for sea. In addition to loading her own stores and water, the *Chesapeake* had to take aboard supplies and equipage for other ships in the Mediterranean squadron. Her upper spars had to be swayed up and rigged, and the studding sail gear for all masts had to be mounted and rigged. The 18-pounder guns for the gun deck had all to be mounted in their carriages, but some of them didn't fit—a problem that was not noticed until later on.[49]

On 15 June the *Spitfire,* having made a round-trip to the Washington Navy Yard, brought the quarterdeck guns, twelve 32-pound carronades. These short-barrelled smashers allowed a lightweight gun to hurl a large ball and were highly effective, but only at short ranges. While at the navy yard, Barron had agreed to try out experimental mountings for the carronades, and fitting the guns on them proved to be troublesome.[50]

There were other problems. The crew was not complete, and new men were coming aboard every day. The ship lacked the most important of her warrant officers: no boatswain had been ordered aboard. The sailing master, whose duties included navigating the ship and keeping the logs, could "neither read nor write [enough] to be understood" and had "no adequate knowledge of navigation."[51] Also, Captain Gordon had been unable to find another gunner to take the place of Hook, who was still under arrest, and a few days before getting under way for the Mediterranean reinstated him in spite of concerns about his competence and the state of things in his department.[52] The guns had just gotten aboard, and some were still incompletely mounted in their carriages and unrigged, so there was no real opportunity to hold satisfactory exercises with them for this raw crew.

Then there was the matter of the condemned powder. And the gun deck was "lumbered up" with crates of Dr. Bullus's furniture and the supplies and equipage being transported for the other ships in the Mediterranean Squadron. In spite of all these drawbacks, Captain Gordon reported to Barron that the *Chesapeake* was ready for sea. In a sense she was: there is little doubt that the ship could have accomplished a peaceful voyage across the summer Atlantic, fixing up the rest of the problems as she went. This, however, was not how things came about.

Toward the end of this period, Captain Gordon had all the guns loaded and the tompions, or muzzle plugs, put in to keep them dry. On some ships this was considered a normal practice prior to going to sea, but in Gordon's mind was the threat from the captain of H.M. Frigate *Melampus* to recover his deserters by force.[53] However, the captain of the *Melampus* was not the only one interested in getting his hands on the deserters. Vice-Admiral the Honorable George Cranfield Berkeley, commander in chief of the British naval forces in American waters, had been complaining without result about the widespread problem of desertions in his command. Lord Townshend's letter about the *Halifax* deserters finally brought him to action.

Like Townshend, Berkeley was a member of one of the great political noble families of England and was, in addition, a member of Parliament himself, having earlier purchased a seat in the Commons at great expense.[54] While in command of the American station he emitted a continuous stream of complaints about the Admiralty and about the American government and sent these missives directly to the prime minister, bypassing his nominal superiors at the Admiralty. This engaging conduct was overlooked because in Parliament, when he was home, he was a strong supporter of the present government, as was his powerful brother, the Earl of Berkeley, in the House of Lords.[55]

The admiral was a beefy, bull-necked man who despised Americans and believed that the United States was conspiring to take over the West Indies trade and the fisheries on the North Atlantic Banks. He had a one-sided picture of the political situation in the United States, partly because he got most of his information from the ultra-right High Federalist newspapers in Boston and from a network of spies in New England that sent him letters in cipher:[56]

> Received yours of the 29th January. 38 in EF18 and 2CH 35AW. 68 his AP76 as well as KW39+37 was BB40ed, and everything is perfectly KG82 AY5 them. . . .[57]

He had a contingency plan in his files for fomenting a slave uprising in Maryland and Virginia as part of a war to liberate New England from the domination of the current American administration headed by Virginians.[58] His surviving papers show that he would not have been unwilling to see a war with the United States begin in 1807, something that was strongly contrary to the policy of the British government.

Berkeley had set up his headquarters ashore in Halifax, Nova Scotia, and used his flagship, H.M. Ship *Leopard,* as just another ship in his command. On 1 June 1807 he issued an order to the ships under his command, noting the desertion problem, asserting that deserters from a number of his majesty's ships had signed aboard the U.S. Frigate *Chesapeake,* and directing his captains to stop her if they caught her at sea outside U.S. waters and search her for these deserters. The list of six ships whose deserters were being sought included the *Halifax* but not the *Melampus.* It is not clear why she was omitted. The order was given to the captain of the *Leopard* to carry down to the squadron at Lynnhaven Bay.[59]

The *Leopard* was a fifty-gun ship, a class of small battleship no longer used "in the line," but still a lot more powerful than the thirty-eight–gun *Chesapeake.* The *Leopard*'s captain was Salusbury Pryce Humphreys, who, although only the son of a Shropshire clergyman, had risen into the minor gentry by marrying an heiress. He was a handsome dog, with strong, classic features and the short tousled hair and long side-whiskers affected by younger naval officers at that time.[60] The order in hand, Humphreys, with the *Leopard,* headed for the Chesapeake Bay.

The *Leopard* arrived off Cape Henry at the mouth of the Chesapeake at 8 A.M. on 21 June, passed H.M.S. *Triumph,* 74, which was anchored just north of the cape, and ran up to Lynnhaven Bay, four miles to the west, where she anchored. Present at that time at Lynnhaven were the *Bellona,* 74, and the frigate *Melampus.* Humphreys reported to Captain John Erskine Douglas, the captain of the *Bellona* and the senior British officer in the area, and showed him Admiral Berkeley's order.

It was common knowledge in Norfolk that the *Chesapeake* was planning to leave the next day, a fact that created some urgency among the British, and the captains of the squadron were brought together to read the order and discuss how it was to be implemented. The order was clear and unequivocal in that it "required and directed" the captains of his majesty's ships meeting the *Chesapeake* at sea to show her captain the order and "to require to search his ship for the deserters from the before-mentioned ships, and to proceed and search for the same. . . ."[61]

The order did not mention the use of force, but it was pretty clear that force was implied, as it was not likely that any American warship would submit willingly to such a humiliating experience. So whichever of the ships present was to bell the cat had to be powerful enough to handle the *Chesapeake.* Of course, all the captains present would have enjoyed this delicious opportunity to humble the Americans and at the same time provide a grim object lesson to potential deserters in their own ships. Captain Hawker of the *Melampus* had bragged in public of his intent to recover his deserters, but his ship was the same size as the *Chesapeake,* and it would be foolish to risk an even contest when the means were available to present overwhelming force. The two 74s, while obviously powerful enough, were a bit clumsy and might not be able to force an action to take place. That left the *Leopard,* and like the small bowl of porridge, she was just right: with fifty-two guns to the *Chesapeake's* forty, she had ample power, and she was nearly as nimble as a frigate.

Now it may have been that Admiral Berkeley told Humphreys in person before he left Halifax that he and the *Leopard* were to handle the job. This, however, is highly unlikely: the evidence is that Humphreys was simply carrying Berkeley's order to the senior officer of the squadron in the Chesapeake and didn't have specific instructions to execute the order himself.[62] This was an era when communications between ships and headquarters took weeks rather than microseconds, and British doctrine called for the senior officer at the scene to have a great deal of latitude in interpreting and executing orders. More likely, some considerable discussion took place among Douglas and his assembled captains, and in spite of the satisfying emotional lift that any of them would get from doing the job, there were misgivings:

Great Britain and the United States had been at peace for almost a quarter of a century, and the action that Berkeley had ordered and the squadron was planning to take—forcing an illegal search upon another nation's ship of war, and practically in her own territorial waters at that—was beyond any right asserted by the British government.[63] The search was almost certain to cause a tremendous uproar, and while an admiral who was an M.P. and the brother of the Earl of Berkeley might come through unscathed, the consequences for a mere naval captain were, at the least, uncertain. The other captains were probably relieved that the obvious choice was the *Leopard* and Humphreys—after all, he was Berkeley's flag captain.

So it was to be the *Leopard,* and at 4 A.M. on the following morning, 22 June, she moved out to a Cape Henry anchorage near the *Triumph,* where she could get under way quickly and get out of the bay even if the winds were adverse. She had taken aboard Mr. Tincombe, a master's mate from the *Melampus,* who could identify her deserters, even though retaking them would exceed Berkeley's order.[64] The *Triumph,* Captain Sir Thomas M. Hardy—Nelson's Hardy— was to be ready to get under way and back up the *Leopard* in the unlikely event that anything went seriously awry. Henry Allen, in a letter written about a month later, said that the *Triumph* had a block under her anchor cable, and an axe handy, ready to cut and run to assist the *Leopard.*[65]

The *Chesapeake* had been minimally ready to go to sea since about 17 June but had been prevented from getting out by an adverse gale from the northeast.[66] Dr. Bullus, with his family and servants, came aboard on the seventeenth, as well as Mrs. Hall, the marine captain's wife. Also aboard were a group of Italian musicians who had served in the U.S. Marine Band until it was decided that they were no longer needed, and they had asked to be sent home. They were considered part of the marine detachment, assigned as "music." Also, as usual, there were a few enlisted wives living on board. By Sunday afternoon, the twenty-first, the storm had passed, Commodore Barron came aboard, and the ship weighed anchor and moved farther down the roads and re-anchored.[67]

The next morning, Monday the twenty-second, was clear, and there was a fresh breeze from the southwest, right for getting to sea. Norfolk civilian pilot Charles Nuttrell was aboard. The *Chesapeake* hoisted in her cutter, brought the jolly boat up to the stern davits, and at 7:15 got under way and stood down the bay on her way out to sea.

Henry Allen had the watch on deck that morning, and at about 9:30, as the frigate passed the *Bellona* and *Melampus,* at anchor on the Tail of Horse Shoe Bank offshore of Lynnhaven Inlet, he saw that the *Bellona* was signaling, apparently to the *Leopard,* which got under way and proceeded out and south around Cape Henry. This, taken together with the rumors about British threats to recover the deserters, alerted Allen's suspicions, always close to the surface where the British were concerned. However, there seemed to be no unusual activity aboard the two ships anchored at Lynnhaven, and Captain Gordon, the threat of the *Melampus* still in his mind, was relieved when she did not get under way as he passed.[68]

The signal from the *Bellona* had told the *Leopard* to "weigh and reconnoitre in the south-east by east."[69] The wind being from a southerly direction, this order put her to windward of the course that the *Chesapeake* would follow in heading to sea. The fresh breeze hadn't been blowing long enough to raise the sea, and the surface was calm. At about noon, just as the *Chesapeake* was at the very mouth of the bay, the wind died and then came back fresh, now from the southeast, forcing her to beat her way out, and she had to make several tacks to do so, always to the eastward. The *Leopard,* carefully staying to windward and holding the weather gauge, tacked in parallel with the *Chesapeake*—very strange behavior in the eyes of those unaware of Admiral Berkeley's order. Henry Allen also noted that the *Leopard,* about a mile away at the time, had her lower-deck gun ports open and took this as more confirmation of hostile intent, although it was a warm day and the *Chesapeake,* and the ships at anchor, all had their ports open for ventilation.[70] Allen didn't tell Commodore Barron of his apprehensions, nor did any of the other lieutenants, who later said that they had had similar suspicions of the British intentions: junior officers are usually reluctant to point out to their seniors things that are visible and seem obvious. Sailing Master Brooke also said nothing, and he was probably the most suspicious and prescient of all, telling Lieutenant Sidney Smith, "This fellow is coming on board of us to demand [his] deserters and if they are not delivered up we shall have **Hell to hold**."[71]

The Norfolk pilot boat had been following the *Chesapeake* to take off Mr. Nuttrell when the ship was safely out of the channel, and at about 3 P.M. the frigate slowed to let the pilot boat catch up and come alongside. At this point the *Leopard,* which had been edging up on the starboard quarter, surged ahead and came abreast of the *Chesapeake,* about fifty or sixty yards to windward. At the least, this was discourteous behavior: a friendly vessel, wishing to speak to another, normally would come up to leeward. But this conduct was now becoming clearly threatening. The *Leopard*'s gun ports were open, and her guns were run out with the tompions removed.[72]

Humphreys hailed across to the *Chesapeake* that he "had despatches from the Commander-in-Chief for the commander of the *Chesapeake*." Barron shouted back, "We will heave to and you can send your boat on board."[73] By this time Barron must have suspected what was afoot, although forever afterward he insisted that he didn't realize until later that they were in for some trouble. He thought that the discussions in Washington between Madison and Erskine had solved the problem with the *Melampus,* and he was not aware that he still had Jenkin Ratford of the *Halifax* on board. It seems to have been beyond his comprehension that he could be attacked in a time of deep peace over such a minor issue. However, it was a common precaution in the U.S. Navy at that time, at least in the Mediterranean squadron, to go to quarters when approaching or being approached by another man-of-war. If Barron had gone to quarters immediately, the events that followed might have had a different outcome.

The *Leopard*'s boat went around the stern of the *Chesapeake* and came up to her lee gangway. Lieutenant John Meade came aboard and was met by Gordon, who took him to Commodore Barron waiting in the cabin. Meade presented Admiral Berkeley's order and a list of the men he was looking for, together with a coolly courteous note from Humphreys expressing hopes that the affair "may be adjusted in a manner that the harmony subsisting between the two countries may remain undisturbed." His probable meaning was that he hoped things could be worked out so that he could execute his admiral's harebrained order without losing his command in the storm that was sure to ensue.[74]

Also in the cabin were the Bulluses, their children, and Mrs. Hall, who was already seasick. When Lieutenant Meade came aboard, they moved into the after section of the cabin, out of sight and out of the way.

Barron called Captain Gordon, handed him the list of men, and asked if any of them were aboard. Without even reading the list, Gordon answered that the crew were all new to the ship and he did not yet know them by name, but that the recruiters had been told not to enlist British deserters. At this point Gordon seems not to have been greatly worried. He had observed the common practice between British and American ships in the Mediterranean to ask for the return of deserters, but not to force the issue if refused. He then left the cabin, not aware of the implication of force in Berkeley's order.

Barron sat down at a table across the cabin from Lieutenant Meade and started to work out a reply to Humphreys. Within a few minutes he asked Dr. Bullus to join him, and they talked earnestly for several minutes, out of earshot of the British officer, and then Bullus went back to his family. What they said has never become known. Barron was hoping for some useful advice from this astute politician but, probably even more, hoping to spread out the responsibility for the actions he might be forced to take. He would be disappointed in the latter: Dr. Bullus was not interested in protecting Barron, was much too adroit to be drawn into any of the consequences, and even avoided testifying at the subsequent court-martial.

Time went by, and after about half an hour the officer of the deck came to the cabin to report that the *Leopard* had hoisted a signal to recall her boat and the officer. Lieutenant Meade became quite restive, but Barron told him the answer would quickly be ready. Within a few minutes Barron gave his completed reply to Meade, for delivery to Humphreys. In it he said that he didn't know of the men described in the list, didn't know of any deserters aboard, and in any event was instructed never to allow the crew of any ship he commanded to be mustered by any but their own officers. It was an excellent reply to an arrogant demand, and it followed the orders given out to the navy after the earlier *Carnatic* incident.[75]

The *Chesapeake* was woefully unprepared for what was to come. Her orders to proceed to the Mediterranean noted that the United States was "at peace with all the world," and nothing in them warned that British-American relations had come to the point that attacks were to be expected.[76] The frigate was encumbered with passengers, baggage, and furniture, plus supplies for the Mediterranean squadron. The crew was raw and, due to the press of getting out of the navy yard and getting loaded for the voyage, had never been put through any training at the guns. Mr. Hook, the gunner, was only marginally competent, tended to become confused at stressful moments, and had a bad stammer. Things in his department were a mess. He had been ordered to fill the powder horns that were used to prime the vents of the guns and had reported this as completed, but in fact had filled only five of them.[77] Only a couple of rounds of cartridges, the flannel powder bags to load the guns, had been filled.

There was another important detail: the gun locks were not mounted on the guns.[78] The gun lock was a relatively new technology at this time and consisted of a device resembling the hammer, flint, and striking plate of a flintlock musket; this apparatus was attached over the touchhole of a great gun and fired with the pull of a lanyard. It made naval guns much more accurate because the firing was made nearly instantaneous, and the ship didn't have a chance to roll much between aiming and firing. More importantly, guns with locks were always ready to fire. Under the old system, pieces of match rope had to be gotten from storage and lighted, or pokerlike loggerheads had to be heated in the galley fire until they were hot enough to ignite gunpowder. When all this was ready, the gun captain, under the old system, aimed the gun, and at his order another man touched the priming powder at the touchhole with a smoldering piece of match rope or a hot loggerhead.

Given the pressure from the Navy Department for the *Chesapeake* to leave for the Mediterranean as soon as possible after getting out of the navy yard, it is not surprising that the locks were unusable: the guns were all new to the ship, and the job of fitting the locks to them in those days before interchangeable parts would take a couple of weeks. However, the lack of gun locks threw the *Chesapeake* back on the old system, which by 1807 was used only as an emergency backup in the event that a lock jammed or a flint broke.

Gordon was on the quarterdeck when Meade came out of the cabin and escorted the British officer back to the lee gangway and his boat. As the boat pulled away, Barron sent for Gordon to come to the cabin. Lieutenant Meade had taken back the only copy of Admiral Berkeley's order, leaving the situation slightly confused, but Barron showed Gordon the letter from Humphreys and his reply, then said, "You had better get your gun deck clear, as their intentions appear serious." Gordon left, found Benjamin Smith and William Crane, the two senior lieutenants, and gave them the order. The astute Dr. Bullus, clearly sensing trouble, took his family down to the cockpit. Captain Hall, warned by the doctor, carried his seasick bride below.

When Gordon returned to the quarterdeck, Barron was standing in the weather gangway, getting his first good look at the *Leopard*. What he saw was not encouraging: she was about sixty yards abeam, her ports were open, the tompions were out of her guns, and the guns were run out and were aimed at the *Chesapeake*.[79]

At last thoroughly alarmed, Barron told Gordon to get the crew to quarters, but quietly, without beating the drum, and without allowing the men to show themselves at the ports. While still standing in the open gangway, Barron was hailed by Captain Humphreys from the *Leopard* but was unable to understand what Humphreys was saying and asked him to repeat it. It is possible that he understood but was playing for more time to get to quarters. It is also possible, even probable, that a British accent with a Shropshire flavor through a mega-phonelike speaking trumpet was simply unintelligible to him. In any event, as the attempted communications were going on, the *Leopard* opened fire.

Gordon had given the order to quietly go to quarters, and the lieutenants started passing the word. But the almost invariable way of getting to battle sta-tions in those days was by beating a drum on the quarterdeck and at the top of the hatch leading from the gun deck to the berth deck. So the *Chesapeake*'s drummer started to "beat to quarters," but Gordon almost immediately stopped him. This created a problem of its own: many of the men hardly knew how to get to their stations in the first place, and when the drum stopped, they were confused and didn't do anything. Of course, by this time all those on board who were awake were aware that something big was happening and were highly alert. However, probably a third to half of the crew were asleep in the berth deck and, without the drum, were slow to be aroused.

Henry Allen, who had recently completed his watch as officer of the deck, was sitting in the wardroom, the officers' space partitioned off at the after end of the berth deck, underneath the cabin area. Some of the officers were asleep in their cabins, which ranged along each side of the wardroom. His friend, Lieu-tenant William Crane, came in and told him that the ship was going to quar-ters. Allen got his sidearms—pistol and sword—from his cabin and ran to his station on the gun deck, where he was in charge of the second division com-prising the middle ten of the guns, five on each side.[80]

Looking out of a port, Henry Allen saw the *Leopard* abeam of him, obvi-ously ready to fire. In spite of the indecision caused by the stopping of the drumbeat, men were beginning to arrive at the guns. Captain Gordon hailed down the hatch to not let the men show themselves at the ports or remove the tompions from the guns, an order that struck Allen as pusillanimous.[81] It was probably unnecessary as well: everyone arriving was thrown into the task of clearing away the mass of clutter that was in the way of working the guns.

Immediately behind Henry Allen's guns was a range of anchor cable, 720 feet of huge hemp cable 6 inches in diameter—impossible to move quickly. Between and around the guns were empty beef and pork barrels, as well as the ship's grog tub. Nine sick men were in their hammocks over and abreast of the guns, together with their seabags, medicines, and other sick-bay necessities. The sick men were carried or helped below to the cockpit, and their bags, the barrels, and everything else movable was thrown down the main hatch into the berth deck. Working with Allen were two midshipmen, John Shubrick and Alexander Wadsworth, and the three of them, with the men who were continuing to arrive, loosened the breeching tackle on three of the guns, which were then ready to shoot, except for powder to prime the vents, and, lacking gun locks, some fire to touch them off.

Henry Allen sent Midshipman Shubrick to the magazine to get some powder horns of priming powder—the horns that the gunner was supposed to have filled, but hadn't. But the magazine was in a state of chaos, the gunner was confused and unable to remember where he had stowed things, and the passage leading to the magazine was jammed with midshipmen and boys trying to get powder horns. Shubrick had to wait his turn. At about this moment came the sound of two guns as the Leopard fired one shot ahead of the *Chesapeake* and one astern, followed shortly by a broadside that went mostly through the sails and masts. This was followed by two more broadsides into the hull, and the damage and carnage on the *Chesapeake* were terrific.

When the firing started, Captain Gordon was on the gun deck, trying to get the guns working, and asked Allen why he wasn't firing. Allen told him that he needed powder horns and matches. Gordon started toward the magazine and met a boy coming up with two horns. He grabbed these and ran forward toward Allen's division and while still several feet away, with the open main hatch between them, tossed them across. The horns lit on the deck and were picked up by the gun crews, who primed three guns.

The lack of gun locks became really critical at this point: had they been mounted, some effective fire could have been returned.[82] As it was, not even matches were available, and Henry Allen ran to the galley, close by his division, where some loggerheads had just been put in the fire to heat. The first one he tried was not hot enough to light the priming powder, and he went back for another. Then he had the inspiration that led to the only defense of American honor that day. He took up a hot coal, went back to the division, and fired one gun with it. He was getting ready to fire one of the other primed guns when

Commodore Barron shouted down the hatch to stop firing because he had struck the colors. Allen was flabbergasted. He could immediately have fired his other two primed guns, and as Shubrick had just returned with five horns of powder, Allen could have fired at least one round from each gun had Barron delayed the surrender for a few short minutes. Disgusted at Barron's hasty capitulation, Allen told Shubrick, "You are too late—the ship has struck!"[83]

Two short generations ago, when the teaching of grade-school history included anecdotes of the heroes of the United States as hortatory examples to American youth, everyone was familiar with the story of the young lieutenant who took a coal of fire in his fingers and fired the only gun for the honor of the flag. Boys visualized the searing flesh and wondered how they would perform if faced with a similar challenge.

Actually, it is highly improbable that Allen picked up the fiery coal with his fingers. He never said that he did—in his journal he said that he "took up" the coal. Under oath at Barron's court-martial he was asked how he fired the gun and replied, "With a coal of fire taken from the galley." At another point in the court-martial he said that he had "run to the galley and got a coal of fire—with this I fired that gun and was about to fire another. . . ." In a letter home, however, he described "snatching a coal from the flames," and the galley was adjacent to his division, so it's possible he did pick it up in his hand. With ladles, cups, and other utensils available in the galley area, it is more likely that he scooped it up in one of these. Captain Hall, not a friend of Allen's, testified at the court-martial that he "observed Mr. Allen attempting to fire a gun, with a loggerhead which was too cold to burn the powder; a man then brought him a coal of fire, with which he fired the gun."[84] The matter was peripheral to the issues in the trial, the apparent contradiction was not pursued, and the truth, perhaps, lost to history. Such is the raw material of patriotism.

The *Leopard*'s three broadsides had taken ten minutes or less. Allen's division, being amidships, caught a good deal of the fire. One shot, twenty-four pounds of cast iron five inches in diameter, struck a sailor at one of Allen's guns in the chest, killing him instantly, and Allen was covered with blood and bone splinters. Five of his men at another gun were severely wounded, one of them having his leg shot away and two others losing arms.[85]

All told, three of the *Chesapeake*'s men—John Laurence, James Arnold, and John Shukly—were killed in the action, eight were badly wounded, and ten less so.[86] Commodore Barron was hit in the right leg by some large splinters of oak that were knocked out of the bulwark by a shot: he was wounded in seven places from thigh to ankle, including having a piece of flesh torn out of his calf.[87] One of the wounded, Robert McDonald, died later in Norfolk and received a hero's funeral.[88]

In spite of the carnage, the crew mostly stuck to their guns, even though there was nothing that they could do to return the fire. Some grumbled at having to stay and "be shot at like sheep." Two or three men in the first division, who were Englishmen, left their gun and went on deck, hoping to avoid the appearance of being taken "in arms against His Majesty," a capital crime in British eyes. Some men in Henry Allen's division left their stations before the firing ceased.[89] Allen was probably too busy to notice or to try to stop them.

There was a considerable amount of damage to the ship. The sea was calm, and most of the *Leopard*'s fire was effective. The first broadside tore up the sails and the rigging. The second and third went into the hull and through the ports, one round shot traveling clear through and lodging in the opposite side of the ship. There was considerable damage to the masts as well.[90]

Viewed from the *Leopard,* these short minutes of confrontation were seen a bit differently. An observer described Captain Humphreys's feelings to be "none of the most comfortable on this occasion." Uncomfortable he might well be. While not the sole holder of the bag, Berkeley having given the orders, Humphreys was still the point man, faced with deciding whether or not to fire into the warship of a peaceful, friendly nation over the issue of a handful of reluctant sailormen. The *Leopard*'s junior officers strongly favored the search and thought that they had a perfect right to use force in the process. Most of the officers in the British Navy held the same views, but for most it was a hypothetical issue, dealt with by ferocious letters to the editor of the *Naval Chronicle.*[91] Humphreys was the only one who ever came face-to-face with the situation.

After the boat returned with Lieutenant Meade and Barron's reply, Humphreys tried once more to get the *Chesapeake* to acquiesce in a search for the deserters. He is quoted as shouting to Barron, who was standing in the gangway, "Commodore Barron, you must be aware of the necessity I am under of complying with the orders of my commander-in-chief."[92] If this oration was actually delivered, it is small wonder that Barron had trouble understanding it when shouted in the accents of Shropshire from sixty yards away. Humphreys repeated his statement a couple of times and, receiving no reply except "I do not understand you," decided that Barron was creating a delay while he got ready to do battle. Humphreys ordered a shot to be fired across the *Chesapeake*'s bow and, when this didn't get a response, fired another. Then he ordered his gun decks to commence firing into the *Chesapeake,* the foremost gun first, then one at a time in succession down the length of the ship.[93]

This order was either misunderstood or, just as likely, overenthusiastically executed, and the result was a broadside rather than the ripple fire he had called for, plus some volleys of musketry from the *Leopard*'s marines, which went unnoticed on board the *Chesapeake* amidst the cannonry and the crashing of the round shot.[94] Humphreys stopped firing for a moment when Barron hailed him but commenced again, sending in two more broadsides. The first had gone mostly into the sails and rigging, the other two went into the hull, and at that point the *Chesapeake*'s ensign and command pennant came fluttering down. The only return from the *Chesapeake* was Henry Allen's one shot, which was delivered just before or just after the colors came down. The *Leopard* reported no damage, but Allen in a letter home said that the round went through her wardroom—a devoutly wished for result, but unlikely.[95]

As soon as the firing stopped, Barron sent a boat with Ben Smith, the first lieutenant, with the message to Humphreys that the *Chesapeake* was now his prize. Humphreys refused to take possession but sent two boats with Lieutenants Falcon and Guise, plus Mr. Preston, the *Leopard*'s purser, who could recognize Jenkin Ratford, and George Tincombe, the master's mate of the *Melampus,* to identify her deserters. They demanded the *Chesapeake*'s muster book, then lined the crew up and for the next three hours interrogated them and searched the ship. They found Jenkin Ratford in the coal hole in the forward hold and brought him on deck.[96] Terrified, he could only squeak that he was not Ratford but John Wilson, an American. He was faced with the purser, who had handled his transfer to the *Halifax* and knew him well. The three *Melampus* men were sorted out even though Berkeley's order had said nothing about them. In addition, the *Leopard*'s officers identified about eight other men or boys who were British but were not known to be deserters. These men were outside the scope of the British officers' orders, so a boat was sent back to get Humphreys's instructions. The boat returned with orders not to take the men.[97] That they found only eight casts some doubt on the contention that something like half of the *Chesapeake*'s crew were British.

The boarding party finally left with four men: Ratford and the three impressed Americans who had deserted from the *Melampus.* Humphreys sent a note to Barron, "deploring" the affair, offered help, and said he was leaving to rejoin the British squadron. By this time it was a bit before eight in the evening and getting dark. Barron made one last attempt to get Humphreys to accept his surrender, sending Henry Allen over in a boat with the message. Allen's description of this incident in his journal does not describe his feelings, but there is no doubt that his humiliation and fury were intense.[98]

While the search was going on, Barron called his officers into the cabin and asked them for their opinions about the affair. After a reluctant pause, Charles Gordon volunteered that the commodore's action had "spared the effusion of blood." Henry Allen said, "We have disgraced the flag."[99] Barron dismissed them without asking for further comments.

As darkness fell the *Leopard* left the scene and, with a level of arrogant effrontery hard to understand after her unprovoked battering of an undefended American ship, went back into American waters and rejoined the

British squadron at anchor in Lynnhaven Bay. She was still in the vicinity more than a month later, at the end of July.[100]

The *Chesapeake,* all three of her masts damaged and her rigging weakened, carefully worked her way back into the bay and up to Hampton Roads. On the way to her anchorage she passed the *Bellona,* by then lying at Willoughby Point. Captain Douglas could see the obvious damage, and in his report of the incident to Berkeley observed that the *Chesapeake*'s "hull, masts, and sails had suffered material injury."[101]

The *Chesapeake* anchored in Hampton Roads at just after noon on 23 June. Within a short time a boat came out from Hampton with Commodore Samuel Barron, James Barron's older brother. James Barron had prepared a report of the incident in which he was very generous in his description of the conduct of Captain Gordon and the other officers, in contrast to his later statements about them.[102] About ten days after the action, in a letter to Dr. Bullus, Barron was highly critical of the lieutenants: The two Smiths, Benjamin and Sydney, he described as showing "an abominable degree of cowardice" and totally lacking "the use of their reason" from the time the firing started until it was over. Also, in Barron's opinion, neither Crane nor Creighton performed well. But he reserved his strongest censure for Henry Allen. Although Barron conceded that Allen "stood his ground" and fired the only gun, he viewed him as "the most infamous and Vindictive rascal of them all . . . with all of the Prejudices that his friend . . . Rodgers could inculcate."[103] Barron believed that "all the Reports now in circulation Prejudicial to [him] originated" with Henry Allen. This may well have been true as Allen had regrettably taken on many of Rodgers's views and attitudes, which probably included an unreasoning dislike of Barron.

At three o'clock that afternoon of their arrival in Hampton Roads Captain Gordon and Dr. Bullus left for Washington in a pilot boat, carrying James Barron's report. They also carried a letter to the secretary of the navy, drafted by Henry Allen and signed by all five of the lieutenants plus the sailing master, requesting "that an order be issued for the arrest of Commodore James Barron . . . on charges which the undersigned pledge themselves to prove true: 1st, On the probability of an engagement, for neglecting to clear his ship for action., 2ndly, For not doing his utmost to take or to destroy a vessel which we conceive it his duty to have done."[104]

It was a terrible mistake on James Barron's part to let Gordon and Bullus carry his report and the lieutenants' letter up to Washington. Somebody was going to be held at fault for what had happened, and if it was not Gordon, it would be Barron himself. Letting the politically well connected Gordon get his side of the story in front of the secretary of the navy first was an act of professional suicide on the part of James Barron. He probably thought that Dr.

Bullus would act in his interest, but he was wrong: Bullus was his "decided enemy" and "injured [him] at the Navy Office."[105] But Barron could not have gone to Washington himself, as he should have: his wounds were too serious. Although they were officially reported as "slight," he could not travel and spent the next four months in bed, lying on his left side.[106]

The repercussions were immediate and became widespread. The citizens of the area were outraged and cut off all communication between the shore and the British squadron—supplies, water, and contact with the British consul in Norfolk. Tenders from the squadron were in Hampton at that time, carrying water casks from the squadron in the process of being filled. Mobs of armed men, led by "the better sort of people," boarded them and "demolished" more than two hundred of the casks—thirty tons of the *Melampus's* water capacity was stove in and destroyed, and one of her boats was burned. This was not a trivial loss, as the *Melampus* and the other ships affected couldn't go to sea until they got new water casks. There was a rumor that the British planned to take the *Chesapeake's* water casks to make up the loss, but nothing came of it.[107]

The militia was called up, and citizens groups passed many excited resolutions. Cut off from the British consul and the accustomed support from ashore, Douglas moved the entire British squadron to a position in Hampton Roads near Norfolk and threatened to cut off all shipping in and out of the town. Mayor Lee stood his ground, and the British backed down, denying any menace. As news of the incident spread, the "lower order[s] . . . [were] much irritated and inclined to violent measures" and the "War [W]Hoop against Great Britain resounded in every State."[108]

James Barron was relieved of his command, and Commodore Stephen Decatur took over the *Chesapeake* on 1 July. Barron went home to Hampton to await the inevitable court of enquiry, which was followed in early 1808 by his court-martial. The whole proceeding was rigged to put the principal blame on James Barron: the charges and specifications for the court-martial were prepared in the Navy Department with a careful eye toward preventing any fault from accruing to the department itself and toward minimizing Gordon's culpability.[109] The president of the court was Barron's archenemy, John Rodgers, and serving as a member was Stephen Decatur, who had openly expressed his opinion that Barron was at fault. To his credit, Decatur tried to be removed from the court, but the secretary of the navy denied the request. Gordon, Marine Captain Hall, and Gunner Hook were also tried. Barron was suspended from duty without pay for five years, Gordon and Hall were reprimanded, and Hook was dismissed from the service.

When the reports of the affair reached England, Canning, the foreign secretary, explicitly disclaimed any British right to search American warships for deserters.[110] The Lords Commissioners of the Admiralty sent to Admiral Berkeley a letter that is one of the finest extant examples of how the English language can be used to flay a human being and recalled him to England.[111] He was replaced by Vice-Admiral Sir John Borlase Warren, Baronet, Knight of the Bath, a bland, urbane, and handsome man. Warren was an experienced diplomat who had been ambassador to the difficult court of Czar Alexander I, and it was presumed that he would be able to keep things settled with the Americans.

As soon as the *Leopard* returned to England, Humphreys was relieved of his command and was never again given an assignment. But the resourceful Captain Humphreys, handed a lemon, quickly made lemonade. He was already married to an heiress, who died in 1808 and left him the estate of Weedon Lodge, Aylesbury. After an appropriate period of grief he remarried in 1810 to an even wealthier heiress and changed his name to Davenport "on his accession to a considerable property in right of his second wife." He was knighted, became a C.B., a K.C.H., and the magistrate for five counties, and fathered eight children.[112]

President Jefferson issued a proclamation on 2 July, requiring all British armed vessels in U.S. waters to depart "immediately and without any delay" and forbidding any support of them by American citizens.[113] In spite of this the British, including the *Leopard,* stayed in Lynnhaven Bay.

Jefferson was concerned that the affair might represent a change in British policy and that more attacks were to be expected. Erskine, the British minister in Washington, assured the president that nothing had changed, but Jefferson decided to privately monitor British actions in the Hampton Roads area. He asked Colonel William Tatham, an acquaintance who had already sent him some letters on the situation, to keep track of British actions and make frequent reports.[114]

Tatham scouted the Lynnhaven and Cape Henry areas by boat and on horseback over the next month. For a few days there was much rushing up and down by the Princess Anne Militia, but by mid-July, only three weeks after the *Leopard*'s attack, Captain Reid of the militia and some of his men, Princess Anne farmers all, were meeting "joyfully" with British officers on the beach at Lynnhaven, offering to sell them fresh beef.[115] Within a few days after that, ships from Norfolk with provisions were holding discreet rendezvous just outside the Capes with tenders from the British squadron.

On 15 July the *Bellona* sailed for Halifax, taking with her the four deserters, now prisoners in irons.[116] On board H.M.S. *Belleisle* in Halifax harbor on Wednesday, 26 August, the power and majesty of the British Navy prepared to destroy Jenkin Ratford. A court-martial consisting of a rear-admiral and six captains had been appointed to try him on charges of mutiny, desertion, and contempt. The court included Captains Douglas of the *Bellona* and Hawker of the *Melampus,* certainly no partisans of Ratford.

Ratford had not been given any counsel to represent him in front of this august, gold-braided group. This didn't matter: the outcome was foreordained. Numb with terror, he presented no defense, asking only a few irrelevant questions during the trial. He was found guilty and the following Monday at 9:15 A.M. was hanged, strangling, from the fore yardarm of His Majesty's Sloop-of-War *Halifax*.[117]

The three *Melampus* men were tried and each sentenced to five hundred lashes. The punishment was remitted, and they, Americans all, were returned to duty in the British Navy.

At least nine duels were fought over matters of honor related to the *Chesapeake-Leopard* affair. Gordon fought three and in the last, in 1810, received a wound in the lower abdomen. Luckily, the ball didn't cut an intestine, the wound didn't become seriously infected, and he was spared a rapid death from peritonitis. But the "air hole in [his] side" remained open and never healed, and he never fully recovered.[118] Much later, in 1820, came the most famous of these duels: Barron, after considerable provocation, most of which was only indirectly related to the *Chesapeake-Leopard* affair, challenged Stephen Decatur and mortally wounded him.

Henry Allen came out of the *Chesapeake-Leopard* incident with more honor than any of the others. He had fired the only gun. He had, without hesitation, expressed his view, albeit biased by his position as a protégé of John Rodgers, that the United States was disgraced by Barron's actions. Although his honor was to some degree served, he felt an excruciating sense of shame. And he gained from the experience a sense of deep distrust and cold fury toward the British Navy.

CHAPTER THREE

Seasoning under Decatur

THE QUESTIONS IN EVERYONE'S MIND in the immediate aftermath of the *Chesapeake-Leopard* affair were, had British policy changed, and would there be other attacks and incidents as a result? A new, harder-line administration had recently come to power in London, opening this possibility. In Washington, David Erskine, the British minister, was himself in the dark and wrote to Berkeley that the "American Government was very anxious to know whether the orders . . . acted [on] had been lately received from England."[1] Like many others aboard the *Chesapeake* and in the Norfolk area, Henry Allen was convinced that the British government had fully sanctioned the attack and that a war was imminent.[2]

On board the *Chesapeake,* anchored in Hampton Roads on the day after the incident, there were feelings of shock and confusion. Commodore Barron was confined to bed in his cabin, suffering from his wounds. The rest of the officers and the crew were making temporary, emergency repairs, first patching up the rigging enough to make it usable, although it was clear from the damage to the masts that the ship would need help from the navy yard.

At 8 A.M. the *Chesapeake* had an unexpected visit from the captain of the French Frigate *Cybele,* who was no doubt seeking information as to whether the British squadron was now likely to come after him right there in Norfolk harbor. In the afternoon, in blowy, rainy weather, the *Chesapeake's* tender returned from Norfolk, and boarding it, Mrs. Bullus and Mrs. Hall, both very shaken by their experience, left the ship and went ashore.

After several more days of hard work by the armorers, sailmakers, carpenters, and indeed the whole ship's company, the rigging was patched, the gun deck cleared, the guns put in order, and the ship made minimally ready to fight if she had to. She moved around Sewell's Point to the mouth of the Elizabeth River, ready to move south, upriver, to a moorage in the stream off Craney Island, nearer to the navy yard. But the wind was from the southwest, foul for sailing up to the yard. From the afternoon of 29 June until the morning of 1 July the crew worked around the clock, "warping the ship ahead." This maneuver involved carrying an anchor out ahead of the ship with the launch, using the capstan and muscle power to pull the ship up to the anchor, then carrying out another anchor, picking up the first anchor, and repeating this slow process.[3]

Then on 1 July, for Henry Allen at least, the sky began to brighten: Henry told his journal, "At Meridian, Stephen Decatur, Junr., Esq., came on board and took command of this ship." At that moment the *Chesapeake* again hoisted the Stars and Stripes and Decatur's broad command pennant. She had been a ship disgraced, without ensign, jack, or commission pennant since the colors came down under fire from the *Leopard*. Now the frigate would be whole again as soon as the crew made the repairs that would erase all visible signs of the attack. At 4 P.M. Commodore Barron, now facing dishonor—most of it undeserved—left the ship to wait at home in Hampton for further instructions from the Navy Department.[4]

While rhetorical bombast still filled the newspaper columns in Norfolk, and the Princess Anne Militia still charged around the county, Josiah Fox, the ship's builder, arrived on 2 July from the Washington Navy Yard with twenty shipwrights and mast-makers to help the navy yard and to expedite the *Chesapeake*'s refit.[5]

Back on board, the crew unreeved the running rigging, completely stripped the ship, then rigged sheers to take the masts out. All three masts—huge, highly-expensive, built-up timbers that were crafted, mortised, tenoned, and rabbeted from long pieces of straight-grain, knot-free pine and fir—had been "badly wounded" by shot from the *Leopard*. The fore- and mizzenmasts were pulled out intact, but the mainmast, "shot through in three places" about twenty feet above the deck, was sawed off five feet above deck level.[6] All three masts were set afloat and towed by the boats to the navy yard. The sails were sent to the loft in the navy yard for repair.

Decatur was still wary of the British and at sunset on 3 July sent the crew to quarters, seriously "expecting an attack from the English squadron." The men and officers stayed at their guns all through the night. On the Glorious Fourth they "fired a salute of fifteen guns in honor of the day." By now spirits were again rising on board the *Chesapeake*.

A few days later, in the midst of the busyness of their refit, Decatur sent Gordon, now back from Washington, with Lieutenants Henry Allen and John Creighton, plus two midshipmen and fifteen men, in the tender "to reconnoitre the English squadron."[7] They returned at half-past ten at night, without having noted any aggressive preparations by the British.

Had they known the reality of the situation in the British squadron, they could have saved a trip. Having knocked over a beehive, the British were busy backing up and swatting. They had plenty of problems to deal with, and now, a couple of weeks after the incident, the furthest thing from the minds of Captain Douglas, the senior officer in the squadron, and Consul Hamilton in Norfolk was initiating an unauthorized war with the United States.

The British officers were worried about the destroyed water casks: their ships couldn't go to sea without water, they couldn't carry anywhere near a full load of water without the casks, and they saw little chance of getting them replaced soon. The British were also concerned about getting supplies and provisions for the squadron from on shore if the present, violent, anti-British mood in Norfolk and Princess Anne County continued, with officers from the squadron being menaced by mobs whenever they set foot in the town. Some expensive ships' boats had been destroyed, and these losses would have to be explained to the bean counters at the Navy Board. And not least, Captain Douglas was worried about how the Admiralty might view his actions in the midst of these electrifying events.

To handle this latter item he wrote a careful, posterior-covering letter to Berkeley, distancing himself from Humphreys and noting explicitly that it was Berkeley's order that had spawned the affair.[8] Then on 15 July Douglas took the *Bellona,* with the four deserters on board in irons, and left for Halifax. This move had been planned weeks earlier, but its timing now turned out to be felicitous: it removed the confrontational Douglas from the scene and left the skipper of the *Triumph,* Captain Sir Thomas Masterman Hardy—a large, amiable, broad-minded, self-assured man—as the senior officer present. Hardy immediately began to smooth over the situation with a burst of conciliatory letters. Relations then came back to normal pretty quickly, although the social climate between the British officers and Norfolk society remained cool: Lady Hardy, the daughter of Admiral Berkeley, told her diary that she spent the winter of 1807–1808 in the Chesapeake Bay, confined on board the *Triumph,* unable to go ashore because of the "exasperated state" of the Americans.[9]

The *Chesapeake* remained moored just downriver from the navy yard for the rest of the summer of 1807. Restored and refitted, she got under way early on 2 September for a short shakedown cruise, described by Henry Allen as "a round turn in the Bay."[10] With Gunboats Numbers 58 and 67 in company, the frigate stood down the Elizabeth River, pausing off the town of Norfolk to send the gig in for Decatur, now being styled in Henry Allen's journal as "Commodore." The frigate and her two consorts came out into Hampton Roads before noon and anchored. It was good for the crew to start working again and get some fresh air through the ship: the *Chesapeake* had an epidemic of "influenza" on board with forty-two men, including Henry Allen, on the sick list.[11]

After "cleansing the ship" and loading and double-shotting the guns, the *Chesapeake* and the gunboats got under way again and headed east, down the bay. They anchored that night in Lynnhaven Bay. The British squadron was not in its accustomed place but was anchored several miles to the northeast, inside of Cape Charles, and not visible because of the dark and the rainy, squally weather. Whether Decatur had meant to find the British at Lynnhaven and assert the presence of his now-recovered and revitalized frigate is not clear. When the *Chesapeake* and her gunboat consorts headed north up the Chesapeake Bay the next morning, they passed the British squadron, the *Triumph* and two frigates, but Henry Allen's journal does not record any contact with them.

The three American vessels cruised up the bay past the Rappahannock River and the Northern Neck of Virginia, past the mouth of the Potomac, and anchored off the Patuxent River, where they met the *Baltimore* packet bringing out a draft of new recruits. New and old, all aboard were pretty rusty and had to learn to be sailors again after three months in port: while the boatswain's crew were swaying up the fore-topgallant mast, a line parted, and this heavy twenty-four-foot-long timber fell like an arrow, cracking one of the gun-deck beams. Luckily, no one was hurt.[12]

After the short shakedown, the frigate was back in the Elizabeth River, moored off Norfolk for several months. The court of enquiry ordered by Secretary Robert Smith "to enquire into the causes of the surrender of the *Chesapeake*" met on board the ship from early October until 4 November. Then from 4 January 1808 until 22 February the court-martial trying Barron, Gordon, Hall, and the unlucky and incompetent Gunner Hook met on board in Norfolk harbor for all but six of its forty-three days.

Henry Allen was greatly relieved that the court did not place any blame on the lieutenants and that the Navy Department found no fault in their actions during the incident. In fact, the secretary of the navy, writing in response to the lieutenants' recommendation, drafted by Henry Allen, that Barron be court-martialed, had told them that their letter "did them honor" and assured them that "it will be attended to."[13]

Henry Allen himself came through it all looking quite heroic, with his professional reputation enhanced. One of the members of the court of enquiry, and his old mentor Rodgers, the president of the court-martial, each offered him a new career opportunity. He wisely declined in order to stay with Decatur.

Stephen Decatur was in every way the opposite of James Barron—bold where Barron was cautious; vital, slender, and dashing where Barron was slow, overweight, and near-sighted. He was Henry Allen's beau ideal of a naval officer, and before long Decatur came to think highly of Allen.

In spite of what he must have been told by James Barron about the lieutenants of the *Chesapeake,* Decatur was apparently willing to keep them all, at least for a while. He could hardly have approved of the actions of Lieutenant Sidney Smith, who stayed behind the mizzenmast during most of the attack.[14] Any questions he might have had about Lieutenant Benjamin Smith were resolved when this unfortunate officer died of "a Billious fever *or Yellow*" in mid-October. He was a townmate of Henry Allen's, from Providence, and Henry handled the postmortem matters of sending home his will and personal effects.[15]

After the courts-martial were over, the *Chesapeake* started operating at sea on a more regular basis, mostly off the Virginia Capes. Her deployment to the Mediterranean had been canceled, and now her usual activity was the enforcement of Jefferson's Embargo Act—the frigate stopped American ships and checked their papers to be sure they weren't engaged in prohibited foreign trade.

This dull and routine duty actually opened a very professionally productive and rewarding period for Henry Allen. Decatur wanted the *Chesapeake* to be brought to such a high pitch of morale and fighting trim that another challenge like the *Leopard*'s would result in a British disaster. Allen was his instrument for gunnery training, and the *Chesapeake* held almost daily gun drills and exercises as she cruised the coastal waters to look for errant merchant vessels. Apparently, part of Henry Allen's gunnery-training and morale-building efforts was allowing the gun crews to give names to their guns, a custom that while not unique was not widespread: at the time of the *Chesapeake*'s capture by the *Shannon* in 1813, the British remarked that each gun had a copper nameplate.[16]

Between her short cruises at sea the *Chesapeake* spent a good bit of time in port in the Hampton Roads area, giving her officers ample opportunities to develop their social lives. However, they apparently did not feel that they were fully welcome in Norfolk society. It is possible that there was some resentment due to the local origin and popularity of James Barron. The mutual animosity, almost loathing, between Barron and his ex-lieutenants, most particularly Allen, was well known. However, in mid-January 1808 Henry Allen attended a "splendid private ball" in Norfolk, where there were "upwards of 60 ladies," and he noted that when rowing off for the ship at 3 A.M. a "cutting north wind" made the boat trip extremely uncomfortable.[17]

He continued to complain about the lack of mail from home—he was "in the dumps" and felt that his family had forgotten him. He asked to be remembered to relatives and friends, "particularly Mr. Jenkins and family," and at that point in the letter Henry specially inserted, "not forgetting Mary. . . ." Mary, probably Mary Jenkins, is a name that appeared in his letters whenever he was feeling lonesome and neglected.[18]

Later in the spring of 1808 he had a brief but unfruitful relationship with a girl from North Carolina, an orphan of considerable property. While walking with her in Norfolk, Allen admired a house that they were passing and was told, "It is in *your* power to have it if *you* choose." He passed the matter off "in jest."[19] But at the same time in a letter home he asked "to hear all about the sweet girls in Providence."

By late summer this was all behind him, and the *Chesapeake* was at sea in New England waters, off Newport Light, still enforcing the embargo. This was an area more familiar and congenial to Allen, but it brought its own problems: Decatur received information that a number of ships from Providence were planning to flout the embargo and run to sea, among them one owned by Peleg Rhodes, Henry Allen's brother-in-law. Decatur then excused Allen from boarding any vessels off the Rhode Island ports. This avoided any conflict of interest and left Henry's sensitive honor intact.[20]

In early February of 1809 Decatur was given command of the frigate *United States,* larger and more prestigious than the *Chesapeake,* and requested Henry Allen as his first lieutenant. The *United States* had been laid up and was "fitting out" in the Washington Navy Yard when Allen, after "anxiously awaiting orders," was sent to her in February 1809.[21] Decatur was away, leaving to Henry Allen the job of equipping her and getting her ready for sea.[22] He had little assistance: most of the midshipmen were tied up, receiving navigation instruction from Mr. Thompson, or were off recruiting. There followed a busy two months in the yard, his head so full of "chain plates, shrouds, boats and ballast" that he turned down all invitations to social events in Washington and even skipped Madison's Inaugural Ball.[23] This last may have been due as much to his family's Federalist political leanings as to his work load on the ship. But Henry Allen found time to help a near-namesake, Midshipman William Howard Allen, an acquaintance but not a relative, who wrote to ask if Henry could help him get orders to the *United States.* Decatur approved, and Henry wrote on Howard's behalf to Mr. Goldsborough, the clerk at the Navy Department, but the effort was not successful.[24]

The end of 1809 found the *United States* fitting new lower rigging in Norfolk, and Allen so well in control of his job that he could write home that "my life is barren of incident at present. . . ." He reported with some pride that the ship had been measured and found to be the largest vessel in the U.S. Navy, 188 feet long on deck and 45 feet in beam—slightly larger than the *President* and *Constitution.*[25] His letters reverted to talk of the attractions of the young women at home in Providence, attractions no doubt enhanced by distance. Whenever the demands of his professional life slackened enough so as not to require his full attention, his mind usually turned to women. He wrote to his sister Sarah, "I must be in love *to be happy*, I must have some little deity to bow down to and worship. . . ." His approach sounds a bit stuffy, even for that time of punctilio and stilted address, but may have served to mask a shyness around women. The southern women of Norfolk apparently considered him to be self-centered and standoffish.[26]

Probably more to blame for his lack of social success was the fact that his interests were intensely centered in his professional life, and the ship and its affairs, especially its gunnery training, were never far from the top of his mind. His early experiences in the Mediterranean, and more particularly the searing effect of the *Leopard*'s attack, gave his life a driving purpose: to be ready to beat the British and to vindicate the humiliation he felt at the disgrace of the *Chesapeake*. The operations of the *United States* in this period, and until the beginning of the war, gave plenty of time for training and thus suited Henry Allen nicely.[27] Decatur strongly encouraged him, and Allen expertly honed the gunnery skills of the *United States* to a fine edge. Morale on the ship seems to have been high and the ship a happy one. A watch, quarter, and station book from Allen's time aboard survives, and the names that were given to the guns indicate a cheerful crew: "Long Nose Nancy," "Brother Jonathan," "Jumping Billy," "Happy Jack," "Hog and Hommany," among others.[28]

The presence of the ubiquitous British Navy gave the gunnery training an extra bite of urgency. The British were always around to freshly remind Henry Allen that they were the enemy. Contacts with them were becoming more frequent in 1811, and while relationships were civil and correct, neither Henry Allen nor Stephen Decatur had forgotten the *Leopard*.

Although most of the cruising British men-of-war were no potential threat to a ship as powerful as the *United States*, Decatur and Allen took no chances and never approached one without getting all ready for action. Off Charleston in early March the frigate ran across the British eighteen-gun brig *Colibri* and the schooner *Jupiter*. The *United States* beat to quarters and then sent an officer on board the brig to politely find out what she was up to.[29]

A few months later, in June, the *United States* had an experience that was eerily reminiscent of the *Chesapeake-Leopard* meeting. On the afternoon of the ninth, sailing out of the Chesapeake Bay, Decatur's lookouts saw two British men-of-war lying to under topsails a couple of miles at sea, in roughly the same spot where the *Leopard* had waited for the *Chesapeake* in the same month, at the same time of the day, four years earlier. As the *United States* passed Cape Henry, the two warships stood toward them "under a press of sail." The *United States* immediately made every preparation for battle and, as the British ships closed, hauled up her lower sails to keep them from catching fire from the muzzle flashes, then beat to quarters and primed the guns.

The two Britishers were a small twenty-six–gun frigate and an eighteen-gun ship-sloop. The frigate's captain hailed the *United States* and announced that his ship was "His Britannic Majesty's Ship *Eurydice.*" His consort was H.B.M. Sloop *Atalante.* They had brought and had sent in dispatches from the British to the United States government. Some other civilities passed back and forth, then a gun was fired from the *United States.* Whether this was an accident or whether some overeager sailor was too ready to avenge the *Chesapeake* is information that has not survived. In any event, after a pause Decatur hailed the British ship and told them "that the firing of the gun was owing to an accident and that he hoped they had sustained no injury." The British captain said that "he was happy to state that there had been none." He was probably also greatly relieved that no harm had been intended: the fifty-plus heavy guns of the *United States* could have reduced the *Eurydice* to toothpicks within minutes. He apparently also felt that at this point the *United States* owed him a favor and asked if he could send his boat over, probably to swap a bundle of month-old British newspapers for some fresh ones from America, as was customary in those times. Decatur replied, "With pleasure," happy to have the incident terminate on a civil note. The boat came, stayed a few minutes, and left. Then the ships parted and went their separate ways, although the British were still in sight to the northeast the next morning.[30]

In February of 1812 the *United States* was moored in Hampton Roads. On the eleventh word reached the ship that a British frigate had come in from sea and anchored in Lynnhaven Bay. That afternoon Decatur sent Henry Allen down in a cutter to find out who the ship was and what her business was. He returned late in the evening to report that she was H.B.M. Frigate *Macedonian,* Captain John Surman Carden, Esquire, commanding, and that she had come from Europe with dispatches from the British government for the British minister at Washington.[31]

The following day the *Macedonian* moved up to Hampton Roads and anchored near the *United States.* Her "dispatches," later disclosed to be more than £600,000 sterling in negotiable bills of exchange, had gone up to Washington by the U.S. mails, Captain Carden being nervous about the security of a British officer-messenger traveling through rural Virginia in those volatile times.[32] The *Macedonian* was now waiting to receive the specie—gold and silver coin—from the sale of the bills.

By this time, in early 1812, the officers and men in both navies were convinced that war was coming in the near future, and with the *United States* and the *Macedonian* in port together, there was a natural urge for each to take the measure of the other. The officers of the two ships exchanged visits, occasions for "much wassail and feasting," and on several occasions Decatur entertained Carden at his house.[33]

Picture them all, wine glasses in hand, conversing with much civility, but warily, like circling, feral tomcats, trying to visualize the outcome of meeting each other in a sea fight. At one of these affairs, while "joking over a wine-cup," Decatur and Carden bet a beaver hat on the result of such a battle.[34] The officers of the *Macedonian,* in common with most of the British, had little but contempt for the American Navy and had no doubt that if a meeting took place, their captain would have the hat. But no beaver were to die on the distant Yellowstone to provide fashion for Captain Carden.

CHAPTER FOUR

Prizemaster of the *Macedonian*

CONGRESS DECLARED WAR on Great Britain in June of 1812 after much debate and at the urging of President Madison. Even today, historians argue over the precise causes of this war. From the perspective of 180 years it might best be viewed, as seen by many at the time, as a Second War of American Independence. The grounds for war emanated from the refusal of Europeans, the most irritating of whom were the British, to treat the United States as a sovereign nation and to stop interfering in American affairs.

From Canada, the British supported Indians in sporadic murderous raids on farms in the old northwest in Ohio, Indiana, and Illinois, and the settlers were outraged. The better-informed of the plantation owners of the South and the newly prospering farmers in the valleys of the Mississippi were aware that their profits were slashed by the interference with American trade and by the seizure at sea and in British ports of the ships carrying American crops. On the other hand, the ship-owning merchants of New England saw the seizure of their ships as a nuisance, expensive and annoying, but acceptable as a cost of doing business and certainly not enough of a problem to make the United States go to war with its best customer. Impressment of American seafarers at sea or in British ports was a very emotional issue, not only with the seafarers themselves but also with the general public. Most shipowners, however, cared little about the impressment of their sailors, so long as there were enough more available at low wages to make up for those taken.

No matter how you view the causes, this little war was probably the most successful of all the wars the United States has fought. This was a war that was neither won nor lost. It cost about $70 million to fight it, approximately 286,000 men were involved, and total casualties were fewer than 5,000. For this the United States got "The Star-Spangled Banner," "Don't Give Up the Ship," Old Ironsides, Andy Jackson and the Battle of New Orleans—signposts on the way to developing an American national character. The war also resulted in real independence, a stable border with Canada, and the impetus to turn west and open up the country, launching one of the most prosperous eras in American national life.

The treaty to end the war, negotiated at Ghent in Belgium by five of the most skillful diplomats the United States ever sent abroad—John Quincy Adams, Albert Gallatin, Henry Clay, James A. Bayard, and Jonathan Russell— did not even mention impressment or the seizure of shipping. These maritime issues, which most consider to have been major proximate causes of the war, were settled not at Ghent but at Waterloo.

When the war started the U.S. Navy was organized into a Northern Squadron under John Rodgers, which was based in New York, and a Southern Squadron under Stephen Decatur, based in Norfolk. The Chesapeake Bay being very easy to blockade, Decatur had moved his ships—at that time the forty-four–gun *United States,* the thirty-eight–gun *Congress,* and the sixteen-gun brig *Argus*—to New York. Rodgers was senior, so in effect he had the overall command of his own ships, the forty-four–gun *President* and the eighteen-gun ship-sloop *Hornet,* plus Decatur's. Rodgers had a plan in mind, and Decatur, although he disagreed with Rodgers's strategy, went along with it.

War was declared on 18 June, and three days later the news reached New York. Within hours Rodgers got to sea on a cruise with everything available in New York—the two heavy frigates, the *President* and *United States,* plus the *Congress, Hornet,* and *Argus.*

He hoped to intercept a British convoy, homeward bound from the West Indies, and the timing was right. In the West Indies trade, ships made one voyage per year. Leaving England in the fall, they delivered their cargoes of British manufactures throughout the islands in the winter and early spring, then in early summer loaded for the return voyage with *Muscovado* sugar, rum, or coffee—or sometimes, but rarely, all three.[1] These were all valuable commodities, and the West Indiamen were rich prizes.

The homeward-bound convoys were usually large, sixty to one hundred ships or more, with only a couple of frigates or brigs as escorts. After leaving the West Indies, the convoys went north, roughly parallel to the North American coast, until near the Newfoundland Banks, then across to England.[2] Although convoys left the islands four times per year, the biggest, richest ones started home in June and July, their departures timed to avoid the peak of the hurricane season in August and September, and to get to England in time to transship much of the sugar up the Baltic to Russia before the ice set in, to sweeten the tea of the Muscovites.

In recent years, most of the danger to these convoys had come from French and Spanish privateers operating in the Caribbean, a marginal annoyance. But now the war with America raised the real possibility of a squadron of enemy warships loose and rampaging amongst a terrified flock of rich merchantmen—an Admiralty planner's nightmare. At the time John Rodgers left New York with his squadron, there was no way that the British convoy commodores, already at sea when war was declared, could know of this new danger. Thus the American squadron had a wide-open, but brief, window of opportunity.

But as often seemed to happen when John Rodgers was in command at sea, the results were disappointing: the squadron completely missed the convoy, was out seventy days, and captured only seven stray merchantmen. Decatur and Allen in the *United States* caught the lion's share of these, three of the seven: on 2 July they captured the brig *Traveller,* on the twenty-fourth the ship *John,* and on 16 August the richest of the three, the schooner *Adaline.*[3] She had left Haiti and San Domingo, bound for Liverpool, with eighty-six thousand pounds of coffee, equal to the entire annual production of a large plantation.[4] The *United States* took twelve prisoners out of her, leaving only the cook and steward, put a prize crew of a midshipman and eight seamen aboard, and sent them off to try to reach an American port. They didn't make it in, and for some time were presumed to be lost.[5] Later it was learned that the British had recaptured the *Adaline* and sent her into Nova Scotia.

John Rodgers's task force saw only one British warship, the thirty-six–gun *Belvidera,* and she was able to slip away.[6] The cruise was, in a tactical sense, a neglected opportunity: the British Navy was stretched very thin, although it had in theory nearly one hundred ships on the American Station, including six ships of the line and thirty-three frigates. Many of these were refitting or in need of work, and only about six frigates, among them the *Belvidera,* and an old sixty-four–gun ship were near the American coast.[7] These were vulnerable to being scooped up by a strong squadron in the hands of a more skillful or lucky sea-fighter than John Rodgers. In a broader sense, the cruise had some benefit in forcing the British to concentrate their available ships more than they might otherwise have done, allowing more American merchant vessels to get safely home without capture.[8] In any event, better things were in store for Henry Allen, Stephen Decatur, and the frigate *United States.*

The *United States* came into Boston at the end of the cruise on the last day of August 1812, and Henry Allen had time for a hasty visit home to Providence—so brief that he was unable to see his sister-confidant Sarah or his "sweet friend Mary"—before returning to the ship to take over while Decatur left for a few days.[9] The crew of the *United States* had suffered from poor health during the cruise: six had died, and thirty-three were sent to the hospital after their arrival at Boston. Then on top of the losses from illness, the *United States* had to send about seventy-five men, sailors and marines, to the *Congress,* receiving a large draft from her in exchange.[10] This left Allen to reorganize the crew, recast their assignments in the watch, quarter, and station bills, and get started on a new training schedule.

The *United States* was in port for just over a month. The navy had by this time been organized into three squadrons, John Rodgers having his own ship, the *President,* plus the *Congress* and the eighteen-gun ship-sloop *Wasp.* Stephen Decatur had the *United States, Chesapeake,* and *Argus.* A third squadron, nominally based in Boston under Commodore Bainbridge, comprised the forty-four–gun *Constitution,* fresh from her victory over H.M.S. *Guerrière,* plus the thirty-two–gun *Essex* and the *Hornet.*[11]

Rodgers and Decatur were planning another cruise, but this time they would not stay together. They slipped out together on 8 October, Rodgers with the *President* and *Congress,* Decatur with the *United States* and *Argus.* Three days out, on the eleventh, they separated, Rodgers's two ships heading in an easterly direction. Decatur headed southeast, and the following day detached the *Argus* to cruise separately.

Lone cruising was much more to Decatur's liking. The *United States* headed for an area near the Canary Islands, just west of the bulge of Africa. In sailing-ship times the favorable combination of the northeast trade winds and an ocean current from the northeast made this area a funnel through which passed ships from Europe heading to the West Indies, to South America, or around Africa to India and the Orient. Decatur hoped to get on the track of the rich British East India traffic.[12]

Early on Sunday morning, 25 October, about 550 miles south of the Azores and 650 miles west of the Canary Islands, lookouts in the tops spotted a sail about twelve miles to windward. Decatur gave orders to clear for action, and while this was going on Henry Allen went aloft, telescope in hand, to try to determine what was in sight. After watching intently for some time, he saw what he was looking for: the long slender streamer pennant, in this case bright red, that identified the vessel as a British man-of-war. From his position in the tops he could see that she was a frigate hull up on the horizon. He came down and joked with the crew waiting on deck that she was their lawful prize.[13] It is not clear whether Decatur and Allen knew at this moment that she was the *Macedonian,* which the officers had visited in Norfolk in February.

The *Macedonian* had left Torbay on the Devon Coast on 29 September, convoying a large East India Company ship bound for India and carrying five hundred troops and money for the army payroll. After a stop at Madeira for wine and other supplies the two vessels sailed together for two more days, then the Indiaman went on her way, and the *Macedonian* broke off to head for a new assignment on the North American Station. Her officers and crew were looking forward to easy prize money off the American coast, and the toast in the wardroom after dinner as the port and madeira went around the table was "To an American frigate."[14]

After dropping her convoy, the *Macedonian* had begun keeping an extraordinarily sharp lookout. Captain Carden "seemed almost crazy with some pressing anxiety" and spent much of his time on deck, constantly hailing the man at the masthead and urging him to keep a good lookout.[15]

The masthead lookouts on the *Macedonian* saw the *United States* at about the same time as their ship was seen. H.M.S. *Macedonian* was in absolutely top shape. She was an oak-built thirty-eight–gun frigate, only two years old, and had recently been through a refit at the Plymouth dockyard, where she had had her bottom cleaned, new rigging installed, and had been completely repainted inside and out. She was described as being somewhat larger than the American thirty-eight–gun frigates, and she was a fast sailer. However, she was no match in size or power for the forty-four–gun *United States,* which carried 24-pounder long guns in her main battery (where the *Macedonian* had 18-pounders), was several hundred tons heavier, and carried a crew of 478 to the *Macedonian*'s 301. The *Macedonian*'s only advantage was her speed: she was well known to be very fast. The *United States* was "the old waggon," not a fast sailer, particularly during the period Decatur was in command of her.[16]

The *Macedonian*'s officers had all had a good look at one American frigate—this one, the *United States*—in Norfolk eight months before, and it was a measure of the contempt with which officers of the British Navy regarded the Americans that they would make toasts to meeting in battle a ship half again as powerful as they were. There was little reason for overconfidence in the British Navy of 1812. Since Trafalgar in 1805 it had been engaged almost solely in blockading. There had been few battles between squadrons, and even the single-ship actions with the French had been infrequent.[17] The British had gotten more interested in polishing their guns than in shooting them, and in no ship of the Royal Navy was this more true than in the *Macedonian* under Captain John Surman Carden.

Captain Carden was born into a family of the minor Irish gentry, a class that contributed many officers to the army and navy, and his father, an army major, had died of wounds received in the American Revolution. Carden had entered the navy at seventeen, a relatively advanced age for those days, and in this fall of 1812 was forty-one years old with twenty-four years of service behind him. In spite of having served through the whole of the wars against the French, he had not seen much action. He had been in only one of the famous battles of the day: serving in the battleship *Marlborough,* he had been "severely injured" during the modestly successful fleet action of 1 June 1794, known as "The Glorious First of June." In a frigate action in 1798, while still a lieutenant, he was commended for his "good steady conduct"—he was apparently brave enough, but this was rather faint praise nonetheless. Other than that, in all of his service during nineteen continuous years of war, he had not come into actual gun-blazing, belligerent proximity to an enemy.[18]

He did run a taut ship, however. He was a strict disciplinarian, wanted a smart crew, and made liberal use of the cat to get what he wanted. His standard dose was thirty-six lashes, but he often handed out many more. He was obsessed with petty thievery and for the alleged theft of a midshipman's handkerchief had one *Macedonian* sailor flogged through the fleet with three hundred lashes. Two or three lashes with a standard naval cat could draw blood, and two dozen or more left a man's back looking like "roasted meat burnt nearly black," so a flogging through the fleet was often "the equivalent of a death sentence."[19] Under Carden's rule on the *Macedonian* this draconian punishment was carried out at least twice.

If the lash failed him in his efforts to encourage smart, sailorlike behavior among the *Macedonian*'s crew, he resorted to another management tool, and in this one he was well ahead of his time. Incorrigibly slovenly or insubordinate sailors were allowed to desert by means of a routine well understood among the crew, for which the code word was "broom." Every so often a small group of these undesirables would be sent ashore to gather material for making brooms to sweep the decks. When Carden told them to go "to cut broom," they knew that they were to keep on going and that no chase would ensue. One man receiving these orders happily answered, "Aye, aye, sir, and I will cut a long handle to it."[20]

Also, a smart ship in any navy whose captain could afford it was likely to have a band. Carden found some musicians among a group of French prisoners of war on a hulk at Lisbon and got eight of them to volunteer for the *Macedonian,* with the provisos that they would not be flogged and that they could stay in the hold during battles—both very prescient requests.[21] The band played in the cabin during Carden's dinner but also performed on deck occasionally—one of the few pleasant elements in the life of this ship's company.

Often in a ship with a flogging captain, the first lieutenant would be a mitigating influence. Not so in the *Macedonian*—Lieutenant David Hope was also an enthusiastic flogger. However, in other ways he was of a different breed than Captain Carden. Hope was a younger son of a family in the Scottish gentry. Two of his three brothers in the army had been killed in the wars. Hope's naval life followed a tougher course than Captain Carden's. David Hope was entered into the navy a month before his ninth birthday as a "volunteer, first class" with a salary of six pounds per year. During the ensuing sixteen years he took part in a very risky amphibious operation, a major fleet action, an action in which two forty-four–gun French frigates were destroyed, and more. He commanded the boats in an action against floating batteries and was commended to the Lords Commissioners of the Admiralty for his bravery in leading a successful cutting-out expedition, a rare accolade for a twenty-two-year-old lieutenant. In spite of his heroism, he apparently was not a pleasant character. He is described as "hot-brained" and "surly."[22]

It was early in the morning when the *United States* and the *Macedonian* sighted each other. There was a strong breeze blowing, and a heavy sea had built up. On both ships, most of the men came on deck to see what was going on. The crew of the *Macedonian* had just finished breakfast and were looking forward to their normal Sunday routine: a muster in dress uniform, a church service read by the captain, then the rest of the day off, with no work required except the routine handling of the ship.[23]

The two ships closed, the *United States* sailing into the wind on the port tack, the *Macedonian* coming downwind toward her but being careful to keep her windward position—a standard tactic. Although by this time the British were fairly sure that they faced an American, they were not certain because the direction of the wind kept the Stars and Stripes hidden behind the sails. At 8:30, when the two ships were about three miles apart, the *United States* wore round and came up on the starboard tack, revealing her colors and heading her to cross the *Macedonian*'s bow. On the *Macedonian*'s quarterdeck, Captain Carden, Lieutenant Hope, and the master—the officer who managed the sail handling—were discussing how to approach the enemy. Hope wanted to get in close as fast as possible, and the master had a similar view. However, Carden was more cautious, excessively concerned with keeping the weather gauge, and decided to change course away so as to pass the *United States* at a distance to windward and then come up on her from astern. He may have been under the mistaken impression that he was facing the U.S. Frigate *Essex*, a thirty-two–gun ship armed only with carronades, an altogether different antagonist from the *United States*. Had his foe indeed been the *Essex*, he would have been wise to stay off, out of range of her carronades but well within the range of his own long 18-pounders. However, the *United States*'s long 24s outranged him. In any event, whether he was simply excessively concerned with keeping the upwind position or thought that he faced the much weaker *Essex*, the decision to stay off was disastrous. With it, Carden threw away whatever small chance he had of winning.[24]

Decatur took full advantage of this mistake and kept away at a distance from which his longer-range, heavier 24-pound guns could batter the *Mace-*

donian, while her smaller 18-pounders could barely touch the *United States.* Now Henry Allen's incessant gunnery training paid off: the shooting was accurate in spite of the heavy seas, and so rapid were the gun flashes that some of the crew on the *Macedonian* thought that the *United States* had caught fire.[25]

The *Macedonian* now faced a nightmare of carnage and destruction. Men were being killed and maimed by the 24-pound balls, by the splinters that they knocked from the sides of the ship as they hit, by the grape- and canister shot poured in by the *United States* as the ships came closer. Lieutenant Hope was wounded in the head but returned to the deck as soon as his wound was dressed, shouting to the gunners to fight on. But it was to no effect—the damage was too great. More than one hundred shot had struck her hull. The carronade batteries on the quarterdeck and forecastle were knocked from their slides and disabled, leaving the ship without her best weapons for close-in fighting. The fore- and main-topmasts were shot away, and the main yard, shot through in the slings, was hanging down in two pieces. When finally the entire mizzenmast was shot away and fell, its wreckage dragging over the side, the *Macedonian* became unmanageable, her guns unable to bear. The firing paused on both sides. The *United States,* almost undamaged, having lost only one of her topgallant masts, pulled ahead, then after Decatur had sized things up came back to finish the job. On the *Macedonian*'s quarterdeck there was a hurried discussion among the surviving officers. Lieutenant Hope urged them not to surrender but to "sink alongside." Carden knew that this was futile, that the battle was over, and ordered the colors to be hauled down. It was 11:15 A.M., and the heavy shooting part of the action had taken about one hour.[26]

Both ships could now assess their losses and examine the damage. Aboard the *Macedonian* the slaughter was extreme: the decks were "covered with blood," and the wounded made "a continu[ous] agonizing yell." Thirty-six men were killed; thirty-six more were severely injured, and most of these were soon to die; thirty-two more were less badly wounded, and some of these would survive. All in all, of the sixty-eight wounded on the *Macedonian,* only fifteen recovered, the most ever killed on a British frigate in a single battle. Two of the *Macedonian*'s dead were impressed Americans, John Card and John Wallis.[27]

On the *United States* there were five killed and seven wounded. Two of the wounded died, one of whom was the junior lieutenant, John Mercer Funck, who had joined the ship from the brig *Argus* just the day before the departure from Boston.[28]

The disparity in the condition of the two ships was much wider than their differences in size and gun power. Henry Allen's relentless and highly effective training of the gun crews on board the *United States* made the major difference, particularly when this program is contrasted with the inferior state of gunnery

training of the *Macedonian*. Decatur, who had a reputation as an indifferent seaman, on this day handled the *United States* in an expert manner, placing the ship
in the best position to use her gunnery skills while reducing the risk of receiving
some crippling item of damage that would have left her at the mercy of one of
the many British cruisers loose in the Atlantic. Carden, by contrast, mishandled
his only real opportunity.[29]

By this point, "every kind of order [had] ceased" aboard the *Macedonian*.
Some of the crew were in shock, others were running around searching for
friends and messmates and too often finding them dead or wounded. The dead
were thrown over the side, tenderly but without ceremony. Some men broke
into the spirit room, helped themselves to the rum, and got gloriously drunk.
Others, sensing an opportunity in the confusion, looted the purser's stores for
new clothing. The large number of wounded so overloaded the surgeon and
his mate that he moved from the cockpit in the hold, to the midshipmen's
quarters in the steerage, then finally up to the wardroom, where he was doing
amputations on the dining table. He wouldn't finish the cutting, sawing, and
dressing of all the wounded until late that night. The officers, stripped of their
authority by the act of surrender, had little control over events in the ship and so
packed their clothes and possessions and waited for their captors to make the
next move.[30]

In the midst of the disarray, Henry Allen and a party from the *United States*
arrived alongside the *Macedonian* in a boat. Decatur had sent Allen to take possession and then to command her on the voyage home. No one on deck would
pass him a rope to enable him to get on board, and he had to climb the side by
scrambling up the main chains, where the rigging of the mainmast attached to
the hull.[31] On the quarterdeck amid the wreckage were the British officers, and
Henry Allen told Captain Carden that he was to go across in the boat to the
United States, where Decatur was waiting for him.

It was a bitter experience for Carden and his officers. British officers had
long been accustomed to enjoying victory over their enemies regardless of the
odds, and it was hard for the Macedonians to accept that they had truly been
beaten. With contempt for the Americans they had gone into the action,
expecting to take them within an hour, and even at the end ascribed the outcome to bad luck.[32] The harshness of their defeat was compounded because,
having not yet heard of the loss of H.M.S. *Guerrière* two months before, they
thought that they were the first and only British frigate to be defeated by an
American.

The moment was as sweet for Henry Allen as it was bitter for the British.
Standing on the deck of the *Macedonian,* surrounded by the havoc created by
his guns, and facing defeated British officers was compensation, five years
delayed, for the humiliation of the *Chesapeake.*

After Carden was taken across to the *United States,* another boat was brought alongside to receive the *Macedonian*'s officers. Henry Allen, determined to show that American officers were gentlemen of "punctilious courtesy and the nicest sense of personal honor," asked them with much civility to get in the boat. Lieutenant Hope, surly to the last, launched this exchange of words:

> HOPE: "You do not intend to send me away without my baggage?"
> ALLEN: "You do not suppose you have been taken by privateersmen?"
> HOPE: "I do not know by whom I am taken." [An intentionally insulting statement, given that the two sets of officers were acquainted from their meeting in Norfolk earlier in the year.]
> ALLEN: "Into the boat, Sir!"[33]

Henry Allen put a guard on the officers' baggage to protect it from the customary looting by the crew and sent it over to them in the *United States* later in the day. This contrasted with the usual behavior of that time: the crew of the victor most often plundered the personal possessions of the vanquished.[34]

The boats shuttled back and forth, bringing to the *Macedonian* the American prize crew and taking back to the *United States* the greater part of the British crew except the severely wounded, plus the surgeon and his helpers. It looked at first as if a melee of fights would break out. The British were still shattered by their defeat and the loss of shipmates and at first wanted to vent their frustrations with their fists. However, the confusion subsided as most of the British were taken to the *United States,* and the American prize crew kept their good humor. Also, there were Americans in the crew of the *Macedonian* and Britishers serving in the *United States,* and members of both crews soon found acquaintances or friends of friends. Some even found relatives in the other crew, but these reunions were not necessarily happy ones.[35]

The British wounded and their surgeon stayed aboard the *Macedonian,* and Henry Allen, now in command as the prizemaster, treated them with particular concern. Allen apparently ran a happy ship: within a few days good feelings prevailed, the battle was largely forgotten, and the American and British sailors were messing and drinking together and swapping sea stories.[36] They worked together to clean up the ship and to get her ready to sail again.

When Carden and his officers arrived on board the *United States,* they were greatly relieved to find themselves treated courteously. Carden offered his sword to Decatur, but it was refused or handed back, and his humiliation was eased when Decatur told him that he was not the first to lose a frigate to the U.S. Navy—Captain Dacres of the *Guerrière* had that distinction. There is no record that the beaver hat wagered in Norfolk was mentioned.

Carden had several casks of good wine on board the *Macedonian,* and

Decatur paid him $800 for the wine and for Carden's investment in the band of French musicians, who now moved to the *United States.*[37]

Their baggage restored, the British officers, warmed by the hospitality of the wardroom, made a well-intentioned but insensitive gesture: they offered to write, sign, and give to the American officers a letter they could show to the officers of any British warship that captured them in the future, to ensure good treatment. The offer was refused. What was said in refusing it has not survived.

Stephen Decatur now had to consider what to do next. The damage to the *Macedonian,* while more than superficial, had by no means left her in a sinking condition. She was a new, fast, oak-built ship, and her addition to the U.S. Navy would increase the overall American naval strength by a healthy 10 percent—38 guns on top of 376.[38] But the ships were a long way from home, at latitude 29° north, longitude 29° 30' west, about 560 miles due south of the Azores and 720 miles off the bulge of West Africa. This was about 2,200 miles from New York by a route that would take advantage of the best winds and currents. Should he send Henry Allen and the *Macedonian* off alone, or should he cut short the cruise of the *United States* and go with him? The Atlantic was swarming with British cruisers, most of them probably lone frigates. Together, the two ships would overmatch anything like that, but alone the *Macedonian* would be easy prey. The importance of Decatur's prize made the decision easier, and given his ego and sense of honor, his vision of bringing into New York the first captured English frigate probably clinched it: the crews would repair the *Macedonian* as well as they could where they were, then try to get home together.

Henry Allen, in command of the *Macedonian,* was in charge of the repairs. His prize crew, plus all the help he could use from the regular crew of the *United States,* handled the work. Good feelings prevailed among all aboard, and the British prisoners of war in the *Macedonian* also pitched in and worked.[39] Although the fore- and main-topmasts were gone, the fore- and mainmasts themselves were still standing and could be secured for use. The mizzenmast was completely down, but its wreckage was lying alongside, as were the other shot-away spars, sails, and rigging. Using this flotsam and spare spars from both ships, Henry Allen, "with great ingenuity," succeeded in rigging a jury mizzenmast and converted the *Macedonian* into a bark, with square sails on her fore- and mainmasts and a fore-and-aft driver sail on the jury mizzen.[40] The two vessels stayed close to each other at the site of the battle for the five days needed for the repairs, then in midafternoon of Friday, 30 October, started for home.[41]

This was Henry Allen's first command of a ship, and he seems to have approached it with much zest and good humor. Even damaged and jury-rigged, the *Macedonian* was a better sailer than the *United States,* and both the officers and men in the prize crew were quick to needle their ex-shipmates about it. There was frequent boat traffic back and forth between the two, and a boat's crew from the *United States,* arriving at the *Macedonian* and waiting to make their return trip, would spend the time on the berth deck, telling sea stories. It was customary in those times for the boatswain's mate on watch to call down the hatch for the crew of a boat soon to depart to man their boat. On the *Macedonian* it went like this:

> BOATSWAIN'S MATE (PIPING): "Away, Wagoneers, Away!"
> OFFICER OF THE DECK: "Boatswain's mate, you rascal, pipe away *United States'* men, not Wagoneers—We have no wagoneers on board a ship!"
> All (except the boat's crew) go into raucous laughter or gentlemanly chuckles, depending on their rank or station.

This, and probably other heavy-handed humor, was repeated over and over until it was run well into the ground.[42]

It was a nine-days' wonder that the two vessels made it home across some 2,200-plus miles of hostile ocean without being seen by one of the many British cruisers then at sea.[43] Although they saw several ships, and even put Mr. Shead, the *Macedonian*'s purser, aboard a Cadiz-bound merchantman to let him get back to England with the pay records for the British crew, Decatur encountered no warships.[44] However, three days in a heavy gale enlivened the voyage. The *United States* rode it out without much doubt as to her safety, in spite of a casualty that nearly carried away her bowsprit. The *Macedonian* with her jury-rig was another story, and Henry Allen thought that she might founder in the high winds and heavy seas. But luck held, and after a four-week passage the ships arrived off Nantucket Shoals.[45] There they parted on 2 December.

The *United States* headed for New London, but Decatur had apparently given Henry Allen permission to go to Rhode Island, Narragansett Bay, and his home, family, and friends, although it was later put about that adverse winds and weather had separated the two. Henry Allen headed for Newport and arrived there on 6 December. This was one of the happiest days of Henry Allen's short life as he brought in a captured British frigate, himself in command, the fifteen stars and fifteen stripes flying above the British red ensign, the whole town of Newport watching. As he came to an anchor, he fired a salute from the guns of the *Macedonian,* and, music to his soul, the naval station ashore returned the salute. On a broader canvas, this was a singular event: only once before had the U.S. Navy captured in battle and brought into the United States a major warship of an enemy. This experience was never again repeated.[46]

It was Henry's good luck that for several days the wind was unfavorable for getting out of port. He invited his family and friends down from Providence to see his ship. He invited the governor of Rhode Island, William Jones, who was his maternal uncle, and gave him a nine-gun salute as he came aboard. It must have been particularly satisfying to fire salutes with captured British powder.

While in Newport, most of the British wounded, now recovering, were taken ashore to the hospital on Coaster's Harbor Island, along with the British surgeon and a British midshipman who had been on board. There was not enough hospital space available for all of them, and Oliver Hazard Perry, who commanded the Newport Naval Station, had to rent rooms in the town to create a temporary hospital for the overflow. Also, in spite of the perhaps half-hearted efforts of the American officers, several of the prisoners of war managed to escape—probably with the connivance of their American shipmates.[47] Once ashore these British sailors found themselves welcome among the townspeople, and some slipped away into the countryside and found new lives, although most of them gravitated back to the ports after a time.

Word of the capture spread rapidly. Upon arrival in New London, Decatur, who had a keen eye for politics, sent one of his junior officers, Lieutenant Archibald Hamilton, who also happened to be the son of the secretary of the navy, to Washington with dispatches reporting the victory and one of the *Macedonian's* large red ensigns. Mrs. B. H. Latrobe, a perceptive observer with a mordant pen, chronicled his arrival in Washington on 10 December. Her letter to a friend, Mrs. Juliana Miller, is worth excerpting at length:

> ... On Thursday last a very splendid Ball was given to the Navy Officers, Hull, Morris, Stewart, etc. My husband could not be absent as he holds an office in the Navy Department, and I was not sorry we went, as it is not likely I shall witness such another scene. At about five in the evening my husband came home and informed me that we must immediately illuminate our house, as the account of a victory obtained by Commodore Decatur had just arrived. My house in ten minutes was prepared for lighting up and we prepared for the Ball. The avenue was very brilliant on our way to the Capitol Hill, and, the company assembling, the crowd was immense. Mrs. Madison was there but not the President. The evening went on with crowding as usual upon the toes and trains of those who did not dance; when at about ten o'clock, a loud huzza announced the arrival of young Archibald Hamilton, who had at that moment appeared with the colours of the *Macedonian*. He was borne into the room by many officers. Good little Mrs. Hamilton, his mother, stood by me, and was so much agitated at the sight of her son, that she must have fallen, had I not stepped forward and offered her my arm. The young man sprung into her arms; his sisters threw their arms around him, and the scene was quite affecting.

The colours were then held up by several gentlemen over the heads of Hull, Morris and Stewart, and Hail Columbia played and there were huzzas until my very head swayed.

The aforesaid colours were then laid at the feet of Mrs. Madison. *O Tempora, Oh Mores.* This was rather overdoing the affair. I forgot to say that the flag of the *Guerriere* was festooned on one side of the room and of some other vessel.

At this point Mrs. Latrobe caught the distinct scent of hubris in the air:

Now, between ourselves, I think it wrong to exult so outrageously over our enemies. We may have reason to laugh on the other side of our mouths some of these days; and, as the English are so much stronger that we are with their Navy, there are ten chances to one that we are beaten. Therefore it is best to act moderately when we take a vessel; and I could not look on those colours with pleasure, the striking of which had made so many widows and orphans. In the fullness of my feelings, I exclaimed to a gentleman who stood near me, "Good Heavens—I would not touch that colour for a thousand dollars," and he walked quickly away, I hearing the gentleman say, "Is it possible, Mrs. Latrobe." I looked around and it was a good staunch Federalist from Rhode Island, Mr. Hunter, the Senator, so that I shall escape hanging after so treasonable a speech. I came home at 12 with a raging headache. . . .[48]

Regardless of Mrs. Latrobe's moment of realism, the general, popular feeling was intense euphoria, and Stephen Decatur's reputation was forever ensured.

In New London, Decatur was probably relieved that the adverse weather kept him from immediately taking the ships on to New York: he was ill when he arrived and moved on shore to recover. Back on board the *United States* in the mouth of the Thames River, the closeness of the shore and the green hills of the town were powerful attractions to the British prisoners, many of whom "were desperate . . . to escape from further British service" under the likes of Carden and Hope. Several of them escaped by making the cold and dangerous swim through the river current to the shore, and one man drowned in this bid for freedom. The sentries on deck tried to prevent escapes and sometimes fired at the men in the water, but it was a half-hearted effort, and they really didn't aim to hit. Decatur asked the local U.S. marshal to take charge of the prisoners, but all that official was willing to do was to turn them over to the British consul. This Decatur didn't want to do: some were impressed Americans, and they hadn't been sorted out yet. Also, some of the prisoners wanted to sign on board the *United States*. When the marshal wouldn't help, most of the prisoners were taken ashore and kept for a couple of days in a not-very-secure barn from which many escaped.[49]

In New York the movers and shakers of the city began preparations to receive the two ships with a great welcome. Committees were formed, headed by names like Vanderbilt, Brinkerhoff, and Fish, and the details of balls and dinners and decisions about how long the bells should ring at the arrival of the ships were worked out.[50] All this would take time, and Decatur was apparently asked to plan his arrival accordingly: there is nothing else to account for the leisurely progress of the rest of his trip.

Henry Allen was happy to stay in Newport, but finally, on Sunday, 13 December, the appointed time arrived, and the wind was right for the passage to New York. He got the *Macedonian* under way and started up the coast to rejoin Decatur and the *United States.* Off New London, he fired a signal gun to call out the *United States,* and within a few hours both ships were on their way up Long Island Sound. This was a pleasant, relaxed trip. How relaxed is evident from the account of Decatur's visiting the *Macedonian* during the passage, during which he was wearing "an old straw hat and a suit of plain clothes," looking more like a farmer than a naval officer.[51] The dangers of the risky Atlantic crossing were past, and they could all, officers and sailors, look forward to enjoying the brief pleasures that a hero's welcome implied—whiskey, women, tobacco, and the cheers of the crowd—as well as the more solid items: prize money and promotion.

The two ships anchored off Riker's Island, outside the Hell Gate, after their leisurely passage through the Sound. The wind was not right for running the Hell Gate, but in any event they needed time to sound and buoy the dangerous, rock-filled channel, and they were not due to move the ships the ten miles down to the city until the day of their formal welcome, still some time off. Still, there was plenty of activity. Shipping going by the two frigates gave them three cheers, which of course had to be returned, and this continued without letup until everyone was hoarse. There was a constant stream of visitors to see the *Macedonian* and the American prize crew, and some of the British prisoners made small fortunes by showing these sightseers around and retelling the details of the battle.[52]

The city's hospitality was enthusiastic. Henry Allen wrote Sarah that the New Yorkers "overwhelm us with invitations to dine, etc., there has not been a day that I have not received three or four."[53] The heroes of the hour were, at this Christmas season of 1812, all present in New York: Isaac Hull, of the frigate *Constitution,* acclaimed for the defeat of H.M.S. *Guerrière;* Master Commandant Jacob Jones, of the ship-sloop *Wasp,* for the capture of H.M. Sloop *Frolic,* in spite of the loss of the *Wasp* and recapture of his prize; and Stephen Decatur, whose victory outshone all the rest, its tangible evidence, the *Macedonian,* being anchored east of the Hell Gate for all to see.

There were honors aplenty for all of them. Hull, Jones, and Decatur were given the Freedom of the City, on vellum and in gold boxes, and their officers and crews given the "Thanks of the Common Council."[54] Sully was to paint Decatur's portrait, to be hung in City Hall. The U.S. Congress voted its thanks to Stephen Decatur and the officers and crew of the *United States,* awarding a gold medal to Decatur and silver medals to the officers.[55] The Legislature of Rhode Island awarded Henry Allen a sword, and Decatur, Allen, and Nicholson were all three to receive "swords, commemorative of the . . . gallant exploit," from the General Assembly of Virginia. Henry Allen wrote a flowery letter of thanks to the governor of Virginia for this sword, which he never received.[56] These trinkets and symbols were only a part of the effusion of honoraria.

The officers of the *Constitution, Wasp,* and *United States* were honored at a public dinner for five hundred—all male, in the fashion of the time—held in the City Hotel, at the corner of Broad Way and Cedar Street, just southeast of where the World Trade Center stands today. The hall was decorated in naval style with masts, sails, ship models, flags, and scenes of battle painted on back-lighted transparencies. Mayor DeWitt Clinton presided, with Stephen Decatur on his right and Isaac Hull to his left. The guests arrived at 4:30 and sat down at five, "to a table . . . covered with every solid and every dainty that the season affords . . . a dessert of delicacies of every description [and] the best liquors and choicest wines."[57] They ate, drank, sang, and speechified until 11 P.M. There were thirteen formal toasts scheduled on the program. These were interspersed with songs, band music, and cheers and were followed, as the evening wore on and the liquor flowed, by twenty-four "volunteer toasts by the prominent persons present." Among these was one given by Oliver Wolcott, leading Federalist and fiscal conservative, that can only be considered as highly prescient: "A Navy, an Army and Taxation. . . ." There is no record indicating that this was followed by wild cheering and songs.[58]

The greats of New York were nothing if not wise in their social planning and, of course, knew that their wives and daughters would never let them get away with just an expensive all-male bash, so they had also scheduled a ball for all the officers present. This took place on New Year's Eve at the same City Hotel, where the decorations were still up. Three hundred ladies arrived to dance with the dashing and intrepid officers and perhaps, in those simpler times, to be dazzled into matrimony by gold epaulets and bullion-trimmed blue uniforms.

But Henry Allen and the officers of the *United States* and the *Macedonian* were unable to attend: the larger plans called for the two ships to arrive off the city for their official welcome on New Year's Day, 1813. The wind was fair for their passage of the Hell Gate, so the officers were all on board, waiting for daylight and hoping that the wind would hold.[59]

In the morning there was a fresh breeze from the northeast, so the ships passed the rapids and rocks of the Hell Gate and made it down the East River, in spite of the *United States*'s accidentally dropping one of her anchors right in the narrows of the Gate: she was forced to quickly cut the cable to avoid being brought up short and run down by the *Macedonian*. This embarrassing mess avoided, the frigates anchored off Peck's Slip, just southwest of where the Brooklyn Bridge would later cross, and were greeted "with great joy." General Morton's brigade fired an artillery salute of twenty-one guns, which the *United States* and *Macedonian* answered. All the ships in the harbor flew the Stars and Stripes at their mastheads, and all the bells of the city were rung for one hour—an enthusiastic, if deafening, welcome.[60]

After the greetings were over, Henry Allen took the *Macedonian* across the East River and into Wallabout Bay near the navy yard to begin her repair and refit. All of New York wanted to see this trophy frigate, and even before she was moored, "the Navy Yard and the surrounding hills were covered with spectators" gaping at the shot holes in her sides and the "fifteen or twenty balls partly buried in her planking."[61]

To refit the *Macedonian,* Henry Allen had the help of an old acquaintance: the person in charge of arranging supplies and managing the logistical affairs of the naval ships in New York was the navy agent, Dr. John Bullus, the politically well connected naval surgeon whom Henry Allen had known as a passenger aboard the *Chesapeake* on that terrible day in 1807. Dr. Bullus was not only the navy's agent but also, in those happy days before the invention of conflict of interest, one of the major contractors selling supplies to it. He and two partners—John P. Decatur, the commodore's brother, and a man named John A. Rucker—were in the gunpowder business, making and selling "Belleville Gun-powder—single, double, treble, fine cannon and canister powder, glazed and rough, manufactured at Belleville Mills. . . ."[62]

A few days before a cartel vessel had arrived from England under a flag of truce and took aboard Captain Carden, his officers, and what remained of the *Macedonian*'s British crew. Only about 115 men were still prisoners—roughly 100 had gotten away, mostly in Newport or New London, although since the arrival in the New York area there had been continuous attrition of one or two every day.[63] The cartel left in late December for a long winter voyage home, and when it stopped at Bermuda and was again under British jurisdiction, the former Macedonians were available for exchange and enabled the release of some American prisoners of war.[64]

In England the inevitable court-martial "most honourably acquitted" Carden, but he was not employed again until 1825, and then only as overseer of a group of laid-up ships. He had ample time to refight the battle in his mind: longevity and seniority promoted him to rear-admiral on the retired list, and he was still alive in 1845. Lieutenant Hope continued in the thick of the fight until the end of the wars in 1815 and then was employed off and on until 1830, when he was promoted to captain and retired on half pay. As a result of the capture of the *Macedonian,* the Admiralty, a few months after Carden's court-martial, ordered that His Majesty's frigates were henceforth not to singlehand-edly engage the big American frigates.[65]

The welcome laid out by the city of New York was not quite over. The best, and certainly the liveliest, celebration was left for the last. On 7 January the city hosted a dinner and theater party for the four hundred–plus sailors of the *United States* and the prize crew of the *Macedonian.* All were able to go—temporary crews from other ships took over all shipboard duties. The officers were included in the invitation but had the good sense to leave early.[66]

The dinner was scheduled to start at 2 P.M., and boats brought the men in at the "New Slip," today called the "Old Slip," where they formed up to parade to the City Hotel. At the head of the procession was the band—Captain Carden's old band, now Decatur's by purchase. Pragmatists all, just as they had dropped the "Marseillaise" and the "Ça Ira" from their repertoire and picked up on "Hearts of Oak" and "Rule Britannia," the French musicians were now ready with "Hail Columbia" and "Yankee Doodle."

Next came a committee of aldermen, then Stephen Decatur, Henry Allen, and the officers, all in full uniform. Then came the crew, two by two in their best Sunday outfits—blue jackets and trousers, scarlet vests, and black glazed hats. Not all of these uniforms would be clean and neat the next day.

Among the assembled ship's company, ready to share the victory dinner, were a few of the vanquished, men from the old British crew of the *Macedonian,* now "escaped" prisoners of war, whom the American crew had befriended, provided with American uniforms, and brought along. After the cartel vessel left for England with the British officers, many of the escaped British crew came out of hiding and gravitated to the waterfront, and some of them social-ized with the American crew and came and went aboard the two frigates.[67] The officers tolerated this, perhaps in the hope that some of the men would sign on.

So they went in procession through Pearl Street to Wall Street, across to Broad Way, and then north to the City Hotel, trooping into the same hall, with the same decorations, left over from the other two more-upscale affairs. The boatswain piped for silence, and after a mercifully brief address by Alderman Vanderbilt they all got their dinner.[68] For a considerable time the only sound in the hall was the clicking of cutlery and the subterranean rumbling of hun-dreds of jaws. Then the dinner was cleared away, the liquor started to flow, and the toasts began. The officers, as custom of the time required, had eaten in another room, but as the dinner in the hall ended Stephen Decatur and Henry Allen came in, were toasted and cheered, then gracefully left. Vanderbilt toasted "Commodore Decatur and Mr. Allen," then the serious drinking got under way. There were several formal toasts, then lots of volunteer toasts from the sailors, most of which were right to the point: "All the pretty girls who like Yankee Tars" and "Success to the Frigate *United States,* and plenty of prize money."[69]

The toasts were still going strong when the time came to leave for the play, which was to start at 6 P.M. at the Park Theater, a quarter mile away. There was some attrition at this point, but "many of them" started up Broad Way to the theater, located just inside the diagonal at Chatham Street, now Park Row. The streets were lined with New Yorkers waiting to see the sailors, and there were cheers and cries of "Jack [is] full three sheets to the wind!" or if there was some shoving and someone fell down, "Save the pieces!"[70]

The theater party was a great success. The sailors filled the house and cheered at everything. The play was named *Fraternal Discord,* but no one paid much attention. The last item on the program was a hornpipe, danced by a Mr. McFarland, a popular comedian. He brought down the house.

They left the play and scattered to be with their friends and continue the festivities or to hunt out the other diversions that the city offered. Sailors had never been more popular than these. Their credit was good—it was well known that they were to receive prize money—and the town was theirs. They were due to be back aboard ship the next day, but it was more than a week before the last of them returned, ragged and red-eyed. Some got into trouble and to preserve the forms of discipline during this tolerant period were brought to the gangway and flogged, but apparently very lightly: an ex–British Navy tar who was familiar with the real thing said that these lashings were "a . . . farce." Usually, though, punishment could be avoided altogether by appealing directly to Mrs. Decatur, who would then intercede with the commodore. Given the prevailing euphoria, that hero was glad to be dissuaded from applying any heavy-handed justice.

Pleasant and solidly heartwarming subjects now came to the fore: prize money and, particularly for Henry Allen, promotion. The law at that time stated that if an American ship captured an enemy vessel of equal or greater force, the entire value of the capture was to be divided among the officers and men of the captor. However, if the enemy was of lesser force, the American captor was to receive "one moiety only," that is, one-half of the value. Two "referees," or a third if the two disagreed, would determine whether the enemy force was greater or lesser and the amount of the valuation to be placed on the prize.[71] Secretary of the Navy Hamilton appointed Captain Jacob Lewis, the naval officer in charge of the gunboat flotilla in the New York area, as one referee and told Decatur to pick the other one himself.

This was quite a sweetheart deal. Jacob Lewis was much junior to

Decatur, and commanding as he did only the small gunboats, mostly manned by "Sea Fencibles"—waterborne militia—that were supposed to provide the local defense of New York harbor, he lacked glamour and was completely overshadowed by Decatur, the national hero and high-spirited commodore. The outcome was predictable: the "referees" determined that the *United States* and *Macedonian* were of equal force, in spite of the obvious differences in tonnage, gun power, and manpower, and set the latter's valuation at $200,000, which was paid over to Decatur, his officers, and crew.[72] Decatur himself received $30,000, the largest payment of prize money to a captain for a single capture during the war.

The Madison administration may have intended it to come out that way. The *Macedonian* was a valuable addition to the navy, and the skillful performance of Decatur, Allen, and the crew of the *United States* deserved the best reward that the country could provide, even if this meant stretching some law passed by Congress in an early fit of parsimony. However, even if it had gone the other way, all was not lost: the second moiety would then have gone into the Sailors' Pension Fund.

Henry Allen's main concern at this time was promotion. He knew that he was due to be rewarded—Decatur's letter to the secretary reporting on the battle gave him credit for the superior gunnery that overwhelmed the *Macedonian*. The secretary of the navy in those days personally handled the details of promotions, and William Jones, who came to the job in January 1813, was particularly interested in promoting meritorious officers ahead of the average. It had become customary to promote by one rank either the commanding officer or the first lieutenant of a ship after a victory that "served the national interest in a spectacular way."[73] Stephen Decatur was already as high as he could go, so Henry Allen's case for promotion was strong. The next rank up from lieutenant was master commandant, but the one beyond that was captain. At that time there were no admirals in the U.S. Navy, and commodore was not a rank but simply a title given to a captain who was commanding a group of vessels, so captain was the top rank in the navy. Masters commandant commanded brigs and ship-sloops, but captains commanded frigates. Henry Allen hoped, in spite of the "one-rank" custom, to be jumped over the rank of master commandant and promoted directly to captain.

He had some reason to think that this might be possible: Lieutenant Charles Morris, the first lieutenant of the *Constitution* during her recent victory over the *Guerrière,* was promoted directly to captain and given command of a small frigate to boot. Navy Secretary Paul Hamilton had, in an impulsive but unwise administrative gesture, ordered the promotion, which propelled Morris over the heads of seven lieutenants and eight masters commandant. Most of them were highly unhappy about it.[74]

However, this double-jump promotion was not likely to be repeated for Henry Allen. The *Constitution*'s victory had, after all, been the first major triumph of the war, and there is nothing like being first. Also, Hamilton was just leaving office, was probably still smarting from the criticism he had received over Morris's promotion, and was not likely to do the same thing again.

Given what might have been, the final upshot had an edge of disappointment for Henry Allen: he was to be promoted to master commandant and given a command. Even this didn't come easily. The new secretary, William Jones, wanted to reward Henry but within the customary limits. He recommended him for promotion to master commandant along with fourteen other lieutenants and moved him up in seniority on the list that was sent to the Senate, where it was delayed for some time. The list carrying Henry Allen's name didn't come out until July 1813, after he had taken the *Argus* out on her last cruise. Henry left without knowing what his status was to be. The fact that Henry was not promoted quickly after the battle, particularly when coupled with Morris's double jump, was a matter of open discussion within the officer corps, and it was thought "that promotions have taken a most extraordinary course."[75]

Henry and his family thought that the delay and the lack of a double jump was due to politics, although this was probably not so. However, the Allen family and their friends were Federalists, and the administration was Republican. These things often mattered in those days, even for navy lieutenants.[76]

In early January Henry Allen was in the process of turning over command of the *Macedonian* to Jacob Jones, hero of the *Wasp,* soon to be a newly minted captain. The matter of Henry's promotion was still completely uncertain, and he was anxious also to know what his next assignment would be. He wrote home that he was "very unwell," a likely result of his anxiety.[77]

At this point the U.S. Brig *Argus,* which had left along with the *United States* in early October, finally returned from her cruise, and her captain, Master Commandant Arthur Sinclair, asked to go on an extended leave. The *Argus* was part of Decatur's squadron, and in mid-January Decatur put Henry Allen temporarily in command of her and asked for confirmation from the secretary of the navy.[78] Now it turned out that the former secretary, Paul Hamilton, had promised the *Argus* to Oliver Hazard Perry but had left office without doing anything about it. Hamilton's successor, William Jones, was embarrassed by the mix-up, but the problem was neatly solved when Perry asked to be assigned to service on the Great Lakes.[79] So Oliver Hazard Perry went on to the Battle of Lake Erie and the immortality of "We have met the enemy and they are ours. . . ." William Henry Allen took the *Argus* on her last, fatal cruise.

CHAPTER FIVE

The U.S. Brig *Argus*
Anatomy of a Ship

THERE IS NO VESSEL AFLOAT and sailing today anywhere in the world that is like the *Argus*. All of the current replica "tall ships" were built with at least some safety features and watertight compartmentation and include modern materials like fiberglass, nylon rope, and Dacron sails. And only a few of the replica ships have the *Argus's* brig-of-war rig—a full set of square sails on two masts, with a gaff-headed "driver," or fore and aft mainsail, that rode on a lightweight "trysail mast" attached to the after side of the mainmast.[1] The true brig rig went out of favor even as a merchant rig, replaced by the brigantine as ships got larger, well before the end of the Age of Sail.

But in the time of the wars of the French Revolution and Napoleon, man-of-war brigs were used in all navies as light cruising vessels and were highly regarded: they were powerful enough to overcome the largest privateers and merchantmen, were fast enough and weatherly enough to get away from frigates under most conditions, and could stay at sea for two or three months. They were particularly effective as commerce destroyers, and the prospect of an enemy brig-of-war loose in the shipping lanes was a recurring nightmare to those in the British Admiralty who planned for convoys and the moving of trade.

During those days the industrial revolution had as yet hardly touched shipbuilding, but the highly sophisticated technology of building ships of oak timbers, fir masts, hemp rope, and flax canvas was at its apogee.

The *Argus* was built in Boston in 1803, one of a group of four small cruisers, two brigs and two schooners, authorized that year by the navy. As built she was 95 feet 6 inches long on her upper, or gun, deck, had a beam of 27 feet, was measured at 315 tons, and cost $37,428.[2]

In the simplest, most basic sense she was a marvelously shaped box, artfully constructed of white-oak timbers and planks. The heaviest piece in her was the twelve-inch-by-twelve-inch keel timber. Coming up from the keel like ribs growing out of a backbone were her frames, sawed into the curved profiles that gave the hull its shape. These frames were covered with thin, three-inch bottom and side planking, cut into the curves and widths that would fit both the narrow and the wide parts of the ship and allow the illusion that the planking went straight along the hull. To enclose the top of the box, slightly arched beams connected the upper ends of the frames and were given strength at the ship's sides where beams joined frames by heavy knee pieces. The beams were then covered over with deck planking. All this was fastened together with copper bolts and wooden treenails.

On all the outside surfaces of the deck, sides, and bottom, the narrow seams where the planks came together were hammered full of oakum caulking, which was then sealed in with sticky, never-drying pitch made from pine tar. The underwater bottom planking was covered with thin rectangular copper sheets in an attempt to defeat the voracious, wood-destroying teredo worms.

Like other ships of her time, the *Argus* had no interior watertight compartmentation—if a bad leak developed, there was nothing to prevent the water from filling the ship.

As a fighting machine and as a living environment for her ship's company, she was considerably more complex. All of her guns—eighteen 24-pound carronades and two British 12-pound long guns that Henry Allen brought over from the *Macedonian*—were on the upper deck, exposed to the sky and the weather.[3] Carronades—short-barreled, short-range guns, lighter in weight than standard long guns of the same caliber—gave a small vessel like the *Argus* the ability to carry more and larger-diameter guns and thus to fire a more powerful broadside.

The *Argus*'s carronades were not mounted on wheeled gun carriages but on "slides," a recent technical innovation that speeded up the rate of fire by allowing the gun to be brought quickly back to its firing position after recoil. The slides were fixed to the deck, nine on each side, at each of the gun ports where carronades were to be mounted. Each slide pivoted on a heavy "fighting bolt" around which they could be swiveled for aiming the guns. The *Argus* in 1813 had ten two-foot-square gun ports on each side, one each for the eighteen carronades and two long guns, plus two bow and two stern chase ports. She had one more port in each broadside than other ships of her size: this was because her tiller, and the rigging connecting the ship's wheel and the tiller, were under the main deck, in the overhead space in the captain's cabin, not above deck, and this allowed room for one more gun to be worked on each side at the after end of the deck.[4] When the guns were not in use, "half ports" fitted top and bottom around the barrels, or "chases" of the guns, closed the gunports to keep the sea from washing in. Like all guns in 1813 the *Argus's* carronades were equipped with firing locks and could be fired with the pull of a lanyard, without waiting for matches to be lit or loggerheads heated.

The two long 12-pounders were on normal wheeled carriages so that they could be moved around the deck to the most effective position, although they were usually positioned at the most forward broadside ports that had been especially cut a couple of years earlier.[5]

The sides of the ship, the bulwarks, extended up to about four and one-half feet above the upper deck, and the iron frame and light rope nettings that served as stowage for the crew's hammocks carried this up another foot or so. The bulwarks and hammock nettings protected the gunners and others on deck during battle from light shot and small arms.

Between the gunports were smaller nine-inch-square rowing ports, each closed with a door to keep the sea out. The *Argus* was designed to be "rowed fast" with long sweep oars—a useful capability on a calm day with a juicy prize or a heavy enemy in sight.

At the bow of the ship, forward of the hull structure itself and built on top of the cutwater, was the head of the ship, formed of side rails and gratings and open to the sea from below. It held down and steadied the bowsprit, jibboom, and flying jibboom, which together extended out about sixty feet ahead of the hull. The Argus had a figurehead, a decorative flourish unusual in a brig-of-war, probably the bust of her namesake, that minor Greek god of a hundred eyes. The head also accommodated the toilet facilities, "seats of ease," for the crew: a couple of round holes in the top of open-bottomed boxes set on either side of the head, open to the sea and weather.

The upper deck was crowded with the guns and with all of the paraphernalia used to handle the ship: the large wooden bitts to take the strain of the anchor cable, the capstan to hoist the anchor and handle other heavy lifting jobs. Then the foremast and mainmast themselves and the heavy, tarred standing rigging supporting them. And the innumerable coils of large and small rope that made up the working parts of the running rigging that controlled the twenty-two yards, gaffs, booms, and bumkins and their sails, up to thirty-two of which could be set to the wind at one time, plus the roughly two hundred belaying points, kevels, and cleats used to secure the working ends of all of these lines.

No detailed plans survive to show the exact location of the deck or interior fittings aboard the *Argus,* but such plans do exist for British and French brigs of the time, and there are enough scattered references concerning the *Argus* herself to allow useful conjectures to be made about how her fittings were arranged.

Between the two masts and amidships were the boats—a launch, a cutter, and a gig—nested together on skids.[6] In racks above and beside the boats were the oars for the boats, the sweeps for rowing the ship, and the ship's spare spars. Farther back, aft of the mainmast, was the quarterdeck, with the ship's wheel, its wheel ropes going through the deck to the pulleys and tiller in the overhead space of the captain's cabin. In the after corners of the quarterdeck were two small houses, toilet facilities for the officers and warrant officers, called the "quarter galleries."

From the upper deck, two hatches with ladder ways led below to the berth deck, where lived, ate, and slept all of the 120 to 155 souls that were normally aboard the *Argus*. The berth deck was lightly constructed and was not intended to be watertight—it was heartily desired that any seawater inadvertently making its way down the hatches from the upper deck not stay on the berth deck but continue on into the bilge of the hold, where it would be less of a stability problem and where the pumps could reach it. The berth deck ran the whole length of the ship, but it was not a solid deck. In addition to several hatches and scuttles leading into the hold below, much of the berth deck's surface consisted of removable panels—about three feet by five feet, with ringbolts at the corners—which gave access to the various storage areas in the hold.

The headroom on the berth deck was about five feet three inches from the deck to the undersurface of the upper deck, and only four feet three inches from the deck to the upper-deck beams, which were spaced only about two feet apart. This meant that all but the shortest men moved about the living spaces in a perpetual crouch. The crew that took the *Argus* on her final cruise averaged five feet five inches in height, and Henry Allen was taller than six feet.

The berth deck was socially segregated. The after part, about one-third of the total space, was allocated to the 14 officers and warrant officers, the forward two-thirds to the roughly 125 men in the crew.

Officers' country was divided into smaller spaces by deck-to-overhead panels of thin wood, or possibly of canvas stretched on wooden frames and painted *tromp l'oeil* fashion to look like wood paneling. The captain got the most space, a truncated triangle in the stern area, about seven feet long and sixteen feet wide at most, with a skylight leading into the quarterdeck above. Forward of his cabin was the wardroom, a ten-foot-by-twelve-foot space used as a mess room and work space by the two lieutenants, the surgeon, and the sailing master. Some of the homey atmosphere of the wardroom was dispelled by the twelve-inch capstan shaft that came down from the upper deck, passed through the wardroom, and fitted into a ten-inch-by-twelve-inch socket block set in the deck. Forward of the wardroom was a smaller room where the four midshipmen slept and ate. On each side of the ship, from the captain's cabin forward, were tiny three-and-a-half-foot-by-six-foot cubicles for the officers and warrant officers, each with a wood-frame, canvas-bottomed bunk with space under it for a trunk or sea chest, a tiny washbasin set in a ring with a slop jar under it, and nearby a water jug, a towel ring, and a candle stand. These cabins were closed with twenty-four-inch-wide canvas-on-frame doors.

Forward of officers' country, the berth deck was just a large open room. This space, roughly 55 feet long and 25 feet wide, served as the living, eating, and sleeping area for the crew, some 138 men on her final cruise—this meant a little less than 10 square feet per man. There were no windows or portholes at all, not anywhere on the berth deck. Such daylight and ventilation as there were came down through the hatches. During warm and moderate weather the windsail, a large canvas tube with an air scoop at the top, was rigged to bring air into the berth deck.[7]

The crew slept in hammocks, slung on hooks set in the overhead beams. Each man was assigned a numbered pair of hammock hooks, but there was simply not enough space for the full crew to be in their hammocks at one time. However, half the crew, minus the cooks and other "idlers," were always on watch when under way, so there was room, barely, for the watch below to turn in. Also, some men preferred to lay their hammocks on the deck, and when the weather was not too rough, many got permission from the officer of the watch to sleep on the upper deck, under the stars. Sleeping on deck had its drawbacks. The planks were hard, even though many sailors had the idea that some were softer than others and would take their knives and "prick for the softest plank."[8] Also, in hot weather the sleeper might find himself, like Gulliver, unable to rise in the morning, stuck to the deck by the softened pitch in the seams. However, the worst hazard was the occasional wave that would break over the deck even in calm weather, soaking everything.

In the forward middle of the berth deck was the galley stove, wood-fired on the *Argus,* with an oven on one side and a couple of large and some small round-bottomed boiling pots, or "coppers," set into the top. Over the galley was a grating in the upper deck to accommodate the smoke pipe and to allow steam to escape.

The navy in those times tried as much as possible to get fresh air into the living spaces of ships, but this was mostly a daytime thing as most people thought that the night air was unhealthy. During the night on ships like the *Argus,* with the watch below asleep, part of the deck watch probably actually sitting on the berth deck around the foot of the after ladder, and most of the officers in their bunks, the air was so fetid and bereft of oxygen that a candle would burn only with difficulty. The malodorous combination of unwashed bodies, Stockholm tar, and rancid bilge water created a reeking and oppressive stench. The heat and humidity generated by a hundred bodies in such a confined space has been described by those who experienced it as "overpowering."[9]

Below the berth deck was the hold, about six feet deep and crammed full with a seventy-five-day supply of stores, all she could carry without riding too deep, plus equipment, powder, and shot. Along the keel on both sides was her ballast, in 1813 comprised of iron bars called kentledge rather than the old-fashioned loose-stone ballast. Between the two masts and amidships in the bottom of the hold there probably were sheet-iron water tanks, fitted to the shape of the hull, and on top of the tanks were stowed perhaps twenty casks that were used to bring water from the shore to fill the tanks.[10] Together, the tanks and the casks held six thousand gallons of fresh water. Also on top of the tanks was stored her supply of salt meat, about thirty-five barrels of salt beef and twenty-four of pork. Aft of the water tanks was the spirit room containing about twenty-one small barrels of whiskey for the daily grog ration.

In its early post-revolutionary days the U.S. Navy had started out serving rum, like the British.[11] But in 1805, during Jefferson's Republican administration, Secretary of the Navy Robert Smith ordered a changeover to whiskey, "pure rye whiskey of the 3rd or 2nd proof, and one year old." It was said to be "cheaper and more wholesome," but there may well have been a political edge to the decision: rum was imported or was made in Federalist New England of imported Caribbean molasses, but whiskey was domestically made in the Republican southern and middle states from nourishing grain raised by the agrarian yeomen beloved of Jefferson.[12] Whether rum or whiskey, when mixed half-and-half with water it was grog, and "splicing the mainbrace" with the twice-daily serving of it was for most sailors—and for many of the officers too—one of the real highlights of their otherwise dangerous and grindingly uncomfortable lives.

But eight ounces of fiery, one-year-old, high-proof whiskey per day, even when mixed with water and doled out in late morning and afternoon servings, was enough to quickly create in most of those early sailors a pathology of alcohol dependence or addiction. Most of the disciplinary problems in the early U.S. Navy, and the British Navy too, had their roots in grog, as did the popular stereotype of Jolly Jack, the drunken sailor ashore. The officers knew it, and the Navy Department knew it, but there was no way to get rid of grog without widespread discontent or even mutiny. Looked at another way, the situation in the navy reflected the larger society ashore: in the early days of the Republic distilled spirits were thought to be healthy, nourishing fare, and Americans were heavy drinkers. The average per-capita consumption of distilled spirits, that is, rum, whiskey, gin, and brandy, was around four and one-half gallons per year in 1810, about three times what it is today.[13] But the U.S. Navy sailor who drank his whole grog ration, 360 days per year, absorbed 22.5 gallons per annum of raw, liver-pickling booze, about 5 times the average consumption ashore, even in those hard-drinking times, and certainly enough to often subvert discipline aboard ship.

The problem wasn't solved until many years later, when the moral uplift and urges toward temperance of the Victorian Age began to reach even the ships, and the men began to be willing to take money in lieu of their spirit ration. On board the *Argus* in 1813 the sailors needed their grog, and so there was seventy-five days' worth of whiskey in the spirit room.

Under the wardroom was the magazine, about eight feet by ten feet, lined with copper, a flameproof lantern set into one side, and filled with about fifty small barrels of black powder and racks of filled cartridges. Forward of the magazine was the shot locker, carrying about twenty-three tons of 24-pound round shot, canister and grape, and 12-pound round shot.

In the forward end of the hold were the sail bins and the bins for the purser's, boatswain's, and carpenter's stores. A little aft of this on both sides were the cable tiers, the stowage areas for the bulkiest items on the ship, the coiled-down anchor cables: three 720-foot, 4-inch-diameter hemp cable-laid ropes, which were the bower cables; the 2.5-inch-diameter stream cable; and a 720-foot, 1.6-inch cablet.

Around and amongst all of this, wherever there was a little space, were stored the barrels, kegs, and bags of dried peas, rice, flour, cheese, butter, molasses, and vinegar that made up the navy ration in those days. The bread, hard sea biscuit, was stored under and aft of the captain's cabin.

So this was the *Argus* when ready for sea. Crammed with guns, shot, men, equipage, and supplies. Not a cubic foot left empty. With twelve tons of guns on her deck, her crew on board, her hold filled with shot and stores, and no watertight compartmentation, she would seem a risky proposition to most modern sailors. Should a butt-end bottom plank work loose at the sternpost from the ship's having gone too long in a following sea, or should any other serious leak develop, she would sink in a few short minutes. Those who sailed in her were conscious of the horrid possibilities, but then all ships were risky, and sailoring was an inherently risky profession. The *Argus* was well liked: one of her captains described her as "this charming vessel."[14] She was an excellent and fast sailer, and in her earlier days during the Barbary Wars she was "universally allowed to be the finest vessel floating in the Mediterranean."[15]

With modern eyes, and from another perspective, she should be viewed as a different thing: at sea, with her rigging taut and all her sails set, she was like a violin, a fragile thing of beauty, held together and in balance by the tensions of her shrouds and stays and the tenuous fastenings of plank to frame to keel. A skilled captain, adept officers, and a trained crew could extract virtuoso performance from her. With a fresh breeze broad on her bow and every rope wind-strummed at its proper frequency, she would be an aeolian orchestra, and all on board would be uplifted and know why they had chosen the sea for their life.

CHAPTER SIX

Captain of the *Argus* and Her Crew

THE *ARGUS* ARRIVED IN NEW YORK on 2 January 1813 after a "long, unpleasant and . . . unsuccessful cruize."[1] Out for seventy days, cruising in an area off Brazil that was usually rich with homeward-bound British merchantmen, she had taken only four prizes. Then on the way home, northeast of Bermuda, she was chased by a squadron of six British battleships and frigates for three days and nights, the moon so bright that she could not shake her pursuers in the dark. She came within a hair of being captured, but such was the sangfroid of her skipper and crew that they paused in the middle of their flight to make a prize of an unlucky British merchantman that was passing by.[2]

Battered by winter gales and strained in hull and rigging by the exertions of the chase, the *Argus* "complained a good deal" and began "to show her age in every joint . . . leaking in every seam and nail head in her upper works." Water coming down through leaky seams in the upper deck drenched the berth deck and everybody and everything in the living spaces, then fell down into the hold, ruined most of the little food that was left, and sloshed around six inches deep in the magazine. She arrived in New York a wreck in hull and rigging, her officers and crew worn out. The ship needed a thorough overhaul before she could cruise again, and all hands needed a rest.[3]

Her skipper, Arthur Sinclair, was given a three-week leave of absence and told that if he didn't return before the ship was ready for sea again, she would be sent out under Henry Allen.[4] Sinclair had no intention of returning to the

Argus: his next service was as chief of staff to Commodore Isaac Chauncey on Lake Ontario later in 1813.

Henry Allen was assigned to supervise the repairs of the *Argus* and then given command of her: subsequently, direct correspondence from the Navy Department to the ship was sent to "Lieutenant W.H. Allen, U.S. Brig *Argus*" or "Commanding the U.S. Brig *Argus*."[5]

A promotion list published in late March advanced Lieutenants Oliver Hazard Perry, Joseph Bainbridge, William Crane, and James Biddle to be masters commandants, but not Henry Allen. He was, however, high up on the next list, which came out in July, after the *Argus* had departed. He never received his formal appointment to the new rank, and his last communication from the Navy Department, the 5 June operation order for the cruise of the *Argus,* addressed him as "Lieutenant."[6] He carried with him on the cruise his February 1807 commission as lieutenant.

Henry Allen took command of the *Argus* on 17 February 1813.[7] He was twenty-eight years old, a young naval officer of great promise. He was a handsome man: his only surviving portrait shows him in profile, with a straight nose, a pleasant half smile, curly hair cut short, and long side whiskers in the fashion of the day. He is in uniform, wearing an epaulet, and the impression given is of a well-made man, rather than one either slender or stout. He is described as "about six feet high, a model of symmetry and manly comeliness . . . and [an] accomplished gentleman." He was more than six inches taller than the average of the ship's company of the *Argus,* although four men in the crew were taller than he.[8]

He was also the pride of his family, but there was also in his correspondence a shadowy, barely seen Providence girl, Mary, to whom he may have represented wasted hopes and quiet exasperation. Her name appeared in his letters to his sister Sarah over the years, when he asked to be remembered to "little Mary." But although always fascinated with women, he was shy with them, and he seems never to have given Mary his serious intentions. If she was waiting for him, she tired of it. Two months before the cruise, he wrote to Sarah that "I hear our 'little Mary' is soon to take a husband . . . if so, the chances are against my marrying in Providence."[9]

When Henry Allen first mustered his crew after taking command of the *Argus,* there were one hundred officers and men in the ship's company—old hands, most of whom had been aboard for a year or more. The ship was shorthanded—her full complement was about 125—but much worse was to come.

It was swiftly becoming apparent to Madison's government that the key strategy of the war for the United States was to take and hold control of the Great Lakes, and the Navy Department urgently began drafting men from the ships in the Atlantic ports to build and crew the ships to do this. The *Argus* was tasked to send "to the Lakes" a lieutenant, Wolcott Chauncey, plus fifty others, including two experienced midshipmen, the ship's sailing master, and a master's mate. This was a severe blow to Allen, coming less than two weeks after he took command. Decatur tried to have the order changed, urging Secretary Jones to take men from the New York gunboat flotilla and from a couple of other ships that were unlikely to be sent out to meet the enemy at sea.[10] But Jones stood firm on his order, and the men all left the ship by 2 March, leaving Henry Allen with the task of replacing them.

There were also the normal losses. Over the next three months several enlistments expired, seven men were lost to the running sore of desertion, three died, and a few were discharged as "unfit." The crew that took the ship on her final cruise included only 23 of the old hands. Among these, the first lieutenant, William Henry Watson, twenty-two years old, had come aboard from the frigate *President* in June 1812. He was a Virginian, and although born in Alexandria had spent most of his life in rural Fauquier and Prince William Counties. He was a sturdily built man just under five feet nine inches, light haired and blue eyed, had entered the navy on New Year's Day of 1808, but was quite new as a lieutenant. The other lieutenant, William Howard Allen, had entered the navy on the same day as Watson and had reported aboard the *Argus* at about the same time. He was Watson's close friend and was only barely junior to him in rank. Howard Allen was from New York State, from the large riverside town of Hudson, and his father was also in the navy, a sailing master. He was twenty-three, a year older than his friend and at five feet five inches a bit shorter. He too was fair haired and blue eyed. He was bony and muscular, with strong features and a keen eye. He was sensitive upon points of honor and, when a midshipman on board the *Chesapeake* in 1808, had wounded an antagonist in a duel over some now-forgotten insult concerning the incident with the *Leopard*. He was from a family that had earlier known considerable prosperity and prominence but was at this time experiencing difficulties. His father had recently been arrested for a "debt that the plaintiff was unable to substantiate" and during this spring of 1813 was in the gaol in Brooklyn.[11]

Both Watson and Howard Allen had known Henry Allen for several years, and the two Allens had served together in both the *Chesapeake* and the *United States*. The two lieutenants filled the complement of fully commissioned line officers, but the *Argus* was short of having the six midshipmen, a surgeon, and a surgeon's mate that were also scheduled.[12]

Other key people who would make the cruise were already aboard when Henry Allen arrived: Midshipmen Temple and Snelson, plus Midshipman Pottenger, who was temporarily on leave at that time; Henry Denison, the purser; some of the warrant and petty officers; Colin McLeod, the boatswain; John Fleming, the sailmaker; Richard Groves, the master's mate; and James Beon and Thomas Hill, two of the quartermasters. About a dozen experienced seamen remained of the old crew, Charles Baxter, William Shaw, James Hunt, and John Henry among others.

Three midshipmen, William Jamesson, Richard Delphey, and William Edwards, followed Henry Allen to the *Argus* from the frigate *United States*. Jamesson came aboard the same day as Henry Allen, and the other two arrived within a few weeks.

For some of these men enough information survives to enable us to see them in the round, but for others we get just a few tantalizing glimpses. Here is Midshipman William Temple from Virginia, twenty years old and two years in the navy, tanned and hazel eyed, with his initials and an anchor tattooed on his left arm and an eagle on his right, the only tattooed man recorded on the *Argus*.[13] And Colin McLeod, the boatswain, at thirty years one of the older men aboard, recorded as born in Philadelphia, but with something, perhaps a burr in his voice, that raised the possibility that he was really from Scotland. Or Midshipman Richard Delphey, from Washington, D.C., the son of a shoemaker. He was just eighteen years old but, with four years of sea service behind him, so expert in navigation and lunar observations that he was used as an assistant by Mr. Thompson, the navy's traveling navigation professor.[14] Richard Delphey was a protégé of Henry Allen's from the frigate *United States*. And there was short, stocky Quartermaster Thomas Hill, a dark and violent man with violence in his future.

After taking command, Henry Allen was fully absorbed with the job of getting the *Argus* ready to go to sea again. She needed to be cleaned up and tightened up, repaired and refitted, and a new crew gotten aboard and trained. Decatur, who had seen before how Henry Allen could refit a ship and pull a crew into shape, was optimistic. On 25 February Decatur wrote to Secretary Jones, proposing a cruise: "The *Macedonian* will be got ready in a month and the *Argus* much sooner . . . as soon as I have had time to consider of a cruise . . . I will submit my ideas of it to your consideration."[15]

But getting the *Argus* ready took longer than Decatur anticipated. With the *Argus* now in the navy yard, it was for Henry Allen a matter of slogging through detailed problems a day at a time. The first new arrivals, Acting Midshipman Ben Eames and Seaman John Barlowe, "a deserter," did not look to be an auspicious start on a new crew. The departure of the experienced men ordered away "for the Lakes" left a huge gap in the work force and experience level, but it cleared the air for Henry Allen. The officers, new or remaining, were people he apparently had chosen or were well known to him. The crew would be men recruited from among the seafarers of uncertain quality currently at loose ends in the port of New York, except for those he would be able to get from the frigate *United States* or from the New York gunboat flotilla.

Given time, he knew that he could train them into an effective ship's company.

Midshipman Delphey came aboard on 8 March. On the fourteenth most of the marine detachment came back from the barracks in the navy yard. A seaman, William Hoventon, and William Taffe, a boy, an eager volunteer, arrived that week. Taffe, thirteen years old, was four feet ten inches tall, one of two or three men in the crew who could move around in the *Argus*'s five-foot-high berth deck in some comfort. On the other side of the ledger, one man had to be discharged as "unfit for service," a carpenter's mate and a seaman died, five men were released at the expiration of their enlistments, and three more men deserted.

The refit was apparently going more slowly than Decatur and Allen wanted because of the short-handed state of the *Argus,* and on 20 March seventy men from the frigate *John Adams* were sent aboard for five days to help out. Then that same week two more officers arrived aboard, Midshipman William Edwards from the frigate *United States* and one of the most important additions to the ship's company, John Hudson, the sailing master. He came from Gunboat Number *108* in the New York flotilla. But the same day Hudson arrived, the New York police came aboard and arrested Acting Midshipman Ben Eames. We are not told what he was accused of doing, and he simply disappeared.

The day after the *John Adams*'s men were sent back to their own ship, twenty-five men were sent from the frigate *United States* to the *Argus* to continue the outside help for the refit. But the *Argus* continued to have serious personnel losses: Thomas Brian, the ship's clerk, and William Bristol, a coxswain, were discharged. Then Daniel Stickell, a marine private, died. A few days later two of the midshipmen and the boatswain became seriously ill. Midshipman Yates had been suffering from a persistent chest pain and was coughing up blood. Midshipman Jamesson was "wounded by Venus" and came down with a bad and complicated case of syphilis, which put him on the sick list for more than two months. Boatswain McLeod had a two-week bout with what was probably viral pneumonia.[16]

But in spite of everything, the refit was somehow getting done, with the help of the working party from the *United States.* Then in the last days of March and the first week of April, twenty-nine new men came aboard, mostly seamen and boys, plus a few petty officers: some were experienced men from the gunboat flotilla and the frigate *Chesapeake,* some were recruited from the New York waterfront.

The British blockade of the coast had been steadily tightening, and in the general vicinity of New York there was usually a small squadron of one or more seventy-four–gun battleships, frigates, and often a brig-of-war. These ships were sometimes in full view, sometimes just a shadowy presence. Not only were they a fixture on the horizon, they were also part of the local economy, buying fresh meat and vegetables over the beach from farmers along the coast.

The other end of Long Island Sound was also becoming tightly corked. The British had taken over Block Island, were using it as a source of water and fresh beef, and were rumored to be building a wharf to accommodate boats from the ships offshore. The squadron usually included the seventy-four–gun battleship *Ramillies,* under Sir Thomas Masterman Hardy, now a rear-admiral, and a changing cast of other 74s and frigates. At this time, in early 1813, these ships normally stayed in Block Island Sound or outside in the Atlantic itself and did not venture through "The Race" that marks the entrance to Long Island Sound a few miles south of New London. However, they often sent small armed vessels inside to pick off local coastal traffic.

This was the case in the first days of April. Reports arrived in New York and Boston that a British brig-of-war or a large privateer brig of eighteen guns, together with a schooner, had been seen off Newport. They were now reported to be cruising in the area between Point Judith and Montauk Point and were a threat to shipping in the vicinity of New London. These clever marauders had captured a number of fishing smacks, manned them with British prize crews and boarding parties, and sent them to intercept unsuspecting merchant vessels. Approached by "harmless" fishermen, several merchantmen were quickly captured and sent on their way to the British prize court at Halifax.[17] These depredations called for a response.

The frigates *United States* and *Macedonian* were in the navy yard, completely dismantled. The *Hornet* was not ready for sea. The *Argus,* on the other hand, was close to finished with her refit but had only about half a crew aboard. It was decided to man the *Argus* with volunteers from the *Hornet* and send the former into the Sound and off New London to look for the intruders and protect the coasting trade.[18]

The *Hornet*'s volunteers, seventy-six men altogether, including Lieutenant John T. Shubrick, Lieutenant John Thomas Newton, and three midshipmen, came aboard on 7 April, and the *Argus* got ready for a short cruise. The next morning Midshipman Jamesson and Boatswain McLeod were still too ill to be returned to duty, so Surgeon Clarke sent them ashore to the sick quarters in the navy yard. Henry Allen got the *Argus* under way at three in the afternoon, beat his way up the East River against an adverse northeast wind, and anchored near Corlear's Hook. The wind was dead against her getting through the Hell Gate that night.[19]

After the ship was anchored, Allen had the crew "beat to quarters," and the officers made sure that each man at least knew where his battle station was. It was, of course, the first time this assorted collection of seagoing humanity— volunteers, new men, with a salting of old hands—had ever tried to work together. Henry Allen's memories of 1807 and the unprepared *Chesapeake* were still vivid, and he wanted no repeat of that kind of humiliation with himself cast in Barron's role.

In the morning the wind was still foul, but at nine it shifted to the southeast, and the *Argus* got under way and passed safely through the Hell Gate—certainly in the crew's untrained state the result as much of sheer luck as of the skill of Henry Allen, the knowledge of the pilot, or the sail-handling abilities of the diverse assortment of sailors on board.

After dropping the pilot, the brig moved down Long Island Sound at a good clip, and the crew trained at quarters, Henry Allen trying feverishly to get them working smoothly together. After a long day the *Argus* anchored for the night off Bartlett's Reef, close to New London.

Under way the next morning, the brig moved along close to the shore into Block Island Sound, off Watch Hill lighthouse, looking for the enemy brig and schooner. Exchanging information with a packet, Allen found she had been fired on the night before by some kind of "light cruiser," and he was also given more information about the decoy fishing smacks. Soon after, he spotted a smack that fit the description the packet had given and chased it through the Race without being able to catch it. All day the lookouts could see some of the large ships of the British squadron to the south and east, around Block Island and offshore—a dismaying sight. After a fruitless day, Henry Allen anchored the *Argus* off New London.[20]

That was the closest she came to any action on this short cruise, and this may have been a lucky thing: she was sent to look for a British brig-of-war plus a schooner, and most British brigs were a good bit huskier than the *Argus* and more heavily gunned. A well-trained, well-handled British brig, together with a schooner, would certainly have been too much for Henry Allen's inexperienced pickup crew to fight.

After spending a few hours of 11 April cruising in the Race, always with the British heavyweights in sight to the south, Henry Allen worked his way back up Long Island Sound toward New York, watching for any enemy cruiser activity but finding none. He made a stop off West Haven to pick up his brother Tom Allen, who had arranged to visit Henry and the *Argus*.[21] They waited outside the Hell Gate for a fair wind for three days before getting through on Saturday the seventeenth. Then the *Argus* anchored off the navy yard in Wallabout Bay, and the *Hornet*'s men all returned to their ship. Henry Allen's first cruise with the *Argus* was finished.

Immediately after arriving back from the Sound, Henry Allen did what all navy skippers do soon after arrival in port: he started getting his ship ready to go to sea again. At about this time a decision was apparently made, probably by Decatur, to have the short-handed *Argus* crew brought up to about 30 men over her normal strength of 125 to provide prize crews during her next cruise, which was now being planned. Henry Allen set up a recruiting rendezvous ashore under the charge of Sailing Master John Hudson, who quickly began to fill out the crew. Thirteen men came in on one day, four on another, seven on another, in a fairly steady stream. Over the next two months the brig received eighty-two men, most of them seamen or boys; but these men included the sail-maker, Sylas Day; a gunner's mate, Robert Conklin, who was quickly promoted to be the gunner; a carpenter's mate, John Sniffen; Quartermasters James Salley, John Young, and Abel Waite; and a real rarity in those parts, a Chinese man named Appene, to be Henry Allen's servant. Appene had been born in Canton and was twenty-one years old when he came aboard. To Henry Allen, training these new men was fully as urgent as recruiting them. Nearly every day they "beat to quarters and exercised the crew."[22]

Also at about this time Dr. Clarke, the surgeon, left the ship, himself ill. The last entry in his clinical journal is for 23 April, and he apparently stopped providing medical care to the crew at that time. He was sent to sick quarters at the navy yard but was not finally detached from the muster list for several weeks.[23]

In early May Decatur received a set of confidential orders from Secretary Jones. The orders told Decatur, who was preparing for a cruise in the *United States,* to take the *Argus* with him to a point off Charleston, then to direct Allen to head for the Gulf of St. Lawrence, where he was to cruise and to intercept British transports and stores ships coming in and out of Canada.[24]

In the days that followed, the *Argus* continued to receive men from the recruiting rendezvous and topped off with stores for the expected cruise. On 8 May she received her priming and battle powder from the magazine at the Wallabout. Gunpowder was usually one of the last items to be loaded, and its loading was an indication that a cruise was imminent. However, the ship was still short about fifteen men.

On that same day Dr. James Inderwick came aboard as the assistant surgeon, and he was to play an extremely important role in the events to come. Inderwick was twenty-three years old, with brown hair and blue eyes, and was described as "heavy set" and with a "cleft forehead." He had graduated from Columbia College in 1808 and attended lectures at its newly reorganized medical school, but he did not take the M.D. degree. Like most American surgeons of the time, he probably earned his basic professional credentials as an apprentice. He had also been a house surgeon at the New York Hospital before joining the navy and being assigned to the *Argus.* Although relatively inexperienced, he was apparently well thought of by the medical faculty at New York and also by Decatur.[25]

On 9 May the *Argus* took a pilot aboard and with the frigate *United States* moved through the Narrows and down to the Lower Bay of New York, near Sandy Hook. Decatur expected to leave on the planned cruise early the next morning, but when daylight arrived, he could see a British battleship and a frigate in the offing. Departure would clearly be foolhardy. Henry Allen put the *Argus*'s crew on water rations of one-half gallon per day, just as if they were already at sea, and spent the day in badly needed training exercises.

The next day, the eleventh, Surgeon Inderwick held his first sick call. It was a large event, eight patients, because of the backlog of medical problems that had built up since Dr. Clarke had stopped work. Midshipman Yates was still coughing up blood. He apparently had tuberculosis, and it became disabling to him at this time. He was discharged to the hospital ashore. Midshipman Snelson came to be treated for a severe sore throat. Seaman John Hamilton had a bad fever and headache. Then three men came in with gonorrhea, one with syphilis, and one with gonorrhea and syphilis.

The *United States* and *Argus,* soon joined by the *Macedonian,* waited for the next five days, hoping that the British would leave or that the weather would change and drive them off. The British squadron now actually consisted of just the seventy-four–gun battleship *Valiant* and her consort the frigate *Acasta,* and with luck and on a rough day Decatur's ships could have taken them. But Decatur believed, wrongly, that there were more of the British just out of sight over the horizon, and his opinion was strengthened when some deserters from the *Acasta,* arriving in New York on the fifteenth, reported that the British had his ships in sight every day and planned an attack on them soon with Congreve rockets.[26]

Henry Allen used much of the time to put his new crew through exercises at their quarters. A new officer reported aboard while the ships were anchored off Sandy Hook: Uriah Phillips Levy heard about the upcoming cruise of the *Argus* and came to New York to volunteer. Levy had commanded his own merchant vessel, and Henry Allen took him on as a "supernumerary" sailing master. The *Argus* already had a sailing master, John Hudson, and a master's mate, Richard Groves; and Henry Allen apparently used Levy as a lieutenant, adding him to the watch list as an officer of the deck.[27] This allowed Watson, Howard Allen, and Levy to stand the much easier schedule of a watch in three, rather than having Watson and Howard Allen doing watch-and-watch.

Uriah Levy was slender and darkly handsome, tall for the day at five feet nine inches, twenty-three years old, and hot tempered. He was one of a relatively small number of Jewish officers in the navy at that time and was an excellent pistol shot. He was the last of the wardroom officers to come aboard and with the two lieutenants, Surgeon Inderwick, and Sailing Master Hudson, formed an apparently congenial group during the upcoming cruise, although rifts later developed between Uriah Levy and the two lieutenants, William Henry Watson and William Howard Allen, as a result of an operational incident.[28]

The *Argus* was still at anchor in the Lower Bay, waiting, when on about 15

May an order arrived from the Navy Department that changed her destiny. In a confidential order issued on 10 May Secretary Jones told Decatur, "The President of the United States having in view a special service for the United States Brig *Argus*, you will direct Lieutenant Allen to await the further orders of this Department with the *Argus*, in a perfect state of efficiency and preparation for departure at a moment's notice."[29]

The new orders for the *Argus*, coupled with Decatur's perception of the size and persistence of the British squadron, forced a change of plans, and Decatur moved his ships back up to New York. The *Argus* was now for nearly all purposes out of his control and was not available to go with him on his overdue cruise. But the *Hornet* was ready for sea, and Decatur, his squadron now the *United States, Macedonian,* and *Hornet,* decided to avoid the British blockade by passing the Hell Gate and escaping through the eastern end of Long Island Sound.

Piloting frigate-sized ships eastward through the Hell Gate was considered to be a particularly tricky bit of work, and in any event seamanship was not Decatur's long suit. First he ran aground in the East River and was delayed for several days, and it wasn't until Monday night, 24 May, that he got under way to go through the Gate and into the Sound. The cruise began with a bad omen: as the ships passed Hunt's Point, lightning struck the mainmast of the *United States,* tearing Commodore Decatur's broad pennant from the masthead and leaving it lying on the deck.[30]

With this upsetting event fresh in mind, Decatur and his little squadron slowly worked their way down Long Island Sound, taking several days to make the passage that had taken the *Argus* one. On 1 June Decatur attempted to get to sea, passing through the Race into Block Island Sound, to go between Block Island and Montauk Point into the open Atlantic. In sight ahead was a British seventy-four–gun ship. Skillfully handled, the *United States* and *Macedonian* together should have been able to take her. But just as they were "congratulating [themselves] on the prospect of doing something handsome," out from behind Montauk Point came what Decatur took to be another seventy-four–gun battleship, plus a frigate and a razee—a battleship cut down by one deck—although in fact the only two British ships in the area seem to have been the *Valiant,* 74, and the frigate *Acasta.* Decatur turned his ships around and ran for New London. The *Macedonian,* a fast sailer, was in little danger of being overtaken, but the *United States* had a close call when her pursuers nearly came up with her.

The Americans got safely into New London, where they later successfully held off repeated British attacks by two 74s and two frigates that came close off the town. The British badly wanted the *Macedonian* back and said they meant to have her if they had to follow her into a cornfield.[31] They huffed and they puffed, but they didn't get either her or the *United States*. The two American frigates were stripped of enough of their guns to fortify the point at Groton, across from the town, and then moved up the Thames River, out of the reach of cutting-out forays by the boats of the British squadron.

The war was over for the frigates *United States* and *Macedonian:* they didn't come out again until after the peace. It was almost over for Stephen Decatur: he went to sea once more, in command of the frigate *President,* on 14 January 1815, after peace had actually been agreed upon at Ghent and the treaty was en route to the United States to be ratified. Getting out of New York Harbor in bad weather, Decatur ran aground, and shortly after he got the *President* off and afloat again, he ran into a small British squadron. After an action that, given his reputation, can hardly be described as brilliant, he surrendered his ship and became, briefly, a prisoner of war. Decatur's 190-year prestige as a Naval Hero comes in part from his burning of the *Philadelphia* during the Barbary Wars, but his major accomplishment was the capture of the *Macedonian,* and Henry Allen's gunnery skills brought him that victory.

Henry Allen and the *Argus* waited at anchor in New York, keeping topped off in stores and water, training the crew at the guns and at sail handling. On about 2 June the expected letter from the Navy Department arrived, telling him "that the service destined for the *Argus* is that of conveying our Minister, the Honorable Mr. Crawford, to France, and from thence immediately on a cruise, for which you will receive orders . . . in due time."[32]

CHAPTER SEVEN

Napoleon's Retreat and the Death of a Poet

THE SECRETARY OF THE NAVY'S change of plans for the *Argus* was the result of an untimely and tragic event that had taken place six months before and left the United States without a diplomatic presence in France.

American problems with France in the years leading up to 1812 were nearly as serious as those with England and in a way were a mirror image of them. The British Navy, acting under a series of Orders in Council, searched American ships at sea, seized any carrying French-owned cargoes, and required those carrying neutral cargoes destined for the Continent to stop in England and pay for a special license. The French, under decrees issued by Napoleon, at first seized American ships in French waters that had touched port in England or that had submitted to search at sea by the British, but later confiscated and sold all the American ships and cargoes that they could lay their hands on, in port or at sea.[1] French privateers were still active, although a British blockade had tightly bottled up what was left of the French Navy. Thus the United States was caught between Napoleon's devil and the British Navy's deep blue sea. Presidents Jefferson and Madison responded, at various times, with the Embargo and the Non-Intercourse Act, and at one point the United States was at the edge of going to war against both England and France.

President Madison had sent a minister to France in 1811 to try to get Napoleon to compensate the United States for the two-hundred-some seized ships and cargoes and to put the trade between the two nations on a basis more favorable to America. The minister was Joel Barlow, a Francophile Connecticut Yankee of strongly Republican sympathies who had lived in Paris during the Revolution, had made his fortune in France, and had many friends there, particularly among those in the more moderate wing of French politics. He had cooled toward the methods of the Revolution after the guillotining of Louis XVI and the onset of the Terror, and he had a strong but concealed dislike of Napoleon, whom he viewed as having stolen the Revolution from the people and destroyed its promise.[2]

Barlow was an early American intellectual, a Yale graduate, and the country's only epic poet of the period. His poems, never very popular, are read today only as historical curiosities. He was the close friend and patron of Robert Fulton and in this role was the midwife of the submarine and steamboat. After his return from France in 1804 Barlow purchased an estate, which he named *Kalorama,* overlooking the capitol in what is now northwest Washington, and he and his wife, Ruth, became popular fixtures in the social and political life of the city during the presidencies of Jefferson and Madison. Joel became a sort of unofficial adviser on foreign affairs, particularly on matters French.

So when in 1811 during Madison's administration it was decided that someone should be sent to France to improve relations with Napoleon's court and to try to solve the chronic problems, Joel Barlow was the clear choice.

Old friends warmly greeted him and Ruth in France, and Joel immediately established what he felt to be a good working relationship with the Duke of Bassano, Napoleon's foreign minister. Barlow met twice with Napoleon himself and each time came away feeling encouraged for the success of his mission.

Barlow was deluded in this: with the archives of those times now open, it is clear that Napoleon never had the slightest intention of paying for the seized ships. He despised the United States and would have liked to see it and its Republican form of government crushed. He hoped to see America embroiled in a war with England and instructed Bassano to give just enough ground in the negotiations with Barlow to keep the United States from invoking the Non-Intercourse Act against France, but not enough to cause England to rescind its Orders in Council against the United States. While Napoleon made only a minor contribution to bringing about America's declaration of war against England in June, that declaration was one of the few things that went right for Napoleon in 1812.[3]

So the deceitful Bassano kept encouraging Barlow to believe that progress was being made toward resolution of the problems. Bassano went so far as to forge and back date by over a year a document stating that two of the most onerous decrees had been canceled.[4] In the late spring of 1812, as Barlow was trying to keep the negotiations moving ahead, Bassano left Paris to join Napoleon, who was moving the Grand Army into eastern Prussia and Poland to position it for his great campaign against Russia.

Bonaparte's general concept for the Russian venture called for the quick conquest of Lithuania, at that time an integral part of Russia, followed by a move toward Moscow on a broad front. He hoped to destroy the separate Russian armies piecemeal before they could join together into a really effective force. This, Napoleon reasoned, would enable him to dictate terms of peace to Czar Alexander I and force him to make some territorial concessions. That achieved, Napoleon would move the Grand Army back to Vilna, in Lithuania, to overwinter and prepare to complete his conquest in 1813. Seldom have plans gone so calamitously askew.[5]

By the end of May Napoleon had about 449,000 men and 1,146 guns ready to open the campaign, more than twice the force that the Russians could put together at that time. But there were bad omens in late June when the Grand Army prepared to cross the Niemen River into Russian Lithuania. First, Napoleon's horse shied from a startled hare, and the emperor was thrown to the ground in front of his troops; then a thunderstorm broke, and torrents of rain drenched the ranks. There were murmurs among the soldiers, "This is a bad sign!"; "Few will return!"[6]

The French and their allies readily overran Lithuania, but although they met almost no resistance, the hot, muggy weather and epidemic dysentery left thousands dead or straggling behind—causing disorder. By the end of July there were more than fifty thousand stragglers and deserters ranging across Lithuania in dangerous packs in the rear of the Grand Army, making travel hazardous and disrupting resupply efforts. Almost worse, the army's draft horses, key to the success of French logistics, were dying from heat, thirst, and overwork, and "the cadavers of 10,000 horses . . . littered the road . . . to Vilna."[7]

Moving deeper into Russia itself, Napoleon was unable to bring on a decisive battle. The Russian armies managed to join together in spite of his best efforts, and now the army and the people themselves fell back before the French, carrying away or destroying everything that could be useful. The humid continental summer weather was a heavy drag on the Grand Army, and widespread sickness continued knocking down men and horses alike.

At Smolensk, Napoleon thought he was finally forcing the Russians to stand. Alexander would surely fight or bargain over this sacred place, rich in the relics of the Russian Church. This city was believed to be the key to Moscow: an old superstition held that if Smolensk was ever captured, Moscow was sure to fall. But after a brief, bloody, and inconclusive fight, the Russian forces torched the city and fell back farther eastward, the army intact.

Alexander ignored Napoleon's repeated urgings for negotiations: the defense of the Russian homeland had by now taken on a mystical, religious character with the czar and the Russian people, and no bargaining was possible while any of the French remained in Russia.

History gives us the hindsight to say that had Napoleon stopped at Smolensk and perhaps wintered there, he might well have succeeded in his conquest of Russia in 1813. But he felt that he still needed a decisive battle to break the spine of the Russian Army, and there was by now no turning back. "The wine has been poured," he said, "it must now be drunk."[8] Also, he was convinced that if he captured Moscow, Alexander would be forced to fight or ask for peace. Following a bloody shambles of an encounter at Valoutina, Napoleon finally met the Russian Army on 5 September at Borodino, about seventy-five miles west of Moscow.

After some maneuvering by both armies the real battle took place on the seventh. Napoleon was sick with a fever during the battle and the days preceding it and in pain from a swollen prostate and difficult urination. His disability reduced the scope of the French victory and contributed to making Borodino "one of the bloodiest battles of the entire nineteenth century." The French lost about twenty-eight thousand men, killed and badly wounded, including forty-nine generals; the Russians lost about fifty-two thousand, half of their line troops. But their army was not destroyed—it was saved by Napoleon's ineffectiveness during those three critical days.[9]

The battered but still-intact Russian Army passed briefly through Moscow, then left the city behind without fighting. A large number of the inhabitants left with the army as it moved out. The army first headed to the east and south, but then came back to the west, flanking the French.

Most of those Muscovites who had not gone with the army were servants of the nobles and now accompanied their masters out into the country, to their big estates. Then Count Rostopchine, the governor of the Moscow area, emptied the "darkest chambers of the Muskovite jails," filling the streets with these "furtive, shaggy, ragtag and defiant" dregs, and placed bombs and combustibles in buildings all over the city to burn Moscow over the heads of the French, "to warm the enemy's stay in their fair city."[10]

The French army came in sight of Moscow on 14 September. It was in bad shape and needed the rest, refreshment, and fresh supplies that the capture of Moscow promised. Their supply line stretched back nearly six hundred miles to Kovno, in Poland, and was not working well. As the French approached from the west they could see people streaming east, out of the city. In spite of this they found it hard to believe that the city was empty and undefended and entered cautiously. Napoleon was convinced that now, at last, Alexander would be willing to negotiate to his terms.

During the night the fires began, first one place, then another, blocks away. Over the next four days the mostly wood-built city burned to ashes, and it was becoming clear to the French high command that their conquest was quickly turning to ashes as well. Wisdom, informed by caution, called for a swift, orderly retreat. The French were in the middle of a hostile country, far from their bases, with winter coming quickly closer. However, Napoleon stayed in the Moscow area until early October, waiting for some message from the czar at St. Petersburg. But Alexander had no intention of talking to Napoleon, and no message ever came.

The delay was calamitous for the French. They were fast using up the food and useful supplies in Moscow. Very little food and ammunition was coming through the supply line, now under constant guerrilla attack, and the country around Moscow was being scoured clean: starving civilians, now trying to live in the forests and nearby villages, and stragglers from the Russian Army were competing with the French for every scrap of fuel and forage. A brief snowfall and dropping temperatures brought new problems: many of the French soldiers had thrown away their winter coats and extra clothes during the hot summer march into the country. Disease and losses to Cossack guerrillas were daily diminishing the French Army, while the Russian Army, drawn up in a strong position at Malo-Yaroslavetz, seventy-five miles to the south and west, was continually gaining new strength in men and horses.

Of the 449,000-some men that Napoleon had brought into Russia, perhaps 175,000 had been sent on other missions or left to guard and handle the supply train. But disease and battle had taken nearly 175,000, and the army in the vicinity of Moscow in late September was reduced to about 100,000.[11] Morale was bad, the senior officers were wrangling among themselves, and the men were tired and apathetic. Napoleon himself was ill and lethargic, only a shadow of the victor of Ulm and Austerlitz. By about 6 October he was planning an orderly retreat, at least to Smolensk. But in truth this was no longer feasible.[12]

Back at Vilna, at this time in early October, there was little solid information about the condition of the army with Napoleon, other than that it was at Moscow and was in some trouble. But from the other direction Bassano heard from Joel Barlow in Paris that the British had canceled their Orders in Council and that this would probably lead to an early end of the war between Britain and the United States, leaving France, which had refused to deal with America's problems, as the target of "the nation's hostility."[13] Stirring these things together, Bassano decided that a commercial treaty with the United States would be desirable after all. On 11 October he wrote to Barlow that if he would come to Vilna, the American problems could be rapidly solved.[14]

To Joel Barlow this proposal was "totally unexpected." He was no longer a young man, and the idea of a 1,400-mile coach trip through eastern Europe in the gathering winter was "disagreeable"—an understatement that could come only from a diplomat. But he felt that there was a fair chance that the trip would, at last, lead to the end so much desired—payment of the indemnities and the signing of a commercial treaty. There was little choice. He had to go. He wrote to Bassano on 26 October that he would be leaving Paris for Vilna the next day.[15]

Although neither Barlow or Bassano could know it, the mission to Vilna was lost from the beginning. The diminished French Army, after beginning the planned move back toward Smolensk over a route not devastated by its earlier advance, ran into the now-strengthened Russian Army at Malo-Yaroslavetz, and a short, bitter fight ensued. On the same day that Joel Barlow wrote to Bassano, Napoleon ended a long and contentious meeting with his marshals and staff by deciding that the Russian Army facing him was too strong to defeat and that he would retreat to the north and west, back along the track that he had fought over and foraged bare—back to Warsaw, out of Russia. From that moment on Napoleon himself focused almost totally on getting back to Paris to save what he could of his political life.[16]

This was an authentically historic day: the high-water mark of the First Empire. Up to this day in October 1812, all had been conquest and advance for Napoleon—any retreats had been brief and orderly, and facing his adversary. This was to be unconditional retreat, his back turned to the enemy, past Mozhaysk and Smolensk, past Vilna and Warsaw, to France itself, then Leipzig, Paris, Elba, Waterloo, and St. Helena.

Ignorant of the events in Russia, Joel Barlow set out for Vilna, after "tearful" good-byes from Ruth and the rest of his household. With him in the coach was his nephew Tom Barlow, who was going as his secretary, and on the box, as driver, was Louis, one of the Barlow servants. The fall rains had turned the roads to mud, and the going was difficult. The travelers got to Berlin on 3 November, then Königsberg on the eleventh, and arrived at Vilna, in freezing weather, on 18 November after passing through devastated country, the roadside littered with broken wagons, dead horses, and dead men.[17] With the countryside overrun with stragglers and deserters from the army, Barlow's party was extremely fortunate to have made such a trip in safety.

Napoleon's lucky star had now deserted him. The winter of 1812–13 came on early and was unusually severe. The Grand Army dragged itself west through snowstorms and over icy roads, with the Russian Army hanging on its southern flank and attacking at vulnerable points. Cossacks and peasant guerrillas killed stragglers and foragers, often with great ferocity. There was little food to be found other than dead horses, and it was almost impossible to keep campfires going. Men dropped from the cold and exhaustion while marching and froze where they fell. They froze around their campfires. On average, the Grand Army lost about 2,500 men per day during the retreat through Russia.

All in all, going and coming, the invasion and retreat cost the French more than four hundred thousand men.[18] The Russians at the same time were losing comparable numbers of soldiers and civilians, perhaps even more. No one knows.

The uncountable millions that have died horribly in the twentieth century, at the Marne and the Somme, in Stalin's purges and gulags, in Hitler's invasion of Russia and his Holocaust, in the fire raids on Dresden, at Hiroshima and Nagasaki, in Cambodia and Rwanda, have numbed modern reactions to the statistics of horrible death, and the human costs of Napoleon's invasion of Russia today seem like small change. But for the hundred years that followed that winter march in 1812, it was the standard by which catastrophes were measured.

It was an unreal world that Joel Barlow found in Vilna. The city believed, or pretended to believe, that Napoleon's conquest of Russia was going well and that the emperor would soon arrive with his staff and his guard to establish a headquarters for the winter. Joel divided his brief time in Vilna between making short trips into the devastated countryside around the city, writing letters to Ruth, and working on his last, most passionate epic poem, "Advice to a Raven in Russia." Joel's advice to the raven was not to bother trying to eat the frozen corpses in Russia because, due to Napoleon, there were plenty of unfrozen bodies all over Europe that would be easier fare for scavengers.[19]

Bassano had set up a temporary foreign office, and the diplomatic corps had moved from Paris to Vilna, ready to do business with Bonaparte. News reporting the Grand Army's retreat was widely ignored in the city, although Joel's letters to Ruth show that he had a premonition of what was likely to come. Even as late as 29 November, at the time the Grand Army was losing thirty thousand men in five terrible days during the crossing of the Berezina River, Bassano was telling the diplomats in Vilna that Napoleon would arrive within a week to set up winter quarters.

In fact, the Grand Army ceased to exist after Berezina, and Napoleon fled alone for Paris in a closed carriage on sleigh runners, leaving Murat in charge of what was left. The survivors still in ranks numbered only about 8,800 as they passed Vilna, although about 40,000 soldiers of the Grand Army finally got out of Russia one way or another.[20]

In Vilna on 5 December the dam broke. Strangers were ordered out of the city, and everyone in Vilna came to the realization that there would be no winter headquarters, that the Grand Army had ceased to exist, and that there was nothing between the city and the advancing Russians, now only about sixty miles away. The diplomatic corps, en masse, took to their coaches and joined the soldiers and other stragglers fleeing west toward Warsaw. Joel and Tom Barlow joined the stream in a carriage drawn by six artillery horses. The roads were frozen and covered with packed snow, and on 8 December the temperature fell to minus twenty-nine degrees Fahrenheit. The Barlows crossed the River Niemen on the ice, leaving Russia and entering the Duchy of Warsaw. They arrived in the city of Warsaw on 17 December. There they met an acquaintance from Paris, Jean Baptiste Petry, an official in the French Foreign Office, who joined them.[21] They left Warsaw early on the eighteenth, headed south for Cracow, Vienna, Munich, and then Paris.

Joel caught a cold on the nineteenth from riding all day in the frigid carriage. He was worse on the twentieth, with headache and fever. During the morning of 21 December the Barlow party came to the tiny village of Zarnowiec, and Joel was too sick to go farther. He may have remembered Ruth's letter to him, received in Vilna, then only poignant but now prescient: "O my *precious,* take great care of your health. I fear that you will fatigue too much and get cold, and of how much more consequence to me is your life than the lives of all the world besides."[22]

The Barlows stopped in the center of the village, and Petry went to look for some warm place that could take in the seriously ailing man. The mayor of the town, John Blaski, took Joel Barlow into his home and gave him a warm bed and kind attentions. By now Joel's cold had become pneumonia, and there was no question of his traveling farther. He became steadily worse, and in spite of all that could be done for him by very kind people and two local physicians, he died on 26 December 1812. He was as much a casualty of the war and a victim of Napoleon's ambition as any French grenadier killed at Borodino or any Russian peasant who starved that winter in his or her own village.

Tom Barlow and Petry made hurried arrangements for Joel to be buried near the local church, then swiftly resumed their journey. A troop of Cossacks was rumored to be in the area, and in any event there was now nothing more to be done for Joel. Later, Ruth, after her grief had abated, arranged for a marble tablet to be placed in the porch of the parish church, styling him in Latin "*Plenipotens Minister a Statibus unitis America. . . .* "[23]

Today, on the left side of the lobby of the State Department building in Washington, there is a tablet of polished gray stone honoring in gold letters the names of American diplomats who have lost their lives under "heroic or tragic circumstances." Joel Barlow's name is the second one listed.

CHAPTER EIGHT

A Georgia Senator
Becomes a Diplomat

BARLOW'S DEATH LEFT THE FRENCH problems unsolved and faced Madison with the question of what to do next. He was skeptical of the chances for success, but Barlow's last letter before leaving for the east had been optimistic that the negotiations could be brought "to a speedy and advantageous close."[1] In any event, the potential benefits to be gained were great enough to call for another try.

At his second inaugural ball, on 4 March 1813, Madison told Monroe that he wanted to get the French indemnity problem straightened out and that he planned to appoint William Harris Crawford of Georgia as minister to France to handle the matter.[2] Monroe's reaction is not recorded, but it may well have been at least mild astonishment. Crawford was not everyone's idea of the model diplomat and was about as different from Barlow as it was possible to be.

Crawford was a powerful national political figure in his own right. He was a U.S. senator from Georgia, and more than that he was the president, *pro tempore,* of the Senate, having been elected to the position in March of 1812 when Vice President Clinton took sick, then after Clinton's death a month later was reelected on a more permanent basis in the next session of Congress. He, rather than John Quincy Adams, would very likely have been elected president of the United States in 1824, except that Crawford became the victim of a crippling illness a few months before the caucuses.[3]

William Harris Crawford was raised in a rough place at a rough time. Rural Georgia in the late eighteenth and early nineteenth centuries was frontier—raw and violent and no place for the weak or faint of heart. He was born into a modestly prosperous farming family with a father who pushed him to get all the education that he could. Crawford grew to be six feet three inches tall at a time when most men were about five feet six inches. He weighed more than two hundred pounds and was built burly, like a large bear.

Crawford was a rough gem and not a polished diplomat, but he was far from being the coarse country primitive that some thought he was. In 1813 and 1814 as minister to France, Crawford was the friend of such sophisticates as the Marquis de Lafayette and of Madame de Staël, who "delighted in his ingenuous conversation and southern charm of manner."[4] Also in 1814, despite the war with England, Crawford was on good terms with the Duke of Wellington, who was in Paris for a brief time after Bonaparte's abdication as the British ambassador to the Bourbon Restoration, and who was "exceedingly courteous" to Crawford. When in the middle of the night of 24 December 1814 word was received at the British embassy that the Treaty of Ghent had been signed, Wellington sent a messenger to wake Crawford with the news and with his congratulations.

He was a strong and early supporter of going to war with England. This and other assistance and advice given to the administration led to a close personal relationship with Madison in the spring of 1813, and in turn led to his appointment to Paris as the "minister plenipotentiary to the court of the Emperor of the French and King of Italy."[5] He resigned his seat in the Senate on 23 May. The Senate approved his appointment to France on 28 May, and his commission was made effective the same day.

Crawford had been planning for the move since he had agreed in early March to take the job and had spent March and April in getting ready. He had asked that his friend Dr. Henry Jackson, who was Professor of "Chymistry and Natural Philosophy" at the University of Georgia at Athens, be appointed as his secretary of legation.[6] Crawford anticipated that his assignment to France would last perhaps a year or a bit more and didn't want to subject his family to the risk of a sea voyage, so in late April he moved his wife, Susanna, and their eight children back to Georgia, to *Woodlawn,* their plantation near Lexington.

On 4 June Crawford, Dr. Jackson, and two servants left Washington at 4 A.M. in a hired carriage, bound for New York, where the *Argus* was waiting to take him to France.

Upon their arrival in New York, Crawford and Jackson located an inn, expecting to stay there during their brief time in the city. Crawford was to contact the navy agent, who was none other than the highly political Dr. John Bullus, and the collector of customs of the port, David Gelston. Dr. Jackson called on Bullus and Gelston to let them know that Crawford had arrived, and the two soon appeared at the inn to see Crawford. For Bullus, this was an opportunity to add a powerful national figure to his collection of useful acquaintances, and he made the most of it, insisting that Crawford and Jackson stay at his house, which would be more private than a public tavern. Henry Allen had lodgings next door, and the Bullus house was near the North River wharf a little above the Battery, opposite to where the *Argus* was anchored out in the stream.[7]

The next day was Saturday, 12 June. Crawford and Jackson met over a midday dinner at Dr. Bullus's house with Henry Allen and Mr. Gelston. Arrangements were made for Gelston to handle some last-minute banking transactions for Crawford. Also, Henry Allen had received his orders for the cruise a few days before from the secretary of the navy, and these were undoubtedly discussed in some detail.[8]

These orders for the operations of the *Argus* were brief, comprising just three hand-written pages, a far cry from the book-sized operation orders of the modern navy. In those simpler days before missiles, radar, and satellite communications, captains of naval vessels were told, usually directly by the secretary of the navy himself, what they were expected to accomplish and were given some guidelines to go by and boundaries to stay within. But once out to sea a captain was on his own and was expected—or rather, required—to make decisions on matters of detail within the scope of his orders, or in matters about which the orders were unclear. He was even expected to override his orders if he was faced with situations that he was fairly sure the secretary had not foreseen.

Henry Allen was told to get to sea at the "first favorable opportunity" after Minister Crawford was ready to go, and then, avoiding risks and "without deviating for any other object," to head for the first port he could make in France. After his valuable passenger was safely delivered to France, Henry Allen was to "proceed on a cruize against the commerce and light cruizers of the enemy." He was given a number of guidelines and constraints for this cruise. He was to destroy ships that he captured and not to try to send them in as prizes unless they were extremely valuable and he was "morally certain" that they could safely reach a close, friendly port—the secretary probably did not want Henry Allen's mind to be diverted by thoughts of prize money or the *Argus*'s crew weakened by the manning of prizes.

Allen was told that "the enemy should be made to feel the effects of our hostility" and that the best way to do this was to destroy British commerce, fisheries, and coastal trade right in their own home waters. Secretary Jones was drawing on his own experience as a merchant and shipowner and was perceptive in telling Allen what to pursue. Convoys were continually entering or leaving British home waters, the coasting trades employed a large number of ships, and the herring fisheries off the northwestern coast of Scotland alone amounted to three hundred to four hundred vessels. All of this shipping was surprisingly vulnerable, and its owners were wealthy, politically powerful men who, along with the insurance syndicates, would be hit in the pocketbooks. This, Secretary Jones predicted correctly, would "produce an astonishing sensation."[9]

Allen was told that his "cruizing ground" was to be from the entrance to the English Channel to Cape Clear at the southwestern corner of Ireland, along the eastern coast of Ireland, up through St. George's Channel and into the Irish Sea, and across to the northwestern coast of England. When he was ready to leave this area, after a month or six weeks, or maybe if it got too hot, he was to pass around the northwest of Ireland and head for the Fair Island passage, north of Scotland, between the Orkney and Shetland Islands, to get on the track of the British Archangel Fleet returning home around Norway from the northern coast of Russia with timber and furs in August and September. Finally, Henry Allen was told, when it was absolutely necessary to return home, he was to pick his own route and head for an eastern port in the United States, like Portsmouth, New Hampshire, but while still in France before starting his voyage of mayhem he was to ascertain whether it would be feasible to reprovision in France and thus stretch his cruise out even longer.

This was a challenging set of orders for any ship in any war. Its only counterpart in modern times are the orders that were given to particularly adventurous submarine skippers in World War II, who like Allen were young and hot headed.

Henry Allen hoped to get under way early on Sunday morning, and so on Saturday evening Crawford and Dr. Jackson sent their baggage on board with one of the servants. Another passenger boarded on the twelfth, a Monsieur Loremy, a French citizen who had permission to return to France in the *Argus*. Henry Allen and the *Argus* crew were handling the last details of getting ready for sea. They received a new gig from the navy yard, and they topped off their tanks and casks with fresh water, bringing them up to the full six thousand gallons. She had aboard her other important stores nearly up to her full allowance of twenty-five barrels of pork, thirty-five barrels of beef, and twenty-two barrels of whiskey.

But in the morning the wind was foul, from the southeast with only light airs.[10] Henry Allen needed a wind from the west or northwest, and more than that, he needed to be confident that he would have a steady, lasting wind that would carry him well out to sea. Light, unsteady winds raised the chilly, career-destroying prospect of finding himself becalmed a few miles offshore with this nationally important person on board, vulnerable to being taken by the boats of the British blockaders. The blockading ships were not in sight at present, but they could be just over the horizon.

Although impatient to get under way, Henry Allen could make good use of a little more time. The *Argus* was still short a few hands. The carpenter, George Harman, a key warrant officer, had deserted on 4 June—a highly unusual action for such a senior person.[11] A replacement had finally been found, James White, at twenty-one a young man for this experience-demanding job. But he hadn't come aboard until the twelfth and needed time to organize his crew and check his stores. The new carpenter probably also had another urgent job to handle as soon as he came aboard: there is no indication that Henry Allen knew in advance that Crawford was so tall and burly, and if the extra berth that had been built for him in Allen's cabin was sized for the average man, James White and his mates must have had to work all night to rebuild it to a larger size.

Three new seamen also came aboard on Saturday the twelfth: Thomas Young, William Knolton, and George Starbuck, of the prominent Nantucket seafaring family. Midshipman Jamesson had finally returned from sick leave two days before, and the brig had just received another key petty officer, John Place, the armorer.[12]

Wednesday's weather was squally with thunderstorms, lightning, and rain as a frontal system moved through the area. Thursday started off with rain, but then cleared off as the leading edge of the front passed out to sea, and on Friday, 18 June, although there were still thunderstorms in the area, the weather that Henry Allen had been waiting for began to arrive, and a light breeze began to build from the northwest.[13] A little after 9 A.M. the *Argus's* anchor was hove short—still holding the ground but now under the ship's forefoot, ready to be quickly broken free of the bottom and hoisted in—and a midshipman was sent on shore with the gig to fetch Minister Crawford and Dr. Jackson.

The midshipman arrived at the Bullus house at about 10 A.M. Dr. Bullus had decided to ride the *Argus* down to Sandy Hook and come back with the pilot, so the three men, plus Crawford's servant, went with the midshipman in the gig, arriving on board the *Argus* at eleven. As soon as they were aboard the upper sails were set, a gun was fired, and the signal hoisted to recall aboard all officers and boats, and at 12:04 P.M. the ship weighed anchor and braced the yards to catch the light northwest breeze. The brig made a swift passage through the Upper New York Bay, the Narrows, and the Lower Bay, and at about 3 P.M. was approaching Sandy Hook when the wind died, leaving a calm with oppressively hot and humid air. Allen anchored the ship near the East Bank to wait for the wind to return, and they all had dinner in the cabin, Henry Allen, Crawford, Jackson, and Bullus. After dinner, Crawford, feeling a landsman's anxieties on making a first sea voyage, wrote a short last letter to his wife and one to a friend, to be taken back and mailed by Dr. Bullus.[14]

Within an hour, an afternoon thunderstorm came up with rain and lightning, bringing a fresh breeze from the west. This was the time for the final parting with the land, and at a little after 4 P.M. Henry Allen got the *Argus* under way. The ship fired a gun to signal the dispatch boat with them to follow and take off the pilot, and at 5:15 Dr. Bullus and James Flinn, the pilot, left, severing the last connection with the shore; and the *Argus* headed out into the Atlantic. None of the British blockading ships were in sight. In fact, they were all clustered off New London, where Admiral Hardy was trying to figure out a way to get at the frigates *United States* and *Macedonian,* now out of his reach, immobilized well up the Thames River.

The sun was still up when the *Argus* passed the lighthouse on Sandy Hook. Crawford watched the sun set over the highlands of New Jersey, and he stayed on deck, seeing the land fade, until he could no longer see the light. He was forty-one years old and expected that it would be some long time before he would see the American shore again.

CHAPTER NINE

The *Argus* Ready for Sea

NEVER ROOMY AT BEST, the *Argus* upon getting to sea for the run to France was greatly overcrowded. There were on board a total of 158 souls occupying space that was inadequate for her normal complement of about 125.[1] First there was Minister Crawford, berthing in the cabin with Henry Allen, and Dr. Jackson, apparently in one of the tiny staterooms, displacing one of the officers, who probably in turn displaced one of the midshipmen into a hammock. The two servants that they brought aboard were out with the crew in the berth deck. Also there was Monsieur Loremy, undoubtedly berthed somewhere in officers' country.

Then there were the ship's officers: the captain, Henry Allen, in his cabin; the two other lieutenants, William Henry Watson and William Howard Allen, in their cubicle staterooms; and Surgeon James Inderwick, Purser Henry Denison, Sailing Master John Hudson, and "Supernumerary" Sailing Master Uriah Levy, all in their tiny rooms, except for those displaced by Dr. Jackson and M. Loremy. The six midshipmen shared a somewhat larger room, the "Midshipmen's Berth," perhaps five feet by six feet.

There were fourteen warrant and petty officers aboard, most of whom slung hammocks in the berth deck with the rest of the crew, although they got the choicer spots, just forward of the wardroom country. Three of the warrants were better off, having microscopic rooms that also served as their offices: Boatswain Colin McLeod, Gunner Robert Conklin, and Carpenter James White.

Everyone else lived forward, in the general open space of the berth deck: seventy seamen, twenty-six "ordinary" seamen, two landsmen, five boys, the six stewards and officers' servants, and the fifteen marines—a sergeant, a corporal, and thirteen private marines. The muster list of the *Argus* for this time did not show anyone rated as cook, but someone had to be doing the cooking, perhaps one of the stewards, or a seaman under a tryout period, expecting to be later advanced into the cook's rating and pay.

Seventeen of the men on board were black, two were described as "mulatto," and one was oriental—Appene, Henry Allen's Chinese servant, born in Canton. The rest were whites of various complexions.

Most of the crew described themselves as American-born; only twelve gave birthplaces outside the United States, in Norway, Sweden, Germany, Prussia, Holland, France, Italy, and China. Also there were at least three men who were probably born in the British Isles: Robert Conklin, the gunner, from Kinsale in Ireland; John Brown, a seaman, also from Ireland; John Robinson from Dundee, Scotland; and possibly the boatswain, Colin McLeod. There may well have been others; as noted earlier there were many British-born sailors in the U.S. Navy at that time. However, the information on the birthplaces of the *Argus* crew comes from British prisoner-of-war records, and it is unlikely that a British-born sailor, even if a naturalized American, would admit to having been born in Britain under examination by the entry clerks at the prison depot, unless a very strong brogue or burr in his voice made denial hopeless. The British government didn't view the process of "naturalization" into American citizenship as relieving a sailor from his duty to the king, and the penalty for a British subject's being "taken in arms against His Majesty" was a perfunctory court-martial quickly followed by hanging.

The 91.4 percent of the crew that called themselves American-born came from the Mid-Atlantic States (37.6 percent), New England (28.4 percent), and the Upper South (24 percent). The new crew was recruited in New York, and thirty-six of the men had been born in New York State, twenty-three in New York City, others in Brooklyn, Jamaica, Hudson, Batavia, and Onondaga. Eleven were from Pennsylvania, eight of these from Philadelphia, and six were from New Jersey. The New Englanders came mostly from the small ports: Wiscasset, Kittery, Portsmouth, Gloucester, Cohasset, Chatham, Nantucket, New Bedford, Newport, Norwich. Only three each were from Boston and Providence, and two from Salem. The Southerners were from Delaware, Maryland, and Virginia—Wilmington, Newcastle, Annapolis, Baltimore, Alexandria, Richmond, Petersburg, Northampton County, Hampton, Norfolk—plus four men from New Orleans.[2]

Nine of the ship's company were under eighteen years old, the youngest being William Taffe, thirteen, who had volunteered for the *Argus* from the frigate *John Adams*. There were two men older than fifty. Benjamin Phillips, a seaman, was the oldest at fifty-six years. He was born eighteen years before the Revolution and gave his birthplace simply as "America." The average height of the *Argus* crew was five feet five and three-quarters inches, but six of the crew were under five feet tall and could, therefore, stand upright in the five-foot-three-inch height of the berth deck, between the beams. The rest of the crew had to move around in a perpetual crouch, particularly the six men, including Minister Crawford and Henry Allen, who were six feet or taller. Quarter Gunner William Smith, the tallest, was just over six feet four inches. To late-twentieth-century eyes, most of these men would have looked rather slight of build; the uniforms from those days now in museums show that these sailors looked more like slender boys of modern times than like short, five-foot-six-inch modern men.

One hundred and eleven of the crew had been aboard three months or less and had received no training together. Only twenty-seven were left of the "old crew," from the vessel's previous sea time under Arthur Sinclair.

With such a large crew on board, the packed, unventilated environment in the berth deck might have produced high rates of sickness or even epidemics. Somehow, this didn't happen. There seems to have been no rampant contagions affecting New York just at that time, to be brought aboard. But very likely much of the good health aboard the *Argus* was due to Surgeon Inderwick, who was not given to excessive bleeding or severe doses of strong medicines.[3] Also, some credit should go to Henry Allen's management.

The Ship's Orders for the *Argus,* issued in 1811 but very probably continued under Henry Allen, were a model of common sense when concerned with the health of the crew, stating that "nothing promotes it more than cleanliness and a free circulation of air."[4] To accomplish the latter, the windsail was to be always kept hoisted and trimmed into the breeze during dry, pleasant weather. The windsail was a large canvas tube, four or five feet in diameter and perhaps twenty-five feet tall, with the top made into an air scoop. It was rigged between the two masts, with the air scoop pointed to catch the wind and the bottom of the tube put down into the open main hatch, and it could create a tremendous rush of fresh air into the berth deck. As a morale builder it must have been just behind grog, good food, and prize money.

Also, the orders pointed out, it was important never to unnecessarily expose the men to bad weather and risky situations, and never to let them sleep in their wet clothes—which in a ship as small as the *Argus* must have been a continuous problem, with waves frequently combing the deck and drenching everyone.

There was apparently no fixed area set aside for a sick bay. The orders speak of letting sick crew members keep their hammocks slung during the day if the surgeon thought this to be desirable, indicating that there were no special bunks for them. There was apparently no staff of medical helpers: a sick man's messmates were tasked to do his washing and to feed him, but "additional attendance may be had . . . by applying to the First Lieutenant . . . in short, no comfort will be withheld from them that the service admits of." However, for most of the illnesses experienced on the *Argus,* the men on the sick list apparently just went on pursuing their normal activities, perhaps on a "light duty" basis or perhaps performing no work at all.

The men on the *Argus* came to Surgeon Inderwick with a wide range of complaints, usually diseases, most of them contagious, plus the traumas consequent from the risky business of seafaring: sprained knees and ankles, a concussion from a fall down a hatch, adz cuts from woodworking, contusions, and later, battle wounds.

Inderwick treated a range of eighteen different diseases and conditions, from tuberculosis, malaria, and erysipelas to colds, diarrhea, and constipation. But his main load came from venereal diseases—primary and secondary syphilis, plus some gonorrhea—and from a complaint called "rheumatismus," which consisted of severe fever with chest pain or headache and often some joint pain. For rheumatismus he often prescribed "Dover's Powders," a mixture of ipecac and opium, plus a cathartic. For syphilis he prescribed what was the standard treatment then and until relatively recent times, mercury compounds: red mercuric ointment to be rubbed into the chancre lesions, and calomel, mercurous chloride plus pure mercury, to be taken internally. In a time when even the working sailor could appreciate a classical allusion, this treatment (and its cause) was mordantly described as "seven minutes with Venus, six months with Mercury."

Even though they presented a large variety of illnesses, the number of men on the sick list was fairly constant at about twelve men, whether in port or at sea, varying perhaps two up or down from this. While the ship was in port in New York, about one new case came in per day, but after the brig got to sea this dropped off to one every other day. Of the man-days lost to sickness on the *Argus,* nearly half—44 percent—were lost to venereal diseases. All of the other sixteen diagnoses made by Surgeon Inderwick accounted for the other 56 percent of lost time.[5]

In spite of prescribing the standard treatments of the day that we now view as ineffective or even poisonous, Surgeon Inderwick, though short on experience, apparently understood that medical science really knew very little, that it was important to do no harm, and that often the best thing was to do nothing.

The prevailing medical theory of the day still looked back to classical times and Aristotle, whose world view held that the elements comprising all things were fire, water, air, and earth. In medicine these correlated to human temperaments classified as sanguine, phlegmatic, choleric, and melancholic, and in turn to the body's four "humors," the fluids that were identified as blood, phlegm, yellow bile, and black bile. In addition, physicians and surgeons were interested in the firmness and response to stimuli of the patient's body, particularly the blood vessels and nerves. So the average medical practitioner of the day viewed good health as the proper balance between the patient's humors combined with a nice firm "tone" of the nerves and veins.

When a patient exhibited symptoms of illness, the physician or surgeon saw the problem not as a specific disease pathology but as an imbalance among the humors or a maladjustment of body tone, and the solution would be to try to readjust the humor balance and improve the tone. The physician would look for excesses or deficits in the related attributes of heat and cold, moisture and dryness. So an excess of heat, indicated by a rapid pulse or an elevated temperature, implied a fever, and the ill-humored patient was given drugs and treatment—say, cold baths—to eliminate the excess of heat, to bring the humors back into balance. Or the patient might be given a "tonic" to improve body tone. If the patient had symptoms like headache and nausea, but without an increased temperature or rapid pulse, the physician would diagnose a "cold."[6]

So this medical system didn't look for specific diseases that might have specific cures but rather treated the symptoms in an attempt to bring the humors back into their proper relationship. This often led to destructive treatments, such as bleeding yellow fever patients, for whom the real problem already was loss of blood. By 1813 the more curious and intelligent physicians and surgeons were beginning to go beyond the humoral system, but in spite of the fact that the Dutch optician Leuwenhoek had a century before seen tiny living creatures through his primitive microscope, the discovery of the relationship between human diseases and microorganisms was still well in the future. Mosquitoes were annoying pests, but malaria and yellow fever were caused by miasma or bad air.

CHAPTER TEN

Atlantic Crossing

AT DAYBREAK OF SATURDAY, 19 June, her first day at sea, the *Argus* was well out of sight of land, about seventy miles east and south of New York. The weather was clear, although there was a fog bank to the south. The sun was just up and bright, and the wind had freshened from the north-northwest, when at a few minutes before eight the lookouts sighted a strange sail, "a vessel of force," off their larboard bow. It was heading for them under a "press of sail" from out of the sun and had gotten to within about twelve miles before the lookouts saw it. Henry Allen speculated that it was one of the blockading squadron known to be off New London. But it was probably one of a group of British warships, a 74 and two frigates, coming from Bermuda to join Admiral Hardy off New London, that had seen the *Argus* before being seen and was hoping to scoop her up.[1] Henry Allen called all hands to make sail, set the studding sails, and turned southeast into the fog bank. It was a close call, and Allen was lucky to have had such a handy bank of fog. The cruise might have been over before it was fairly started, and one of Crawford's claims to historical notice would have come from being the highest-ranking prisoner taken in the war.

Henry Allen sailed southeast for an hour but then came back to his course. The *Argus* was in the fog for several hours, but when it finally burned off, her pursuer was no longer in sight. Allen was acutely aware that his job was to get Minister Crawford safely to France as quickly as possible and had the *Argus* carry the maximum amount of sail at all times. He also set a course to France that took advantage of a favorable ocean current of more than half a knot, over which the winds for that time of year were usually fresh and from westerly directions—in the early part of the passage from the southwest, and closer to Europe from the west and northwest.

But for the first days the winds were variable and often from the east, requiring frequent tacking—which kept the sail handlers busy and gave the *Argus* a bumpy ride. Crawford was seasick and "cascaded copiously," but he stayed on deck in the evening as long as he could before retreating to his berth in the cabin. Once in bed he found that the retching subsided, and by the second night out he slept very well.[2]

Early the next morning the lookouts sighted a westbound sail, a clearly non-threatening merchant brig, and the two vessels went through a brief minuet of flags, the *Argus* hoisting British colors and the merchant brig then hoisting Portuguese. Henry Allen's purpose was probably to convey a confusing message to any of the British blockaders that might stop the brig to ask her what she had seen during her crossing. The next morning the lookouts sighted a large ship to the northeast that tried to close with the *Argus*. Henry Allen turned away, to open the distance between them, and hoisted, one after the other, British, Portuguese, and American colors. There was no response from the stranger, which was probably a British warship. The *Argus* detoured around her, and the brief meeting passed without incident.[3]

By the twenty-fourth Henry Allen had more favorable winds and was setting every sail on the ship, not only the courses, topsails, topgallants, royals, jib, and fore-and-aft mainsail, but also all the staysails, the studding sails, and the rarely set skysails, flying jib, and gaff topsail. The *Argus* bowled along, truly a cloud of canvas, often logging eight or nine knots, and was accompanied by porpoises. Minister Crawford was feeling much better, although left with a taste in his mouth of grease, tar, and soft soap, and to him the whole ship smelled of the same—sensations familiar to anyone who has experienced the gradual recovery from seasickness.[4]

Crawford spent many hours with Henry Allen and came to like and respect him as "an accomplished officer and a gentlemanly man," and later on looked back "with great pleasure" on his days with Allen aboard the Argus. Crawford apparently talked to all of the officers, particularly the lieutenants, and was impressed with the discipline aboard. He gave Henry Allen high marks for the "silence and order which attended the execution of every order" and praised his professional skill in a letter to the secretary of the navy. He complimented the officers on their skill and on their "suavity of manners."[5]

As the voyage went on, Crawford more and more identified himself with the *Argus* and her ship's company, and had she been drawn into a battle, he would have wanted to serve in the fighting.[6] Even after his passage in the *Argus* was over he felt a kinship with her officers, recommending Henry Allen and his lieutenants to the secretary of the navy's "particular favor" and calling attention to Midshipmen Delphey and Jamesson as being "from the neighborhood of Washington" and "poor and friendless."[7]

The weather held pleasant for several days, and the ship had by this time settled into a routine existence, with almost continuous sail handling to take full advantage of the winds, plus training at the guns every afternoon. The *Argus* was not alone on the ocean. One afternoon there was a distant ship on her starboard beam, and late on 27 June the lookouts sighted a fleet of fifteen or sixteen sail to the south. This Henry Allen took to be the Barbados Convoy on its way to England, and it would have been a great opportunity for him and the *Argus,* except for the restrictions of his orders.

The crew was, by and large, enjoying good health, and Surgeon Inderwick had little to do. Thomas Young, a seaman, complained of headache, and Abel Waite, a quartermaster, came to Inderwick with "rheumatismus." One crew member came down with primary syphilis.

The pleasant weather ended on the twenty-eighth. Every sea voyage should have a storm, and for the *Argus* it began as the sky clouded over, the temperature dropped, the wind freshened from the north, and a heavy sea began to build. The next day after a calm of several hours in the early morning, the wind shifted to the southwest and began to blow a gale. The seas increased, and the rain came down in sheets. Every heavy wave combed the deck, and the lee-side guns were constantly under water. The upper sails were taken in and their yards sent down, and the lower sails reefed, then all were taken in except the foresail, and with it alone the brig scudded along at eleven knots. During this dangerous, high-wind sail handling, one of the best topmen, James Hunt, fell from the main yard forty-five feet above the deck, hit the starboard gunwale, and then went overboard and was lost. He was probably killed by hitting the gunwale, and any attempt to save him would have been futile. In any event, the weather precluded any try at a rescue. At eight that night, 1 July, Henry Allen took in all sail and for five hours scudded under bare poles, rolling, pitching, and corkscrewing. While he and the entire crew were using all their energies to keep the ship under control, Minister Crawford was dividing his time between trying to hold his seasickness in check and observing this rampage of nature, far outside of anything in his previous experience. He stayed on deck until chased below by the rain and the seas. In the cabin, the deck overhead was leaking, but fortunately not over his berth. As long as he stayed in bed he could stay dry and keep his nausea under control, but then his curiosity would bring him on deck again. To him the storm was a "spectacle," both "grand and magnificent," and it fully met his previously imagined expectations of what a storm at sea would be like.[8]

Finally, in the early morning of 2 July, the storm began to subside, and Henry Allen and the crew were able to spread a little sail. But like proverbial ill winds, this one had blown some, even much, good: the *Argus* had been carried about 525 miles in the right direction during the three days of bad weather, the best speed that she made during the entire voyage.[9]

Saturday, 3 July, was a fine day. The wind was fair, from the northwest, and Henry Allen again had every sail on the ship set. The storm had proved his training of his new crew—not a mast or spar had carried away. The loss of James Hunt was tragic, but officers, ship, and crew had passed through their shakedown period and were now working as an effective team.

The next day was Sunday, the Fourth of July. As was customary for Sunday, the crew was lined up in clean uniforms, the muster roll called, and the Articles of War read to them. Henry Allen, his officers, and the passengers later drank a glass of wine to celebrate the anniversary of independence. It was the best Madeira, but to Crawford, his stomach still queasy, it tasted "like salt and weak vinegar."[10]

Only about a third of the journey was left to go, and thoughts began to turn to what was waiting in Europe. Late Tuesday afternoon, the sixth, a westbound merchant schooner showed up to the northeast, and Crawford asked Henry Allen to close and speak her, to get the news from Europe. Allen viewed Crawford's request as releasing him for the moment from the orders to take his passengers straight to France without deviating or taking risks. He maneuvered the *Argus* to get to the weather side of the schooner and began the minuet of flags. First, the *Argus* ran up Portuguese colors, and the schooner hoisted British. Then the *Argus* hoisted British colors, and the schooner did the same. Henry Allen then fired a shot ahead of the schooner and one astern of her, ran up the Stars and Stripes, and fired one gun directly at her. Then the *Argus* prepared to fire a broadside, but before the gun crews could get ready, the schooner hauled down her British colors. Henry Allen sent Lieutenant William Howard Allen in a boat to take possession of her and get her ready for burning. The prize proved to be the *Salamanca,* now British, but formerly an American vessel known as the *King of Rome.* She was new and had been captured on her first voyage by a British cruiser in the Bay of Biscay only a few months earlier and sold as a prize. As a Britisher she had carried a load of fish from Newfoundland to Oporto in Portugal, food for Wellington's army in Spain, and was on her way back to Newfoundland in ballast when she had the bad luck to coincide in time and place with Minister Crawford's need for news.[11]

The boat made several trips back and forth, bringing to the *Argus* Thomas Roe, the master of the *Salamanca;* Alexander Roche, the mate; and her fourteen crewmen—now prisoners of war—and all their baggage, plus some of her stores wanted by the *Argus.* The wind and sea had picked up, making these

transfers difficult, and it was nearly eight in the evening before they were completed. Then Howard Allen and his men set the *Salamanca* afire, and the *Argus*
got back on her course for France.[12]

Surgeon Inderwick was having a busy week. Two days before the *Salamanca*'s capture, Francis Eggert, a seaman, had received a bad bruise on one
foot from a gun slide during a drill, Boatswain's Mate Thomas Thompson
went into convulsions, and Seaman James Kellam had come down with
rheumatismus. It also turned out that two of the prisoners had active cases of
syphilis and needed treatment. On the heels of that, Midshipman Temple came
in to be treated for a bruised testicle.[13]

Two of the *Salamanca*'s crew decided to join the *Argus*. Neither had any
patriotic reason to become a prisoner of war on behalf of the British: Peter
Neho, a sixteen-year-old seaman, was from Bordeaux, France, and Seaman
John Peter Hanson, nineteen, was a Swede from Gothenburg.[14]

After the excitement settled down, the master of the *Salamanca* related the
European news, satisfying Crawford's itch for information, probably not
knowing that except for this he and his vessel would still be on their way to
Newfoundland.

His latest news, of course weeks stale, told the Americans that in Spain,
Wellington had turned the line of the French at the River Ebro and that a
major battle was expected. By the time this information arrived on board the
Argus, the battle, fought on the plain of Vittoria on 21 June, was over, and the
French under Napoleon's brother Joseph were streaming in defeat over the
passes of the Pyrenees, back into France, with Wellington on their heels.[15]
Napoleon himself was with his next-to-last army in Prussia. The Armistice of
Breslau was in effect but would soon be terminated by the Austrian-Prussian-
Russian-Swedish allies, Napoleon's defeat at Leipzig would ensue, followed by
his ten-month retreat ending in the Battle of Paris, abdication, and Elba.[16]

The *Salamanca* adventure was an excellent drill for Henry Allen, his officers, and his crew and was a foretaste of things to come.

The wind and weather stayed favorable, and by Saturday, 10 July, the *Argus*
was approaching the coast of France. When the first daylight came at 3 A.M.,
the lookouts sighted a sail on their lee bow, to the south. Henry Allen tacked
to bring the *Argus* closer to the wind, to keep the all-important weather gauge.
As the stranger got closer and full daylight came, he saw that she was an eighteen-gun brig of war, and she soon ran up British colors. To keep her guessing,
Henry Allen hoisted no colors at all. There were other ships in sight at the
same time, one on the windward bow and another on the quarter, possibly
men-of-war and, like the brig, units of the British blockading squadron. Henry
Allen kept on under all sail, trying to maintain his course as well as possible
while still getting around the enemy brig without a fight. His orders, of course,

required him to deliver Minister Crawford to France without taking unnecessary risks, but Allen and the *Argus*'s crew, and even Crawford, would all dearly have loved to take on this brig.

Henry Allen had the ship cleared for action, and as she came within gunshot of the British brig, Crawford climbed up on a gun to better see what was going on. He presented a large target, and Allen quickly asked him to get down. Even on the deck, Crawford's head stood above the bulwarks, and Allen, who could visualize himself explaining to the secretary of the navy how the minister to France got killed on his quarterdeck, asked him to go below to the cabin and, when he returned to the deck, ordered him below.[17]

The British brig hoisted a succession of flag signals, but the *Argus* hoisted no colors and made no response to the signals. Although the two brigs passed within gunshot, the Britisher did not choose to open fire, and the *Argus* passed on her way up to the coast, with Henry Allen undoubtedly much relieved, in spite of having missed his first opportunity to command in an action of near equals. What was said to the skipper of the British brig by his admiral after this lost opportunity is not recorded.

The *Argus* was still out of sight of land, and the leadsman had been sounding and finding no bottom. Now in the early afternoon of the sea day of the eleventh the leadsman found bottom at eighty fathoms, and the *Argus* was finally back on soundings and approaching the land. The wind held, and the next morning the lookouts sighted land, first from the masthead a hazy line on the horizon, then from the deck the headlands of the south side of the Quimper Peninsula. There were other vessels in sight, including a British cutter from the blockading squadron, but no attempt was made to interfere with the *Argus*. She passed a small port and fired a gun for a pilot, but there was no response, and no pilot came out. So, with a chart of the coast of France on the navigator's table Henry Allen made his own way, passing south of the Iles de Glenans, then heading southeast along the coast, inside the Ile de Groix, toward Port Louis and L'Orient, in the estuary of the Blauvet River. Just before 6 P.M. the brig came to in Port Louis Roads. In anchoring, Richard Groves, the master's mate, caught his arm in a turn of the heavy hemp cable as the anchor was dropped and was severely bruised, giving Surgeon Inderwick employment for the evening. In spite of this accident the *Argus* got successfully anchored, and the voyage across was over.[18]

The reaction of all aboard must have been great relief: Henry Allen relieved that he had safely made it across and that Minister Crawford and Dr. Jackson would be safely off his hands in another day or so; Crawford relieved not only to have safely arrived but also to be nearly back on solid earth again, safe from further seasickness; the officers and crew relieved to have a rest from the backbreaking routine of 'round-the-clock sail handling; Monsieur Loremy relieved to depart this ninety-foot sardine box and be back at home in France.

Henry Allen had more than this to be pleased about. His ship and crew were functioning well together, and he had faced several challenges to his seamanship and to his tactical skill in the presence of the enemy and had surmounted them. Last, but hardly least, with his important passengers leaving, he would soon have his ship—and his cabin—to himself again. Crawford had been a nearly ideal passenger, friendly, enthusiastic, and supportive, but Allen by this time probably felt that enough was enough.

At eight the next morning a harbor pilot came aboard, and the *Argus* moved up into Port Louis. By nine thirty she was moored to two anchors in the harbor. At noon officers from the police and several customs officials came aboard, and a message from the local maritime prefect welcomed Minister Crawford. But then the Americans were treated to a civics lesson on the difference between the open society enjoyed in the United States and the authoritarian regimen of Napoleon's France. Henry Allen was interrogated "in a manner totally disagreeable to his feelings" and was so incensed that he finally refused to answer the questions of the French officials. All the mail that the *Argus* carried that was addressed to private French citizens was taken. Crawford was required to show his commission as minister and to deliver over the dispatches and letters to the French government that the ship was carrying as a favor to the French legation in Washington. The whole process and the style in which it was carried out made Crawford feel that he "was now in a country where the Rulers were everything and the people nothing."[19]

The French finally left, clearing the Americans of quarantine, and Minister Crawford, Dr. Jackson, and their servants prepared to leave. At about six in the evening they made their good-byes to Henry Allen and the officers and crew of the *Argus* and entered the boat waiting for them at the gangway. Howard Allen was in the stern sheets as boat officer. As the boat pulled away the *Argus* fired a salute of seventeen guns for Minister Crawford. In his turn Crawford was undoubtedly already feeling some nostalgia for this brief period, now over, of kinship with the seafarers of the *Argus,* brave men, honorable and direct in their actions—a brief respite for Crawford in his life of dealing with the politically devious and diplomatically mendacious.

Portrait of Lieutenant William Henry Allen: This engraving of Henry Allen was done shortly after his death and is probably based on a self-portrait sketch done by Henry Allen himself. (Courtesy of the Franklin D. Roosevelt Library)

Portrait of Captain William Bainbridge, USN: Bainbridge was Midshipman
Henry Allen's first commanding officer, in the frigate *George Washington,* during
her voyage to Algiers with the tribute, then to Constantinople. (Courtesy of the
U.S. Naval Institute)

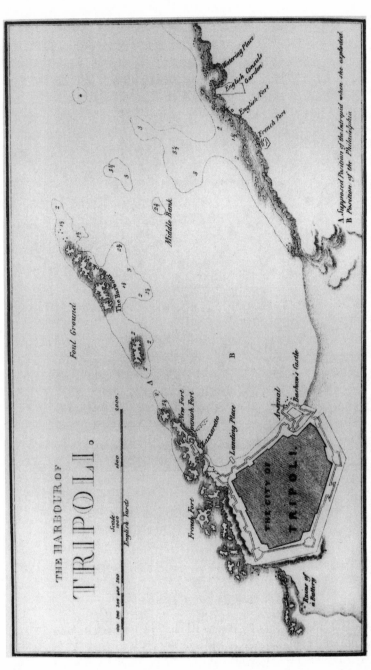

A chartlet of Tripoli Harbor as it appeared during the Barbary Wars, showing where the *Philadelphia* was anchored after her capture and where the *Intrepid* blew up. (From the 1839 European edition of J. Fenimore Cooper's *History of the U.S. Navy*)

Portrait of Commodore John Rodgers, USN: Rodgers was Henry Allen's commanding officer and mentor during two deployments to the Mediterranean during the Barbary Wars. (Courtesy of the United States Naval Academy Museum)

RIGHT: Pen-and-Ink Sketches by Henry Allen: The top sketch is the *Intrepid,* which Decatur used to burn the *Philadelphia* in Tripoli. It is enlarged from a sketch in a letter to Allen's father. The other two, the brig *Boston* and a "lateen vessel," are from Henry's 1802 journal. (Sketch of the *Intrepid* reproduced by permission of the Huntington Library. The *Boston* and "lateen vessel" sketches are courtesy of the G. W. Blunt White Library at the Mystic Seaport Museum.)

sance ⟨Decatur boa

nnew   the

foremast ⟨contained

tatssails ½ past 10 took a
them up—

Brig Boston

ssing N W B N D ½ W Eaj

Bound to   Cadiz

Commodore Stephen Decatur, USN: Allen served under Decatur in the *Chesapeake* and was his first lieutenant in the frigate *United States* during her capture of HMS *Macedonian*. Thomas Sully painted this picture soon after the battle. (Courtesy of the U.S. Naval Institute)

Commodore James Barron, USN: James Barron was the commodore aboard the unlucky frigate *Chesapeake* during the attack on her by HMS *Leopard*. Henry Allen fired the *Chesapeake*'s only shot in defense. (Courtesy of the Earl Gregg Swem Library, College of William and Mary)

Poet and Diplomat Joel Barlow: Barlow was the American minister to France. His death in Poland in December 1812, during Napoleon's retreat from Russia, precipitated the fatal cruise of the *Argus*. (Author's collection)

Senator and Diplomat William Harris Crawford: Crawford, a senator and power-
ful political figure, was sent to France to take the place of the dead Barlow. The
Argus carried him over, then went on her rampage in the Channel. (Courtesy of the
National Portrait Gallery, Smithsonian Institution)

A model of the U.S. Brig *Argus*. (Courtesy of the Mariners Museum, Newport News, Virginia)

Captain John Fordyce Maples, R.N., C.B.: The portrait of John Maples was painted about 1815 and shows him wearing the ribbon and medal of a Companion of the Bath. The artist is unknown. (Courtesy of Count Godwin Spani)

John Maples's Midshipman's Dirk: Prince William Henry, who was later King William IV, presented the dirk to John Maples in 1786 aboard the frigate *Hebe*. (Author's collection)

Vice-Admiral Sir Hyde Parker, Knight: Hyde Parker was commander in chief of the Jamaica Station during much of John Maples's service in the West Indies, and later commanded the British fleet at Copenhagen in 1801. (From a pastel portrait by Sir Thomas Lawrence, courtesy of the National Maritime Museum, London)

Captain William Henry Jervis, formerly Ricketts: William Henry Ricketts was Maples's commanding officer in the *Magicienne*. He was a highly skilled and lucky frigate skipper but a heavy flogger. Ricketts changed his name to Jervis upon being named heir to his famous uncle, John Jervis, Admiral the Earl of St. Vincent. (From *The Naval Chronicle* for 1808)

Memorial Stone to Captain Jervis/Ricketts: This picture is one of the few personal traces of Captain Ricketts. The boy-midshipman is Lord George Rosehill, Ricketts's nephew, lost at sea in 1807. (By permission of the British Library)

Portrait of Rear-Admiral Horatio Nelson, K.B.: Nelson's portrait, taken from the painting originally painted by Lemuel Abbot in 1797 and later produced in several versions, shows Nelson shortly after the Battle of the Nile. (From volume III of *The Naval Chronicle*)

John Jervis, Admiral the Earl of St. Vincent: St. Vincent is shown in full dress, wearing all his honors, shortly after serving as First Lord of the Admiralty. (Author's collection)

The Battle of the *Argus* and the *Pelican:* This is the best known contemporary print of the battle, engraved by Sutherland from a painting by Whitcombe. (Author's collection)

THE HEADSTONE RECORDING THE INTERMENT
HEREBY OF WILLIAM HENRY ALLEN & RICHARD DELPHEY
WAS RESET ON THIS MONUMENT & THE ANCIENT DOORWAY
ADJOINING RESTORED BY THE NATIONAL SOCIETY
UNITED STATES DAUGHTERS OF 1812 TO PERPETUATE
THE MEMORY OF THESE OFFICERS & TO RECORD AN
APPRECIATION OF A HUMANE & CHIVALROUS ACTION
OF THE ENGLISH PEOPLE.

SACRED
to the MEMORY of
WILLIAM HENRY ALLEN Esq.
Aged 27 Years.
Late Commander of the
United States BRIG ARGUS,
who died August 18th 1813,
In Consequence of a Wound
Received in Action,
with H.B.M. BRIG PELICAN
August 14th 1813.
ALSO in Remembrance of
RICHARD DELPHEY, Midshipman
Aged 18 Years.
U.S. NAVY, Killed in the same action
Whose remains are Deposited
on the Left.

HERE SLEEP THE BRAVE.

And the fruit of righteousness is sown in
peace of them that make peace.
James iii. 18.

THE DOOR OF UNITY

The Tombstone of Henry Allen and Richard Delphey: Allen and Delphey's grave marker in St. Andrews Churchyard in Plymouth, England. The stone is now mounted on a wall near the grave. (Courtesy of the rector of St. Andrews)

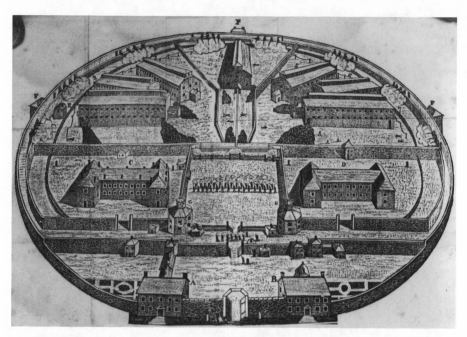

A Birds-Eye View of Dartmoor Prison: The prison depot is shown in 1815, at the time of the prisoner riot and the "Dartmoor Massacre." (From *A Journal of a Young Man of Massachusetts,* Boston: Rowe and Hooper, 1816)

PART TWO

John Fordyce Maples, Royal Navy

CHAPTER ELEVEN

The Training of a Sea Dog

THERE WAS NO WAY for Henry Allen to know it, but he was arriving in Europe for his cruise at a lucky time, during a brief window of opportunity. The British admiral in Cork, Ireland, whose command covered the area where Allen planned to operate, was short of ships and in poor shape to cope with the threat posed by the *Argus*.

It happened that most of the British warships under Vice-Admiral Edward Thornbrough, the commander in chief of the Irish Station, had earlier been sent far to the north to chase an American privateer that turned out to be a will-o'-the-wisp.

There had been chronic problems with American privateers in the area, the most recent about a month earlier. So when rumors began to come in that a large American privateer brig was committing depredations around the northern end of Ireland and the west coast of Scotland, Thornbrough sent all of his force, except a couple of ships already assigned to the convoys, up to the north to hunt for the predator.[1] While he was making these dispositions, the *Argus* either was still innocently crossing the Atlantic or was moored to two anchors at L'Orient.

Then on 19 July Admiral Thornbrough received a letter from the captain of H.M. Sloop *Port Mahon,* one of the ships he had sent north. The letter stated that the area had been scoured, that there was no American privateer, and that a British Revenue Service brig had inadvertently created the whole affair from thin air. That there was no privateer in the area was confirmed by the arrival at Cork of H.M. Brig *Stork,* which had just sailed clear around Ireland without falling in with any trouble.[2] So Thornbrough started the slow process of getting his ships back into more useful positions.

Even without this false alarm and the maldeployment of his force to the north, Thornbrough in this late summer of 1813 faced more problems than he had ships to solve them. He was expecting the arrival from Barbados of a large convoy of valuable ships loaded with rum, sugar, and molasses, probably the same convoy the *Argus* had seen in the distance during her trip across. Many of these rich ships would be heading up St. George's Channel toward Bristol, and he would have to protect them as they passed through his area. Another group of merchant vessels was assembling in the Cove of Cork to form a convoy to Portugal, Spain, and Gibraltar and would need at least one of his warships to escort it. As if that was not enough, transports with the 76th and 84th Regiments already on board, bound for Spain and Wellington's army, were nearly ready to need escorts, and a twenty-nine–ship convoy for the West Indies was in the process of assembling.

All that the Admiral had at his disposal at this time—and these were mostly spread off to the north—was one frigate, the *Leonidas,* and several smaller vessels of war, H.M. Sloops and Brigs the *Brisk, Resolute, Port Mahon, Helena, Teazer, Jalouse,* and *Pelican.*

The *Pelican* was a brig-of-war and had been built at Topsham, in Devon, in late 1811 and commissioned in 1812.

The captain of the *Pelican* was Commander John Fordyce Maples, forty-three years old in 1813, an officer of great experience who had seen all the varied action that twenty years of continuous war could offer. He had entered the British Navy in October 1782, two years before Henry Allen was born.

Maples's career had lagged in recent years, and promotion had been slow in coming. This was a fairly typical situation for British sea officers at that time, except for those with exceptional influence. After Trafalgar the navy had faced no serious challenge at sea. By 1813 the long war against Napoleon was finally winding down, and even with the American War to fight, the Admiralty was reducing rather than expanding the fleet. Promotion was beginning to stagnate and employment at sea becoming difficult for many officers to obtain.

In the British Navy of the late eighteenth and early nineteenth centuries, personal influence—the term used at that time was "interest"—was of vital importance for a "young gentleman" wanting to become an officer and for a sea officer hoping to rise in the profession. Interest could flow to an ambitious young man in several ways. The best way by far was to be born into the right family, preferably into one of the large landowning families of the peerage or gentry. Or a family without pretensions to nobility but having members, even fairly distant cousins, in powerful positions in the navy, army, or church could usually provide enough interest to launch and even sustain a naval career. Interest could also flow from a political obligation, public or covert. In any event, having the favor of some powerful patron, in or out of the navy, was necessary to get one into the navy and doubly necessary to keep the promotions coming. At an earlier time John Maples had been favored with a certain amount of interest, but it had dissipated in recent years.

How John Maples came by the influence that got him into the navy and moved his early career is not clear. He was born, probably in January of 1770, in Colchester, a small city in Essex about fifty miles northeast of London. There is a baptismal certificate stating that on 21 January of that year, in the parish of the Holy Trinity, was baptized "John Fordyce, [son] of John and Ann Maples."[3]

His parentage and background apparently were not based in the gentry or even in one of the more socially acceptable professions of the law, the military, or the church. The evidence for this is sketchy and negative in nature. Later on, well after the wars were over, two different editors collected together biographical sketches of officers who had served in the Great War. These short pieces were really autobiographical—the officers themselves were asked to provide them. Officers with any claim whatever to family prominence and social standing described their family background in their submissions to the editors, usually with some inflation.[4] But John Maples provided nothing at all on his family, an almost certain indication that there was no socially acceptable background to provide. Yet there was some "interest" available to him through the patronage of a powerful family with naval connections: the Afflecks.

The Affleck family was definitely "gentry." Their estate was Dalham Hall in Suffolk, about twenty-five miles northeast of Colchester. The senior member of the family in the late eighteenth century was Sir Edmund Affleck, an admiral, formerly active and of much distinction, who in 1782 became the member of Parliament for the borough of Colchester. Also in 1782 John Fordyce Maples entered the navy, and Captain Philip Affleck, Sir Edmund's younger brother, provided Maples's all-important first appointment to a ship.

What was the link between John Maples's family and the Afflecks? No firm evidence could be found, but a scenario that fits the little that is available goes like this: Perhaps John Maples, Senior, was a prosperous merchant or businessman of some kind. If this was so, if his father was "in trade," John Fordyce would have been unlikely in those particularly snobbish postwar times to list this socially less-than-acceptable family background in his biographical sketches. However, John Maples, Senior, could have been an important political supporter of Edmund Affleck's parliamentary affairs in Colchester, and this connection would have provided the link that gave young John Fordyce Maples his interest. Also consistent with this scenario is the supposition that the

Maples family, if prosperous and successful in business, would have had the necessary money to provide John Fordyce with the extra income needed to pay his way as a young gentleman in the navy.

In any event, on 5 October 1782 Captain Philip Affleck appointed twelve-year-old John Maples as a "Captain's Servant" aboard his ship, the *Triumph*, a seventy-four–gun battleship, then in the Chatham dockyard. The rating of captain's servant was at that time the preferred way of entry into the navy for young gentlemen on their way to becoming officers. Philip Affleck had earlier been in command of the *Triumph*, but 5 October 1782 marked the start of a new commission for her, with a new crew. She was still being refitted, and John Maples, if he was actually on board and not just carried on her books, had the early experience of seeing her being rigged, watching her cables and stores come aboard, and observing her being ballasted.[5]

It is very probable that he was bewildered and homesick and didn't absorb much of this seamanlike knowledge. Also, a ship like the *Triumph* normally carried a schoolmaster to teach the young officer candidates, and Maples probably spent a good part of his days in receiving instruction in the three R's. Certainly, either before he entered the navy or during his early time in the navy, or more likely both, John Maples learned spelling, grammar, and penmanship and learned how to express himself lucidly in complete sentences. He normally wrote in a clear, plain, highly legible hand but when he wished could write in a fancy, embellished style. His signature is a showpiece of calligraphy; it is hard to see how it could have been written with a quill pen.[6]

Captain Philip Affleck seems to have been a kindly person for his rank and his times, and his portrait shows a rather grandfatherly appearing man.[7] In a day when senior naval officers had nicknames like "Mad Jack" or "Dismal Jimmy" bestowed on them behind their backs by their juniors, Affleck was called "Uncle Phil."

When young John Maples joined the *Triumph*, England was at war with France, Spain, and Holland and was still trying to cope with the American Revolution, but the *Triumph* did not see any action after he came on board, she being either moored at the Nore anchorage or acting as the guard ship in Portsmouth. By late 1783 England was at peace again with all the world. Thus Maples's service aboard was probably relatively unexciting. If John Maples kept a journal of those times or left any personal reminiscences, they have not yet turned up, and there is no way to know what imprint this first shipboard duty left on an impressionable twelve year old. He probably took away some ideas about how a ship should be run, and if so the log of the *Triumph* can provide a clue. One indicator of the state of morale and command effectiveness aboard ships of that day was the frequency and severity of punishment. The *Triumph*'s log during Philip Affleck's time in command shows an apparently well run ship with a comparatively low incidence of punishment, an infrequent infliction of two, or occasionally three, dozen lashes for "disobedience of orders" or "neglect of duty."[8]

Philip Affleck left the ship in mid-1784 and was replaced for a short period by another of the Afflecks, William, a cousin. He was followed after a brief time by a Captain Faulkner, and John Maples then got to see what punishment could really be like in the British Navy: just two weeks before Maples left the *Triumph* a court-martial aboard her sentenced an unfortunate man, James Baptister, to "200 lashes, ship to ship."[9]

John Maples was detached from the *Triumph* on 19 September 1784, soon after the Afflecks left her and, in a move that they probably arranged, was sent aboard H.B.M. Frigate *Hebe,* part of the Channel Fleet. The *Hebe* was commanded by Captain Edward Thornbrough and had the reputation of being "one of the finest frigates in the British Navy."[10] As it was peacetime, this reputation was most likely based on smartness in appearance—brilliant brass, snowy-white decks, crisply executed sail handling, and precision maneuvering—rather than, say, aggressive boarding tactics.

But the Admiralty apparently thought highly of her; and when a suitable ship was needed for a new duty assignment for the only naval member of the Royal Family, the *Hebe* was chosen, and Prince William Henry was sent aboard for his first tour of duty as a new lieutenant.

Prince William Henry was the third son of George III and would come to the throne himself in 1830 for a few years as William IV, the "Sailor King," a bluff, good-natured, and popular monarch who in the long parade of British rulers just precedes his niece Victoria. In mid-1785 the prince had served off and on for six years as a midshipman, had passed his examination for promotion, and was assigned to the *Hebe* as her third lieutenant.[11]

For John Maples, and for most of the officers of the *Hebe,* the seven months that the prince was aboard were an eye-opening time as they got a glimpse into the rarefied life-styles of the powerful and well-born of the kingdom. The *Hebe* went on a cruise around England and the Orkney Islands, ostensibly hunting smugglers, but stopping frequently, the prince being feted and honored, wined, dined, and adulated in every port. How much of this festive activity trickled down to the *Hebe*'s officers and young gentlemen is not clear, but some undoubtedly did: the nobility and gentry of England have usually had numbers of daughters, and these balls and dinners must have welcomed the attendance of these eligible young sea officers of the navy.

Prince William Henry left the *Hebe* in February of 1786 and in parting, as was his occasional habit, gave swords or dirks to the officers with whom he had been associated. Two of those presented on the *Hebe* survive: a sword given to a Lieutenant Lock and a midshipman's dirk given to John Maples.[12] The brass ferrule of the scabbard of John Maples's dirk is engraved on one side, "Prince

William Henry," and on the other, "I.F. Maples, 1786." John Maples was apparently very proud of this brief contact with royalty: he kept the dirk all his life and passed it on to his heirs.

John Maples remained aboard the *Hebe* until February of 1789, serving for most of that time, about twenty-two months, rated as "Able Seaman," although still living aft with the officers. This was a common practice in officer training at that time, with the purpose of giving the young gentlemen some concentrated experience in practical seamanship, and it enabled John Maples to become intimately familiar with how a sharp, taut ship was run in peacetime. About ten months before he left the *Hebe,* John Maples was appointed a midshipman—an indication that he had learned enough to pull his weight and was capable of being given more serious shipboard responsibilities.[13]

He was nineteen when he left the *Hebe* and Channel Fleet for what turned out to be eleven years on the Jamaica Station. He was entering the most professionally intensive, physically hazardous, and financially rewarding period of his career. He was appointed at this time as master's mate aboard the frigate *Blonde,* commanded again by a patron, this time William Affleck.

The political arrangements in the West Indies when John Maples arrived there in the spring of 1789 differed considerably from what they are today. The English held Jamaica and had a naval base on the southern coast at Port Royal, near the present-day city of Kingston, and they held Barbados, the most eastward and windward island of all the Windward Islands and, in the days of sail, one of the strategic keys of the Caribbean. The English also held eight more of the smaller islands in the Leeward and Windward chains, including Antigua, with its naval base at English Harbor, Grenada, and the rich sugar islands of St. Vincent, St. Kitts, and Nevis.

The French held Saint-Domingue, the western one-third of the Island of Hispaniola—roughly the same domain that is now Haiti—plus the islands of Guadeloupe, Martinique, and Saint Lucie in the Windward Island chain. The Dutch held Curaçao and its neighbors, plus a couple of the smaller Leeward Islands.

The Spanish owned everything else: Cuba, Santo Domingo (the other two-thirds of Hispaniola), Porto Rico, Trinidad, the adjacent mainlands of South and Central America known as the Spanish Main or as the Caraccas and New Granada, as well as New Spain (now Mexico), Louisiana, and Florida.

These European colonial powers were currently—temporarily—at peace with one another. But that didn't mean that all was peaceful in the region. In this spring of the year of the fall of the Bastille and the onset of the French Revolution, the focus of trouble in the West Indies was Saint-Domingue, and trouble was to continue there for all of the time that John Maples served on the Jamaica Station, and for long afterward.

The Island of Hispaniola is shaped like a huge, open lobster claw, facing west. The two pincers of the claw plus the area between them made up French Saint-Domingue; to the east, the body of the claw was Spanish Santo Domingo.

Saint-Domingue was the bright green jewel in the crown of France, its richest colonial possession by far, providing two-thirds of France's tropical produce and one-third of all French overseas trade. With the wealth of its plantations and cities, its excellent harbors, fertile soil, and well-developed artificial irrigation systems, it was the most productive of all the European colonies in the West Indies. The richest part of the colony, with the most productive land of its three provinces, was the North Province, which occupied the northern pincer of the lobster claw and whose main port, Le Cap François, was the cultural center of the colony. The West Province, with the fertile Plaine du Cul-de-Sac that stretched along the great bay between the two pincers, was nearly as productive as the North. The West's port and main city was Port-au-Prince. The South Province, comprising the lower pincer, the southern peninsula, was rocky, more arid, and much less productive. All along the coasts of the colony and stretching back up the valleys and into the foothills of the mountains were more than three thousand plantations producing sugar, coffee, cotton, indigo, and cacao.[14] Saint-Domingue was a marvel of economic geography: the labor resources of Africa were exploited on the arable land of this Caribbean Island for the profit of a few wealthy men in Europe.

The troubles, now imminent, came from the highly pyramidal, racially divided social structure of the colony. At the top of this pyramid were the whites: first the high government officials, sent out from France, called the *bureaucrats,* then the *grands blancs,* a group comprising the plantation-owning white colonists, styled the *colons,* plus the bankers and rich merchants. Below them were also some lower-class whites, the *petits blancs,* who were the plantation managers, shopkeepers, mechanics, small farmers, sailors on the beach, etc. Altogether, the whites in the colony numbered about twenty-four thousand, and although quite a few of them lived in the cities of Le Cap François or Port-au-Prince, most of the landowners, plantation managers, and overseers, and many of the artisans, lived in the countryside, on the plantations.

At the bottom of the society, making up the huge base of the pyramid, were more than four hundred thousand mostly male black slaves. Few of these were relatively docile plantation-born slaves. Nearly all were Africans captured and enslaved as young adults, still retaining strong, although diverse, tribal memories, tied together by the cultural thread of their voodoo religion. Most of the men had been warrior-trained from their young boyhood until their capture.

All of them, the men and the fewer women, fiercely resented their captivity, their bondage, and the brutally oppressive labor regime they worked under—a regime in which the planters found it more profitable to work their slaves to death and replace them rather than to coerce them into reproducing. To keep the labor force replenished, an active slave-trading system imported West Africans to Saint-Domingue—more than twenty-nine thousand had been brought in during the single year of 1788.[15] The mortality of this procurement system was so dreadful that some eighty-seven thousand men, women, and children had to be captured each year in the interior of Africa just to provide the annual input needed by Saint-Domingue alone.[16]

Just above the blacks and below the whites in the social pyramid of Saint-Domingue were a few free blacks and about twenty thousand free persons of mixed race, classified into more than a hundred jealously guarded gradations of color and parentage. They were generally spoken of collectively as *gens de couleur* or as *mulatres* or mulattos. Many of them were landowners, small planters, or merchants, particularly in the south and west. Others worked on the plantations as overseers, clerks, and artisans.

The plantation owners and managers, and their overseers, outnumbered seventeen-to-one by the blacks, maintained control over the vast slave population through a brutal and horrifying system of discipline and punishment. The slaves could be whipped or mutilated for the slightest breach of the draconian rules under which they lived. A slave could be "tortured in official investigations and sentenced to a grotesque death" or could be killed out of hand at the whim of his or her owner.[17]

This stew of humanity was, in 1789, roiling with racial tensions and social discontents. The white plantation-owning *colons* bitterly resented the home government in France and the mercantilist laws, dating from Louis XIV, which kept Saint-Domingue from legally trading with any country but France. The *colons* hated the rich French merchants in Nantes and Bordeaux who kept them in debt, skimmed tremendous profits from their sugar and coffee, and then overcharged for the manufactured goods sent out to the colony. Closer to home, the *colons* looked down on the *petits blancs* and despised the *mulatres*. The *petits blancs* in their turn hated the *mulatres*. The *mulatres* craved equality with the whites and despised the blacks. The blacks longed for their freedom and an end to their incessant labor but were held in check by the ferocious discipline imposed on them by all those above in the pyramid.

The explosion was some time in coming. At first the *colons,* although Royalists at heart, liked the news that came out to them of the Revolution that had started in France because they expected it to bring them more economic freedom. But then on 28 March 1790 came a decree from the National Assembly giving the right to participate in the local colonial assemblies to all property owners and taxpayers over twenty-five years old. The mulattos of Saint-Domingue promptly demanded representation in the new Colonial Assembly, and when the whites refused, an uprising of mulattos took place, which the whites put down with great cruelty.

After a complex series of events in which the whites and mulattos plotted against one another, and the National Assembly in France enfranchised one category of mulattos but not others, the mulattos planned to rise again on 26 August 1791.

But three days before then, on the twenty-third, the black slaves exploded in revolt all over the North Province, putting the torch to the plantation houses and cane fields and slaughtering all the whites that they could find—men, women, and children—returning in full measure the ferocity and cruelty that they had long received.

The slave revolt spread through all of Saint-Domingue and went on through month after year of horror piled on horror, with shifting alliances and enmities between whites, mulattos, and blacks. The struggle swayed one way and then another, with troops coming out from France to try to stabilize the colony, and commissioners from the National Assembly making belated offers of freedom to the blacks, who by that time had their freedom and wanted political hegemony and independence.

The opening in Europe of the Great War in 1793 brought a British invasion of Saint-Domingue, supported for three years by the Spanish from neighboring Santo Domingo until Spain changed sides and became an ally of France.

Saint-Domingue proved to be a morass for the British. For five years, until 1798, they poured troops and treasure into a struggle that was doomed nearly from the beginning. They were decimated and their morale was corroded by yellow fever and malaria, they were worn down by jungle guerrilla tactics with which they were unable to cope, and they were finally outgeneraled, outfought, and defeated by François Dominique Toussaint—Toussaint Louverture—a former slave, the son of a "petty African Chieftain" and his army of black former slaves.[18]

The French did no better against Toussaint and the other black leaders, Jean Jacques Dessalines and Henri Christophe, and the *mulatre* Benoit Joseph Rigaud. Toussaint's maneuverings infuriated Napoleon, and black success in controlling Saint-Domingue was seriously compromising his plans for empire in North America.

In 1802, when during the brief Peace of Amiens he did not have to face the British Navy, Napoleon sent out his brother-in-law, General LeClerc, with a large army and fleet. Bonaparte's plan was to regain control of the colony, disarm the blacks, and then reenslave them. He had obtained the ownership of Louisiana by retrocession from Spain and expected to make Saint-Domingue the base and stepping-off point for a French empire in the Americas that would include Florida, Louisiana, and the American West. The colony was vital to these plans, which he envisioned putting into effect as soon as he was successful in uniting the neutrals of Europe and using them, plus the United States, to counter Britain at sea.

This effort was doomed in the end: the black military forces and their leadership were highly effective by 1802. They fought the French to a standstill, then the yellow fever spread through the French Army in a major way. Soon after, in May of 1803, the war between France and England was renewed, and the British Navy began to support the black armies. The French in Saint-Domingue, cut off at sea from any reinforcement, their numbers decimated by the continuous fighting and the yellow fever, left in defeat.[19]

Saint-Domingue itself did not escape the doom that these events brought to all the participants. At first, under Toussaint, the plantations were made to work again, trade increased, principally with the United States, and the economy of Saint-Domingue again became prosperous. But in 1802 and afterward nearly all the whites left the country or were butchered. The former colony, soon divided between the principally mulatto Republic of Haiti in the south and the black-ruled Kingdom of Haiti in the north, languished slowly into poverty after the deaths of the revolutionary leaders. Eventually the kingdom and the republic coalesced, and over the years what had been the rich and productive jewel of the Caribbean evolved into the impoverished and agriculturally barren Haiti of today, hagridden by *caudillos,* and futureless.

As the earliest of these events were unfolding, British policy toward Saint-Domingue was vacillating and uncertain. In 1791, just as the slave revolt was exploding into its full fury, the French Colonial Assembly asked the British governor of Jamaica to take the colony under British protection. The governor not only lacked the authority to do this but also wanted to be in a position to pick off this rich plum for Britain. The British home government was horrified by the slave revolt and didn't want it to spread to the British sugar islands, particularly not to close-by Jamaica, where 30,000 whites tenuously controlled 250,000 slaves, and hill settlements of escaped blacks—*maroons*—already provided a focus for revolt.[20] So the senior naval officer in Jamaica was told to increase the patrols and surveillance off Saint-Domingue to prevent contact between there and Jamaica, only 115 miles distant.

Of course, the richness of Saint-Domingue was attractive to Britain. But also important was its strategic position. The northern coast of Saint-Domingue faced the Atlantic, and the western end of the northern peninsula—the western tip of the upper pincer of the great lobster claw—formed the eastern shore of the fifty-five-mile-wide Windward Passage, the gateway in the shortest route between Jamaica and the Atlantic Ocean. The eastern tip of Spanish Cuba formed the other side of the Windward Passage.

In the same way that the British at Barbados controlled the entrance to the

West Indies from Europe in sailing-ship days, the holder of the northern peninsula of Saint-Domingue could control traffic entering or leaving the western Caribbean through the Windward Passage. Most vessels coming from the United States to Jamaica or Saint-Domingue used this passage, and it was an extremely important exit for shipping leaving Jamaica for England. At the western tip of the northern peninsula of Saint-Domingue, right on the Windward Passage, was the excellent fortified harbor of Môle Saint Nicolas, the "Gibraltar of the Antilles." The British wanted it badly.[21]

John Maples's first years in the West Indies aboard the frigate *Blonde* were unexciting peacetime years for the British, although during his latter months in the *Blonde* the slave revolt in Saint-Domingue was fully ablaze. The ship was based in Jamaica and patrolled off the coasts of Saint-Domingue and in the Windward Passage, stopping ships and checking their papers, looking for violations of the Navigation Acts, watching out for the small-scale pirates then operating in the Caribbean, and preventing any infection from the slave revolt in Saint-Domingue from crossing over to Jamaica.

His tour on the *Blonde* ended abruptly: The ship was moored in St. Ann's Bay in the Ochos Rios area on the northern coast of Jamaica. On the day after Christmas 1791, a stormy, rainy day, "at 3/4 past 2 PM, Captain [William] Affleck departed this life suddenly, without a groan." He was buried ashore the next day in the churchyard, to the sound of minute guns from his ship. John Maples had lost a friend and a patron. He left the *Blonde* a couple of weeks later, reporting next aboard the battleship *Centurion,* the flagship of his major benefactor, Philip Affleck, now a rear-admiral and since 1790 the commander in chief on the Jamaica Station.[22]

John Maples was now twenty-two and still a master's mate, but he had put in well over the required six years' time to be examined for lieutenant. After about six months on board the *Centurion* he was sent to England to undergo his examination, carrying his journals from the *Hebe, Blonde,* and *Centurion* and certificates from their captains as to his competence. He was examined on 2 August 1792 and given a passing certificate dated 30 July.[23]

By this point in his career it was becoming clear that John Maples's "interest" was limited. The Afflecks were his supporters, but they were apparently only willing to help him to a certain degree and were not willing to expend a lot of political capital to advance his career. An officer with good, solid family connections in the navy would have been quickly appointed to a lieutenant's billet and promoted right after passing his exam. John Maples was not promoted until nearly two years later. However, many, many officers—those without any interest—waited several years or forever for promotion after passing.

When John Maples returned to the West Indies after his lieutenant's examination he was appointed as master's mate in the thirty-two–gun frigate *Pene-*

lope, commanded by Captain Bartholomew Rowley, a member of another one of the great naval families of England.[24] This was important to John Maples and the other officers of the *Penelope:* a ship whose captain had interest and family connections usually got the better assignments. It was especially important in wartime because a ship with an influential captain would usually be assigned to cruise on hunting expeditions in areas with plenty of loaded enemy merchant-men to be taken. Such assignments, of course, meant prize money and the chance to become rich. Ships whose captains lacked influence were assigned to hard and frustrating, or dreary and boring, jobs, like protecting convoys of way-ward merchant vessels with obstreperous and headstrong skippers, or backing up the army and ferrying soldiers and supplies from place to place.

John Maples seems nearly always to have been appointed into ships com-manded by influential officers. This could hardly have been coincidence. But his interest with the Afflecks seems at this time to have been not only limited but waning. However, it appears that John Maples was achieving a reputation as a young officer of promise. Even influential captains needed hard-working subordinates who were good fighters, and this probably helped to make up for his declining interest until he found another patron.

The long wars of the French Revolution and Napoleon were now immi-nent. The revolution in France was having a major impact in England. At first, in 1789, the more liberal English middle classes—professionals, merchants, and artisans—welcomed the aspirations of *liberté, egalité, fraternité,* and were impressed by French progress in real political and social reform. The British government and the aristocracy viewed the early revolutionary events in France with caution but without much worry. But as increasing numbers of Royalist *émigrés* arrived in England and described in alarmist terms the seizure of their properties by the Revolutionary government and the disappearance of aristocratic privilege, the English upper classes began to see the increasingly radical events in France as potentially dangerous to themselves. They could compare the actions of the *sans-culotte* mobs in Paris to their own Gordon Riots of a few years earlier and see that mob violence was possible in London as well as Paris. But when Austria and then Prussia invaded France in April of 1792, getting badly bloodied in the process, England stood aside.

British uneasiness increased when the Austrian invasion of France triggered the unseating of Louis XVI and the declaration of the French Republic, then in January of 1793 the English people were shocked by the guillotining of the deposed Louis. Not only was this an assault on the stability of monarchial gov-ernment everywhere, but also England's own unhappy experience with regicide in 1649 was still fresh in the national memory. War became inevitable when the French invaded Holland and the Austrian Netherlands—today Belgium—in violation of French treaty obligations, threatening Britain's commercial interests.

France, already engaged with Austria, Prussia, and Spain, declared war against Holland and England on 1 February 1793. This war, or wars—there was a short break in 1802–1803 under the Treaty of Amiens—was to be the world's first modern war and would last twenty-two years, until 1814, then the "Hundred Days" in 1815, finally ending at the Battle of Waterloo.

Britain was not ready for what was now ahead. The army in 1793 was small, poorly organized, and antiquated. The navy was in better shape, although nowhere near as professional and effective as it would be in a few years. Across the Channel the French Army was becoming a highly effective citizen-manned mass army, with an extremely potent artillery arm officered by holdovers from Royalist times. The French Navy, on the other hand, was suffering badly from the Revolution, its officer corps being gutted by the flight or arrests of the aristocrats.

The British government's strategic concept was to financially subsidize others to conduct the land war in Europe, committing a minimum number of troops, and to use the navy to pick off France's overseas colonial possessions, particularly in the West Indies.

At the outbreak of the war the British Navy on overseas stations was very weak. The force on the Jamaica Station, which was expected to cover all of the western Caribbean, consisted of one fifty-gun ship, the *Europa,* plus the thirty-two–gun *Penelope* with Captain Rowley and John Maples, two small twenty-eight–gun frigates, five sloops and brigs of from fourteen to twenty guns, and a cutter. The senior naval officer on the Jamaica Station was now Captain John Ford, who had relieved Admiral Philip Affleck in 1792. Ford flew a commodore's broad pennant in the *Europa*.[25] There was another small British squadron in the Leeward Islands area about one thousand miles east and upwind from Jamaica. The French, however, were just as weak. As neither power had a fleet in the West Indies at this time, there was no likelihood of a major naval battle.

To these few British warships in the West Indies, to ships like the *Penelope* and to young officers like John Maples, the onset of war opened delightful prospects of prize money and promotion. There were swarms of French merchant vessels loaded with valuable tropical products, plus neutrals that would be fair game if carrying contraband or French-owned cargoes. Also, French privateers sprang up like mushrooms in the small ports and remote bays of Saint-Domingue, Santo Domingo, and Porto Rico to prey on the rich British commerce. These privateers were tougher game for the British but provided spice, variety, and challenge.

So there was to be no lack of action, the real risks were minimal, and the rewards could be great. One of the usual toasts in British wardrooms as the wine went around the table after dinner was dedicated to promotion, to "a bloody war or a sickly season." But while single-ship actions and cutting-out forays in defended harbors produced some casualties, the havoc of yellow fever and malaria created the real opportunities for advancement during the late spring and summer seasons, when the rains enabled the mosquitoes to breed.

John Maples's experience in action started early: he fought in the first actual naval engagement of the war, the first of the thousand or so actions that were fought between French and British warships during the entire course of those twenty-plus years of war. Late in the afternoon of 16 April 1793 the *Penelope* sighted a French brig-rigged sloop-of-war a few miles off Grand Cayman Island, west of Jamaica. The frigate overhauled the sloop, and after several broadsides were exchanged, the Frenchman struck her colors. She was *Le Goe-lan,* fourteen guns, and she had been badly cut up by the fight, being greatly overmatched thirty-two guns to fourteen. The *Penelope* put her boats in the water and sent an officer to take charge of the prize, plus the *Penelope'*s carpenter and boatswain and a repair party. *Le Goelan* was leaking badly from shot holes at the waterline and had considerable damage in her sails and rigging. After working all night the working party got the leaks stopped, and after daylight the *Penelope* took her in tow and carried her into Port Royal, the first blood of the war.[26]

There is no surviving record of how much prize money John Maples earned during his West Indies service, but it must have been a considerable amount. Just over a month after the capture of *Le Goelan,* the *Penelope* encountered two very lucrative prizes. On 4 June she intercepted a French slaving brig from Guinea, bound for Saint-Domingue with 124 slaves on board. As Captain Rowley was taking her into Port Royal, the frigate came across another French brig with 139 slaves on board and took her in as well. The price of slaves was inflated then because of a shortage of supply, and a strong, healthy man might bring close to 3,000 livres, roughly £124 sterling. This amount of money was about equivalent to the annual pay of the captain of a frigate the size of the *Penelope,* or nearly two years pay for a lieutenant, and the prize money from the capture of a loaded slaving vessel was definitely a sum worth having.[27] The sale after the prize court's condemnation of the two brigs, their equipage, and their human cargo of 263 souls provided a substantial amount to be shared among the Penelopes. John Maples as master's mate shared one-eighth of the total with the lieutenants and the warrant officers, about twelve people altogether. The captured slaves were no doubt sold to British planters in Jamaica.

In line with the overall British strategy of picking off the French colonies overseas, an invasion of Saint-Domingue was planned for the fall of 1793. Other factors were also at work. With Spain now at war with France, the British government worried that troops might move across the border from Spanish Santo Domingo and take over French Saint-Domingue. To forestall this possibility, the British made an agreement with Spain for both countries to invade the French possession, the Spanish by land, the British from the sea, and to divide the colony between them.

Also, the French planters, not only in Saint-Domingue but in all of the French West Indian colonies, wanted to join England. They were by now frightened of the Revolution and terrified by the slave revolt in Saint-Domingue. They felt that if there was any security for them it lay with the British. With these fears in mind, the planters of Saint-Domingue in 1793 renewed their previous requests to the governor at Jamaica for British protection, and this time, when the governor informed the home government, he was given "the King's commands to accept terms of submission" from the parts of Saint-Domingue that asked for British protection.[28] The French planters also promised to cooperate with the British invasion and to provide troops to help.

The British command in Jamaica gave these promises considerable importance, and there was at least some expectation that the British would gain the ownership of Saint-Domingue in the end. But the real drive behind the decision to invade was the British government's fear that the slave revolt might cross the channel to Jamaica. There had been sporadic slave uprisings in Jamaica since 1673, and any anxiety about infection from Saint-Domingue was real. The British believed that invasion was the preventative.[29] Seldom has a major, thoroughly considered decision turned out to be so wrong: the British were to find that they had overestimated the extent of French planter support, grossly underestimated the fighting ability of the blacks and mulattos, and embarked on a long, costly fight with an expensive defeat at the end.

The task of invasion, which was expected to be initially an occupation, was given to General Sir Adam Williamson, with a detachment from the 13th Regiment of Foot. He was to be supported by Commodore John Ford with a small squadron of ships: his flagship the *Europa,* fifty guns; the *Penelope,* thirty-two; the *Goelan,* fourteen; the *Penelope's* recent prize, now under British colors; the schooner *Flying Fish,* which was another prize of the *Penelope's* and possibly one of the small twenty-eight–gun frigates. They were to go in at Jérémie, the main town at the western end of the southern peninsula. The way had been prepared by contact with the planters in the area, and little or no resistance was expected—General Williamson and M. de Cadushé, of the town of Jérémie, had signed an agreement or "treaty" on 3 September, putting the South Province under British protection for the duration of the war. Some French planter troops were to support the British ashore.[30]

On 9 September at Port Royal the *Europa* loaded 870 soldiers, and on the twentieth the little expedition arrived off Jérémie. All went according to plan, at least at first: the British troops under Lieutenant Colonel Whitelock, plus the French planter troops, occupied Jérémie without a struggle and were received with "every demonstration of joy and fidelity." With things apparently well in hand at Jérémie, Commodore Ford took part of his squadron and headed north to attack Cap Saint-Nicolas Môle, which he captured on 23 September, at last giving the British control of the Windward Passage.

Ford apparently detached the *Penelope* and one or two other ships to operate independently before he left Jérémie—John Maples does not mention being present at the taking of Môle Saint Nicolas. The *Penelope* took this opportunity of independence to cruise around the tip of the peninsula and sweep up French and neutral shipping anchored in the small bays near St. Louis on the south side—a highly profitable enterprise: John Maples told of the capture of two thousand tons of shipping loaded with tropical produce in the period following the Jérémie episode.[31]

Later that year Captain Rowley caught up with a tougher adversary when on 25 November the *Penelope,* in company with the *Iphigenia,* another thirty-two–gun frigate, ran into the larger French frigate *L'Inconstante,* thirty-six guns. At this early point in the war the French were still formidable fighters at sea, and even with two of the British it was a "warm action." The *Penelope* lost one man killed and had seven wounded in the half-hour action before the Frenchman was captured.[32]

The British invasion of Saint-Domingue was by this time experiencing some exhilarating success. General Williamson had experienced a brief rebuff in October when he failed to capture Tiburon, a small port city about thirty-five miles south around the tip of the peninsula from Jérémie, but by now both the army and the navy were receiving reinforcements from England, and the British were able to bypass Tiburon and throw in more troops in other landings. By the end of 1793 the British had more than five thousand regulars and colonial militia ashore, had captured important places along the bight of the coast between the two peninsulas—Jean Rabel, Saint Marc, Arcahaye, and Léogane—and were threatening an outnumbered French force at Port-au-Prince. On 2 January 1794 Ford sent the *Penelope* into Port-au-Prince under a flag of truce to carry the British terms for the surrender of the city and port. When his terms were refused, Ford had the city tightly blockaded from the sea.[33]

Early in 1794 the British went back to Tiburon by sea to try again. John Maples and the *Penelope* were there to cover the debarkation near the town by Lieutenant Colonel Whitelocke and his troops. This time they had better luck. On 2 February Whitelocke attacked, captured Tiburon, and chased the defenders east along the southern coast toward Les Cayes. The *Penelope* followed at sea, engaged in a gunnery duel with the batteries at Les Cayes, then sent in her boats and brought off as prizes several loaded merchantmen. Whitelocke's troops were stopped briefly at Les Cayes, but then swept past and on to the east to capture a fort at L'Acul.

In April 1794 John Maples finally got the break for which he had waited two years: he was transferred to Commodore Ford's flagship, the *Europa,* and promoted to acting-lieutenant. This was a very short assignment, and he spent most of it ashore, serving in a sailor-manned battery of guns at Cap Saint-Nicolas Môle, called Fort Ford. In mid-May a lieutenant's billet opened up on board the thirty-two–gun frigate *Magicienne,* and twenty-four-year-old John Maples was assigned to her as third lieutenant.

Thirty-two–gun frigates were going out of style by 1794, and the new-construction programs in all navies were featuring the larger thirty-six– and thirty-eight–gun, or even forty-four–gun, vessels. The smaller thirty-two–gun ships, however, were just fine for the service required around Saint-Domingue at that time. They were handy and maneuverable, and their relatively shallow draft—the *Magicienne*'s loaded draft aft was only sixteen feet ten inches—enabled them to get into the little coves and harbors where the numerous French privateers and their prizes liked to hide.

Aesthetically, these small frigates were the prettiest and most graceful of all the classes of warships of the Great War, and the French-built ones, like the *Magicienne,* were the prettiest small frigates of all.[34] She was only 136 feet long at the waterline, but if the length of the bowsprit and jibboom are added in, plus the end of the spanker boom extending over the stern, the tip-to-tip length of the *Magicienne* was about 190 feet. She was very tall of mast. She carried twenty-eight 12-pound guns on the gun deck plus ten to twelve carronades and a couple of 6-pound long guns on the quarterdeck and forecastle.

The *Magicienne* had been built in 1777 and was captured off Boston from the French during the American Revolutionary War and added to the British Navy.[35] She was described several years later by a British officer who had served in her as "possess[ing] . . . very excellent qualities . . . viz., sailed extremely fast, very stiff under sail, easy draft of water, long floor, a fine entrance, and a very superior run, and a most weatherly ship in a gale of wind."[36] Her plans show that her underwater hull form was almost clipper-like—certainly very advanced for her time.[37] She was also described as having a rather extreme amount of tumblehome—meaning that the sides curved inward quite sharply above the waterline—an old-fashioned attribute. This brought the guns closer to the centerline, which improved the ship's stability but also decreased the angle of the shrouds and their ability to support the masts.[38] Stability, shroud strength, and gale-weatherliness were to be crucial at least once in her life under British colors.

The *Magicienne* should have been one of the most elite frigates on the Jamaica Station. Her skipper was Captain George Martin, a member of another large naval family with powerful service connections. But in spite of this he had somehow gotten crosswise with his boss, Commodore Ford. While

it is obviously not good for a skipper anywhere to be out of favor with his commodore, it spelled disaster for a frigate captain on the Jamaica Station because
it meant that he and his ship got the hard, boring assignments with little opportunity for easy captures and prize money.

John Maples continued to serve in the *Europa* for a couple of weeks after he
was assigned to the *Magicienne*. An invasion of Port-au-Prince was in the
works, and Commodore Ford apparently kept him on board the flagship as an
extra officer until it was over.[39] The British were lucky in their timing: the
mulatto and white defenders of the city had just been involved in a debilitating power struggle in which many of the whites were slaughtered and the city's
ability to resist had been weakened.[40]

Since mid-May British forces had been assembling in the harbor at Môle
Saint Nicolas: three battleships, a 74 and two 64s; ten transports with soldiers;
several frigates and sloops; plus miscellaneous support vessels—with Commodore Ford in the *Europa* commanding the whole group. The battleships put
to sea on 22 May, followed on the twenty-third by the transports and the
Europa with Ford and Maples. This fleet arrived in the Bay of Port-au-Prince
on 31 May and the next day attacked with more than 1,400 soldiers under
Brigadier General Whyte, supported by plenty of naval gunfire. A bad storm
interrupted the operation, but in the confusion and bad visibility the British soldiers rushed and carried the fort.[41] On 4 June 1794 the city surrendered.

The *Magicienne* had not participated in the invasion, being kept back at the
Môle to defend the British position there, but a prize-sharing agreement had
been signed by all the ships in the area, and the Magiciennes would be in on the
division of the prize money. Port-au-Prince was one of the biggest prize hauls
ever made by the British Navy: estimates of the total involved run up to
£500,000.[42]

The capture of Port-au-Prince was the high point of British military affairs
in Saint-Domingue. From this time onward the road led downhill. The British
hardly noticed the real turning point of the war at the time. It came on 6 May
1794, ten days before John Maples was assigned to the *Magicienne* and a month
before the capture of Port-au-Prince, when ex-slave Toussaint Louverture, the
charismatic leader of the black army, the most effective politician and general
on any side of the struggle, shifted his allegiance from the Spanish to the
French.

Toussaint had joined the French in opposing the Spanish invasion but
became convinced that the French government intended to restore the old
order and reenslave the blacks. The Spanish promised freedom and also
offered Toussaint himself a knighthood and a military title. So Toussaint
joined the Spanish, taking his army with him, and fought so effectively that he
soon held most of the West Province, including the territory inland from Port-

au-Prince. His change of allegiance back to the French in May 1794 resulted from changes in the French government in Paris: Robespierre, although soon to die, was now in power, and his Jacobin faction favored the elimination of slavery. With this impetus, the Convention quickly passed a resolution that "slavery be abolished in all the territory of the Republic, including Saint-Domingue."[43] This convinced Toussaint to change sides.

Once he had made the shift, Toussaint moved swiftly. Without warning he attacked the Spanish as they came from Mass on Tuesday, 6 May. He drove them eastward toward the mountains and then started to chase the British back into the sea.

At Port-au-Prince the British were trying to consolidate their victory. In the harbor at Môle Saint Nicolas the *Magicienne* reembarked her sailors and marines from Fort Ford and sailed for Port-au-Prince. Coming in on 26 June, she passed an outbound group of ten prizes—part of the rich haul captured in the port—convoyed by the battleship *Sceptre*. John Maples apparently actually joined the *Magicienne* at this time, moving over from the *Europa*.[44] The urgent task for the ships in the harbor was to take control of the prizes, put prize crews aboard, and get them ready for sea. The *Magicienne* had the task of manning four prizes and sent over her gunner and thirty-one men to get them ready and sail them to Jamaica.

British fortunes now began to deteriorate. Toussaint was attacking the British nearly everywhere, and there was much dissension between them and their French-planter allies. The English asserted that the planters often refused to join the fighting, while the French felt that the British took all the credit. Cruel behavior by the British (and particularly by their Spanish allies) was reducing the chance of any eventual victory by turning the population against them: after the fall of Port-au-Prince General Whyte threatened to execute insurgent blacks who refused to surrender, but then many of those who did surrender were killed anyway. There were rumors that the British were sending their black and mulatto prisoners of war to Jamaica to be sold as slaves.[45] Even with these difficulties, there might have been a chance for an ultimate British victory had it not been for the yellow fever and, to a lesser degree, malaria.

Port-au-Prince was surrounded on the land side by a long, woody marsh, or swamp, where millions of mosquitoes bred, particularly the malaria-carrying *Anopheles*. And in the town, open water barrels in the houses, discarded pots, and other containers filled with rain water, provided the breeding environment preferred by *Aëdes aegypti,* the more fastidious, specialized breed of mosquito brought over from Africa, which carried yellow fever. Nearly all of the indigenous blacks, whites, and mulattos had been exposed to yellow fever in their childhood, and many had died, but those who had had light cases and survived to be adults now had long-term immunity to the disease. The British troops had no such immunity and died in large numbers.[46]

The ships in the harbor were not safe: the afternoon land breezes carried clouds of mosquitoes out to them. On shipboard there were always open containers of water: slop jars, water casks, the scuttled butt of water set out on the berth deck for the ship's company's drinking water. If infected yellow fever mosquitoes managed to establish themselves on board in these places, the ship would carry her means of contagion with her wherever she went. The terrible yellow fever epidemic that decimated Philadelphia in 1793 was apparently brought there from Saint-Domingue by a trading vessel in just this way.[47]

The onset of a malignant attack of yellow fever was terrifying to its victim and frightful to watch for shipmates who knew that they might be next. First the afflicted sailor would develop a severe headache with pains in his arms and legs, followed by general, overall weakness. Then to the victim's horror and that of onlookers, he would begin to show the characteristic greenish-yellow tinge in the whites of his eyes and his skin. His eyes would sink back in his head, and the fever would begin. Then there would be chills. Terrible, continuous pain would grip his lower bowels. His tongue would be swollen, bright red at the edges and thickly furred with white. The pain would spread; there would be dark vomit and tarry feces marking the onset of internal hemorrhaging. Within a few days, usually after a period of wild delirium, death would ensue.

The physicians and military surgeons of that time had no idea of the real cause of the disease; the first connection between mosquitoes and yellow fever was not surmised until much later, in 1848.[48] But doctors had pragmatically observed that if a ship was moved away from the land, the outbreak aboard would often subside, and this was the officially recommended action. Of course, if the mosquitoes were breeding in shipboard water containers, even anchoring farther out or going to sea could not prevent or end an outbreak.

Treatments ran from such harmless, inoffensive remedies as drinking vinegar and water mixtures, bathing the victim's feet in warm water, and taking "James's Powders," on up to the frighteningly aggressive measures favored by most of the British (and French) military surgeons: plenty of mercury compounds, plus bleeding.[49] Modern medicine shuns the use of heavy-metal compounds in most circumstances as much too toxic, particularly mercury. But in the 1790s many practitioners viewed mercury as the "Samson of the *materia medica*" and prescribed it for yellow fever with great enthusiasm. They gave mercury by mouth as calomel (mercurous chloride compounded with pure mercury) or "by clyster" (in enemas) and rubbed large quantities of "the strongest mercurial ointment" into the patient's skin. Those who survived the fever may well have died later from mercury poisoning. Bleeding these yellow-fever patients to "restore internal tone and energy" was even more wrong-headed because they were already suffering from internal hemorrhaging.[50]

Some captains had their ships frequently "washed and smoaked between decks."[51] The washing certainly was beneficial, and the "smoaking," done by burning pots of sulfur or tobacco, probably did no harm and may have killed some mosquitoes. It did not, however, stop the yellow fever.

Within a week after the *Magicienne*'s arrival at Port-au-Prince, John Maples began noting deaths in his journal nearly every day. The victims were hurriedly buried ashore. On 7 July the efforts to control the epidemic took a setback when Samuel Sinclair, the surgeon's mate, died and was buried. Captain Martin sent the carpenter and nine men, all sick, to the hospital ashore one day, then eight more a few days later, followed by three more after that. On 2 August 1794 John Maples wrote, "From the returns of the Hospital here we have lost upwards of thirty men, exclusive of those that dyed on board."[52]

In August the outbreak subsided. The *Magicienne* had moved to the outer harbor on 23 July—which probably put her beyond the range of the daily cloud of mosquitoes carried by the afternoon land breeze and, therefore, cut down on new malaria cases. It seems likely that at this time, for some reason, the yellow-fever mosquitoes had not established their breeding in the *Magicienne*'s shipboard water. Also, the "sickly season" was waning; it usually ended in September. But the *Magicienne* lost about seventy men to yellow fever while supporting the army in Saint-Domingue.[53]

Although the British now held Port-au-Prince, the country surrounding it to the west and north was by early July of 1794 under the control of Toussaint and his black troops. To the south, General Rigaud and a mulatto army held the countryside in the southern peninsula, except for British forts at Léogane, Tiburon, and Jérémie. During this period the *Magicienne* and *Hermione,* another thirty-two–gun frigate, were running mates, both ships being stuck with the thankless and disease-ridden job of supporting the army, and both skippers being out of favor with John Ford, their boss, who had just been promoted to rear-admiral. In mid-July John Maples on board the *Magicienne* saw the "brigands" setting fire to the plantations just up-country from the port. Fort Bezonton, one of the British-held positions, and the *Hermione* fired several shots at them—very probably a total waste of powder. By early September Toussaint's forces had cut off the water supply to Port-au-Prince, and the *Magicienne* had to get her water from the wells in the fort.[54]

Ashore, losses among the soldiers from the fevers had reduced the army to just manning defensive positions and to hiring black slaves from the planters to fill the ranks. To attract the blacks, the British promised them their freedom, and the spreading word of this offer complicated the British problems in Jamaica. The ships in the harbor were so short-handed that they had to loan working parties to one another to get one ship under way. The *Magicienne* sent a master's mate, fifty seamen, and fourteen marines to the *Hermione* so that she could go to sea for a week in late September. Out of these lamentable events came a piece of good fortune for John Maples: in fulfillment of the wardroom toast to promotion, the "sickly season" apparently carried off an officer on the *Magicienne* senior to him, and on 2 October 1794 John Maples became her second lieutenant. Less than two months later the first lieutenant, Andrew Thomson, was transferred temporarily to the *Europa,* and John Maples became first of the *Magicienne.*

The British made a strong effort to retake the countryside behind Port-au-Prince, but Toussaint met them with guerrillas and ambushes. As the British offensive began to bog down, Toussaint attacked frontally and drove them back to Port-au-Prince. Then Rigaud and his mulattos attacked and overran Léogane, and the British defenders retreated headlong to Port-au-Prince after butchering about one hundred captives that they held. In early December Rigaud was strong enough to attack Port-au-Prince. John Maples described hearing the gunfire from the fort on 5 December and sending reinforcements of eighteen seamen and sixteen marines under a lieutenant. The *Magicienne*'s returning boats brought off the wounded from the fort. Two days later the fort was under attack again, and the Magiciennes were again called on for reinforcements. Rigaud was finally beaten off and Port-au-Prince saved for the time being, but he then took his troops west along the southern peninsula and attacked Tiburon, which the British had garrisoned with a small detachment from the 23rd Regiment of Foot. The British, outnumbered and encircled, tried to break out. Most were slaughtered in the process.[55]

The first months of 1795 brought no improvement in the British position. In April 1795 most of the British naval force attacked Léogane, anchoring close to the fort and bombarding it for several hours. But the return fire from the mulatto-held fort was heavy and accurate, and the ships were forced to give up the attack and haul off. The *Magicienne*'s messenger cable parted while she was trying to get her anchor up, and she had to cut and run, leaving the anchor behind. The breeze was light, and the *Hermione* was unable to get clear fast enough, so the *Magicienne* sent boats to tow her out.[56]

The attack on Léogane was John Maples's last involvement in Saint-Domingue for some time. He was now first lieutenant of the *Magicienne.* The ship would be away from the West Indies for fifteen months, and when it returned most of its time would be spent in cruising rather than supporting the army.

Three months after the *Magicienne* and John Maples left, the British received another major blow. In Europe, in July of 1795, Spain made peace with France with the Treaty of Basle. As part of the agreement Spanish Santo

Domingo was ceded to France, and Spain officially ceased to be allied with Britain in Saint-Domingue and the next year became an ally of France and Britain's enemy.

The British continued to struggle on, pouring more and more men into Saint-Domingue to die of yellow fever or to be killed in fruitless battles against Toussaint and Rigaud. The inscription on a monument in an English church to the memory of a British Army officer who survived several campaigns, only to die at sea on his way home, expresses the frustration:

> Thrice had his foot Domingo's island prest,
>   Midst horrid wars and fierce barbarian wiles;
> Thrice had his blood repelled the yellow pest
>   That stalks, gigantic, through the Western Isles ![57]

This was clearly a depressing time for the British. In the autobiographical sketch written for O'Byrne, John Maples apparently wanted to put it out of his mind and covered the whole period after the taking of Port-au-Prince up to the time he left in April 1795 by saying that he "was for some time employed in co-operating with the Army in a vain attempt to complete the conquest of the French posts in St. Domingo."[58]

CHAPTER TWELVE

Convoying, Storm, and Peril

IN LATE APRIL OF 1795 John Maples and the *Magicienne* left Port-au-Prince and took a small convoy from Jérémie to Port Royal in Jamaica. After arriving there, the *Magicienne* prepared for a long trip: she cleared her hold, repaired her water casks, took in provisions for three months, and pressed some men.[1] She was scheduled to go to England for a major refit and, along with the *Europa,* to escort a large convoy bound from Jamaica to Bristol, Liverpool, and London. Her old boss, Rear-Admiral John Ford, in the *Europa,* was to command the convoy.

Early in the morning of 29 May the wind was from the east-southeast, fair for the first leg of the trip, and at 4:30 A.M. Admiral Ford made the signal for the convoy to get under way. Ford did not plan to take the convoy through the Windward Passage but intended instead to take a longer route, sailing west from Port Royal along the southern coast of Jamaica, north through the Yucatan Channel around the western tip of Cuba, then east along the northern coast of Cuba, and through the Straits of Florida. Then he planned to turn north to pass along the east coast of Spanish Florida, up the east coast of the United States to the Grand Banks of Newfoundland, then across to England. Spain and England were not at war at this time and were still allies against the French in Saint-Domingue, so Ford didn't have to worry about attacks by the Spanish from Cuba and Florida.

The *Magicienne* had been waiting at a single anchor in the fairway at Port

Royal since early on the twenty-sixth and within half an hour after the admiral's signal was under way and heading out the channel. John Maples, now her first lieutenant, would get a hard but thorough education in how to escort a convoy: captains usually left to their first lieutenants all the tedious hour-to-hour details of shepherding perverse, unruly merchantmen.

The convoy made good speed, and 30 May found it off Black River Bay, well along the southern coast of Jamaica. Here the *Magicienne* and John Maples had their first taste of real convoying. In midmorning one of the convoy ships "made the signal of distress" and fired several guns to get attention. The *Magicienne* sent over a boat with an officer and several men to find out what was wrong and provide help. The distressed vessel proved to be the *Mary* of London, which had "sprung a leak, had eight feet of water in her hold and her pumps choaked with coffee."[2] The *Magicienne* took her in tow and tried to help her crew clear the pumps. Captain Martin cast off the tow later in the afternoon, but the next morning the *Mary* was again signaling distress. There was no answer to her problem, and as she was obviously sinking, the *Magicienne*'s boats towed her ashore near Savanna la Mar—the first casualty of the convoy.

All went quite smoothly for the *Magicienne* over the next few days, then on 6 June she answered another cry of distress from one of the convoy ships. This time Captain Martin came within hail to find out what the problem was, and the merchantman ran on board the frigate, damaging the *Magicienne*'s quarter galleries and breaking her spanker boom. This was a real calamity: the officers' washroom and toilets were in the quarter galleries.

The days stretched endlessly on, the *Magicienne* firing shots at ships in the convoy to get them into their stations, towing stragglers, answering distress signals, chasing strangers that came near the convoy, sending working parties to repair sprung masts. As the convoy got closer to home, some of the faster merchantmen dropped out and went on their own so that by 30 July, when the ships were about halfway across the Atlantic, the convoy was down to 123 ships. The Magiciennes were struggling with another problem too: the mosquitoes of Saint-Domingue had apparently established themselves in the *Magicienne*'s water supply, and the frigate continued to have a high death rate, losing ten men to disease, most probably yellow fever, during the trip across. At one point Captain Martin had some empty water casks sent on board the *General Elliot,* a transport, possibly passing her some infected mosquitoes as well.[3]

Finally, the convoy was in sight of Ireland, and on 9 August off Dungarvon Admiral Ford told the *Magicienne* to part company and take charge of the ships bound up the Irish Channel. With thirty-seven ships under convoy, Captain Martin broke away and headed up toward Liverpool. Two days later he released his dwindling convoy, now down to twenty-nine vessels, and headed south, around Cape Cornwall, for Portsmouth. John Maples would soon be back in England for the first time in three years.

The *Magicienne* arrived in Spithead on 17 August and was immediately back in the punctilio and ceremonial of the Big Navy, the ship's company giving three cheers to the flag of Admiral Sir Peter Parker, as was customary for ships returning from overseas. Five admirals, their flagships, and most of the Channel Fleet battleships were present in port for a visit by the Prince of Wales the next day, and the event itself brought on a great extravagance of twenty-one–gun salutes. After the ceremonies were over, the *Magicienne* moved into Portsmouth harbor, and the ship was stripped for her major refit. When the *Europa* came in at the end of the month, Andrew Thomson came back aboard the *Magicienne* as first lieutenant, and John Maples moved down to being second for the time being. But the convoying voyage was a valuable though hard-earned part of his experience.[4]

The refit lasted nine weeks, and in late October the *Magicienne* left Portsmouth harbor and dropped down to Spithead. She was clean and newly painted inside and out, her masts were overhauled and newly woolded, she had new rigging, her water casks had been made tight, and she had new, clean ballast. On 4 November she was ordered to move out to Saint Helens and join Admiral William Cornwallis, who was going to take his flagship, the *Royal Sovereign,* four other battleships, and a convoy of merchant vessels to Gibraltar.[5] The *Magicienne* and John Maples's old home, the *Hebe,* were added to repeat signals and run errands for the admiral and to whip the merchant ships into line. After the convoy's arrival at Gibraltar, plans called for the *Magicienne* to be released to proceed back to the West Indies and the Jamaica Station.

At this time, on Friday, 13 November 1795, a Captain Moubray replaced Captain Martin. This was truly a day of bad omen for Captain Moubray. His tenure aboard the *Magicienne* was to be short, unlucky, and hair-raising.

As Admiral Cornwallis and his little fleet headed south across the Bay of Biscay, that cradle and nursery of storms, the weather was unusually moderate. It was well into the season for strong westerly gales and bad weather, which usually started in late September and often forced the blockading squadrons off France to fall back to the Devon coast. By 17 November Cornwallis's fleet was some thirty miles off Cape Finisterre at the northwestern corner of Spain. At noon the admiral signaled for Captain Moubray to come aboard the flagship. When he returned an hour later, the *Magicienne* broke off and headed southeast, apparently to pick up some recent local intelligence by stopping random merchant vessels. Relations between Spain and England were quite delicate at this time. Spain had in July 1795 signed the Treaty of Basle with France and dropped out of the war, but although no longer an ally of England, Spain was not yet an active enemy.[6]

The *Magicienne* spoke an American merchant brig bound for Bilbao without learning anything useful and by 5 P.M. on the eighteenth was only nine miles off Cape Finisterre. The weather was moderate and cloudy, with an easterly wind. At around midnight it grew calm, and then the wind shifted to the southwest and freshened. The air was hazy. The frigate began to tack to the northwest to get off what was now a lee shore only a few miles away. The wind became stronger as the morning wore on, and Captain Moubray first brought down the topgallant yards, then furled the mainsail and struck the topgallant masts, telescoping them down along the topmasts.

By noon he had managed to work the ship about thirty miles off the coast, but then the wind increased to a strong gale from the southwest, and the frigate was being hit by squalls as well. The captain took in the fore-topsail and soon also the foresail and set the main-staysail to steady the ship. Soon the early evening darkness and driving rain added to the difficulty of handling sails and conning the ship in the increasingly heavy seas. It was "blowing remarkably strong," the wind a heavy gale, with drizzling rain and haze, and a heavy swell had developed from the southwest. The *Magicienne* rode through the night under fore-staysail, close-reefed main-topsail, and mizzensail, with the ship secured as tightly as possible. Then at 4:30 A.M. the wind abruptly shifted to the northeast, and a heavy, driving rain began. The wind, still a strong gale, was now blowing counter to the heavy seas from the southwest. What had been difficulty now became danger: the ship was "labouring very much" because of the counterswell. Captain Moubray set the foresail and tried to find a course that would ease the strain on the masts and the hull from the violent motion of the ship, but without success.

Shortly after 8 A.M. disaster struck. A rapid chain of events started when the collar gave way on one of the standing bobstays that held down the outer end of the bowsprit. This left the entire strain from the upper masts, transmitted through the foremast and forestays, to be carried by the now-unbraced tip of the bowsprit. This was too much for the bowsprit, and it broke upward at the gammoning, releasing the forestays and leaving the foremast without forward support.

Immediately, the foremast snapped off sixteen feet above the deck and fell aft over the larboard side. In crashing down it stove the launch, crushed the gangway, carried away the iron stanchions of the hammock nettings, and damaged some of the side planking. Within minutes the main-topmast, having lost its forward support when the foremast went, broke off and fell over the starboard quarter, before the crew were able to rig any sort of jury stay to save it. By now they were all—Captain Moubray, Lieutenant Thomson, John Maples, and all hands—driven by terror, working frantically to clear the wreckage, "swifftering in the main rigging and not omitting any other endeavour" to save the mainmast. But because of the violent motion of the ship, all was in vain: the heavy main yard swinging from side to side overstrained the mainmast, and it broke in the partners, at deck level, and went over the starboard quarter. It was immediately followed by the now-unsupported mizzenmast, which carried away twenty feet above the deck.

The *Magicienne* was now completely dismasted. The first order of things was to try to keep her out of the trough of the sea; and their energies focused by the danger of their situation, the crew worked to rig a spare fore-topgallant sail on the stump of the foremast and to cut away the wreckage so that the ship could respond to the sail and her helm to wear her stern around into the wind. But this effort failed, and the frigate was soon rolling heavily in the trough, the storm blowing "remarkably severe," with violent squalls and heavy rain.

They were now truly in peril. If the ship could not be gotten out of the trough and on an easier course, her brutal rolling and twisting motion would soon make her planks slip and grind against one another—which would destroy the caulking and open her seams. She would then quickly fill with water, the weight of her guns and ballast would take her under, and she would sink like a stone, very likely taking all hands with her.

By now, because of the earlier wind shift to the northeast, there was a strong cross-swell running and making the sea confused. Captain Moubray next tried to bring the ship's head into the wind. He lowered the jury sail from the fore-mast stump, "put the helm a-lee," and hoisted a fore-topmast staysail fore-and-aft on the stub of the mizzenmast. This was finally successful; and weather-cocked, with her head into the wind, the *Magicienne* began to ride a little more easily. Moubray now had the situation under at least tenuous control and felt secure enough to send most of the hands, exhausted by the terrible efforts of the last hours, below to get some rest. Those on deck worked at clearing away the wreckage and better securing the boats and the spare booms and other spars: these would soon be needed to make the jury rig.

As the Magiciennes labored in the middle of that difficult night they had a near-supernatural experience, an event to terrify the superstitious: a strange ship came scudding eerily out of the storm, riding ahead of the gale like a spectral apparition. The ship and her phantom crew passed them close aboard, then quickly disappeared again into the murky darkness without speaking them or offering help.

As the first daylight made effective work possible, all hands were called to the task of putting together a jury rig of masts and sails that would enable the ship to get into port. The weather was still "strong gales and squally." It must have seemed incredible to John Maples and the other Magiciennes that only twenty hours had passed since their troubles had started.

The first job now was to get out the spare masts, booms, and other spars stored above the waist along the centerline between the main- and mizzen-masts. The wreckage of the launch, the largest boat, smashed beyond repair by the fall of the foremast, was on top of the boom stowage. So the crew broke it up to get at the spars underneath. The boatswain's gang got out spars to lash together to form a set of sheers, an A-frame arrangement to act as a crane, to lift the jury foremast into position alongside the old stump. The carpenter's crew worked at fitting out jury fore- and mainmasts. Another group of hands, using spare shroud hawser from the boatswain's stores, put together the rigging for the jury masts. Moubray had decided to set up jury foremast and fore-top-mast, and mainmast and main-topmast, and to use the remaining twenty-foot stump of the mizzen as it stood.

At noon the weather briefly moderated, although the ship was still laboring heavily, and she urgently needed to get on a course that would be easier on her. Moubray rigged the sheers at the foremast stump and set the fore-topgallant sail on them. With this he was able to wear the ship and get the wind sharp on her larboard quarter. Then he set one of the royal sails on the stump of the mizzen and was able to scud along on a more comfortable heading.

The weather again picked up to "strong gales and squalls," but by now the Magiciennes were slowly getting more able to cope with it. By midafternoon they had stepped the jury foremast alongside the old stump and were rigging it. By evening they were able to take down the sheers and set sails on the foremast. By early morning the weather had eased considerably. At daylight all hands were called, and the sheers set up to hoist and step the jury mainmast. By noon the weather could be described as "pleasant," although there was a long swell from the north. The crew spent the day in getting more yards and sails on the jury foremast, getting the rigging on the jury mainmast, getting up a jury main-topmast, and placing a spare jibboom as a jury bowsprit. Moubray set the spare main-topsail as a mainsail and other of the smaller sails in proportion.

Thanks to the skill and effort of them all, the *Magicienne* had been saved from the worst, and some of her maneuverability had been restored. But because of the limitations of her jury rig, she could not effectively sail close to the wind. By about seventy-two hours after the accident Moubray felt sufficiently recovered to begin to consider what port he should head for. The closest port where major repairs would be available was Lisbon, 120 miles to the south. Plymouth, the closest English port, was about 640 miles to the north. But the wind was from the southwest, and the *Magicienne* with her jury rig couldn't sail into it to make for Lisbon, so there was little choice. Captain Moubray headed north for England, probably with much reluctance. He was in a vulnerable condition: another severe storm might quickly finish off the ship, or any French warship of significant size could easily capture her.

By noon on 23 November the wind had picked up to a fresh gale, there were squalls in the area, and it looked as if the *Magicienne* might be in for another serious storm. Moubray stowed the spare booms again and secured the boats and got as ready as he could for more bad weather. Then that evening he had the only good luck of this difficult cruise: the wind shifted to the north and settled down to strong, steady breezes. Moubray wore ship and headed south for Lisbon.

The frigate had a relatively easy forty-eight–hour run down to Lisbon, and early afternoon of the twenty-fifth found her crossing the bar and heading into the River Tagus. She moored off the naval arsenal and spent the next three months, from 26 November 1795 until 3 March 1796, in repairing the damage from the storm.[7]

The bad luck of Friday the thirteenth was not quite through with poor Captain Moubray. The *Magicienne*'s refit was practically completed in early February when on a wet, windy day with a strong ebb tide and the Tagus swollen from rain, a Spanish frigate, poorly moored upstream, dragged her anchors and came down broadside against the bow of the *Magicienne,* carrying away her new bowsprit. Insult was added to injury the next day: although the *Magicienne* had shifted position on her mooring, the Spaniard got loose again and slammed against the Britisher's starboard side, staving in her cutter and sinking a shore boat alongside that was carrying an expensive new hawser.[8] This time Captain Moubray got under way and moored again at a safe distance from danger.

When the refit in Lisbon was finally over, the *Magicienne* was ordered to take a small convoy of twenty-two merchant vessels to England and arrived in Spithead on 16 March. Six days later Captain Moubray was replaced. The reasons are not clear. Whether the storm had been too much for him (not likely), whether the Admiralty found fault with his handling of the ship (a good possibility), or whether his health became bad, is unknown. He simply disappears from history.

Moubray's replacement was Captain William Henry Ricketts, who was entirely another breed of cat. Ricketts had enormous interest. His grandfather was a prominent Jamaica landowner, his sister's husband would shortly become the Admiral the Earl of Northesk, Captain Ricketts himself was married to the sister of the Earl of Cavan, and, best of all, he was the nephew of Admiral Sir John Jervis. Admiral Jervis was, even in 1796, one of the most powerful officers in the navy and on his way to much greater things: less than a year later, on Saint Valentine's Day in 1797 off Cape Saint Vincent on the coast of Portugal, John Jervis's young subordinate, Commodore Horatio Nelson, won a victory for him that resulted in Jervis's being made the Earl of St. Vincent and later First Lord of the Admiralty. Jervis had no children, and he later selected Captain Ricketts, his sister's child and John Jervis's favorite nephew, to take his name and be his heir.[9]

Among his social equals in polite society, Henry Ricketts had the reputation of being "generous and urbane," well-mannered and "polished," although "at times . . . somewhat whimsical." He was not handsome. His eyes were too big for his face, and he had a large, beaked nose that gave him the appearance of an alert, predatory bird. His portrait suggests that he was slender and perhaps also small in stature. But Henry Ricketts was also a remarkably capable young frigate captain and was lucky as well as skillful.

Like his famous uncle, Henry Ricketts was the strictest of disciplinarians. He used the cat freely during his twenty-three months in command of the *Magicienne,* one of his best days being 19 October 1796, when he had nine marines punished with thirty lashes each. John Maples apparently took a firm lesson from this example: when he got his own commands he hardly used the lash at all.[10]

In particular, Captain Ricketts was a bear about alcohol abuse by the ship's company. Of the 118 floggings that he handed out during his time aboard the *Magicienne,* 46, or 39 percent, were for drunkenness. A good many of the other offenses that he punished, such as fighting, disrespect to a superior officer, and neglect of duty, were probably related to alcohol in some part.

It is no surprise that many of those British sailors of the late eighteenth and early nineteenth centuries had alcohol-dependency problems. They were crowded together in small ships under the hard conditions prevailing in the British Navy of those years and given the equivalent in rum or brandy of about two stiff whiskeys-and-water on an empty stomach every day before their noon meal, and then the same again in the afternoon, year after year, as their only pleasant experiences of the day.

But even with the acknowledgment that the way grog was used created fleetwide problems, it seems clear from the surviving journals that the *Magicienne* had more than a normal level of alcohol-related troubles. Shortly after leaving Spithead in late May 1796, the men were hoisting a cask of brandy out of the hold for the crew's grog when the tackle gave way; the cask dropped back into the hold, where it shattered and spilled its precious contents.[11] Now of all the operations carried out in the daily running of a ship, the one that would normally be the most painstakingly handled was getting up the liquor for the grog. Could it be that some of the crew had earlier found a way to tap that cask, a little at a time, and that the cask was really drawn well down and no longer contained its full sixty-six gallons? Once the cask was brought on deck and under the supervision of an officer, the shortage would quickly be discovered, and investigation and punishment would follow. Was there a conspiracy among the crew to drop and smash that cask to conceal such a theft? There is no way to know, but when this incident is connected with later events, the possibility becomes stronger.[12]

After Captain Ricketts took command at Spithead on 22 March 1796, the *Magicienne* operated off the Atlantic coast of France for several weeks, coming back to the Portsmouth area in early May to refit, to be recaulked, and to take on provisions for six months for her return to the West Indies. Andrew Thomson, the senior lieutenant, left the ship, this time for good, and John Maples became, briefly, the first lieutenant. But then on 18 May Captain Ricketts brought aboard a cousin, Lieutenant Tristram Robert Ricketts, who was senior to John Maples. Maples was pushed back to second. But there were better days ahead for John Maples and the *Magicienne*.

The Admiralty rarely neglected the chance to get more work out of its ships, especially the frigates, and the *Magicienne,* on her way back to the West Indies, was ordered as part of a small squadron to take a convoy to Gibraltar. Shortly after he delivered the convoy, Captain Ricketts's luck began to show. He had been notified that a French cutter had captured an English merchant brig and a Portuguese schooner in the area. Now two strange sail were sighted in the distance. The wind was calm, so Ricketts ordered the boats hoisted out and sent, manned and armed, in pursuit of the strangers. Sure enough, they were the French prizes. The Magiciennes boarded and took them, making prisoners of the fourteen Frenchmen in the prize crews, and sent the vessels into Gibraltar for prize-court adjudication.[13] These were not remarkably valuable prizes, but they were the first for the *Magicienne* in a long time, and they were a foretaste of the exciting and profitable days to come.

Finally, on 30 July, Ricketts was released and ordered to head for Jamaica. The frigate had an uneventful passage until 9 August when in midocean, about halfway between the bulge of Africa and Barbados, the early morning light revealed a ship ahead to the west. The *Magicienne* chased and overtook her, and Captain Ricketts had her boarded early that afternoon. She proved to be a Spanish ship from Cadiz, bound for Vera Cruz in Mexico. Relations between England and Spain were touchy in the fall of 1796—Spain would declare war on the sixth of October—and Captain Ricketts had been told in Gibraltar to detain and send in any Spanish vessels showing any suspicious features. So when the boarding party searched her and found "sealed papers which appeared to be of consequence," this was enough for Captain Ricketts. He ordered forty-nine men of her Spanish crew taken out of her and brought to the *Magicienne* as prisoners, then sent John Maples with ten men and two boys on board her with orders to make the best of his way to Jamaica.[14]

No record survives to describe John Maples's trip in the Spaniard. It must have been unrelenting hard work for the small British prize crew, although probably a few of the Spanish crew had been left on board to help. The *Magicienne* went on her separate way and after a stop at Barbados sailed on down to Saint-Domingue, finally arriving at Cap Saint-Nicolas Môle on 9 September. John Maples and his men delivered the Spanish ship to Port Royal, Jamaica, and then rejoined the *Magicienne* at the Môle on 15 October 1796.[15] It was John Maples's first experience of an independent command, and he apparently handled it well.

CHAPTER THIRTEEN

Scourge of the Mona Passage

THE *MAGICIENNE* AND JOHN MAPLES faced an entirely new situation when they returned to the Jamaica Station in late 1796. England was now fighting three of the four European nations that had colonies in the western Caribbean: France, Spain, and Holland were arrayed against Britain; and Saint-Domingue, Santo Domingo, Cuba, Porto Rico, and the adjacent Spanish mainland areas in South America, Florida, and Mexico were all now enemy territory. Only Denmark, owners of the Virgin Islands, remained neutral. The Dutch and French colonies in the Lesser Antilles, however, were the problem of the British admiral on the Leeward Islands Station, not of the commander in chief at Jamaica.

This situation created some problems for the admiral commanding the Jamaica Station: the Spanish now could be expected to cooperate ashore with the French in Saint-Domingue, convoys to England no longer could safely take the easy route around Cuba, there was more coastline to patrol, and the depredations of Spanish privateers would be added to those of the French. But the increased opportunities for prize money took most of the sting out of the changed order of things for the individuals in line for these juicy rewards.

The first in this line was, of course, the admiral, "The Commander-in-Chief of His Majesty's Ships and Vessels employed at and about Jamaica," who received, right off the top, one-eighth of the value of all prizes taken on the Jamaica Station. Late in 1796 a new officer arrived to take this job: Vice-Admiral (of the Red

Squadron) Sir Hyde Parker, Knight. In his younger years he had shown a good deal of enterprise and daring and had won his knighthood in action during the American Revolutionary War. But his fire had cooled over time, and by 1796 he was, at fifty-seven years of age, a conservative officer who rarely took chances and saw problems where he should have seen opportunities. The command at Jamaica, however, did not call for a dashing young sea admiral but rather for a good administrator, one who could manage resources. The job of the admiral at Jamaica was to get the loaded, outgoing merchantmen assembled into convoys; get the convoys and their escorts off on time; and keep his frigates, sloops, and brigs efficiently patrolling at the key choke points in the area to spot hostile warships and to capture enemy merchantmen and neutrals carrying enemy cargoes. He also had to stay one jump ahead of the bureaucrats back in the Admiralty and at the Navy Board. Hyde Parker was passably good at all these things. But he was not a particularly attractive person. He was the son of an austere, sour, and humorless admiral whose nickname was "Old Vinegar," and he seems to have been a chip from the same block.[1] He was a harsh disciplinarian and had little sense of justice, particularly when it came to fair trials and equitable punishment for sailors or lower-ranked officers. He kept grudges: once someone got in his bad books, it was difficult to get out. Also, he had little sense of fairness in his treatment of the captains and ships in his command. He played favorites, and those he favored got good assignments with opportunities for prizes and wealth. Those out of favor got to run convoys or support the army ashore.

On the Jamaica Station his favorites were three sharp young frigate captains: Henry Ricketts of the *Magicienne,* Hugh Pigot of the *Success* and later the *Hermione,* and Robert Otway of the *Mermaid* and later the *Ceres.*[2] All three were officers with important connections and much interest.

Ricketts's influence through Admiral John Jervis has already been mentioned. Hugh Pigot was the son of an admiral and the nephew of a prominent general and of a Member of Parliament, plus he had connections with the Staffords, one of the great landowning families. Robert Otway was the son of a rich Irish landowner. Ricketts was the oldest, thirty-two in late 1796, and the most senior in rank. Pigot was next oldest at twenty-six and next senior. Otway was only twenty-four but became the most successful of the three, making more than two hundred captures during his six years in the West Indies. In his portrait he appears to be a thoughtful, sensitive man, looking rather like the late Leslie Howard, the actor.[3]

In contrast to these three young captains, John Maples, who was twenty-six at this time and with comparable experience, but lacking the level of influence held by any of the three, was still a lieutenant and would remain so for many years to come. Maples and Otway had been shipmates on the *Blonde,* John

Maples as master's mate and Otway as a midshipman. But Otway was promoted into a lieutenant's billet in August 1793, while Maples waited until May 1794 for his advancement to lieutenant. Then Otway's interest really showed itself: he was made a commander in 1794 and in October 1795 was given the all-important promotion to post-captain and command of the frigate *Mermaid*. From then on he had relatively smooth sailing. However, all three of these young captains—Ricketts, Pigot, and Otway—were to meet violent or tragic ends.

That these young captains were popular with Sir Hyde Parker is not surprising: all three were highly aggressive and capable skippers, and their success at capturing prizes made them and Sir Hyde rich.

The *Magicienne* was experiencing problems with morale and discipline in the fall of 1796. A week after John Maples was sent aboard the Spanish ship as prizemaster in early August, Ricketts ordered punishment for three sailors and five marines for neglect of duty, all on one day, giving them twelve lashes each. Other punishment followed every few days, including flogging two sailors and having two marines "run the gantlet," a punishment usually reserved for thieves or incorrigibles.[4] On 11 September six men were flogged with twelve to thirty-six lashes for "neglect of duty" and "drunkenness," and on the fifteenth, three more with twenty-four lashes each. More punishment followed on the twenty-seventh and on 12 October.

Then on 19 October, just a few days after John Maples had returned to the ship, Ricketts ordered a mass punishment of the *Magicienne's* marines, giving nine of them thirty lashes each for "neglect of duty at their posts."[5] On the following day the ship received sixteen new marines but apparently didn't transfer off the offenders. One marine, the unfortunate George Jackson, was a particular target of the captain's wrath. Between August 1796 and January 1797 he received, at various times, 150 lashes, plus having to run the gauntlet.

These problems may have been strictly specific to the *Magicienne,* but they could have also contained an element of the widely based discontent that was then current among the crews of the British Navy. Long-festering navywide problems were coming to a head in late 1796 and 1797: Sailors' pay, always much lower than pay on merchant ships, had not been raised for more than a hundred years—but the army and militia had recently received more money, and that rankled the sailors and aggravated the problem. The food served in the navy was not only badly prepared, unhealthy, and usually disgusting, but was of often execrable quality when delivered to the navy because of cheating contractors and was always issued in short quantity because of the rules allowing the purser to take part of it for his profit. On most ships, men served years of hard service without being allowed to go ashore on liberty because the officers knew that they would desert if given the slightest opportunity. On some ships, cruel and inconsistent discipline by captains and officers who had little but contempt for the men under them made for almost unbearable living and working conditions. Then also, the makeup of most crews had recently changed slightly—not much, but enough to create problems: The cause was that with wartime expansion some less docile men, usually not career seafarers, had been caught up in the net of impressment or sent to the navy by the courts as an alternative to other punishment. These newcomers formed nuclei of discontent on many ships.

These things taken together culminated in two fleet mutinies in England. The first was a genuinely patriotic mutiny at Spithead, presenting the Admiralty with real grievances and asking for modest, fair redress. But the second mutiny, at the Nore fleet anchorage, had a more political context and finally had to be put down with some force, and the principal mutineer, Richard Parker, was hanged, as were some thirty more of the ringleaders. Hundreds more were flogged or transported.

Besides the fleet mutinies there were three ship mutinies in the West Indies, as well as some in other locations. The consciousness of the widely shared discontent tended to sharpen the focus of problems on board individual ships, pushing them closer to open revolt than would have otherwise been the case. Examining the punishment given on board the *Magicienne* in late 1796 and 1797 gives the feeling that Captain Ricketts was probably skirting the edge of real trouble.

The *Magicienne*'s active schedule and Captain Ricketts's skill and luck with prizes, plus his apparent concern for the health and feeding of his men, may well have been what kept the lid on any violence. In late October the frigate was ordered out to cruise off the southern coast of Saint-Domingue, together with the *Quebec,* another thirty-two–gun frigate, and the sixteen-gun brig *Drake.* Ricketts was the commodore, in command of this little squadron. It got under way from the Môle on the twenty-fourth, and on the twenty-seventh off Cap Dame Marie the captains, officers, and crews signed a prize-sharing agreement for the cruise. The intent was for the ships to cruise separately most of the time, rather than as a squadron, but to share the profits of whatever they caught.[6]

The *Magicienne* rounded the southern peninsula, cruising eastward along its southern coast, and in midafternoon on 2 November off Altavela Rock she came across a French brig flying the tricolor and a white flag of truce identifying her as a cartel vessel with the right of free passage. Ricketts sent John Maples and a boarding party over to examine her anyway. She was the *Cerf Volant,* bound from Aux Cayes to France, and was carrying several "passengers of consequence," delegates from the South Province to the National Assembly. But also on board were a British midshipman and six British seamen, prisoners of war captured several months earlier from H.M. Ship *Hindostan.*[7] They were undoubtedly delighted to see John Maples and his men.

It was now late in the day, and as darkness was coming on, the *Magicienne* detained the French brig overnight. In the morning Ricketts sent over the first lieutenant and a party of men to search her hold. After several hours the search party found a tin box with "voluminous" dispatches from the mulatto General André Rigaud, who controlled the South Province, to the Directory in France. This, as well as the presence aboard of the British prisoners, violated the *Cerf Volant*'s cartel status, and she was clearly a fair prize. And a very nice one she turned out to be: further search of the hold turned up a box marked "Claret," which actually contained seven tin boxes of money probably being taken by the delegates to the relative security of France for safekeeping. Hyde Parker later had the *Cerf Volant* surveyed by the officers of the yard at Port Royal and purchased into the navy—which meant that the captors would receive a top price for her.[8]

Ricketts didn't waste any time in standing by the *Cerf Volant*. Leaving John Maples and the search party aboard her, the *Magicienne* went off in chase of a strange sail. She was an American from Baltimore, one of the many trading with the parts of Saint-Domingue held by Toussaint Louverture at that time, and Ricketts let her go. As he was leaving her the lookouts saw another stranger, and late in the afternoon the *Magicienne* captured a Spanish sloop that was coasting from Santo Domingo to Jaquemel, Saint-Domingue.

Captain Ricketts was not one to let all this action interfere with the internal running of the ship, and while he was waiting for the *Cerf Volant* to be searched the ship's company was called to witness punishment, and three men were flogged—one John Brown, a seaman, with a terrible number of lashes, forty-eight, for "neglect of duty and insolence to his superior officer," and two others with twenty-four for "drunkenness."[9]

The day after capturing the Spaniard, Ricketts stopped a passing vessel loaded with livestock for Jamaica and bought five bullocks from her to provide fresh meat for the squadron, then followed that act of consideration for the welfare of the crew by giving two men a dozen each of the cat for "neglect of duty." The next day was Sunday and was quiet except for mustering the ship's company, reading the Articles of War, and exercising the crew at small arms.

The next morning the tempo picked up again. The *Magicienne* chased and captured a Spanish schooner, and while Ricketts was dealing with her, another schooner appeared. The wind had died away, and he couldn't get up to her, so Ricketts sent the boats, manned and armed, to catch her. She proved to be Spanish, loaded with livestock, bound from "the Main to Santo Domingo," and the boats brought her back to the *Magicienne*. At about this time the lookouts spotted some vessels in "a small nook near Port St. Louis," and the boats, still in the water, manned and armed, were sent in to see if they could bring the vessels out. The boats soon came back with a French coaster, loaded with wine and other cargo, no doubt a welcome haul. That was enough for one day, but in the morning the captain put the crew to work and shifted the cargo of the small prizes into the largest one, put a three-man prize crew aboard her, and sent her off for Jamaica.[10]

A few days later, on the fourteenth, Ricketts sent the boats of the *Magicienne* and *Quebec* in to the coast on another cutting-out foray. They brought back a French sloop loaded with fifty-six hogs and took out twenty of them to give the ship's company the welcome rarity of a few meals of fresh pork. While all hands were hungrily contemplating the pigs, another sail came in sight, and the *Magicienne* went after it. She was an American schooner, and the boarding party "found her suspicious." That was enough for Captain Ricketts, and he put a midshipman and four men aboard her and sent her to Jamaica for judgment by the prize court. This course of action could be risky: if the prize court found her innocent, and they sometimes did, the captors would be liable for demurrage and any damage to the vessel and cargo.[11] Early the next morning the *Magicienne* caught a French schooner, took her crew out as prisoners, and sent her too with a midshipman and four men into Jamaica.

By this time the frigate was becoming short-handed from sending off prize crews. But Captain Ricketts's luck held, and the *Drake* rejoined the *Magicienne* and *Quebec,* bringing twenty-six seamen recovered from the French in a prisoner exchange. He sent eleven of them to the *Quebec* along with some French prisoners who were still aboard and kept the other fifteen aboard the *Magicienne* to add to the crew.

Sandwiched in with all this activity, Captain Ricketts found time to carry out a harsh schedule of punishment: between 10 and 15 November three men were given thirty-six lashes each for "insolence," "disobedience," and "neglect of duty," and one seaman received forty-eight lashes for "drunkenness and striking his superior officer."[12] But the crew was too busy to have much time to think of mutiny and were probably amazed at Ricketts's skill and luck at getting prizes.

Within a few days there was another display of Ricketts's luck. Off Jaquemel, just after noon on the seventeenth, he fired a couple of shots to bring to a schooner flying American colors. She turned out to be the *Romp* and had been detained a few days earlier by H.M.S. *Rattler.* The *Rattler* had found the American carrying a cargo of naval stores for the French and had put a lieutenant and some seamen aboard and sent her for Jamaica. The Americans managed to retake the ship from the British prize crew, then locked them in the hold and went into Aux Cayes, where they turned the lieutenant and some of the seamen over to General Rigaud's forces. When the *Magicienne* took the *Romp,* two of the Rattlers were still aboard, whether as captives or volunteers is not clear. The American owner was with the vessel, and Ricketts took him, the captain, and the crew out of her but decided to keep her in company for the time being, rather than sending her to Jamaica. After removing the American crew, the Magiciennes gave the *Romp* a search and found a chest and a trunk with money: $2,632.50, plus 259 pieces of eight—not a large, but a very nice, windfall.[13]

The *Magicienne* was getting to be a well-known presence along the southern coast of Saint-Domingue. Sitting a few miles off Jaquemel, at daybreak, the morning after sending away the *Romp,* the lookouts saw a sail inshore coming out toward them. As it got closer they found that it was a French schooner showing a flag of truce. It had come out of Aux Cayes, about sixty miles west along the coast, and was carrying dispatches from General Rigaud to Captain Ricketts, asking for an exchange of prisoners. The *Magicienne* sent over the nine French prisoners who were still on board and sent the schooner into Jaquemel, where Ricketts knew that some British prisoners were being held. Then he settled down to wait for her return. With nothing in sight to chase, and an empty afternoon ahead, Ricketts kept the ship's company busy with drills, "exercising the great guns."[14]

He was still waiting off Jaquemel the next day, in calm weather, when at dusk in the evening the lookouts saw a small vessel to the west and seaward. The captain sent the boats, manned and armed, after her. After a long wait, the boats returned at 2 A.M. with their quarry, a Spanish schooner, bound from Cuba to Spanish Santo Domingo. Later in the day the French cartel schooner came out from Jaquemel and sent over nine English prisoners in exchange. Then with H.M.S. *Drake,* the *Romp,* and the Spanish schooner in company, the *Magicienne* moved eastward along the coast to the watering place at Anse-à-Pitre, a bay where a little river came down from the mountains some miles east of Jaquemel. Anchoring close in, Ricketts sent ashore a party of men to fill the water casks and cut wood for the galley stove.

While working parties spent the next three days in filling the casks, rafting them off to the ship, and cutting wood, several of the officers went ashore to "divert [themselves] with some pleasant walks, shooting, etc." This seems incongruous because the mood and temper aboard was apparently still edgy and tense: eight men deserted from the wood-cutting party and headed into the countryside. Four of these had been flogged in the past for various offenses and presumably had more than the usual reasons to want to get away, but the other four seem to have had clean records. That they would desert ashore in Saint-Domingue at all indicates a good deal of desperation. The southern part of Saint-Domingue was at that time filled with roving bands of guerrillas—black, mulatto, and white—each racial group eager to kill anyone of the others. White British sailors ran a high risk of murder, while black sailors were likely to be murdered or enslaved. Even though the loss of eight men was serious,

Ricketts apparently made no effort to catch them; perhaps the level of discontent aboard was high enough that he was willing to get rid of a few who were obviously eager to escape.

Captain Ricketts was, at this time, trying to raise the morale aboard by such small actions as he could take to improve the food served to the ship's company. A series of journal entries, unusual in that they state what was served to the crew, note on the morning of 24 November, "Served fish to the people"; two days later, "Served goats flesh to the ship's company"; and on the twenty-seventh, "Bought 14 bullocks" to be shared among the squadron and then, "Served fresh beef to the ship's company." Also, on the twenty-eighth Ricketts had the money found aboard the *Cerf Volant* distributed to the squadron. But on the same day all hands were called to witness the punishment of George Jackson, the marine, who received the incredible number of sixty lashes. His offense this time had been "sleeping at his post, insolence, contempt and disobedience of orders to the Captain."[15] The post at which he had been sleeping was probably just outside Captain Ricketts's cabin, and the draconian penalty might well have reflected Ricketts's fear of being left unguarded at a time when his crew was ripe for mutiny.

George Jackson was either incorrigible or deep in the captain's bad books for some other reason. He had been flogged and made to run the gauntlet a little over two months before and on 19 October had been given thirty lashes for "neglect of duty at his post." His back must have still been raw, unhealed and covered with scabs from that flogging, when he received the sixty. How he survived the experience is difficult to understand.

The next morning the ships were under way again, with the *Quebec* and four prizes in sight. The *Magicienne* chased a sloop that ran into a little bay called Mary Gut, where she went for protection under a two-gun mud fort. Never lacking courage when a prize was involved, Ricketts went in after her in five and one-half fathoms over a rocky bottom but, even after firing several broadsides at her, was unable to get her out—one of the *Magicienne*'s few failures. The next day was better: at first light there were a brig and a schooner in sight. The cutter was sent after the brig, which was closer by, while the *Magicienne* made sail after the schooner. The schooner turned out to be the *Vigilant,* a Dane carrying a French cargo. The captain sent a mate and four men over to take charge of her and took out eight prisoners. The area continued to be ripe with prizes. Just before dark the next evening, 3 December, the Magiciennes took a large Dutch sloop loaded with dry goods and headed for Jaquemel from Curaçao. Ricketts sent some hands to take charge of her and took out sixteen prisoners.[16]

The rest of Ricketts's little squadron had done well too. The *Drake* showed up with an American brig, the *Punch,* which had been found to be carrying a "valuable French cargo." The *Quebec* captured a really useful prize, a French warship, the corvette *African Queen,* which had been hanging off to the west of the British squadron to pick off such prizes as were sent toward Jamaica or strayed too far from the protection of the frigates. She had, a day or two earlier, captured and sunk the *Magicienne*'s prize, the coasting sloop loaded with wine, earlier sent to Jamaica. When the *Quebec* captured the *African Queen,* the three Magiciennes of the prize crew were retrieved.[17]

The reassembled squadron spent a day to organize the prizes, which were then sent off to Jamaica and the prize court under the care of the *Quebec;* then the *Magicienne* and *Drake* headed back to Cap Saint-Nicolas Môle. Soon after the *Quebec* left, the *Magicienne* captured a Spanish sloop, which was taken in tow. But she was apparently leaking, and when she got "too heavy," Ricketts sank her.[18]

The *Magicienne* arrived back at the Môle on 10 December and found that there had been several changes during her absence. Sir Hyde Parker had arrived at the Môle, bringing four line-of-battleships with him, and had picked up the ships lying there and gone with all of them on a cruise off the northern coast of Saint-Domingue. Also, there was a forty-four–gun frigate newly arrived from England, the *Regulus,* Captain William Carthew.

The admiral had left orders for the *Magicienne* to join him, so Ricketts loaded water and provisions, sent the French prisoners to the prison ship, sent a few sick men to the hospital, and was under way again two days later. There followed a not very productive period, with Sir Hyde and his fleet rushing up and down the northern coast of Saint-Domingue without achieving much in the way of tangible results. This was not what the Magiciennes were used to, and it certainly wasn't Ricketts's cup of tea—he liked the freedom and profit of cruising after prizes on his own. While the *Magicienne* was with the fleet, the first lieutenant, Tristram Ricketts, was promoted into Sir Hyde's flagship and replaced by a Lieutenant Trelawney. John Maples was junior to him and had to wait yet a few more months before working his way back up to being first again.[19]

The flogging continued to go on, with three seamen punished with a dozen on 30 December and two on 5 January, all for "neglect of duty." The next day something unusual happened: James Leggatt, a sailmaker—a senior petty officer—was given thirty-six lashes for "insolence." Petty officers were rarely flogged in the British Navy. For most offenses—and it was not often that a petty officer got into trouble—they were disrated and reduced to seamen. On board the *Magicienne* under Captain Ricketts, two boatswain's mates and the ship's cook were flogged at different times, in addition to Sailmaker Leggatt.[20]

On 5 January 1797 the *Magicienne* was released to go cruise on her own off the western end of Porto Rico, then back along the southern coast of Saint-

Domingue. These were both very productive areas, and Ricketts crowded on all sail and headed east, leaving Sir Hyde and the fleet behind.

By the tenth the *Magicienne* was in the Mona Passage. Just before noon with a fresh breeze blowing, the lookouts sighted a large schooner downwind, and Ricketts bore up to go after her. After a short chase he caught up with her and fired a shot at her. She was the French privateer schooner *La Fortune,* of eight guns and seventy-four men, on a cruise out of Curaçao. Captain Ricketts took the prisoners out of her, put a small prize crew aboard, and told her to stay in company.[21] In the night the lookouts saw another schooner to leeward, and Ricketts took off in chase of her. But at first light, about 4 A.M., the lookouts saw that there was also a ship-rigged vessel ahead, so the Magiciennes quickly picked off the schooner, took out her crew, put a small prize crew aboard, and then shifted quarry and went after the ship.

This new chase turned away and made all sail, but the *Magicienne,* now in full pursuit, soon overhauled her and at 7 A.M. began to fire at her with the bow guns. The chase now hoisted French colors, but struck them within the hour and surrendered, and the *Magicienne* took possession of her. She was the *Brutus,* a French privateer—and a large one—of 20 guns and 127 men.

It took some time to shift the prisoners across, and at that point Ricketts had more than two hundred prisoners aboard. As the *Magicienne's* ship's company was probably down to 150 or thereabouts, the British were well outnumbered. To guard against a prisoner uprising, Captain Ricketts took the highly unusual step of issuing side arms to the crew. This was almost never done and was considered to be highly risky. In navies of that day, and especially the British Navy, only the marines normally had access to arms, and their main job was to keep the crew in line and prevent any thoughts of mutiny. Other weapons—muskets, pistols, cutlasses, and tomahawks—were kept strictly locked up and out of the hands of the sailors. So Ricketts's action was a significant gamble, especially in 1797, the "year of mutinies."[22] But with the excitement of the action and the anticipation of prize money, the Magiciennes were probably reasonably content and stable just then.

The last chase had taken the frigate well to the west along the southern coast of Spanish Santo Domingo. Things had barely settled down aboard when the lookouts saw another schooner to the west. After chasing her all afternoon and all night, the *Magicienne* caught up to her at a little after four in the morning and fired several shots at her. She came to, and the *Magicienne* took her over. She proved to be the *Poisson Volant,* a Dutch privateer from Curaçao, mounting fifteen carriage guns and carrying eighty men. As had become routine, Ricketts put a prize crew aboard her and took the prisoners into the *Magicienne,* where there were now close to three hundred: French, Spanish, Dutch, and whatever—a seagoing Tower of Babel. The *Magicienne's* ship's company, reduced a few more because of the prize crew sent in this latest capture, was in a fair way to be overwhelmed by their captives if the situation should turn mean. To even the odds somewhat, Ricketts ordered one hundred of the prisoners put in the hold and locked down. Most of the rest were probably herded into the forecastle area, and a couple of the quarterdeck guns, loaded with grape, trained on them.[23]

It now became urgent to get into a port where Ricketts could profitably get rid of the captives before, locustlike, they ate up all the stores aboard. So with his prizes, a ship and two schooners, in company, he headed for San Domingo city. Arriving off the port on the fourteenth, Captain Ricketts hove to and sent John Maples in the cutter with a flag of truce to try to arrange an exchange of prisoners.

Maples and the cutter were barely away when a French schooner was sighted a few miles east along the coast from the *Magicienne,* and off she went in chase. The schooner ran into a bay near Cape Caucedo and anchored in six fathoms of water, probably feeling that she was in shallow enough water to be safe. But the *Magicienne* went in after her, ran alongside her, boarded her, and brought her out. She was a French privateer, of "two guns, six swivels and 50 men." By this time Ricketts must have felt that his ship had reached the breaking point for prisoners. So he took this latest capture back to San Domingo and, after picking up John Maples and the cutter and finding that his exchange mission had been successful, set the new prize up as a flag of truce, put 173 Frenchmen aboard (in addition to the 50 of her crew, who had apparently been left on board), and sent her in. Soon a flag of truce came out of the port with the French prisoner agent aboard, and agreement was reached to release the rest of the prisoners, 116 mixed French, Spanish, and Dutch, in exchange for British prisoners to be picked up at Jaquemel.[24] It had been a very successful, even exciting, week.

Much of the *Magicienne's* water had by now been used up: 300 prisoners in addition to the crew of about 170 had put a heavy drain on the supply of cooking and drinking water. So as the frigate headed west along the coast to retrieve the British prisoners at Jaquemel, her prizes in company, she stopped at the watering place at Anse-à-Pitre. This time Ricketts took no chance with further desertions, and armed marines guarded the watering party. During this brief breathing space, Ricketts sent the three prizes off to Jamaica, two of them, the *Brutus* and *Poisson Volant,* to be sold after condemnation by the prize court. *La Fortune,* the big schooner privateer, he manned with a larger crew, planning to make her the *Magicienne's* tender as soon as she returned from Jamaica, because she would be capable of running errands and capturing smaller vessels, particularly upwind, that the *Magicienne* herself was unable to catch.[25]

Also, as was done with terrible frequency in Captain Ricketts's *Magicienne,* he found time on 20 January to call all hands to witness punishment. Both victims were repeat offenders. Joseph King, a seaman, received twelve lashes. He had been punished with a dozen less than three weeks before. The other was the unfortunate George Jackson, who was given the appalling number of forty-eight lashes on his raw, unhealed back, just three weeks and a day after being punished with sixty. His offense this time was "insolence, drunkenness and striking his superior."[26]

It is difficult to understand why Captain Ricketts kept Jackson on board. If he was as incorrigible as the record makes him appear, it would have been wise to simply put him ashore or trade him to another ship after his second or third offense. Men were hard to get at that time in the West Indies, but the damage to the relations between the captain and his officers, on the one hand, and the ship's company on the other, from the repeated brutalization of this man must have been considerable.

As soon as the crew completed watering, the *Magicienne* moved on west to Jaquemel. John Maples was sent ashore in the cutter to make arrangements for the release of the British captives that had been traded for. There were some eighty-plus English prisoners—merchant-ship skippers, seamen, and soldiers—who had been held "in close confinement . . . enduring the greatest hardships" for more than two years.[27] Maples and the cutter returned the next morning with the promise that all the English captives would soon be sent out in a cartel.

While waiting, Captain Ricketts again ordered punishment, and two seamen, Sam Richards and Thomas Pine, each got four dozen of the cat for "drunkenness and neglect of duty." At last, on the twenty-sixth, a Danish schooner came out of the port, carrying eighty-two liberated British prisoners, no doubt the happiest of men as they saw the British red ensign flying from the gaff peak of the *Magicienne*. Soon after, another schooner arrived from Aux Cayes, bringing twenty-six British sailors, earlier captured from H.M.S. *Salisbury*. These men may have been less overjoyed: some of them were immediately taken into the *Magicienne*'s ship's company, under a flogging captain.

Under way again and cruising, the frigate headed back east along the curve of the coast. The lookouts spotted a brig anchored close in to the northwestern side of Beata Island, and Ricketts worked his way up to her and anchored nearby, with the brig under his guns. She was a Dane, from Santa Cruz to Curaçao, and apparently had some contraband aboard as she was taken over and sent to Jamaica. The just-exchanged English prisoners, except for the *Salisbury*'s sailors, were put aboard her for the trip.

The Dane had told the Magiciennes of a well of good drinking water a short distance inland from the beach near the anchorage, so the *Magicienne* spent a day in filling some casks. Her usual luck held, and while the men were watering, a French schooner carrying passengers from Aux Cayes to Santo Domingo came into the anchorage "in distress," probably with a leak, as the weather was not threatening. Although she was fair game, distressed vessels were often allowed to enter and leave port without capture, and Captain Ricketts was apparently in an expansive mood and let her go. Perhaps he didn't like the prospect of filling his ship with a herd of passenger-prisoners, many of them very likely women and children, so soon after cleaning up after the last batch of captives.

The *Magicienne* was well known by this time as the scourge of the southern coast and the Mona Passage. She got under way again on 5 February and headed east, running a few miles off shore. At daylight on the ninth off Catalina Island she saw a brig and a schooner ahead of her. The brig ran for awhile but then headed inshore and anchored close under the island. The *Magicienne* left her for the moment and went after the schooner, firing several shots at her. This was too much for the schooner. She ran into the mouth of the Romaine River and quickly anchored, and the crew abandoned her and went ashore. The *Magicienne* sent John Maples in the cutter to bring her off. She was a nice prize indeed—a Spanish schooner loaded with mahogany, worth a fortune to the furniture makers in London.[28] The frigate now headed back to give her attention to the brig, still at anchor under the western end of the island. Ricketts anchored near her and sent a boat over, but she proved to be a Dane, innocent and anyway in ballast, so he left her and got under way again.

As soon as he was clear of the island, the lookouts saw a sail heading into Saona, to the southeast, and the captain started after her. The chase, a sloop, didn't wait to be taken. Her crew ran her on shore on the western end of Saona Island, then left her stranded there while they made off in a boat. Ricketts sent John Maples with the cutter in to get her off, and she turned out to be Spanish, armed with eight guns and loaded with hides, oil, tallow, and cotton—not so glamorous as mahogany, but still saleable. The Magiciennes were still dealing with this prize when another sloop came in sight, headed in toward the land, and they took off after her. As they were closing in, her crew abandoned her and headed for the mainland of Santo Domingo in a boat, hoping to escape capture. It was to no avail. The *Magicienne* paused long enough to put a prize crew aboard the sloop, then went after the boat, quickly overtook it, and brought aboard nine unhappy Frenchmen. The sloop was English, having been captured earlier by a French privateer. The *Magicienne* took her in tow. Captain Ricketts apparently did not want the problem of loading up again with prisoners, as he gave the Frenchmen back their boat and turned them loose to go ashore. He also sent the Spanish prizes off to Jamaica but kept the sloop.[29]

While all this prize-capturing activity was taking place, life aboard the *Magicienne,* with its day-to-day problems, went ahead pretty much as usual.

Sails split and were repaired. A crack weakened the mainmast, and it had to be "fished"—braced with a long, heavy splint fitted over the damaged area and tightly lashed in place with woolding of small rope. When the weather and schedule permitted, Ricketts sent the boats out with a seine net to catch fish, and they were often lucky enough to be able to feed the entire ship's company with fresh fish. The crew was exercised at the great guns or with small arms nearly every day. Punishment continued: every few days one or two men would be given twelve to forty-eight lashes, usually for "drunkenness" or "neglect," but once for "rioting." And sometime in mid-February or early March John Maples was advanced to be first lieutenant, this time permanently. This seems to have resulted from Lieutenant Trelawney's being sent off to Jamaica as skipper of the schooner *La Fortune* when Ricketts decided to make her the *Magicienne*'s tender whenever she returned after her condemnation by the prize court.

The *Fortune* would be away in Jamaica for some time, so Ricketts worked the newly captured sloop into his plans for his next venture. The ships were now just west of the Mona Passage, and across it on the western end of Porto Rico was Roxo Harbor, a bay and harbor about eighteen miles north of Cape Roxo, today called Mayaguez Bay.[30] Roxo Harbor was a favorite hangout for French and Spanish privateers and their prizes. There was a good reason for this: the harbor was protected by shallow, unmarked rocks and a bar or reef that shoaled in places to about two fathoms, making risky the entry of even a small, relatively shallow draft frigate like the *Magicienne*. There was also a two-gun battery at the entrance to the harbor and another at its head.[31] But if the *Magicienne* could find a safe path into the harbor and out again, she could make a nice killing: there were always several vessels inside.

The *Magicienne* crossed the Mona Passage and just before noon on the thirteenth worked her way cautiously toward the entrance to Roxo Harbor. The captain soon noticed that his position was getting ticklish: the surge of the sea coming into the harbor mouth was feathering and almost breaking on hidden rocks just below the surface very close to the frigate. The bottom had shoaled to ten fathoms, which was plenty of water for the ship; but the concealed rocks made things very chancy, and Ricketts decided to anchor and try to get some better information by sending the sloop ahead to run soundings and see if a channel into the harbor, deep enough for the *Magicienne,* could be found.

He had earlier put a set of signal flags aboard the sloop and now told her to go ahead and signal the water depths with the numeral flags. The soundings were irregular, but the *Magicienne* got under way and followed the sloop in closer. She anchored again late in the afternoon before the light failed, in six fathoms, with breakers about a mile to the south and east to seaward, but still well beyond gun range of the harbor. When day broke the frigate got under way and headed for the sloop, which was closer in toward the harbor. The *Magicienne* passed over a bank with only four feet of water under her rudder and then into a deeper, six-fathom spot, where she anchored.

Captain Ricketts had apparently decided that the water ahead was just too uncertain to risk the ship. He ordered the sloop to come alongside, put two 6-pounder guns in her, plus ammunition, manned her and the *Magicienne's* launch with "near 100" seamen, marines, and officers—all under the command of Acting-Lieutenant William Parker—and sent this little expedition in to cut out some of the vessels they could see.[32]

William Parker was a peculiar choice for this job. He was at this time only sixteen years old and inexperienced, with less than four years in the navy, nearly all of it as a boy-midshipman. Any of the other officers would probably have been better. But Parker had great family interest and was ambitious for glory.[33] Perhaps Ricketts was having one of his whimsical moments when he gave the task to Parker. In any event, things turned out badly.

When the sloop and the boat got into the harbor, they found that they were outnumbered and outgunned. There were four enemy privateers mounting several guns each, plus the two shore batteries, and a crowd of armed men. After the British got well inside the range of the enemy guns, the sloop went aground, and there she stuck. Lieutenant Parker and his party were in this predicament for several hours, trying to get loose and get in closer to press home the attack.

Finally, in midafternoon Parker sent the launch back to the *Magicienne* to tell Ricketts what was going on and find out what he wanted to do. The decision was made to abandon the attempt, and the launch was sent back in to help the sloop get free. This was done, and the "retreat was effected with some difficulty." The expedition arrived back at the *Magicienne* late in the evening, with marine Lieutenant Perry and three seamen wounded. Ricketts brought the guns back on board and got to sea. One of the seamen later died of his wounds. This kind of defeat and failure was not a familiar experience for the Magiciennes, but the next morning they were back in chase of prizes.[34]

Around midday the lookouts saw two brigs being chased by a schooner, apparently a privateer. The frigate cut off the schooner, which then ran into the shallow water under Cape Calabash to get away. The *Magicienne* followed in as close as she dared, anchored in five fathoms of water within gunshot of the schooner, manned and armed the boats, and sent them to take possession of her. The schooner apparently showed signs of further resistance, and Ricketts, who had run a spring line to the *Magicienne's* anchor for just such an eventuality, hove the ship around to bring her broadside to bear, to cover the boats. That threat did the trick, and the boats took possession of the schooner. She was the French privateer *Flying Fish,* of six guns and fifty men.[35]

While this was going on, the two brigs parted company, one heading out to sea, the other into the shallow water inshore. Ever practical when it came to prize taking, Ricketts let the first one go and followed brig number two in, anchored near her, and sent the boats to cut her out. She made "little resistance" and turned out to be a Spanish merchant brig carrying six guns. It was now evening, so the frigate stayed at anchor overnight, with the two prizes.

Early in the morning the *Magicienne* was under way again, this time headed back to the Môle, this cruise over. Two men were punished for "drunkenness" soon after the ship got under way that morning: William Barnett, the ship's drummer, with forty-eight lashes, and John Miller, a seaman, with twenty-four. Such punishments were taking place about once per week.

Ricketts went west around the northern side of Hispaniola and arrived back at Cap Saint-Nicolas Môle on the twentieth, and worked his way up into the harbor, to an anchorage off the town. Vice-Admiral Sir Hyde Parker was in port in his flagship, H.M. Ship *Queen,* plus several other line-of-battleships and a frigate. The *Magicienne* immediately began to reload to go to sea again and took the opportunity to make a better repair to her weak mainmast and to caulk the main deck. Seaman John Vining was punished with two dozen for "drunkenness and neglect."[36]

Just a week later, on the twenty-seventh, she was ordered out on another cruise, this time in company with the *Regulus,* which she was to meet at Irois Bay, on the tip of the western peninsula. The *Magicienne* made a one-day stop at Dame Marie Bay and sent a party ashore to pick oranges on one of the plantations, to keep the scurvy away, then slipped ten miles down the coast to Irois. The *Regulus* was already waiting in the bay, and the *Magicienne* anchored for long enough to transfer some stores to her, then Captain Ricketts ordered them both under way.

They were to cruise along the southern coast of Saint-Domingue and Santo Domingo, on into the Mona Passage, then off the western end of Porto Rico. This had always been a productive area, swarming with French and Spanish merchantmen, but this time it was strangely empty. The British boarded a few neutrals but were unable to find anything that they could take as a lawful prize. Ricketts's luck seemed to have abandoned him. The lack of prizes apparently increased the problems with morale and discipline aboard the *Magicienne.* The floggings now came every day or so, for "neglect," "drunkenness," "disobedience of orders," and, ominously, "rioting."[37] Ricketts at this time was particularly hard on drunkenness, handing out twenty-four, thirty-six, or forty-eight lashes for this offense.

The ships had worked their way along the entire southern coast and were off the western end of Saona Island when on 28 March, a squally rainy day, the *Regulus* saw a schooner and went off in chase of it, and soon after two brigs were sighted from the *Magicienne,* to the east, heading through the Mona Passage. The *Magicienne* started after the closest one and, after catching up, fired a couple of shots to bring her to. Then Ricketts saw that the other brig was being chased by a large schooner flying English colors. He didn't recognize the schooner at first but soon realized that she was the *Fortune,* his own tender, formerly the French privateer *La Fortune,* now returned from Jamaica. The *Fortune* fired on the brig, which promptly struck, then brought her prize down to where the *Magicienne* was taking charge of the first brig. The two brigs were Spaniards, from La Guayra, "on the Caraccas" in what is now Venezuela, one headed for Cadiz, the other for Bilbao. They were loaded with coffee, cacao, hides, cotton, and indigo—a nice haul. It looked as if Ricketts's luck had returned. All the vessels anchored together under the northwestern end of Saona Island—the *Magicienne,* the *Fortune,* the two Spanish brigs, and, soon after, the *Regulus.* Boats passed back and forth, and the *Fortune'*s ship's company was no doubt giving out to all the news from Jamaica. But the news was not all they brought: sailors of that time were tremendously skillful and ingenious at smuggling liquor aboard their ships, and sometime on the evening of the twenty-eighth a "keg of spirits" was slipped aboard the *Magicienne* from the *Fortune'*s boat.[38]

Early on the twenty-ninth the Spanish prisoners were given a boat and three days' provisions and turned loose to go into Santo Domingo. Then at noon the little flotilla got under way, the *Magicienne,* the *Regulus,* the *Fortune,* and the two prize brigs, all sailing peacefully westward. But the spell was broken that night. Down in the *Magicienne'*s lower deck, or maybe below in the hold, the keg was broached. How many men were involved is not clear: at least six or eight. Neither is it clear exactly what was in the keg, although most likely it was raw, high-proof, skull-busting local rum from one of the prizes, or perhaps from Jamaica. In any event, some fair-sized group of Magiciennes had a drunken spree, a bacchanalia, an event of signal magnitude that could be recounted over and over in lower-deck yarn-fests throughout the fleet, growing each time and becoming legend.

But in a crowded ship-of-war, such happenings cannot be run quietly or without being noticed, and word of the event soon made its way aft. Captain Ricketts went into a tremendous, towering rage. First, he held John Maples, as first lieutenant, responsible for letting the liquor get into the ship in the first place, and Maples was "put under an arrest" in his stateroom. Then the captain had as many of the culprits as possible rounded up and sentenced seven of them, six seamen and one marine, to sixty lashes each. One man, apparently less culpable, was to get eighteen, and John Vining, who had about a month earlier been flogged with twenty-four, was now to get twenty-one lashes. Vining, his recent experience at the grating fresh in his mind and the scabs on his back not yet healed, could not face being flogged again and escaped punishment by telling how the keg had been gotten aboard. The others received their full, dreadful measure, a session of continuous punishment that must have lasted at least two hours, sickened all but the most hardened of the observers, and left the victims crippled for weeks and scarred for life. Vining's confession apparently got John Maples off the hook, as no court-martial or other adverse action toward him followed—quite the contrary.[39]

At this point Captain Ricketts had apparently decided to make another run at Roxo Harbor, "the great Receptacle for French privateers and their prizes," and this time to do it right.[40] Perhaps he felt that such a move would take the minds of the ship's company away from the recent unpleasant events and raise their spirits with thoughts of action and prize money. First, however, he was going to take a swing through the Mona Passage and around the western end of Porto Rico and see what else there was: there were small anchorages along the coast that might be sheltering some easy pickings. He told the *Regulus* to meet him at Calabash Bay three days hence, on 5 April, then took the *Magicienne* north past Aguada Point, then east several miles along the northern coast. There wasn't much to be had, but he did take a Spanish sloop carrying coffee and barley and a schooner loaded with wine, brandy, and dry goods. The pickings were sparse along the northwestern coast of Porto Rico partly because, unbeknownst to Ricketts, the frigate *Hermione,* Captain Hugh Pigot, had just ten days before cleaned out a group of privateers near Punta Higuero, a few miles north of Calabash Bay.[41]

The *Magicienne* returned to Cape Calabash early in the morning on the fifth and while running up to her anchorage went aground on the tail of a sand bank—not an auspicious start to the planned adventure, but, as it happened, their only bit of bad luck. After some delay they carried out the stream anchor with the launch and hove the frigate off, then anchored in five fathoms in a safer spot. The *Regulus* came in too. Visible in Roxo Harbor was a forest of masts.[42]

The raid was planned for that night, and the day was spent in getting ready for it. The six largest boats of the *Magicienne* and *Regulus* were loaded with pistols, muskets, cutlasses, tomahawks, knives, grenades and combustibles, grappling hooks, extra rope, axes to cut cables, etc. Last-minute organizational details were taken care of: this time Ricketts was putting his most experienced people in charge, and John Maples, as first lieutenant of the senior ship, was in overall command of the expedition. His second in command was Alexander M'Beath, first of the *Regulus.* Then there were Charles Cheshire and James Reid, the masters of the two ships; Philip Perry and George Frazer, marine lieutenants from each; plus John Jordain and Abraham Adams, the surgeon and purser of the *Magicienne,* to cope with the problems of any that might be wounded. The number of men is not given in any of the sources, just that they were "volunteers." Probably around 150 to 175 took part.[43]

The French and Spanish were alert for an attack and also getting ready. They knew that the *Hermione* had struck just up the coast less than two weeks earlier, and they could see the *Magicienne* and *Regulus* now getting out their boats and loading them. One obvious thing to do was to take ashore all the sails from the vessels in the harbor, to make it impossible for the attackers to sail them out. Another was to moor them with lines running several feet underwater, from ringbolts on the stem below the waterline to an anchor or to an underwater point on a pier. There was very little iron chain or cable available in those days, and practically all mooring lines and anchor cables were just large hemp ropes, easy to cut with an axe if they could be gotten to.

From the *Magicienne,* with a long glass, it was easy to see that the yards and booms of the vessels in the harbor were bare of sails, and John Maples was prepared to burn those that he couldn't easily tow out.

At eight in the evening, well after dark, the boats assembled at the *Magicienne,* then left for the harbor. Apparently, on the way in John Maples briefly diverted a couple of the boats to take and destroy the shore battery at the entrance of the harbor, to prevent it from interfering with his exit later on. The men in those boats chased out the defenders and spiked the two guns, a 6-pounder and a 4-pounder, then rejoined the expedition. Once in the harbor Maples's forces managed to cut loose a Spanish schooner and a sloop, plus one other vessel, and got them in tow. Then he and his men overran the shore battery at the head of the harbor, spiked its two 4-pounder guns, and by about 2 A.M. had set fire to all eleven of the "square-rigged vessels and schooners" that they couldn't bring out, completely taking or destroying all the shipping in the place except one neutral Dane. John Maples led his expedition back to the frigates, victorious, without having lost a man, at about 4 A.M., towing his three prizes. The boats were hoisted in, and an hour later the *Magicienne,* the *Regulus,* and the week's prizes all got under way and went to sea.[44]

The Glorious Expedition, coming as it did on the heels of the Incident of the Keg, seems to have lanced a boil for the Magiciennes, and afterward things aboard were apparently a little less tense. Captain Ricketts was happy with John Maples and a week after putting him "under an arrest" was praising him and the others who took part in the night of cutting out for a "service . . . admirabl[y] well-executed" in a letter to Sir Hyde Parker. Sir Hyde thought the incident important enough to forward the letter to the Admiralty, which in turn was pleased enough to have it published in the semiofficial *London Gazette.*

The earlier taking of the *Cerf Volant,* the action in Roxo Harbor, plus three similar adventures to come, also all led by John Maples, give Captain Ricketts his claim to the few short paragraphs in the more detailed naval annals of the period that are his only appearance in history. Three of these were the only actions for which Ricketts was "gazetted."[45]

The cruise was now nearly over, and the *Magicienne* worked her way west along the southern coast of Hispaniola, on her way back to Môle Saint Nicolas. The *Regulus* and the tender, the *Fortune,* were in company. The prizes had been sent off to Jamaica.

Since returning to the West Indies under Ricketts's command eight months before, the *Magicienne* had had no direct involvement in the failing British struggle to conquer Saint-Domingue, although some of her captures off the southern peninsula had kept useful supplies out of the hands of General Rigaud and his army.[46]

The British at this time in the late spring of 1797 were being fought to a standstill by Toussaint and his black army in the central area around Port-au-Prince, and by Rigaud and his mulattos in the south. Although a new British commander, Lieutenant General John Simcoe, had just arrived and had more than thirty thousand men to work with, the armies of Toussaint and Rigaud now held the initiative.

On the southern peninsula the British and their French-planter allies held the port town of Jérémie on the northwestern corner and had a weak grip on the area at the western end called the Grand Anse, which included a few of the bays on the western tip: Donna Maria Bay, Carcasse Bay, and Les Irois, where the British had a small fort, and some of the plantations near the coast. These positions were important to the British: Jamaica was just 115 miles across the channel. Jérémie, the main British strong point on the peninsula, had just narrowly repulsed a major attack by Rigaud.[47]

As the *Magicienne* and her consorts came around Cape Carcasse at just after noon on 24 April, and the view into Carcasse Bay opened up, there came into sight a large armed sloop flying Danish colors and three heavily loaded schooners close in to the beach a bit south of the fort at Irois. The beach was covered with casks of provisions, and a "numerous body of troops" was assembled close by. Ricketts suspected that Rigaud's forces from Tiburon were getting ready to attack the fort. This was confirmed a few minutes later when a gun was fired at the fort and a red and white flag hoisted on the fort's flagstaff, a signal that the enemy was nearby. The luck of Ricketts and the *Magicienne* was still running strong.[48]

The *Magicienne* immediately headed in toward the landing site, clearing the guns and getting ready to anchor, with springs to the cable on each side. Within forty minutes the frigate was anchored about 1,500 feet from the sloop and was taking her under "heavy fire" from her broadsides. This was too much for the people on the sloop, and after firing six or eight guns, they abandoned her and hastily went ashore. The troops on the beach ran up the embankment fronting the beach and behind some hillocks, out of sight, leaving all the provisions and munitions behind. Ricketts signaled the *Regulus,* which was becalmed some way to seaward, to send her boats, manned and armed.

Without waiting for them, Ricketts ordered the *Magicienne*'s boats into the water, called away the boarding party with John Maples in charge, and ordered the *Fortune* to go in with the boats. At first it looked like a piece of cake: the sloop was abandoned, and there was no one left on the beach. But as soon as Maples and his party boarded the sloop, the enemy soldiers came back to the top of the embankment, above and only fifty yards from the sloop, and started firing on the British. First it was a brisk fusillade of musketry, but then the enemy dragged up two brass field guns and began to let go with round shot and grape. John Maples and his men were trying to tow out the sloop with the boats, but they couldn't get her moving. The enemy fire cut the tow ropes a couple of times and wounded some people in the boats. The *Magicienne* couldn't effectively shoot at the soldiers ashore without endangering John Maples and his party.

This went on for most of half an hour before Maples figured out what the problem was: the sloop was tied to the shore with an underwater rope that proved to be too deep to cut. So he abandoned the attempt to tow her and returned to the *Magicienne*. His force had taken a bad bruising. Four men were killed and eleven were wounded, including Mr. Morgan, the master's mate. At about the time Maples got back, the *Regulus* arrived and anchored near the *Magicienne,* and both ships commenced a heavy broadside fire on the troops ashore. This was effective: the soldiers "retreat[ed] precipitately," heading over the mountains toward Tiburon, leaving everything behind—the brass field pieces, all their ammunition, provisions, and camp equipment, including the general's tent, and a number of dead. In the course of all the heavy gunfire from the two frigates the sloop was sunk, and thus no longer a feasible prize, so Ricketts battered to matchwood the part of her that remained above water and then sent in the jolly boat to set fire to the little that was left.

By now evening was coming on, and during the course of the night the boats from the *Magicienne* and *Regulus* brought out all the abandoned provisions, ammunition, and equipment, as well as the two obnoxious brass field guns that had caused so much trouble. The men also, without incident, towed out three schooners loaded with provisions and fired one that couldn't be brought out. At daylight there were none of the enemy anywhere in sight, and Ricketts sent in the boats again to bring off whatever had been missed in the dark and to destroy anything not worth bringing out. It was a complete victory, and not an unimportant one. Ricketts had rescued the fort at Irois and, for the time being, saved the British position in the southern peninsula. Again, John Maples had carried the major part of the action.[49]

As soon as things calmed down a bit, Ricketts sent the *Fortune* around to Jérémie with dispatches for General Churchill, giving him the news of the recent events. Then the ships spent a couple of days in getting cleaned up and doing odd jobs. The *Magicienne*'s carpenters were sent to Irois to build a new carriage for a large mortar at the fort, and some of the captured provisions and ammunition were transferred to the garrison there.

The *Fortune* returned after two days, bringing the news of the recent attack on Jérémie and a message from the general there asking for any gunpowder that could be spared by the ships. Ricketts had thirty half-barrels of powder loaded aboard the *Fortune* and sent her back to Jérémie within a few hours of her arrival. Then the *Magicienne* and *Regulus* got under way and themselves headed north around the peninsula toward Jérémie. At daylight the next morning the ships saw two strangers between them and the land, but as the light got stronger they were recognized as H.M. Frigates *Hermione* and *Ceres,* captained by Hugh Pigot and Robert Otway. Ricketts sent the *Regulus* inshore to speak them, no doubt ready to regale them with the accounts of their victories at Cape Roxo and Irois. It was a good thing that Ricketts had this news to relay, as Captain Pigot had his own exploit to brag on: he had just run a successful cutting-out operation on the northern coast of Saint-Domingue. He and Otway were now on their way to patrol off the Caracas, an operation that would be aborted by the *Ceres*'s running aground so hard that she was barely gotten off.[50]

At Jérémie the *Magicienne* met with a hero's welcome. The saving of Irois, when added to the recent repulse of Rigaud's army at Jérémie, had prevented the mulatto and black forces from overrunning the white French planters and their farms in the area. The grateful local people brought gifts of fruits, vegetables, and coffee for the ship's company, and the mayor presented Captain Ricketts with a scroll describing "the most lively gratitude" of the inhabitants and a fancy map of the Grand Anse area.[51]

By 10 May the frigate was back at the Môle, and although Captain Ricketts, John Maples, and the rest of the Magiciennes couldn't have known it then, their glory days were now behind them. It looked at that time, however, as though just the opposite were true: Sir Hyde Parker had received some intelligence that a Spanish squadron loaded with treasure would soon be heading from Vera Cruz to Spain, through the Straits of Florida. He put Ricketts and the *Magicienne* in charge of the *Regulus, Thunderer, Severn,* and *Diligence,* with the *Fortune* tender, and sent him off to intercept the treasure ships. This could have been the best venture yet for him, had his luck held.

But the cruise was fruitless. The ships covered the Florida coast and up as far as Charleston, plus much of the Bahamas, before discovering that their quarry had run into Havana and showed no intention of coming out. Ricketts tried to outwait the treasure ships and at one point ran low on rum and had to serve a weakened "three water grog" to the ship's company to avoid running out.[52] Given the *Magicienne*'s problems with liquor and Ricketts's propensity to punish drunkenness heavily, this may have been a good thing. It certainly illustrates his determination to hang on until the Spanish came out. But he finally ran so low on provisions that he had to return to the Môle empty-handed, on 21 July.

Captain Ricketts's other cruises that summer and fall were no more successful. On one six-week cruise, as part of a squadron under the command of the captain of the *Carnatic,* who was senior to Ricketts, the Magiciennes had two weeks of "intolerable bad weather," with continuous rain and heavy squalls, leaving them with no opportunity to get the fresh vegetables and meat that Ricketts was usually careful to provide. As a result, the *Magicienne* had an outbreak of scurvy, the only one during his command.[53]

During the fall of 1797 there were few opportunities to chase prizes. Instead, the *Magicienne,* Captain Ricketts, and John Maples were involved in the aftermath of the bloody and murderous mutiny on board H.M. Frigate *Hermione.*

The *Hermione* had undergone two changes of captains since the days in 1795 when she and the *Magicienne* were assigned together to handle the scut work of supporting the army around Port-au-Prince and was now commanded by the harsh and vindictive Captain Hugh Pigot, formerly of the *Success.* As a flogger, Pigot was on a par with Ricketts, but he was inconsistent with his discipline and did little for the comfort of his crew, matters to which Ricketts paid close attention. Pigot was described by a contemporary British historian as "one of the most cruel and oppressive captains belonging to the British Navy."[54]

In September of 1797, while the *Hermione* was cruising in the Mona Passage, Pigot's fear-inspired hold over his crew was finally shattered.[55] Two minor mistakes in sail handling enraged him, resulting in the death of three topmen in a fall from the rigging. Two nights later the crew mutinied and murdered and threw overboard Pigot, all the lieutenants, a midshipman, and all the warrant officers except the gunner and carpenter—ten in total. The young sharks of the Mona Passage dined well that night.

The leaders of the mutiny took the *Hermione* to La Guayra, on the Spanish Main, in what is now Venezuela, and gave it to the Spanish authorities.

Word of the mutiny did not get back to Admiral Parker at the Môle until 31 October. Sir Hyde immediately wrote a letter to the Spanish governor at La Guayra, demanding the return of the mutineers, and ordered Captain Ricketts in the *Magicienne* to proceed to La Guayra and see what he could do to get back the *Hermione*'s crew.[56]

For the next several months the *Magicienne,* with Captain Ricketts and John Maples, acted as Sir Hyde's agent in dealings with the Spanish, without success. The whole matter soon became moot as the mutineers left their safe havens on the Spanish Main; thirty-three were caught and tried by courts-martial in Port Royal or at the Môle, and twenty-four were hanged and one transported. But more than a hundred of the Hermiones managed to fade into anonymity and escape arrest, including some of the worst of the mutineers.[57]

To throw fear into potential mutineers in the fleet, the executions by hanging that usually followed these courts-martial were done on board different ships, to give each ship's company, in its turn, a close-up view of the majesty of the law in operation. Right after the *Magicienne* returned to the Môle in early May of 1798, three of these executions were scheduled to be done on board her. At 6 A.M. on the seventh a signal was made for a boat from each ship present "to attend while sentence of a court martial on three of the *Hermione's* men was put into execution." John Maples noted in his journal that "at 7 o'clock the prisoners swung off."[58]

The execution was the end of the *Magicienne's* involvement in the *Hermione's* mutiny, and a few days later an era ended aboard the ship as Captain William Henry Ricketts was detached and given a leave of absence to go to England to handle some important personal affairs. He was replaced by a Captain Ogilvy, who as a commander had been captain of the *Lark*, a sixteen-gun brig also on the Jamaica Station.

Had John Maples had family influence or a strong patron, he might well have been given the command, which would have given him the all-important promotion to post-captain directly from lieutenant. In fairness, however, Ogilvy and others like him, waiting as commanders of small ships for promotion into post-rank ships, deserved first consideration.

Things aboard changed under Ogilvy. He was not a flogger, but he didn't have enough influence with Admiral Parker to get cruising assignments that would bring in prizes.

William Henry Ricketts surely must have felt that his cup was running over. He had just finished a highly successful and profitable tour as a frigate captain, and now he was going home to complete the legal and administrative details with the College of Arms and the Herald's Office that would set in place his position as the heir of his powerful uncle, Admiral Sir John Jervis, Earl of St. Vincent. The admiral, although married, was childless. His beloved sister, Mary Ricketts, a widow, had two sons and two daughters, all of whom he loved. But William Henry Ricketts, Mary's older son, was the closest thing the admiral had to a child of his own. Jervis had taken Ricketts to sea as a young boy-midshipman, had treated him sternly but with love, and had guided his career. His pride in the way Henry had become the successful frigate captain was enormous.

So John Jervis, Admiral the Earl of St. Vincent, decided in 1798 to follow his long-held intention and make William Henry Ricketts heir to his title, the income that went with it, and his fortune. This involved setting up an irrevocable line of descent from John Jervis to William Henry Ricketts, who was to change his name to Jervis, then to his sons. But if William Henry died without male issue, the title and fortune would go to the younger brother, who also changed his name to Jervis.[59]

To Captain William Henry Ricketts, now Jervis, and his young wife it must have seemed that wonderful vistas were opening. Their first two children were girls, but they were young enough to have others and would surely have a boy. Other emoluments came Captain Jervis's way, the kind of fruitful sinecures that were distributed to the families of the nobility: he was made the treasurer of Greenwich Hospital and was appointed to be one of the verdurers of the New Forest. But in 1799 a cloud passed over his life: his marriage was "dissolved" as his wife left him to marry another man, a clergyman.[60] Perhaps she had been left alone and lonely too long, while Captain Ricketts chased prizes around Saint-Domingue.

In January 1805 Captain Jervis, then captain of H.M.S. *Le Tonnant,* an eighty-four–gun battleship, was serving in the blockading squadron off Brest. He had received information that the Rochefort Squadron had escaped and needed to pass this news on to the commander in chief of the Channel Fleet. A heavy gale had been blowing for several days, but on the twenty-fourth, as the *Tonnant* arrived at the fleet, it abated somewhat, and Captain Jervis took the *Tonnant's* gig, a four-oared boat, and set out for the flagship. Then two heavy seas broke over the bow of the boat and upset it. The coxswain, John Jones, a good swimmer, supported Captain Jervis for some time, until he was exhausted and had to let him go. Captain William Henry Jervis then sank and drowned. He was forty years old.[61]

Sir John Jervis, Admiral the Earl of St. Vincent, never fully recovered from this stunning blow, made worse for him by the fact that the younger nephew, to whom the title would now descend, had married a woman that St. Vincent detested.[62]

In the Jervis Papers in the British Library is a curious family memento, one of the few real traces of William Henry Ricketts-Jervis as a person. It is a beautifully detailed watercolor sketch showing an urn-topped monument memorializing his death, shaded by a weeping willow tree. The stone is engraved

TO THE MEMORY OF
CAPT[n] W.H. JERVIS
Who was unfortunately
Drownd on the 24th of Jan[y]
1805
Cut off from Nature's and from
Glory's course, which never
Mortal was so Fond to Run[63]

Also in the picture is a boy in midshipman's uniform, one arm draped over the monument: Captain Ricketts-Jervis's fifteen-year-old nephew, who was lost at sea in 1807.[64] In the distant background, behind the monument, is the sea, and on the sea a frigate.

In writing this book I tried to consider thoroughly the few, scattered pieces of information that tell us all that we can know about this complex man: the brave frigate captain who sailed in between the rocks to reach his quarry; the harsh disciplinarian, judge and executioner in one, who could order five men in a day flogged with sixty lashes; the father-captain who would send half the crew on shore to pick oranges to keep them well and who went to great lengths to get fresh fish or a herd of pigs for the ship's company.

It is often and truly said that the past is a foreign country to which we cannot journey. While we can understand the words that these men said and how they sailed and fought their ships, we cannot get inside their thoughts: the cultural and social gulfs are too wide.

CHAPTER FOURTEEN

With Nelson at Copenhagen

THE AUTUMN OF 1798 SAW THE complete collapse of the British position in Saint-Domingue. The British government sent Brigadier General Thomas Maitland out to cut its losses and make the best deal that he could with Toussaint Louverture. But events had gone too far, and Maitland had to let go of everything. The British couldn't even keep the Môle, and by the end of the year Sir Hyde and his squadron, including the *Magicienne* and John Maples, were based in Port Royal, Jamaica. Although it was the end of direct British military involvement in Saint-Domingue, England's indirect influence was decisive: British sea power stood squarely in the way of Napoleon's later efforts to reestablish French control of the island. Saint-Domingue was now on the way to becoming Haiti.

John Maples continued on as first lieutenant of the *Magicienne* for another year. Then in mid-1799 a piece of good luck came his way. Some incident, just what is unclear, brought him to the favorable attention of Sir Hyde Parker, and Maples was transferred to the flagship, H.M.S. *Queen,* a ninety-eight–gun battleship. This was an important break for John Maples: the lieutenants in the flagship normally received such promotions into small commander-rank ships as became available on the Jamaica Station. In the flagship, life for the lieutenants was much more formal than in a frigate. Uniform requirements were stricter, and there was more punctilio on the quarterdeck. The competition among the flagship lieutenants for preferment was cutthroat. Life was lived and duties done right under the eye of the admiral, and for an officer like John Maples with no family influence but with experience and competence, it was an opportunity to earn a little of the great man's patronage. John Maples apparently impressed Sir Hyde as worthy of his support: Maples noted in his autobiographical sketch for Marshall that he "followed the fortunes" of Admiral Parker for the next few years.[1]

John Maples couldn't have known in 1799 that he had tied his fortunes to a star that was soon to fall. But no other opportunities were available to him, and he was fortunate to be counted among Sir Hyde's protégés. By now the Afflecks were dead, Edmund since 1787, Philip in late 1799.

In the early summer of 1800 Sir Hyde was relieved of the command of the immensely profitable Jamaica Station and recalled to England. Earl Spencer, the First Lord of the Admiralty, told him, in effect, that he had enjoyed the lucrative, easy Jamaica Station for a long time and had made himself rich, and that it was now time to give someone else a chance. And rich he was. When Parker had arrived on the station in 1796, he had had no significant personal fortune. Leaving it in 1800, he was worth more than £200,000, the equivalent of more than $5,000,000 in today's values.[2] It was the best kind of wealth: cash, not real estate entailed through to the next generation. Also, it was honorable money, from prizes of war, not grubbed out in trade or from plantations.

There was more to the timing of his relief than the mere matter of giving another admiral a chance to become rich. Sir Hyde strongly opposed the British government's policy of giving up all of Saint-Domingue and over the last two years had become increasingly querulous in his letters to the Admiralty, and Earl Spencer was beginning to show some small symptoms of irritation.[3]

The Queen, with Sir Hyde and John Maples, arrived in Plymouth in mid-September 1800. Sir Hyde, age sixty-one, a widower with grown children, was planning to be married within a few weeks to an eighteen-year-old girl, the daughter of an Admiral Onslow. It may not have been a bad match: he was rich, and she apparently lacked something in appearance and sparkle, being described as "ample" and referred to in gossip as "batter pudding."[4] With wealth to enjoy and connubial bliss close in the offing, Sir Hyde was understandably not eager for an immediate assignment at sea.

Other senior admirals tended to view Hyde Parker with something like contempt tinged with envy. Most of them had been doing tough jobs at sea in cold, bad weather, fighting real battles, with very little prize money to show for it. In particular, John Jervis, Admiral the Earl St. Vincent, in command of the Channel Fleet, was very open in his letters, reminding Spencer at the Admiralty of Hyde Parker's easy service in Jamaica and urging that Parker be sent out to handle the Channel Fleet at sea, while he, St. Vincent, would come ashore and set up his overall Channel Fleet headquarters at Tor Abbey in Devon for the winter.[5]

So preparations were made for Sir Hyde to shift his flag from the *Queen* to the more sea capable battleship *Royal George,* and Captain Robert Waller Otway, Parker's number one protégé, was sent to take command of her. John Maples was transferred to the *Royal George* on 1 November 1800. But before Hyde Parker got to sea to relieve St. Vincent, Spencer was writing to that irascible admiral that "Sir Hyde Parker has no hesitation . . . to serve as your second . . . but I am sorry to say I do not think at present his health [is] in a fit state for an autumnal cruise off Brest. . . ."[6]

The Admiral the Earl St. Vincent, four years older than Hyde Parker and probably in no better health after being almost continuously at sea for several years, was fit to be tied. As it ended up, St. Vincent set up his headquarters at Tor Abbey, but Hyde Parker stayed ashore on leave, and the fleet at sea was commanded from the *Royal George* by Vice-Admiral Sir Henry Harvey as second in command. This had its consequences: Harvey left his station off Brest and came across into Tor Bay on 20 January because of bad weather. While he was off station a French squadron in Brest got out and headed for the Mediterranean and Egypt—a troublesome thing.[7] Would Hyde Parker have handled the situation better? Perhaps not, but there was no test of this: he was on leave ashore rather than exerting his command at sea. Admiral the Earl of St. Vincent was not pleased by these events.

Also in that fall of 1800, in early November, Rear-Admiral Sir Horatio Nelson returned to England after a long absence—his first appearance at home since his victory in the Battle of the Nile two years earlier. His arrival set off a tremendous outpouring of public acclaim and affection for him.

Although well connected and having some family influence, Nelson had been a relatively unknown captain until 14 February 1797. On that Saint Valentine's Day, off Cape Saint Vincent at the southwestern corner of Portugal, he was in command of H.M. Battleship *Captain* and acting as commodore, in charge of the rearmost ships of Admiral Sir John Jervis's fifteen-ship line of battle as it tried to cut through a twenty-seven–ship Spanish fleet.

The battle was heading toward being the sort of inconclusive brush-by on opposite courses common to eighteenth-century naval warfare until Nelson noticed that a gap had opened up toward the rear of the Spanish line. He perceived that if he could get over there right away with a few of the ships from the rear of the British line, he could cut off several of the Spaniards and destroy them before the van of the Spanish line could turn around and come to their assistance. This would accomplish what Admiral Jervis was trying to do, and it was a unique opportunity that had to be seized immediately or it would be gone. But British rules were very strict about leaving the line without orders, and this could have been the end, rather than the beginning, of Nelson's rise to fame.

He didn't hesitate but headed his ship for the gap. Then others followed, and they soon turned the day into a victory, capturing four large battleships, two of which were taken by Nelson who himself led a party of boarders into the *San Nicolas* and from her boarded the *San Josef.*

Nelson's ship, H.M.S. *Captain,* was badly mauled in the process, her "sails and rigging being almost cut to pieces," her fore-topmast and the foretop itself shattered and hanging in wreckage, and "the mainmast having three shot through the heart." Then while the *Captain* was still immobile and entangled with her two prizes, the captors "found the *San Nicolas* to be on fire . . . in her hold"—a very dangerous circumstance—but "it was happily extinguished by our Firemen," as noted by the obviously relieved lieutenant writing the journal. Then the frigate *Minerve* towed the *Captain* clear of the fracas as the battle ended.[8]

Admiral Jervis was lavish in his praise of Nelson. The Admiralty and the government were happy: England needed a victory just then, even a meager one. John Jervis was made Earl of St. Vincent and given a cash grant, plus a generous income to maintain his new social station. Nelson was made a Knight of the Bath. Soon after, the inexorable workings of seniority brought him promotion to the lowest of the nine grades of admiral, Rear-Admiral of the Blue.

An important outcome of the action off Cape Saint Vincent was that from then on Admiral the Earl of St. Vincent had boundless confidence in Nelson's ability to perform miracles. This confidence was more than justified and had much to do with Nelson's being placed in positions that led to the string of victories that defined the brief balance of his life and, indeed, defined the golden age of naval warfare under sail.

Nelson was a natural genius in the Art of the Admiral. He was able to look out across the surface of the sea at a confusing jumble of moving ships, his and the enemy's, and see quickly how to exploit the fluid opportunities that the situation offered. He also understood the strategic framework into which his tactical actions and innovations fitted. But as important as any of this, he radiated the charisma and empathy that made all ranks worship him, and he skillfully used this natural leadership ability to build the fleets that he commanded into enthusiastic fighting instruments. He did this by spending much time with his captains, discussing tactics with them, working out his plans with them, encouraging them to innovate, to be bold, and to swiftly seize unforeseen opportunities. The cabin on his flagship was always full of captains who had come over in their boats while the fleet was cruising, and they all understood his simple doctrines: seize the moment and its opportunities, get alongside the enemy, and don't quit until the enemy's force is annihilated. These ideas were not widely held in 1798, but Nelson's captains shared his enthusiasm for them.

Nelson's career is usually defined in terms of the three great sea fights that he planned and directed: the Nile in 1798, Copenhagen in 1801, and Trafalgar in 1805. John Maples fought in two of these celebrated actions, Copenhagen and Trafalgar.

Because of its impact on later events it is necessary to describe briefly the events surrounding the Battle of the Nile, even though it took place while John Maples was still in the West Indies:

The British had abandoned the Mediterranean during reverses in 1796 caused by young General Napoleon Bonaparte's conquests in Italy, in the months before the Battle of Cape Saint Vincent. But in early 1798 there were strong rumors that the French planned a major naval and military campaign, probably aimed at Egypt. The British had to counter this threat and prepared to send a fleet back into the Mediterranean.

There were, of course, many available admirals senior to Nelson who would have given their eyeteeth for the job, but both Admiral the Earl of St. Vincent and the First Lord, Earl Spencer, agreed that Nelson should have it. He was given thirteen battleships plus two frigates, a ship-sloop, and a brig and told to find out what the French were up to and to defeat them.

The French were indeed mounting a major expedition aimed at Egypt but also had grandiose ideas of digging a canal at Suez, then moving on to attack the British in India. Napoleon was at this time a twenty-nine-year-old general with a short string of battle successes behind him. Although still serving the Directory, he was on his way to becoming its master, his contribution to the coup d'état of *18 Fructidor* fresh in the past.

Napoleon was in overall charge of the Egyptian expedition, and under him Admiral Brueys commanded the fleet. He left southern France in May of 1798 with thirteen battleships, seven frigates, some gunboats, and about three hundred transports. Loaded in this armada were 30,000 infantry, 2,800 cavalry, and detachments of sappers and bridge builders, plus plenty of artillery. Also on board were scientists and savants of every description, ready to extract from Egypt and the East all manner of information for the benefit of France.

The French force paused long enough at Malta to overwhelm, with a little inside help, the decadent Knights of Saint John of Jerusalem and to seize and carry off the gold and silver treasures that the knights had accumulated since the Crusades, plus twelve thousand barrels of gunpowder. Napoleon also garrisoned the nearly impregnable defenses of the island with tough French soldiery. Then the force headed east.

Because of an error in judgment by one of the British frigate captains, the two frigates and the sloop that were Nelson's scouting eyes separated from the fleet and were gone during the next crucial weeks. Nelson and his battleships were left to grope blindly around the Eastern Mediterranean, on two occasions passing quite close to the French armada without detecting it. The effect on

local and world events of Nelson's loss of his frigates is simply incalculable: had
he met the French at sea it is highly probable that he would have defeated and
utterly destroyed them. There is a good possibility that he would have captured
the person of Bonaparte. Had Napoleon Bonaparte spent the war years after
1798 as a prisoner in England, the world of the nineteenth and twentieth centuries would have been quite different.

But by the time Nelson caught up with the French, Napoleon and his army
were ashore, the Battle of the Pyramids had been fought, and the French Army
controlled Egypt. Nelson arrived off Alexandria in the middle of the day on
the first of August, but the French battleships were not there. He sailed east
along the coast and later that afternoon found them anchored in a line in
Aboukir Bay, close in to the shore. Admiral Brueys thought that his position
was secure and that in any event, as it was late in the afternoon, he would not be
attacked until the next morning.

He was wrong on both counts. Nelson immediately swooped down on
Brueys's forces, attacking the ships in the van and the center of the French line
from both sides from ranges of one hundred feet or so and, as the darkness
closed in, utterly annihilating them. The 120-gun French flagship *L'Orient,* the
largest warship afloat at the time, soon caught fire and provided light for the
battle. Admiral Brueys was killed, nearly cut in two by a shot. At a little after
10 P.M. the fires on the *L'Orient* reached her magazines, and she blew up with
a tremendous explosion heard fifteen miles away in Alexandria. Destroyed
with her were the ancient treasures of the crusading knights, taken at Malta
and stored in the *L'Orient*'s hold, and born were the legends of treasures that
survived.

After the *L'Orient* exploded, the battle became a cleanup operation. Soon
after daylight two relatively undamaged French battleships and two frigates
were able to get under way and escape. They were under the command of a
junior admiral, M. Pierre Villeneuve, who from then on had a healthy respect
for Nelson bordering on paranoia. The British captured both of these battleships less than two years later. Except for these, the entire naval battle force of
Napoleon's expedition was captured or destroyed during the night of 1–2
August 1798. Some of the British ships were damaged, but all were repaired on
the spot.

It was a victory of tremendous proportions. No naval action of the eighteenth century had been so thorough. Napoleon and his army were stranded in
Egypt with no possibility of rescue or resupply. Napoleon deserted his forces in
July 1799, slipping through the British blockade and back to France in the
frigate *Muiron.* The French Army was later defeated by a British force sent out
to clean them up, with some help from the Ottomans. The Mediterranean
became a British lake again and remained so for the rest of the war—indeed,

until after World War II. Nelson went back and laid siege to Malta, which with a French garrison proved a tough nut to crack.

Back home in England months had gone by without any information about what was going on with the French expedition and Nelson. Uncertainty ran high: the British, up to this point, had seen few victories against the French. Then came the reports of the Nile. The country exploded with joy and celebration, and Nelson's popularity with the British public soared to heights from which it never receded. Nelson's rewards for the Battle of the Nile seem strangely minor. Where Jervis had been made an earl for the Battle of Cape Saint Vincent, which Nelson had in any event won for him, Nelson received only a barony, the lowest rank in the peerage, for his smashing victory at the Nile. He also received from the king of the Two Sicilies the Dukedom of Bronté and an estate in Sicily.

Nelson didn't come home for more than two years. During that time there were many changes. The coup d'état of *18 Brumaire* took place, and Napoleon was soon first consul and in most ways dictator of France. A British and allied force recaptured Malta and kept it for the British instead of returning it to the knights. The czar of Russia, who had been elected grand master of the knights, was infuriated by this, with consequences to come. But Malta remained under British control until given its independence after World War II.

Basing his squadron at Naples, Nelson was unwisely drawn into the internal struggles of the Kingdom of the Two Sicilies. And it was during this time that his love affair with Emma, Lady Hamilton, began. She was the young wife of sixty-five-year-old Sir William Hamilton, British ambassador to the court at Naples.

Nelson was finally relieved of his command and ordered home in mid-1800, and he chose to travel overland rather than by sea. Nelson, Sir William, and Lady Hamilton traveled together by coach, skirting the eastern edge of the French conquests, stopping to public acclaim in Vienna, Prague, and Dresden, a four-month trip that finally ended at Hamburg. The travelers took the mail packet from Cuxhaven for the last leg to England.

They arrived on 6 November 1800 in Great Yarmouth, where Nelson was greeted with immense enthusiasm. Repeatedly, the horses were taken from his carriage at city boundaries, and the citizens themselves drew him through their towns.

But much of the aristocracy did not share this popular enthusiasm, disapproving of his open affair with Emma Hamilton and his rejection of Lady Nelson, his wife of fifteen years. The minor level of gossip surrounding Sir Hyde Parker and his marriage to Miss Onslow was nothing compared to the delicious high-voltage tales and rumors about Nelson and Lady Hamilton that flooded upper English society.

Meanwhile, another crisis was developing in the war, this time in the Baltic, which was an important area to Britain. From the Baltic came the best mast timber available in Europe and naval stores like turpentine, Stockholm tar, and rosin, plus hemp for cordage, flax for sails, and the best iron. The countries around the Baltic were good customers for British exports, particularly tropical products like coffee, tea, and sugar. Russia was an especially important customer.

Czar Paul, the Emperor and Autocrat of All the Russias, was the most deranged of the mad monarchs in Europe at that time.[9] Among other things, the czar was fascinated with the idea of the crusading knights of Malta and the Order of Saint John of Jerusalem and had gotten himself elected as grand master of the nearly defunct order. No one involved seems to have been bothered by the idea of the most puissant member of the Russian Orthodox Church heading up a Roman Catholic order with fealty to the pope.

To try to keep Russia in the gradually crumbling Second Coalition against France, the British government had earlier promised to restore Malta to the knights. But when the czar suddenly dropped out of the alliance, charmed by a wide-ranging proposal from Napoleon for a "League of Armed Neutrality," which was to be an association of neutral nations to oppose Britain at sea, all bets were off. When the British at last retook Malta, it was the British flag that flew over the islands. Czar Paul was furious and turned against England totally, seizing British ships and other assets in Russia and sending some British sailors off to the wintry interior in Siberia.

The proposed League of Armed Neutrality was part of Napoleon's grand design to defeat or at least nullify the British at sea while he reoccupied Saint-Domingue, put down the slave rebellion, then stepped off with an army for that "superb territory," Louisiana, and created a French empire in the American West. The Second Treaty of San Ildefonso, signed with some secrecy in Spain on 1 October 1800, giving Louisiana back to France, was preparation for this grand design.[10]

Napoleon also hoped to get the United States to cooperate with or even become allied with the league, but the Americans, although not fully aware of the total scheme, accurately smelled a rat and declined. The idea of Napoleon and a French Army ashore at New Orleans and the mouth of the Mississippi was frightening to President Jefferson and all in power in the United States.

The concept and details of Napoleon's proposal for this League of Armed Neutrality came straight out of the Convention of Môrtefontaine, the as-yet-unratified treaty that ended France's Quasi-War with the United States. This convention included items that dealt with several facets of "Freedom of the Seas," and Napoleon had these principles written into a manifesto and widely published in Europe to stir up neutral support for the proposed league. This cut right across Britain's belligerent rights and, in addition, had the effect of shutting Britain out of its Baltic trade.

Helping to feed the push toward this league of neutrals was the growing tension between Britain and Denmark. At issue was Denmark's assertion that Danish merchant vessels, convoyed by a Danish warship, should be free from search by the British for French contraband—an idea right out of Napoleon's manifesto. There was some gunfire over this matter in July 1800, when the frigate *Freya* opposed a British search of a Danish convoy and the British took her and her six-ship convoy into England.

In the Baltic, Czar Paul, after some heavy-handed prompting from Napoleon, took the lead in setting up the "League of Armed Neutrality" and urged it on his neighbors. Russia was the most massive power in the Baltic by far, so it was an offer that the Scandinavian and Baltic nations found difficult to refuse. John Quincy Adams, writing from Berlin, called it "rape by seduction." Some found it ironic that Russia, "a power not possessed [of] as many commercial ships as our Salem [Massachusetts]," should be out front in defending the freedom of the seas.[11]

Denmark joined the league willingly, as a quid pro quo for Russian protection against Britain. Sweden and Prussia also joined, although under some pressure, in mid-December 1800, and the stage was set for the Battle of Copenhagen.[12]

The British reaction was to try diplomacy for a few months. But then after judging that this wouldn't do the job, at least not without the backup of some force, plans were swiftly put afoot for a naval expedition to the Baltic. The strategy was straightforward: It was by now midwinter, and the Russian fleet was icebound in its eastern-Baltic ports and would not be able to get out until spring. The western Baltic around Denmark and Sweden was mostly ice free. The admiral commanding the British fleet would bear a message giving the Danes the option to disarm and enter an alliance with the British, who would then provide a fleet to protect them from the Russians. If this proposal was rejected, the admiral was to destroy the Danish Navy, the shipping in the harbor, and the arsenal at Copenhagen. Put bluntly, the Danes could change their mind, join the British, and rely on their protection or be battered into submission. In their turn the Swedes would be threatened, which was likely to be sufficient, and the British fleet would then move east to be off the Russian ports to take on the czar's navy a piece at a time, as the ice broke up. This strategy required, of course, that the British move rapidly, to accomplish it before the spring thaw.

Now, who was to command this force, which was to be about twenty battleships and six frigates, plus numerous sloops, brigs, bomb vessels, and fire ships? The admiral to be chosen obviously would need to be experienced at handling a large fleet in confined waters, should have a good bit of skill in diplomacy, should be bold and enterprising, and above all should be strategically flexible and tactically innovative, to take advantage of unforeseen opportunities as they arose. Nelson fit the prescription, except that he had never handled a fleet quite that big, and Admiral the Earl of St. Vincent felt that he wasn't quite ready to do so yet. But there were several senior admirals who had handled fleets under difficult conditions in European waters and were aggressive and enterprising, one example being Admiral William Cornwallis, who was available at the time.[13]

But Sir Hyde Parker was chosen for the job. Sir Hyde had none of the qualities needed: his only experiences at handling groups of ships at sea had been when he commanded the four ships of the rear of Hotham's fleet during the "unsatisfactory victory" of March 1795, plus his infrequent cruises around Jamaica and Saint-Domingue with the five or six battleships of his command. He had no diplomatic skills—he even found it difficult to get along with other British admirals and had always been at loggerheads with the army generals sent out to Saint-Domingue. He was sixty-one years old, cautious, and rigid in his ways. He seemed always to find difficulties rather than opportunities. To top it all off, he wasn't interested in having a sea command at this time.

So why was he chosen? It was principally the doing of the ever-powerful Admiral the Earl of St. Vincent. Early in December 1800 while still head of the Channel Fleet he wrote to Earl Spencer, saying, "Sir Hyde Parker is the only man you have to face [the Northern Powers]. . . ." St. Vincent called Spencer's attention to the fact that Parker (then a captain) had been involved in the Russian Armament of 1791, an incident of fleet mobilization when a disagreement with Russia looked as if it might lead to war. St. Vincent said that Parker was "in possession of all information obtained during the Russian Armament" and gave this much importance. Yet any such information held by Hyde Parker was stale by nearly ten years, and in any event Parker had not played a key role at that time. In spite of this seeming praise, St. Vincent's true feelings toward Parker seem to have been dislike and a mild contempt.[14]

The truth seems to be that Lord St. Vincent, always a harsh and ruthless man, had privately decided that Hyde Parker, having so far had an easy and profitable war, deserved to be given a really tough assignment. If he failed, his career would be ended, and that would be a just, if hard, outcome. To ensure that the expedition would accomplish its first major objective of knocking the Danes out of the League of Armed Neutrality, St. Vincent urged that Nelson go as Parker's second in command. Nelson could perform miracles, and one might be needed. Spencer publicly announced the appointments of Parker as commander in chief and Nelson as second on 27 January.[15]

Within a few weeks the Pitt government fell in a disagreement over an Irish religious question. Addington became the new prime minister, and on 18 February Admiral the Earl of St. Vincent became First Lord of the Admiralty, replacing Spencer. St. Vincent's protégé, Captain Sir Thomas Troubridge, not a friend of Parker's, was also appointed to be one of the Lords Commissioners of the Admiralty, one of the two Sea Lords.

Before long St. Vincent, now carrying the full responsibility of the Admiralty, began to have doubts about the appointment of Parker. He remarked to his secretary that "he was quite sure of Nelson and should have been in no apprehension if he had been of [sufficient] rank to take the chief command; but that he could not feel quite as sure about Sir Hyde, as he had never been tried."[16] This seems to have been a considerable change of view from a few months earlier, when from the Channel Fleet he was recommending Parker to Spencer.

The expedition was to assemble in Great Yarmouth on the east coast of England. Sir Hyde Parker's flagship was to be the *London,* a three-decked battleship of ninety-eight guns. On 10 February Sir Hyde's protégés, including John Maples, left the *Royal George,* and they reported aboard the *London* the next day.[17] Captain Robert Otway took command of the *London,* and a new senior captain, not a connection of Sir Hyde's, Captain William Dommet, was put aboard by St. Vincent to be captain of the fleet, a job roughly equivalent to that of chief of staff today.

The *London* did not go to Great Yarmouth for nearly a month. Sir Hyde did not go aboard her until much later, staying instead at his house in London. On 23 February he and young Lady Parker traveled by coach to Great Yarmouth, where they moved into a hotel. He established his flag aboard H.M. Frigate *Ardent,* pending the arrival of the *London.*

Nelson moved aboard his assigned flagship, H.M.S. *St. George,* on 12 February in Portsmouth, with Captain Thomas Masterman Hardy as her captain. In January Lady Hamilton had borne Nelson's child, a girl that they named Horatia. Shortly after hoisting his flag in the *St. George,* Nelson went up to London for a first look at the baby.

The *St. George* was under repair, and it wasn't until late February that she was anywhere near ready to go. Nelson was impatient to get to sea and in addition to constantly hurrying the workmen on the *St. George* kept the pressure on the repair authorities to make ready some ten other ships in Portsmouth that were part of the Baltic force. On 27 February he rapidly embarked the eight hundred plus army troops that were to be the main landing force and got the whole group under way at daylight on the twenty-eighth, nearly carrying some workmen from the yard to sea with him.[18] The army officer commanding the troops was Lieutenant-Colonel the Honorable William Stewart, an aristocrat with friends and access in all high places. He and Nelson immediately became friends, and Stewart was to play a key part in the political events that followed the battle.

In early March the expedition was still assembling in Great Yarmouth. Nelson and his ships arrived on the third, and the *London* not until the ninth. By now, time was critical: the Baltic winter had been mild, and the ice was expected to break up and release the Russian fleet by mid-April or at the latest early May. Nelson was eager to get going, but Sir Hyde showed no urgency. He ignored Nelson and told him nothing of his plans and, in fact, seemed more interested in a ball that Lady Parker was planning in Great Yarmouth for Friday evening, 13 March.

But Friday the thirteenth was not to be Lady Parker's lucky evening. Nelson, frustrated and disgusted, wrote a private letter to Troubridge at the Admiralty, and two days later, the minimum time in which mail could reach London and be turned around, Sir Hyde received a thinly disguised threat from St. Vincent to get under way immediately or face very uncertain consequences.[19] The ball was quickly canceled, and Lady Parker was packed up and sent back to London. Sir Hyde went aboard the *London* on the eleventh, and signals were soon flying to get under way at midnight.

The whole fleet, some fifty ships large and small, was at sea and assembled by midmorning of the next day. Later, a packet ship saw them heading generally northeast, with the faster-sailing ships towing the slower.[20] The distance to be run to arrive in the Skaggerak, outside the entrance to the Kattegat and the Baltic, was about 450 miles, and with a gale from the west-southwest for a day, followed by steady fair winds, the ships should have made the passage in three days at the most. Of course, an admiral in those pre-radar days needed to be conservative with his navigation, but Sir Hyde was excessively cautious: it was not until the morning of 19 March that the ships passed the Skaw, the northernmost point of Denmark's Jutland peninsula, and entered the Kattegat. From there it was only 160 miles up the Kattegat and through the Øre Sound to Copenhagen. Having already frittered away much precious time, Sir Hyde brought the fleet to anchor in Wingoe Bay on the Swedish coast, still 150 miles from Copenhagen.

At this point Sir Hyde had made no plans whatsoever as to how he would carry out his orders from the Admiralty. These orders, which Sir Hyde had not shown to Nelson or Rear-Admiral Graves, the junior flag officer with the expedition, were simple and unequivocal. He had been given a letter, written by the foreign secretary, that he was to deliver to Mr. Drummond, the British chargé d'affaires at Copenhagen. The letter, which Drummond was to present to the Danish government, told the Danes, in effect, that they were to quit the League of Armed Neutrality and have their warships join the British to assist in their own protection against the Russians, or war and destruction would be the consequence. Drummond was to get the Danish reply into Sir Hyde's hands as soon as possible, and if it was adverse, or if no reply was received from Drummond within forty-eight hours, Sir Hyde was to attack.

Sir Hyde then proceeded to make a major strategic blunder—not his last in this campaign. He sent the frigate *Blanche* to carry the letter to Drummond. The *Blanche* was to go to Cronborg Castle, which guarded the four-mile-wide entrance to Øre Sound, Copenhagen, and the Baltic, and send in a boat with an officer. After calling on the castle's governor, the officer was to hire a carriage and carry the letter to Drummond at Copenhagen, about twenty miles to the south.

The letter, arriving by carriage in the hands of a lieutenant, had none of the impact that it would have had if properly delivered: Immediately upon arrival in the Kattegat, Sir Hyde should have taken his fleet past Cronborg Castle, staying on the Swedish side of the channel, out of the effective range of the Danish guns should they choose to fire, then sailed up the sound to Copenhagen. Then with the fleet in full view of the city, he should have sent in his barge carrying a senior officer in full uniform with the letter and its accompanying papers in a dispatch case, to deliver to the British embassy. Drummond could then have gone to the Danes from a strong position, and while the foreign minister and the crown prince read the British ultimatum they could look out their windows at the fifty-ship fleet and be thereby encouraged to come around to the British point of view.

Delivered as it was by Lieutenant McCulloch, the letter had no such impact, and the Danes gave it the most insulting treatment possible: because it was written in English, not the French language traditional in the diplomacy of the period, the Danes returned it without reply. However, without a doubt they read it, and while they had been getting ready for war at a steady pace, they now began to mobilize with all speed.

War now being imminent, Chargé d'Affaires Drummond and Nicholas Vansittart, a senior British government official who was in Copenhagen, having been sent over from London to make a last attempt at negotiation, decided to return with Lieutenant McCulloch and go aboard the fleet. With them went some British families living in Denmark and the British consul. They all crowded aboard the *Blanche,* and by late on the twenty-second had rejoined Sir Hyde and the fleet, now somewhat closer, but still fifteen miles from Cronborg Castle and the entrance to the sound and forty miles from Copenhagen.

Vansittart, whose charter from the government included the authority to give orders to Admiral Parker, immediately sent his secretary over to the *London* with a letter telling Sir Hyde that Drummond had been handed his passport and saying, "This proceeding . . . may be considered as equivalent to a Declaration of War. You will therefore consider all Negociation as at an end, and proceed to execute such Instructions as you have received." These instructions told Sir Hyde firmly and without wiggle room "immediately [to] proceed to vigorous hostilities."[21]

Up to this point no one present in the British fleet had any clear idea of what defenses the Danes had either at Cronborg Castle or at Copenhagen. But with the arrival of the *Blanche* the fleet received several people who did: Mr. Drummond had served for some time at Copenhagen and from a nonmilitary man's point of view knew the city and its defenses well, and he had often been to Cronborg Castle. Nicholas Vansittart and his secretary, also men without a military background, had been several days in Copenhagen and had just passed by the castle while aboard the *Blanche*. Then there were Captain Hamond and Lieutenant McCulloch of the *Blanche*. Hamond had been anchored off the castle for two days, ample time for a good long-glass look, and had also called on the governor of the castle, whose reception rooms overlooked the battery. Lieutenant McCulloch had seen all this and had also had a good chance to observe the defenses at Copenhagen. Both, of course, knew a good bit about what they were looking at when they saw cannon, forts, and harbor defenses.

In the meetings that followed the return of the *Blanche,* Sir Hyde completely ignored Hamond and McCulloch, the most expert observers, and never asked them to describe what they had seen. Instead, late that night Parker signaled for Drummond to be sent over to the flagship. Drummond was well informed on the subject and described, but in uncritical terms, the two hundred guns at Cronborg, the one hundred guns in the Trekroner fort at the northern end of Copenhagen, and the line of warships and armed hulks that extended south in front of the naval arsenal. After hearing these descriptions, Sir Hyde began to see difficulties, and the strength of the Danish defenses seems to have loomed ever larger in his mind. Before the return of the *Blanche* he had appeared determined on sailing past Cronborg Castle and on to Copenhagen. Now he became despondent and defeatist, paralyzed by his appraisal of the enemy's force. But he sent for Nicholas Vansittart and Nelson to discuss what options they had in carrying out the Admiralty's orders.

Nelson came alongside the *London* in a gig and was hoisted aboard in a special chair: a one-armed man could not climb up the wooden cleats nailed to the sides as a ladder—the normal way of coming aboard at sea—and in any event, many admirals had themselves hoisted aboard in this way. The officers of the *London* would have been lined up on the quarterdeck to receive him, and this and two other trips by Nelson to the *London* during the next days gave John Maples his only opportunities for glimpses of the national hero.

Parker, Nelson, and Vansittart met in the *London*'s great cabin. This meeting, plus meetings between Nelson and Parker on the following days, finally cleared up Sir Hyde's doubts and uncertainties and put the expedition back on track. First, Nelson pointed out to Sir Hyde that the real enemy was the czar and that timing had become urgent because the ice would soon be breaking up in the Russian ports. Then Nelson questioned Vansittart more closely about what he had seen of the Danish defenses, and it became clear that while these were formidable, they probably could be successfully attacked. Denmark had not been at war for eighty years, and the state of training of its sailors and gunners was likely to be backward. Many of the guns in the forts were perhaps a hundred years old, had not been fired in years, were encrusted with thick coats of rust and paint, and were probably more of a danger to their crews than to their targets.

Nelson then proposed a tactical approach that led Sir Hyde to gain some confidence in him, and then, back on his own flagship, Nelson turned this concept into a plan. The idea was to avoid, at least initially, the supposedly powerful fixed fortresses at the northern end of Copenhagen's defenses and instead use a squadron of the more shallow draft ships of the fleet to attack the southern defenses. These defenses consisted of a line of moored ships, hulks, and floating gun platforms. The few charts that the British had showed the water in front of them to be shallow but adequate for sixty-four–gun ships and the lighter draft of the 74s. A large shoal called the Middle Ground ran roughly parallel to the Danish line about one thousand yards in front of it, severely limiting the movements of the attackers.

The southern squadron of 74s and 64s was to be under Nelson's command, and while it was attacking, the *London* and the three-decker 98s plus the heavier of the 74s were to move into position off the northern end of the Danish defenses, where the water was deeper, to threaten the forts and fixed batteries.

Sir Hyde was still reluctant to take the fleet past Cronborg Castle. The channel between Denmark and Sweden at this point was only four miles wide, and there was also a fort of unknown potency on the Swedish side. He seriously considered going west and south through the Belt, around the back side of the Island of Sjælland, a distance of two hundred shoal-filled miles. Luckily, he was talked out of this, perhaps by Robert Otway.

Nelson reminded Sir Hyde that the Danish guns at Cronborg Castle had an effective range of only about a mile, that the guns on the Swedish side were thought to be few and small, and that it was unlikely that the Swedes would fire anyway. After this discussion the plans were settled: the fleet would pass the fort at Cronborg, go up the sound, and attack Copenhagen, using Nelson's plan.

At this point the wind was foul for a few days, giving the British time to get prepared. The fleet organization was changed to give Nelson a squadron of twelve ships—74s, 64s, and 50s—plus several frigates, bomb vessels to lob shells into the naval arsenal, and fire ships to torch the Danish line if conditions were right. Nelson shifted his flag to the seventy-four–gun battleship *Elephant,* commanded by Captain Thomas Foley. Sir Hyde retained direct command of the rest, the heavier and deeper-draft ships plus some frigates and brigs.

More officers and men were needed to fill out the crews of Nelson's squadron, and John Maples volunteered for this service. He probably served in charge of a division of guns in one of the battleships. His biographical sketch doesn't give the name of the ship or just what service he provided.

Early on 30 March the wind finally shifted around to the west, fair for passage into the sound. The fleet stayed well over to the Swedish side but received no fire from the Swedes. Cronborg Castle fired, but the shot fell short and the fleet came through without a scratch. By noon the ships were anchored off the northern end of Copenhagen, in full sight of the city but out of range of the guns in the Trekroner fort.

In early afternoon Sir Hyde, Nelson, and Graves, plus Captain Foley and Captain Fremantle, who was in charge of the flat boats planned for carrying Lieutenant-Colonel Stewart's troops, boarded the frigate *Amazon* and sailed over to reconnoiter the Danish line. This was a lot of eggs to risk in one basket, but all went safely—they drew some Danish fire but without harm. They found that, among other things, the industrious Danes had removed all the channel buoys and other navigational markers, making it extremely risky to go anywhere without some likelihood of going aground. When the *Amazon* returned, Nelson mobilized the masters and quartermasters of the fleet to sound the areas that he had to sail through to get into position south of the Danish defense line, correct his charts, and place anchored kegs as temporary buoys. This took all night and a good part of the next day.

The reconnaissance trip in the *Amazon* left Sir Hyde again alarmed at the strength of the Danish defense. Nelson's view was "I think I can annihilate them."[22] But it was clear that the Danes had effectively used the extra time they had been given by Sir Hyde's delays.

At about four o'clock in the afternoon on 1 April Nelson got his squadron under way—twelve battleships, several frigates, plus bomb vessels and fire ships, to a total of thirty-three. There was a light wind from the northwest, and by about 5 P.M. the ships were anchored south of the Middle Ground shoal and about two miles from the lower end of the moored Danish line of ships, gun platforms, and hulks. The view from the *Elephant* looked edgewise along a lineup of some hundreds of gun muzzles—not a sight to cheer the faint of heart.

Nelson badly needed some information about the water depths close along the front of the Danish line. Captain Thomas Hardy had left the command of the *St. George* to serve as a volunteer in Nelson's squadron, and as soon as it was dark Nelson sent him and a party of men in a muffle-oared boat to take soundings as close as possible to the line. Nelson would have liked to fight the battle with his ships practically muzzle-to-muzzle with the Danes. Hardy found good water close to the enemy line but shallow spots and uncertainty farther off, nearer to the Middle Ground shoal. It was Hardy's great good luck that the Danes sent no boats out that night and he was able to sound the whole line without being detected. He returned to the *Elephant* about midnight and reported what he had found.

The rest of the night was taken up with writing detailed operation orders for the individual ships. These orders were written on pieces of card to make them easy to handle on the quarterdeck during the battle and gave information about which ship to follow, how to anchor, and which ships in the Danish line each was to attack. As at the Nile, it was Nelson's intent to concentrate on the first several ships in the line and destroy them, then move on up the line and repeat the process.

Early the next morning the wind shifted to the southeast, fair for the attack. At about 7 A.M. Nelson called all the captains to come to the flagship. Each was given his copy of the operation order for the attack, then Nelson answered questions until it was clear that every captain understood what he was expected to do.

The ships began to get under way at about 9:30 A.M., and by ten the first British ships were anchoring abreast their Danish antagonists and the battle was on. Nelson's plan was briefly disrupted when one of his battleships went aground on the tail of the Middle Ground, out of range of the enemy. He had hardly adjusted his assignments for this bit of bad luck when two more vessels bottomed on shallow spots, and the plan had to be adjusted again. These two were where their guns could reach the enemy but were too distant to be really effective. The battle now settled down into a slugging match, and the dense white smoke from the black powder obscured most of the battle and, according to a contemporary print, made a heavy cloud rising about a thousand feet above the action. Nelson would have liked to have fought at a closer range than the roughly two hundred yards that he ended up at, but the pilots with the ships were afraid of finding shoal water closer to the Danish line, in spite of Captain Hardy's survey of the night before.

The Danes were a more determined and tenacious adversary than Nelson had run into before, and he began to realize that he had underestimated them. Not all of those manning the Danish line were professional sailors or soldiers. Many were civilians swept up in the mobilization—carpenters, shoemakers, and grocers. They were in a completely literal sense defending their homes and families against what was in their view an unprovoked attack by a powerful aggressor, and they fought with a strong sense of outrage and desperation. Overshot cannonballs were landing in their houses, and their wives and children were watching the battle from the quays and house balconies, anxious for the fate of their men. But raw power began to tell, and by early afternoon the Danes were beginning to weaken.

The night before the battle Sir Hyde had anchored his squadron about six miles north of the Trekroner fort. This choice of anchorage is difficult to explain except as a truly deplorable lack of foresight: a wind from the south that would enable Nelson to attack the Danish line, thus starting the battle, would be directly foul for Parker's squadron, which would have to tack laboriously back and forth to get up to its objectives, the forts at the northern end of Copenhagen.

So while Nelson's squadron was slugging it out with the Danes, Sir Hyde and his ships were sailing into the wind, tacking frequently and making almost no headway. The battle was over well before he had attained a position near Copenhagen.

But Sir Hyde could see the battle in the distance, even though much of the detail was lost in the smoke. He could see that one battleship was aground completely away from the battle, and he could see that the Danes were still keeping up a heavy cannonade. He began to see difficulties again and thought that the battle was going badly for Nelson. His reaction was to want to signal Nelson to pull out of the battle, and although his advisers, Captains Dommet and Otway, thought this was a bad idea, Sir Hyde persisted and at about 1:15 P.M. made the signal for the whole fleet to "discontinue the action." It was an incomprehensibly stupid order. There was no way that Nelson could have disengaged without being shot to pieces and running probably half of his ships aground.

The only major ships to obey the signal were three of the frigates at the very northern end of Nelson's squadron. On one of these, the *Amazon,* the result was tragic. As she turned away to disengage, a shot tore her captain in two. He was Edward Riou, a promising officer, and Nelson took his death as a personal blow.

On the *Elephant,* when Nelson was told of Parker's signal, he ordered that it be acknowledged as received but not repeated to his ships for compliance. Instead, he made sure that the *Elephant* kept flying the signal for "Close Action." Then he turned to Captain Foley and created another highlight in the Nelson legend: "You know, Foley, I have only one eye—and I have a right to be blind sometimes." Then he put his telescope to his blind eye and said, "I really do not see the signal!"[23]

Up to a couple of generations ago schoolboys were inspired by such casual heroism and insouciance.

Not only would it have been disastrous for Nelson to disengage at the time of Parker's signal, but the battle was now clearly beginning to favor the British. Within an hour after the signal, several of the ships and hulks in the Danish line had struck. Some that had not given up had almost ceased firing, and there were fires burning on board a few of them. The British line, although battered, was still firing most of its guns.

At this point a flash of Nelson's genius changed the course of events. He wrote a note to "The Brothers of Englishmen, the Danes," saying in effect that he had orders to spare Denmark when no longer resisting, but if the firing continued from the already surrendered and the clearly beaten ships, he would have to set them afire—a move that would kill a lot of helpless wounded men still in them.

This note was taken ashore in a boat with a flag of truce by a Danish-speaking British officer. On shore, the crown prince, the actual ruler of Denmark, was personally directing the Danish side of the battle, his father the king being long insane. The crown prince, accompanied by his staff, was standing at the waterfront, watching the battle, when the note was delivered. He knew that a number of his ships had surrendered and that others were so battered that they could no longer fight. He could see the British bomb vessels moving into position to loft ten-inch explosive shells into the arsenal. And he could see Admiral Parker's squadron of fresh battleships slowly approaching from the northeast. So he sent his aide-de-camp back with the British officer in the boat to find out what Nelson's proposals might be.

This exchange led to a truce. The Danes stopped firing, then the British, and the *Elephant* hoisted a large flag of truce. The battle was over.

The losses were terrible: about 450 Danes were killed in the battle or died of their wounds shortly afterward, and another 550 were less severely wounded. For the British it was 254 killed and 689 wounded. The suffering among the wives and children who had watched the battle and whose husbands and fathers would not be coming home was indescribable.[24]

Although Sir Hyde was slow in getting his squadron into action, he was lightning-fast in grasping for himself and his protégés the rewards of victory. These rewards should have been turned over to Nelson to be distributed among those who had really fought the battle. But this was not Sir Hyde's way.

The first was the honor of bearing home to England the dispatches of victory. The officer who served in this pleasant and honorable role could usually expect to be given a substantial reward, perhaps a promotion, or something of similarly satisfactory weight. This task should have gone to Captain Foley, skipper of the *Elephant,* but Parker gave it instead to his favorite, Captain Robert Otway, who had not had any part in the fighting. So Otway set off for London with the good news.

There were a few promotions and appointments possible, where battle deaths created opportunities for commanders (and occasionally lieutenants) to be moved into all-important post-captain commands, and for others below them to move up. It was here that John Maples received a break of good fortune. He was appointed by Sir Hyde on 4 April to command H.M. Fire Brig

Otter, a fire ship.[25] With the command came a step up in rank to acting-commander. John Maples at least was more deserving than most of the other of Sir Hyde's protégés: he had fought in Nelson's squadron throughout the battle.

Then Sir Hyde had all but one of their prizes burned, and with this disappeared any chance of even a slight reward for the seamen who had fought the action. Nelson was furious. For the first time he began to openly criticize Admiral Parker in his letters home and in his conversations with others in the fleet.

Negotiations for a more permanent truce went on for several days after the battle, with Nelson speaking for the British, nominally on behalf of Sir Hyde. On 8 April the crown prince and Nelson were alone in a room at the Amalienborg Palace, trying to iron out two last sticky points in an armistice agreement, when Captain Lindholm, the aide-de-camp, came in and whispered in Danish into the prince's ear, "The Czar is dead." The crown prince was a cool hand. He didn't change expression and went right forward with the discussion of the armistice.

It was true. In the early morning of 24 March, while Hyde Parker, Horatio Nelson, John Maples, and the British Fleet were still sitting out in the Kattegat, some members of the court at St. Petersburg, fearful for their safety under the unpredictable rule of the ever more erratic Paul I, entered his bedroom and strangled him. The czar's grown son and successor tacitly approved. Alexander I was altogether a different animal. He was, within limits, sane and rational, but he was devious. Napoleon considered him Byzantine, and others said of him, "Alexander is as sharp as a pin, as fine as a razor, and as false as sea foam."[26]

Alexander wanted no part of an alliance against England, with whom he wanted a closer relationship. So in reality the "Armed Neutrality" had collapsed at 4 A.M. on 24 March. The Battle of Copenhagen had been unnecessary, more than seven hundred lives had been wasted, and countless other lives needlessly blighted by crippling wounds or the loss of loved ones. However, the destruction of the Danish warships served short-term British policy—the Danes remained a potential enemy and the problems between Britain and Denmark were simply papered over in 1801, not solved.

The Danes kept the czar's death secret, although it undoubtedly had an effect on their approach to the final negotiations of the armistice. The British Fleet in front of Copenhagen didn't hear of the fortunate event until 22 April, and then by a letter direct from St. Petersburg.[27]

A few days after Otway had gone to England with the news of the victory, it became necessary for Sir Hyde to send another high-level messenger to London, this time with a copy of the proposed armistice negotiated by Nelson. Lieutenant-Colonel Stewart asked to go. He had been present at most of the negotiating sessions and so was a logical choice. He was, of course, also thoroughly familiar with all that had gone on in the fleet, including Sir Hyde's delays and misjudgments, and the fact that Parker as commander in chief had been a hindrance to the expedition's mission and totally superfluous as far as the battle itself was concerned.

Stewart had excellent access to those in power, so after he arrived in England and had given over the armistice documents, he visited Addington, the prime minister, St. Vincent at the Admiralty, and the foreign secretary, among others. The result was that a few days after Captain Otway had left London with messages of approval and the thanks of both Houses of Parliament for Sir Hyde, the Admiralty and the Foreign Ministry itself, based on what Lieutenant-Colonel Stewart had reported, reopened discussions and decided to sack Sir Hyde and give Nelson the command in the Baltic.[28]

So when Stewart returned to the fleet several days later than Otway, he brought Parker the surprising news that he was to lose his command and was ordered home. It was a major shock to Sir Hyde: he had been hoping to be raised to the peerage for the victory. After all, when Nelson won the Battle of Cape Saint Vincent for Admiral Jervis, Jervis received an earldom.

Parker arrived home to find himself at the center of a storm of criticism, much of it unjustified. He was bewildered and did not understand how this could be happening to him. He nearly disappeared from public view and kept his resentments private within his circle of friends and supporters.

Admiral of the Blue Sir Hyde Parker, Knight, was never employed again, and as his influence waned, John Maples again lost a sponsor. Parker lived only a few years after his public disgrace and died in 1807. Captain Otway, the skilled frigate captain, Sir Hyde's closest protégé, went on to become an admiral, a Knight of the Bath, and a baronet, but in old age he experienced that tragedy most feared by the ancient Romans: his two eldest sons died before him.[29]

Napoleon's grand design for Saint-Domingue, Louisiana, and his American empire had received a near-fatal setback from the Battle of Copenhagen and the death of Czar Paul. Napoleon made one more major effort toward Louisiana when he sent General LeClerc and a twenty thousand–man army to retake Saint-Domingue in 1802, when during the brief Peace of Amiens he did not have to face the British at sea. But the British declared war again on 18 May 1803. Now cut off at sea by the British Navy, and defeated by the black armies, yellow fever, and the death of LeClerc himself, the French surrendered in Saint-Domingue. Napoleon finally saw the overwhelming difficulty of his venture and, needing money, sold Louisiana to the United States.

Within hours after Sir Hyde left Copenhagen in the *Blanche,* Nelson got the fleet under way and headed up the Baltic. Acting-Commander John Maples in H.M. Fire Brig *Otter,* along with the other smaller vessels, followed in the wake of the battleships. First they went across to Sweden and stopped off the naval base at Carlskrona, where the Swedish Fleet was visible at anchor. Nelson sent in a letter, courteously phrased but leaving no doubt that if he found the Swedish Fleet at sea, he would destroy it. Then he headed up toward the Russian ports of Revel and Kronstadt. His intent was to make sure that Czar Alexander was indeed going to be friendly to England and that the British ships, sailors, and assets seized by Czar Paul were going to be promptly released. This accomplished, Nelson's role in the Baltic was completed. His health, always frail, was particularly bad at this time. He was relieved by Admiral Pole and returned to England in late June of 1801. He was made a viscount for his services in the Baltic, but his reward in terms of public approval far transcended that elevation—he was the most popular man in England and a true national hero.

For John Maples, the *Otter* was his first real command. It was not the sort of command that would have been given to a rising sprig of the nobility with family interest, but it was a welcome step to John Maples. However, the *Otter* was laid up in September 1801, and the Admiralty did not make John Maples's appointment as acting-commander permanent—probably a reflection of Sir Hyde's waned influence. Maples was transferred to H.M.S. *Ganges,* a seventy-four–gun battleship commanded by Captain Thomas Fremantle, a favorite of Nelson's. John Maples was still a lieutenant and at thirty years was now getting a little long in the tooth.[30]

CHAPTER FIFTEEN

The Frigates at Trafalgar

EARLY IN HIS DRIVE TO PERSONAL POWER and his campaign to extend the hegemony of Revolutionary and Imperial France across Europe and the world, Napoleon Bonaparte realized that Great Britain was the major obstacle in his path. There stood Britannia, less than thirty miles away, but across a strip of water that had not been successfully crossed by a conqueror since 1066.

The population of Britain in 1793 was a little under thirteen million, much less than half of the roughly thirty million of France. Although the British had an army, it was at that time small and old-fashioned. Given the demographics, the British Army could never hope to compete with the French in sheer manpower. Also the French Army soon became the world's best, a citizens' army in the modern sense, with an officer corps in which promotion depended on ability not birth and with the most effective artillery and logistics—an army that drew upon the mobilized resources of the nation. The British regular Army, even at its peak under Wellington late in the wars, when man for man it had no superior, never reached 150,000 in size, and no more than about 40,000 British troops ever actively campaigned against the French at one time. The French Army at its full strength under Napoleon was able to field more than half a million men.[1]

But there was the British Navy. In size, when mobilized for the long wars of 1793–1815, it was nominally not much larger than the navy of France. But in leadership, training, seamanship,gunnery skills, morale—everything that counted—the British Navy was greatly superior to that of France. It was also more than the equal of any combination of fleets—Spanish, Dutch, Danish—that the French could put together with their own. As long as the British Navy existed and could be brought to bear, the Channel might as well have been as wide as the ocean. It blocked Napoleon and kept England, the implacable adversary that stood between him and world conquest, beyond his reach.

This was not all. England was rich: its manufactories of iron products, textiles, and other goods dotted the countryside and cities of the north. Shipyards, commercial ports, and fisheries crowded the coasts. The riches of the overseas colonies in India, the West Indies, and Canada flowed in, and English manufactured exports flowed out, aboard hundreds of British merchant vessels, manned by that most important of England's maritime assets, the resourceful and sagacious British seafarer.

All of this was under the shield of the navy. The same shield that protected the Channel kept the French Navy blocked up in its anchorages. At the same time that it covered the passage of the British merchant fleets, it prevented the deployment of French traders on other than short coastal voyages between French-controlled ports. The British Navy cut the French off from putting down the revolution in Saint-Domingue, France's richest overseas possession. And Napoleon himself received a sharp personal object lesson in the use of sea power at Aboukir Bay in 1798.

Thus the British, unable alone to field an army to beat Napoleon, but beyond his reach, could use their wealth to subsidize France's natural enemies in Europe—Austria, Prussia, Russia—to bring their armies against him. This was eventually to wear him down, and Napoleon understood that this could happen. Of course, like anything in war, subsidizing armies was expensive. In 1800 Britain was paying its allies about £200,000,000 per year to keep their armies in the field—a sum equivalent to perhaps £18 billion today, about the size of the total annual British defense budget in the late 1980s.[2]

Because he foresaw that the British strategy could eventually succeed, Napoleon in May 1803, when the war was resumed after the brief "Peace of Amiens," set plans in motion aimed at the invasion, military defeat, and occupation of England. Troops were moved to the Channel ports, particularly Boulogne, which stands near the narrowest point for crossing, and fleets of flat-bottomed boats were built to ferry men and horses across the twenty-seven miles of water. A contemporary print shows the rows of tents on the hills behind the town and a forest of masts in the port itself.[3]

Napoleon's Grand Plan was that the squadrons of his navy would break out of the ports in which they had been blockaded by the British for years and would make a feint to the West Indies, drawing the British Navy away from

Europe in the process. The French squadrons would then coalesce into an effective fleet. This fleet would come up the Channel, driving off any of the British Navy that was left there to oppose them, and would then hold control of the narrow waters between France and England for some brief days while the French Army crossed and Napoleon the Corsican repeated the feat accomplished by William the Bastard at Hastings.

There were some basic flaws in this plan, but on the other hand, with some luck—and in those earlier days Napoleon had luck—it might have succeeded to the point of getting the French Army across.

The flaws—and here only a couple of the major ones will be mentioned—were, first, that Bonaparte's navy had been blockaded in its harbors almost continuously since 1793, the crews were untrained and unskilled in seamanship, and the ships themselves were mostly in poor shape. Most of his admirals were inexperienced and without much ability, were overawed by the British Navy, and were paralyzed by the prospect of having to meet the British at sea. The chances were slim that these admirals, crews, and ships could successfully carry out Napoleon's complex plans.

Then also, Napoleon did not have any clear idea of how the British might react to his moves, apparently assuming that they would fruitlessly scatter their fleets in pursuit. But Admiralty doctrine, understood by all British admirals, called for just the opposite. If a blockaded fleet escaped and got out of sight so that it could not immediately be brought to battle, the blockading squadron would normally fall back and reinforce the Channel Fleet. Only if there was an excellent reason for doing so and firm intelligence about the enemy's intentions would a blockading squadron chase after a vanished blockadee. So if the French managed to coalesce their squadrons into a fleet and come up the Channel, they would very likely meet a large and determined British fleet waiting for them.

The British, while alert and wary, were confident. As St. Vincent put it in speaking to the House of Lords, in an utterance that was as close as he ever came to humor: "I don't say the enemy cannot come; I only say they cannot come by sea."[4]

In late 1804 Spain was again drifting toward an alliance with France. After an unprovoked attack by the Royal Navy on four treasure ships arriving from South America, Spain took the opportunity to declare war on Great Britain on 12 December.[5] By a prewar agreement between France and Spain made earlier that year, the Spanish were by 30 March 1805 to provide Napoleon with twenty-five to twenty-nine battleships and four thousand to five thousand Spanish troops.[6] Before this agreement the French had thirty thousand troops and transports in the Texel, in Holland. At Boulogne and nearby French ports were flotillas of flat boats to carry 120,000 men and 25,000 horses, with many more than this number of men and horses billeted in the area or under canvas.[7] At Rochefort were six battleships and four frigates with four thousand troops on board; at Brest, twenty-one battleships, plus frigates and transports and twenty-five thousand troops; at Toulon, eleven battleships and eight frigates, plus transports with nine thousand troops on board. So, taking the French and Spanish forces together, the invasion began to look like it might possibly work—again, with a little luck.

Napoleon, just crowned emperor of France on 2 December 1804, now at the beginning of 1805 decided that the time was right to put in motion his Grand Plan for the invasion. He had at his disposal about sixty-eight to seventy battleships, not counting the Dutch Navy. The British had, nominally, 116 battleships, but probably only about 83 of these could actually be sent to sea, and there were other worldwide commitments besides Europe.[8] So counting just the numbers of ships, without considering training and condition, Napoleon could view his naval strength as roughly the equal of Great Britain's.

Things started off well. As a curtain raiser, Rear Admiral Missiessy escaped from Rochefort in bad weather on 11 January 1805 with 5 battleships, 3 frigates, 2 brigs, 3,500 troops, stores, and artillery. He headed for the West Indies, where he was supposed to stop at Martinique and Guadeloupe, conquer British Dominica and ransack the smaller British colonies, then await the arrival of Admiral Villeneuve and the squadron from Toulon, forming the initial coming together of the invasion fleet.

But soon things began to unravel. Missiessy attacked Dominica but failed to take it and harassed St. Kitts, Nevis, and Monserrat.[9] Then Villeneuve was delayed, and Missiessy received new orders from Napoleon to return to Europe.

On 20 May Missiessy was back where he started from, anchored in Aix Roads, just outside of Rochefort, and blockaded in. This was a foretaste of the future as the Grand Plan began to go awry.

The next to move was Admiral Villeneuve at Toulon. He was blockaded in by Nelson, but it was not exactly a blockade because Nelson with his battleships usually stayed well off the port, leaving a couple of frigates to watch, in the hopes of drawing the French out to sea where he could get at them. Villeneuve had barely escaped with his life from the Battle of the Nile, and his dread of meeting Nelson at sea was acute. But on 17 January 1805, finding his way clear and the wind fair, Villeneuve got under way with 11 battleships, 7 frigates, and 2 smaller vessels, with 3,500 troops on board, to try to carry out his orders from Napoleon: to go to Cartagena, pick up several Spanish battleships there, proceed through the Strait of Gibraltar to Cadiz, drive off the British blockaders and pick up several more Spanish and a French battleship there, then head for the West Indies. Once in the West Indies he was to do as much damage to British interests as he could while waiting forty days for the Brest squadron under Admiral Ganteaume to arrive. Then with Ganteaume in charge, the combined Rochefort, Toulon, and Brest Squadrons—an imposing fleet of about forty battleships—were to head for the English Channel, arriving there between 10 June and 10 July.[10]

But as Villeneuve headed southwest across the Golfe du Lion, he ran into a heavy storm; and short on sea experience because of being continuously block-aded in port, most of the ships were damaged in their masts and rigging. Vil-leneuve decided to go back into Toulon for repairs.

On the evening of the seventeenth, as he first came out of Toulon, he was immediately sighted by Nelson's two frigates, which kept contact with him until the middle of the following night and estimated that he was headed south. Then the frigates headed off to give Nelson the good news.

Nelson and his eleven battleships were anchored in a bay on the northeastern corner of Sardinia, about 230 miles from Toulon. When he got the information that the French were heading south, he began to think they were bound for Egypt—Nelson was mildly obsessed with the idea of French attacks on Egypt. So he headed south along the eastern side of Sardinia and sent his frigates ahead, to go west around the southern end of the island, to see what they could find.

Information was scanty, so he headed east, passing the volcanic island of Stromboli glowing in the dark during the night of the twenty-ninth, then on through the Strait of Messina and eastward, arriving off Alexandria on 7 Feb-ruary. Of course, he found nothing there and no word of the French. So he headed back to the west and sometime after the fifteenth received solid infor-mation about what had happened to them. By 15 March Nelson was off Toulon, relieved to note that Villeneuve was back inside.

By this time Nelson's ships were in much need of replenishment, so he ordered his storeships to meet him in the Gulf of Palma, on the southwestern side of the island of Majorca. On 27 March he began his refit and replenish-ment, which lasted until 1 April.

But Villeneuve was again ready to get to sea and, when he found his exit unguarded, got under way on 29 March and headed south-southwest, to pass to the east of Minorca and Majorca, because he thought Nelson was off Barcelona. Villeneuve was again spotted by Nelson's frigates, which tracked him briefly before losing him.

At about the same time, on 1 April, that Nelson got the information from his frigates, Villeneuve had a stroke of luck: he met a merchant vessel that had seen the British off the southern end of Sardinia just a few days earlier. So Vil-leneuve changed course to go close along the Spanish coast, to the west of Majorca. Nelson, meanwhile, still concerned about Egypt, headed southeast and took up a position between the southern end of Sardinia and Africa. Nelson's Egyptian biases were apparently becoming a subject of discussion within the British fleet: Rear-Admiral George Murray, Nelson's captain of the fleet, wrote to a friend, "Perhaps [Villeneuve] is only come out to make a flourish—supposing L[or]d N[elson] will again go to Egypt and leave him command of these seas."[11]

Both Murray and Nelson were, of course, wrong. Villeneuve was not making a feint, neither was he heading for Egypt—this time he was really on his way. But when he stopped off Cartagena, the six Spanish battleships there refused to join him.[12] Villeneuve did not waste time but left immediately, passing through the Strait of Gibraltar on 8 April and arriving off Cadiz late the same day. He chased off the small British blockading squadron and was quickly joined by one French and five Spanish battleships, plus a frigate and a couple of smaller vessels. Another eighty-gun Spanish battleship tried to join him but went temporarily aground. Villeneuve, holding in his mind the specter of Nelson on his heels, just over the horizon, did not wait but headed west early on the ninth, telling the unfortunate Spaniard to follow him. He now had seventeen battleships, seven frigates, and four smaller vessels.

Nelson was actually far to the east, off the western end of Sicily. He had finally gotten the imagined threat to Egypt out of his mind and on the ninth headed west. But the winds were foul, and his progress was slow. On 16 April, a whole week after Villeneuve had started across the Atlantic, Nelson was off the southern end of Sardinia, planning to head back up to Toulon. At that point he finally got firm intelligence that Villeneuve had passed Gibraltar and headed after him. But the winds were against Nelson, and it wasn't until 7 May that he was able to pass Gibraltar.

But where to go? He was pretty well convinced that Villeneuve was headed for Ireland, but he admitted that he could be wrong, as he had been before. The French could feint briefly to the west and then come back to raise the blockade on some of the French ports, or they could be headed for the West Indies or, less likely, for India. Nelson badly wanted to catch the ships that had escaped from his blockade, but he needed better information.

While waiting for the wind at Gibraltar, Nelson received the intelligence that he needed. Donald Campbell, an old friend who was serving as a rear admiral in the Portuguese Navy, came aboard and met with him. Campbell had apparently gotten information about Napoleon's orders to his squadrons and convinced Nelson that Villeneuve's destination was the West Indies. A good easterly wind came up later in the day, and Nelson moved out into the Atlantic with ten battleships and three frigates. It was 12 May, and Villeneuve had more than a month's head start.

Meanwhile, another piece of Napoleon's Grand Plan was coming unstuck, a very important piece. In Brest was the largest of all the French squadrons, twenty-one battleships plus assorted frigates and smaller fry, along with transports loaded with troops, under the command of Admiral Ganteaume. This squadron was blockaded in by the main part of the British Channel Fleet, about seventeen battleships. The emperor's orders to Ganteaume, issued on 2 March, were to get to sea as soon as he could and lift the blockade at Ferrol, in Spain, to release about twelve Spanish battleships there. With his enlarged fleet of thirty-three, he was to head for the West Indies, meet Villeneuve and Missiessy, take them in charge, and with this great fleet return to the Channel, completing the plan and enabling the invasion. It was not to be.

On 23 March Ganteaume sent word to Napoleon that he was ready to go, that there were only fifteen British ships holding the blockade, and that he was sure he could beat them and get out. In return Napoleon ordered him to "go to sea without fighting."[13] The British blockade at Brest was nearly always very tight and close in, so there was no way Ganteaume could get out without a battle. But the emperor's orders had to be obeyed, so Ganteaume stayed put in Brest. None of the Brest fleet got to sea until long after Trafalgar was fought.

Villeneuve arrived at Martinique on 13 May. In spite of his orders to attack British interests in the West Indies, he did nothing at all for more than two weeks, then attacked the Diamond Rock, a small British outpost just off Martinique that had been aggravating the French since early in 1804 by firing at the shipping going in and out of Fort-de-France. Then on 1 June Villeneuve received fresh orders from the emperor: seize Antigua, St. Vincent, and Grenada. The admiral was also told, in Napoleon's words, "Why not take Barbadoes?"[14] After capturing these British islands, Villeneuve was to force contributions from them, remove all their artillery, and take away one-half of their black inhabitants to be sold as slaves in Martinique and Guadeloupe. So much for *liberté, egalité,* and *fraternité.* While creating all this havoc, Villeneuve was to wait thirty-five days for Ganteaume and then return to Europe.

So Villeneuve started to threaten Antigua but then heard that a British convoy was nearby and went after it, capturing fifteen merchant ships—no great exploit for a fleet of battleships and frigates, and certainly no substitute for taking Antigua. From some of the prisoners taken in this adventure he learned that Nelson had arrived in the West Indies and was looking for him. No doubt he remembered afresh his narrow escape after the terrible night at Aboukir Bay. So his dread of Nelson, close by, overrode his fear of disobeying the emperor, who was far away in France, and Villeneuve quickly headed back for Europe. Of course, although he didn't know it, there was no point in waiting for Ganteaume, who was snugly blockaded in Brest.

Nelson had nearly caught up with Villeneuve. Having made a faster passage across the Atlantic and picked up the reinforcement of two battleships at Barbados, and despite having followed some false leads, Nelson arrived in the

Antigua area just a few days after Villeneuve had left. Nelson was quite sure that the French had headed back for Europe, although with his prejudice toward the Mediterranean he thought they were going toward Cadiz or Gibraltar. Actually, Villeneuve was headed for Ferrol or the Bay of Biscay.

On 12 June Nelson ordered away H.M. Sloop-of-War *Curieux* to make the fastest possible time to England to carry dispatches giving the Admiralty the best information that he had available. The next day Nelson was headed out of the West Indies with his fleet, bound for Gibraltar.

One week after leaving Nelson, Commander Bettesworth, skipper of the *Curieux,* had a nice piece of luck: he sighted the edge of the French fleet 150 miles east and north of Bermuda—seventeen battleships and "sailing badly." He tracked them long enough to determine their course, then slipped around them and raced on to England, arriving in Plymouth on 7 July. At 11 P.M. on the eighth he appeared at the Admiralty, but no one was willing to wake up Lord Barham, the First Lord. But as soon as Barham awoke in the morning, Bettesworth gave his information. Lord Barham was furious at not having been aroused the instant Bettesworth arrived the night before and without dressing sat down and penned orders to Admiral Cornwallis, commander in chief of the Channel Fleet—orders that he hoped would result in Villeneuve's being intercepted.[15]

Cornwallis was told to reinforce Vice-Admiral Calder, then blockading Ferrol, to bring his squadron up to fifteen battleships, and to order him to cruise west from Cape Finisterre at the northwestern corner of Spain for 90 to 120 miles, for about a week. Cornwallis himself was to cruise at the same time with his remaining force across the front of the Bay of Biscay, from Ushant to Cape Finisterre. Barham closed his letter to Cornwallis with, "Time is everything."[16]

There were some risks in this strategy: To strengthen Calder, the blockading squadron in front of Rochefort had to be taken off its station, and Cornwallis's patrol across the face of the Bay of Biscay left a reduced guard in front of Brest. The French didn't try to get out of Brest, but the Rochefort squadron, five battleships now under Admiral Allemand, did seize the opportunity and came out, hoping to join Villeneuve.

As it turned out, Calder and Villeneuve did sight each other on 22 July, a foggy day, at 11 A.M. Both started to maneuver to form battle lines in the old-fashioned way, and it was after 5 P.M. when the engagement started. It was a desultory action: both sides were in disarray, unable to see well in the fog and smoke. Calder dismasted and captured two of the Spanish battleships at about 8 P.M., during the long twilight, but shortly after this, with night falling, signaled to "discontinue the action."[17]

Neither side seemed interested in renewing the fight the following day, although they were still in sight of each other. Calder seems to have been more interested in making sure that his two prizes were secured and that his ships got back to their blockading duties, and Villeneuve was presumably following his instructions to avoid losses. He took his fleet—now eighteen battleships, six frigates, and two brigs—into port at Vigo, and then Ferrol.

In spite of his orders to Villeneuve to "avoid battle," Napoleon was quite unhappy with this outcome: he was politically embarrassed by the fact that both captured ships were Spanish and that Villeneuve made no significant effort toward recovering them the next day—a bad omen for the alliance.

Three days before all this happened, on 19 July, Nelson and his fleet arrived in Gibraltar. So a case can be made that if he had followed a more northern track he might well have caught up with Villeneuve at sea. In that event an interesting encounter would have taken place: Nelson would have been out-numbered two to one. He had earlier considered this possibility, however, and was determined "to stop [Villeneuve's] career, and to put it out of his power to do any further mischief."[18]

In Gibraltar Nelson set foot on shore for the first time in more than two years. His ships received badly needed stores and repairs. Then after five days, on 24 July, he was under way again, headed back through the strait and then north. At this point he had no firm knowledge of where Villeneuve had gone or what had happened to him. Adverse winds and weather slowed Nelson's progress. On 15 August he joined Admiral Cornwallis and the Channel Fleet off Ushant and received all the news of recent events. Then, with the knowl-edge that Villeneuve was securely blockaded in port at Ferrol, Nelson left most of his fleet with Cornwallis, took the *Victory* to Portsmouth, and there struck his flag. He went on shore for a much needed rest. It was to be the last time.

The next month was probably the happiest period of Nelson's life. He spent it at his recently purchased estate, Merton, near modern Wimbledon, with Lady Hamilton, now a widow, and their daughter, Horatia, surrounded by assorted cousins and other relatives. But Merton was only eleven miles from the Admiralty at Whitehall, and Nelson spent many days of this, his last leave, in town, talking to the Lords and the Admiralty staff about what should be done next.

Shortly after going into Ferrol, Villeneuve learned that Allemand was at sea and looking for him. Villeneuve sent the frigate *Didon* ahead to locate Alle-mand, then followed with his fleet, now twenty-nine battleships, a couple of days later, on 11 August. Villeneuve apparently firmly intended, after meeting Allemand, to go to Brest and raise the blockade there, freeing Ganteaume and his twenty-one battleships, and then to go to Boulogne and shield the crossing of the army and the invasion.[19]

Villeneuve didn't find Allemand but was himself spotted by H.M. Frigate *Iris* on the thirteenth. One reason he had trouble finding Allemand was that the frigate *Didon* had unwisely accepted a fight with H.M.S. *Phoenix,* a smaller British frigate, and had been captured. The *Phoenix* was busy towing the *Didon,* now her prize, to safety, covered by H.M.S. *Dragon,* a seventy-four–gun battleship. At this point the *Dragon* was spoken by a Danish merchantman, and the *Dragon's* skipper, his wits firmly about him, put on some theatrics for the Dane. First, he told him there was a twenty-five–ship British fleet nearby, then hoisted signals and fired guns to communicate with this nonexistent fleet. Within hours, and with the *Dragon, Phoenix,* and *Didon* still in sight, the Dane was stopped by one of Villeneuve's scouting frigates and passed along the false information.

The frigate returned to Villeneuve and his fleet, signaling as she went, and shortly thereafter the French and Spanish fleet turned south—away from the Channel, away from Brest, away from the Grand Plan of invasion—and late on 20 August 1805 entered Cadiz. The preliminaries were now over, and the stage was set for the Battle of Trafalgar.

Up until about this time Napoleon had been daily, almost hourly, expecting the combined French and Spanish fleet to appear off Boulogne and was prepared to go forward with the invasion. But other factors were beginning to have weight in his thinking, the principal one being that two of his old enemies to the east, Russia and Austria, with English money, had formed a new coalition and were assembling troops to attack him.[20] Threatened on land from the rear, Napoleon on 27 August suddenly ordered his Grand Army, 180,000 strong, to break camp at Boulogne, at Brest, and in Holland and head east. The threat of invasion was over.

Napoleon took this action several days before he received word, on 1 or 2 September, that Villeneuve was in Cadiz and would not soon be coming to the Channel. So the hypothetical possibility exists that Villeneuve could have found Allemand and raised the blockade on Ganteaume and that the whole, great fleet would have arrived off Boulogne on, say, 31 August to find the army gone and the admirals' lengthy and complicated endeavors made ridiculous.[21] But Napoleon knew his admirals and no doubt after his long wait and the stream of mishaps discounted the possibility of such an outcome. So he headed east on the campaign that would lead to his victories at Ulm and Austerlitz.

The facts were that Napoleon's own orders and unrealistic expectations, particularly his conviction that his admirals could get out of their blockades and roam the oceans without having to fight the British, were mostly responsible for the failure of his plans. But he ever afterward blamed Villeneuve and, when leaving for the east, gave orders for him to be relieved by Admiral Rosily, a staff officer in Paris, and for the fleet to leave Cadiz and enter the Mediterranean to support the southern flank of the new land campaign. Napoleon accused Villeneuve of "excessive pusillanimity" and ordered him to return to

France to account for his conduct.[22] Again, as befell so often in Napoleon's naval ventures, the outcome was not to match the plan.

At 5 A.M. on 1 September Nelson at Merton was already up and dressed when a post chaise came into his drive. It carried an old friend, Captain the Honorable Henry Blackwood, captain of the frigate *Euryalus,* en route from Portsmouth to the Admiralty with the news that Villeneuve's fleet was now blockaded in Cadiz. Nelson was excited by this turn of events and followed Blackwood into town, where Prime Minister Pitt insisted that Nelson take command of the fleet in front of Cadiz. At the Admiralty, Lord Barham told Nelson to choose any officers that he wanted and gave him an almost unlimited appointment that included all of the Mediterranean plus Cadiz. H.M.S. *Victory,* at Portsmouth, was ordered to be prepared as his flagship.

At 10:30 P.M. on 13 September, after kneeling at the bedside of the sleeping Horatia and praying for her to have a happy life, Nelson "drove from dear, dear Merton, where I left all that I hold dear in this world . . . ," down the road to Portsmouth.[23]

Passing through cheering crowds on the morning of the fifteenth, Nelson made his way to the beach at Southsea, where his barge was waiting with Sir Thomas Hardy, his flag captain and captain of the *Victory.* The next morning the *Victory* was under way on a light but favorable breeze, with Blackwood's *Euryalus* in company. The ships sailed down the coast to Plymouth, where the battleships *Ajax* and *Thunderer* met them off the port. Then they all headed for Cadiz.

Nelson sent the *Euryalus* on ahead to warn Vice-Admiral Collingwood, in command off Cadiz, that he was coming and not to fire any salutes or display any flags that would warn the enemy of his arrival and the reinforcement that he brought. Nelson arrived on 28 September and took over the command from Collingwood, a friend of long standing, who remained on as second in command. The captains of the ships in the fleet greeted Nelson's arrival with joy: this was not only a matter of Nelson's unequaled professional reputation as a winner of battles, it was also that Collingwood was a strict disciplinarian and had banned any intership visiting for exchanging dinners and the like, which was one of the few pleasures to be had while blockading. Nelson was more relaxed and immediately removed the rule.

The fleet Nelson had at this point consisted of twenty-seven battleships but only two frigates, the *Euryalus* and *Hydra.* To conceal his exact strength from Villeneuve and to tempt him to come out, Nelson kept most of his force about fifty miles to the west, out of sight from the land, leaving only the two frigates to watch the port, with four or five battleships forming a signaling chain between the frigates and the fleet.

By 1805 signaling had become quite sophisticated. For tactical signals like

"Prepare for Battle" (number thirteen) or "Come to the wind on the starboard tack" (number ninety-nine), there was the *Signal Book for the Ships of War,* an official publication that used combinations of one to three numeral flags to convey the standard tactical messages that were coded in the thin, thumb-indexed, 7 by 9–inch book, easy to handle on the quarterdeck. To supplement the signal book the British used a book just recently out, a semiprivate publishing venture, Sir Home Popham's *Telegraphic Signals or Marine Vocabulary.* Although slightly larger than the official publication, this book was also thumb-indexed and easy to use. The vocabulary section of the telegraphic signals used a special flag, to indicate that the message was "telegraphic," together with combinations of the numeral flags to signal the commonly used words and phrases that were coded in the book. The book also had a section coding the individual letters of the alphabet so that words not coded in the vocabulary could be spelled out. Words like "England" and "expects" were listed in the vocabulary and could be sent with one flaghoist, but words like "confides" and "duty" were not and had to be spelled out from the alphabetical section with a flaghoist for each letter. While all of this was a great advance over what had gone before, it took a great number of flaghoists to convey anything very complicated.

In the days that followed his arrival, Nelson spent much time with his captains, hosting half of them for dinner on 29 September and half on the thirtieth to explain his concept for fighting the battle, when and if they could get the French and Spanish to come out.[24] The general idea was simple and classically Nelson: From a windward position the fleet would be sailing in two roughly equal groups, one under Collingwood, one under Nelson. No attempt would be made to form a standard line of battle—the order they were sailing in would be the order they would fight in.

Collingwood's group was to cut through the enemy's line about one-third of the way from the rear and destroy everything in the rear. Nelson's group was to attack in the center, attempting to cut the enemy line at Villeneuve's flagship, to immobilize and capture him, and to prevent the van and center of the enemy from getting back to help the rear, while at the same time creating havoc in the center. Then later, if feasible, both groups could move up and polish off the enemy's van. But one of the key sentences in Nelson's memo describing his plan emphasized that in the confusion of battle, each captain had to depend largely on his own initiative: ". . . no Captain can do very wrong if he places his Ship alongside that of an enemy."[25]

The captains loved the plan. They could see the risks: the enemy would be able to concentrate fire on the leading British ships before all of the British could get into the action. But the captains, like Nelson, were familiar with the lack of skill among the French and Spanish and knew that the risks were worth taking.

The British fleet was also busy repainting. The word had been informally passed that Nelson wanted all the ships painted in the same style as the *Victory* to enable them to easily identify one another during the battle. Prior to this time individual captains had been given considerable leeway to paint their ships in eclectic styles, but from this point on until the end of the Age of Sail, all British ships, and later those of nearly all navies, were painted *à la Nelson*. The new look showed a black hull with broad yellow stripes along the rows of gunports, with the outside of the port lids painted black—giving the ship a checkerboard appearance. The lower masts were also painted yellow—they were the easiest feature to see through the smoke of battle. The upper masts and spars were varnished. This is the painting scheme that H.M.S. *Victory* wears today in her dock in Portsmouth. With some variations, principally the later use of white instead of yellow, the same pattern is worn by the U.S. Frigate *Constitution* in Boston.

The arrival in Cadiz of the roughly 27,500 men in Villeneuve's fleet approximately doubled the population of the city and put a tremendous demand on the food supply in the area, not to mention straining the relations between the French and the citizens of Cadiz, who "seemed to be glad of any circumstance that would deprive them of the French."[26] To remedy this problem Napoleon ordered shipments of food and other stores from Nantes, Bordeaux, and other Bay of Biscay ports. Ships wearing Danish flags carried these cargoes, although most of the vessels may actually have been French. These nominally Danish neutrals unloaded in small Spanish ports near the Portuguese border, and small coasters, running close inshore, then took the cargoes to Cadiz.[27]

Nelson would dearly have loved to stop this resupply traffic, although it was not the biggest issue on his mind. He thought that putting Villeneuve's ships on short rations might be an additional encouragement for them to put to sea. But for the first two weeks after taking the command, Nelson was desperately short of the frigates and brigs that he needed for all kinds of tasks and that could have stopped this inshore traffic as well. Then at the end of the first week in October came a happy event: the frigates *Phoebe, Sirius, Juno, Niger,* and *Naiad,* plus a couple of smaller fry, arrived from the Channel Fleet. Captain Thomas Dundas commanded the *Naiad,* and John Maples was her first lieutenant.

Nelson put the *Euryalus, Phoebe, Sirius,* and *Naiad* into a special squadron under Captain Blackwood, who was tasked with watching the French and Spanish fleet in Cadiz and establishing a communications chain out to the British fleet to relay any information that he gained. Captain Blackwood was just right for the job: he had Nelson's full confidence, and being very senior for a frigate captain—senior in fact to many of the battleship captains—his orders usually got the full attention of those to whom he gave them.

The *Juno, Niger, Hydra,* and smaller ships were set to work at cutting off the coasting traffic and handling other frigate-type errands.

Shortly after his arrival at Cadiz, Villeneuve had written to Napoleon that he would soon be ready to come out with the fleet and head for the Channel. But events had already overtaken him. Napoleon was headed east, the fleet's new orders were for the Mediterranean, and Rosily was on his way to replace Villeneuve. Initially unaware that he was to be relieved, the new orders looked like a godsend to Villeneuve: they gave him another chance, and they appeared to be possible of accomplishment. On 9 or 10 October he moved the fleet up to the entrance to the harbor, to be able to get out when the wind became favorable. Villeneuve's Spanish allies had agreed in a formal council of war that they would go to sea again if the British divided their force or were scattered by a storm—making it feasible for all of them, French and Spanish, to get out and giving them some chance of success in a battle.

On 2 October Nelson had detached Rear-Admiral Louis with four battleships to go to Gibraltar for water and supplies. When word of Louis's departure reached Villeneuve on 18 October, he felt that this diminution left Nelson at the lowest strength he was likely to have and thus could serve as a pretext for ordering the fleet, including the Spanish, to sea under the agreement. The French admiral had received the surprising news that Rosily was being sent to replace him and had arrived in Madrid several days before, on 12 October. So Villeneuve determined to get to sea as quickly as possible and start executing the new orders to save himself from disgrace. Villeneuve was not a physical coward, in spite of his obsession about Nelson. But the Frenchman was a realist and knew that anything like an equal contest with the British would lead to his defeat.

From here forward our viewpoint will shift to that of the frigates, particularly the *Naiad* with John Maples, who after all is our principal interest. The story of the Battle of Trafalgar is nearly always told from the viewpoint of the actions of the battleships as they engaged their antagonists in the melee. We will see it from the perspective of the frigates, principally of course the *Naiad,* but with only occasional attention to what the individual battleships were doing. The logs of the *Naiad* for this period survive, as well as a much more detailed officer's journal. Based on the near-identity of the handwriting, this journal is considered to have been written by the ship's master, Henry Andrews.[28]

As soon as the new frigates arrived, Captain Blackwood organized his squadron to watch the enemy fleet from close off Cape San Sebastian, the outer point of the long spit that forms the seaward side of Cadiz Bay, but kept them prepared to quickly string out in the direction of Nelson's over-the-horizon fleet, first the *Sirius,* Captain Prowse, and close to her Blackwood's own ship, the *Euryalus,* then the *Naiad,* Captain Dundas, and the *Phoebe,* Captain Capel. There were not enough frigates to make the chain, so Nelson had assigned four of the faster-sailing battleships, the *Defence, Agamemnon, Colossus,* and *Mars,* to make up the final links. It took about two to three hours for a message to pass flaghoist to flaghoist, along the chain, out to Nelson. Blackwood now also had three smaller vessels, the brig *Weazle,* the cutter *Entreprenante,* and the schooner *Pickle,* which he normally kept close to the *Euryalus* and used to run errands around his squadron and the fleet.

From 15 to 18 October the squadron operated together, about ten miles west and a little south from Cadiz. The winds were moderate but from the west, so there was no chance that the French and Spanish could get out. H.M.S. *Defence,* the next link in the signaling chain, was in sight to the west of the frigates. Late in the afternoon of the eighteenth Blackwood sent the *Naiad* and *Phoebe* close inshore off Cadiz to reconnoiter the enemy's fleet. They counted twenty-nine battleships "in the same state," not ready for sea.[29] If Blackwood was acting on a hunch that something was breaking, he was a bit early, but not by much: during the night he saw signals being passed back and forth between Cadiz and Rota, to the north. Overnight the wind had shifted around to the east-northeast and, although described as "light breezes," was sufficient to let Villeneuve start to come out.[30] As daylight came on 19 October the frigates saw that the enemy fleet had topgallant yards in place, and eight of the ships had their topsail yards hoisted to the masthead, ready to get under way. By 7 A.M. the northernmost of the enemy ships were under way.

Blackwood immediately stretched his squadron out into a signaling chain, sending the *Phoebe* farthest out to be in solid touch with the *Defence.* The *Phoebe* went off to her station, firing a gun every three minutes to alert the ships farther out. At 8:10 A.M. the *Euryalus* came within hail of the *Naiad,* and Blackwood told Captain Dundas to repeat signals between the *Euryalus* and *Phoebe.* By 9:30 A.M. the signal that the enemy was coming out of port had reached Nelson on board the *Victory,* forty-eight miles west-southwest of Cadiz. He was fairly certain that the French and Spanish were going to head south, for the Strait of Gibraltar, so he signaled the fleet, "General chase to the southeast," a course that would take him to the Strait, to cut them off. The wind was light and had shifted around to the south, so progress was slow.

After giving the *Naiad* her orders, Blackwood telegraphed the *Weazle* to go to Gibraltar with the news, and to see if he could catch Admiral Louis's squadron and get them to return. He ordered the *Pickle* to go off Cape Spartel, a British rendezvous point on the northwestern corner of Africa, to tell any ships in that area that the enemy was out. He then kept the *Sirius* and *Euryalus* close in to Cadiz to track the detailed moves of the French and Spanish.[31]

During the morning the *Naiad* received signals from the *Euryalus* and repeated them to the *Phoebe.* The *Naiad*'s station was about ten miles west of the San Sebastian lighthouse at Cadiz, but from the masthead at noon the lookouts observed that eleven of the enemy's ships had gotten out of the harbor. To the west-northwest they could see the next three ships in the signaling chain stretched out toward the British fleet, which was now moving slowly to the southeast with all sail set.

The eleven enemy ships that had come out were becalmed for a few hours just outside the harbor; but early in the afternoon a light westerly breeze came up, and they moved northward, trailed closely by the *Euryalus* and *Sirius*. Blackwood kept up a steady flow of signals from the *Euryalus* to the *Naiad,* but by late afternoon the distance between them had opened so far that the flaghoists were hard to read, and just before dark the *Naiad* left her station and headed toward the *Euryalus* to close the distance and keep in touch.[32] At 11:40 P.M. the *Naiad* burned a blue light as a signal for the *Euryalus,* and at midnight the *Naiad* reestablished firm contact with the *Euryalus* and *Sirius,* now to the east and a little south.

Daylight on 20 October brought a cloudy day with rain impending. The *Naiad* found herself about twelve miles to the west and south of Cadiz. The *Euryalus* and *Sirius* were in sight to the north, and from the masthead were visible twelve of the French and Spanish ships under way off Cadiz. To the west and south the lookouts could see twenty-three of Nelson's fleet. By 8 A.M. the rest of the enemy fleet was coming out of Cadiz "as fast as possible," and by about nine, thirty-four of the enemy were outside the harbor. The *Euryalus* and *Sirius* hung very close to the French and Spanish fleet, only two or three miles to windward of the enemy. At one point the *Sirius* got too near them, was fired on by one of the battleships, and only narrowly avoided capture.

During the forenoon the breeze strengthened and came around to the northwest, it began to rain, and the weather thickened. The frigates lost sight of the enemy in the murk, but shortly after noon the weather cleared a little and the *Euryalus* saw the French and Spanish ships again, quite close and headed west. Blackwood at this point decided to leave the other frigates to maintain contact with the enemy, while he headed to the southwest to find the *Victory* and bring Nelson up to date with more detail on what was happening than could be readily signaled.

The weather had cleared considerably by late afternoon, and at 4 P.M. the *Naiad* again had the enemy fleet in sight. The French and Spanish were formed in "three lines" and were to the north of the *Naiad.* The British fleet, now heading north to close the enemy, was also in sight from the masthead to the south and west. The *Naiad* signaled to Nelson that she had thirty-one sail in sight, on the starboard tack, headed generally south.[33]

The *Euryalus* returned in the early evening. Blackwood had given the admiral his information, and the *Euryalus* was leaving the British fleet when Nelson signaled him, "I rely on your keeping sight of the enemy." Blackwood took this trust seriously, and the *Euryalus* and *Sirius* spent the night within two or three miles of the French and Spanish fleet, burning blue lights and "false fires" and shooting skyrockets to show Nelson the enemy's position.[34] The *Naiad* and *Phoebe* stayed three or four miles to windward of the *Euryalus*, repeating the lights and rockets, and, being between the two fleets, could see the lights of both.

Morning twilight on the twenty-first came at a minute after 5 A.M., and as the light strengthened, both fleets were in full view from the *Naiad*. To the east, silhouetted against the growing dawn were the French and Spanish—thirty-three battleships, six frigates, and two brigs, the battleships in a rough line stretching north and south. Twelve miles beyond them were the headlands of Cape Trafalgar. To the south the *Naiad* could see Nelson's fleet of twenty-seven battleships. The two fleets were about nine miles apart.[35] The wind was very light from the west-northwest, so the British held the favorable windward position. A heavy swell from the west was beginning to build, warning of a storm to arrive later.

At 6:10 A.M., as soon as it was light enough for signal flags to be read, Nelson ordered his fleet to form into two divisions and head to the east-northeast, then a little later to the east, to cut the enemy off from returning to Cadiz. Although the French and Spanish were still heading south, he estimated that they would soon wear and reverse course.

Villeneuve was also waiting for enough light to signal and tried to get his fleet into a proper, tight line of battle. But the wind was too light for easy maneuvering, and his ships were rolling heavily in the beam sea from the increasing swell from the west. It was soon clear to him that Nelson was in a position to cut off the rearmost French ships and was moving to prevent any retreat into Cadiz. Villeneuve knew that if he continued to the south he would be forced through the Strait with Nelson close on his heels and another British squadron, under Admiral Louis, somewhere ahead.

At 8 A.M. Villeneuve decided to turn to the north to preserve his ability to get back into Cadiz. He ordered his fleet to wear together and form a battle line in reverse order. This move turned Villeneuve's fleet from a line into a ragged jumble of ships, with gaps and overlaps, and made inevitable just the sort of melee battle that Nelson wanted. Many in the French and Spanish fleet recognized that Villeneuve's action would be fatal. Spanish Commodore Chur-ruca said, "The fleet is doomed. The French Admiral does not understand his business." A little later he put it more succinctly, "Perdidos."[36]

The British battleships were now closing on the enemy line as fast as the light wind would carry them. They were in two columns ranged roughly east to west, about a mile apart, the one to the north led by Nelson in the *Victory*, the one to the south under Collingwood in the *Royal Sovereign*. The frigates worked their way west to get to windward of the impending battle but in position to repeat signals for the admiral.

At 7:50 A.M. the *Naiad* received a signal calling Captain Dundas to come aboard the *Victory*. Nelson brought all four of his frigate captains aboard the flagship to tell them what he expected of them during the battle. While their captains were in the *Victory,* the four frigates, under command of their first lieutenants—the *Naiad* under John Maples—took stations on the larboard quarter of the *Victory*.

The first task of the frigates during the battle was to stay to windward, clear of the smoke, but close enough to be able to read signals from Nelson and Collingwood and repeat them so that they could be read by other British ships. The frigates also could be called on to carry written messages between ships in the fleet, and when the battle got heavy, they might be needed to tow disabled ships clear of the fight, to safety. This sounds like a risky business, but there was an unwritten agreement among enemies in those days that frigates, other small ships, or boats were not to be fired upon during battles unless they took some aggressive action.[37]

Nelson kept the frigate captains with him on the quarterdeck of the *Victory* until about 11:45 A.M., when the *Victory* was about two miles from reaching the enemy line. A few minutes before leaving to return to their ships they witnessed the hoisting of the most famous naval signal of all time. Nelson remarked to Blackwood that he would now "amuse the fleet with a signal." After some discussion with the signal lieutenant on words to use that would reduce the number of flaghoists needed to convey the message, using Popham's telegraphic code book, Nelson settled on "England" and "expects," which were words in the vocabulary section, rather than "Nelson" and "confides," which were not and would have had to be spelled out a letter at a time. Thus the signal went out and into immortality as "England expects that every man will do his duty." It required twelve flaghoists: one for each word except "duty," and one for each letter in *duty,* which had to be spelled out from the alphabet section of the book. The *Naiad* and *Euryalus* repeated the signal as they pulled away from their positions near the *Victory*.

The frigate captains had barely returned to their ships when the Great Fight began. Collingwood's *Royal Sovereign,* a fast sailer with a clean bottom, was well in advance of the *Victory* and came within long range of the enemy line at 11:58 A.M. She was fired on by several of the French and Spanish line, but with little effect. At about 12:10 the *Victory* was within long range of the enemy and began to receive some fire. Both British flagships, and the battleships that followed them, held their first, carefully loaded, double-shotted broadsides until they were close enough to be devastating. Then the action really began.

When the *Royal Sovereign* was first fired on, the ships of the two fleets were spread over a broad area. The French and Spanish were strung out in a rough line about five miles long, north to south, bent somewhat convexly toward the east. The British were in two roughly parallel columns about a mile from each other, stretched out northeast to southwest from the enemy line for about four and one-half miles.

As planned, Nelson hit the center of the enemy line, and Collingwood cut off the rear. The enemy rear soon began to pile up on the center, the British ships arriving chose opponents close to their flagships, and soon both fleets were jammed into a smoke-clotted melee covering a space of about one and one-half by two miles. The five lead ships in the French-Spanish line didn't wear around to come to the aid of Villeneuve in the center, as they should have, but kept on sailing north. When they finally turned around, four of these ships and French Admiral Dumanoir kept to windward well clear of the battle and left the area, headed south.

The frigates stayed about two or three miles to the west, to windward of the melee. The *Euryalus, Sirius,* and *Phoebe* were to the east, and the *Naiad* was the westernmost of the four but soon moved closer and to the south of the other frigates. From the *Naiad,* through the smoke, John Maples saw masts falling and French and Spanish ships striking their colors to their British antagonists.

At 3:30 P.M., with the action at its height, Captain Blackwood in the *Euryalus* ordered the *Naiad* to take a disabled ship in tow, the seventy-four–gun H.M.S. *Belleisle.* The *Naiad* moved into the battle and found the *Belleisle* badly battered and completely dismasted.

The *Belleisle* had been the second ship in Collingwood's division, arriving at the enemy line shortly after the *Royal Sovereign* and going through the same gap. She had engaged no less than seven of the enemy battleships, and within an hour her mizzenmast and main-topmast were shot away. Soon after her mainmast fell over the larboard side, and the toppling of "this ponderous mass made the ship's whole frame shake." The foremast and bowsprit followed, and the wreckage from all this timber and rigging made the ship unmanageable and blocked most of the guns. She had not given up, however, had the British jack hoisted on the six-foot stub of her mizzenmast, and continued to fire her quarterdeck guns at such enemy ships as passed within range. The butcher's bill on the *Belleisle* was one of the worst in the British fleet: thirty-four were killed, including two lieutenants, and ninety-six were wounded.[38]

The *Naiad* took her in tow at 4 P.M. The ships were at the southern end of the battle area, and nearby, about a quarter of a mile distant, the French battleship *Achille* was seriously on fire. The fire had started in her foretop from some exploding small-arms ammunition, then British gunnery had brought down all her masts and destroyed her boats and her fire engine. The fire had quickly spread below decks, and now those of her crew who were not disabled by wounds were jumping into the ocean to escape the flames and the expected explosion. Right after taking the *Belleisle* in tow, the *Naiad* put her three largest boats in the water and sent them to rescue as many of the *Achille*'s crew as they could. Leaving the boats in charge of a lieutenant, the *Naiad* with her tow worked her way north about three-quarters of a mile to a position near the *Victory* and sent an officer across in a boat to get the admiral's instructions about where to take the *Belleisle.*

This was at about 5 P.M., and the firing had slackened and now ceased. About ten minutes later all of the ships present saw the *Achille* "blow up with a dreadful explosion."[39] Aboard the *Naiad* there was some worry for the men in the three boats. When last seen from the ship as she was towing the *Belleisle* off in the direction of the *Victory,* the boats were only a few hundred feet from the burning ship. But this concern was soon overshadowed when the *Naiad*'s officer returned from the *Victory* "with the Melancholy News of the Death of our Commander in Chief." Nelson was dead.

Early in the battle the *Victory* had become entangled with the French seventy-four–gun *Redoubtable.* This was very bad luck: Lucas, the French captain, had spent much time drilling his crew in the use of small arms and boarding. He was especially keen on having marksmen stationed in his tops, invisible behind special canvas screens, over which they appeared just long enough to aim and fire before crouching down again to load. These marksmen, armed with smooth-bore muskets, were creating a lot of havoc among the men on the *Victory*'s upper decks, and modern common sense would have had Nelson remove himself from danger until the *Victory*'s marines had taken care of the problem. But the fashions of war in those times required that the admiral remain exposed to whatever danger presented itself, and to do so with cool nonchalance.

Nelson was an obvious target: he wore on his uniform coat the large, bullion-embroidered Star of the Order of the Bath and three other similar decorations. But he walked the quarterdeck with Captain Hardy, seemingly oblivious to the French marksmen above and only about forty-five feet from him. At 1:35 P.M. he was struck by a musket ball, which entered his neck near the back, cut an artery in his chest, then lodged in his spine. He was taken below to the cockpit with the other wounded, where every effort was made to keep him comfortable. The surgeon, Dr. Beatty, recognized immediately that the wound was fatal and that he had no effective treatment to give.

Nelson's dying concerns were for the fleet to obtain a great victory—he hoped for the capture of at least twenty of the enemy—and for the future of Lady Hamilton and his daughter, Horatia, whom he left "as a legacy to my country."[40] As his strength faded he could be heard whispering, "Thank God, I have done my duty." There has rarely been a greater understatement. At 4:30 P.M. the surgeon found that he was dead.

Seldom has it been given to a public man, even a military hero, to die at exactly the peak moment of his glory. But this was granted to Nelson. The tremendous victory at Trafalgar completed his work, and there was no more scope for the Art of the Admiral during the Age of Sail—there were to be no other major, significant sea battles between fleets of oak and hemp, with iron ball and black powder. He lived for glory, and had he survived the battle to live out his life at Merton, his glory would certainly have dimmed. As it was, his memory was preserved, bright and ever untarnished, as part of the moment of victory. It remains so today.

The *Naiad* now headed south and east, to pass by the site of the recent explosion of the French *Achille* and pick up her boats, and then to tow the *Belleisle* to Gibraltar. The frigate was about ten miles off Cape Trafalgar, and the remains of the battle were mostly behind her. To the west, Admiral Dumanoir and his four ships that had not joined the battle except to brush by it were now escaping. Admiral Sir Richard Strachan's squadron would capture them all two weeks hence. To the northeast John Maples and all on board the *Naiad* could see fourteen of the Spanish trying to escape into Cadiz.

At the other end of the towline, all on board the *Belleisle* were trying to cope with the nearly one hundred wounded and were throwing the dead overboard. The two dead officers, the first lieutenant and the junior lieutenant, were laid side by side in the gun room, and their messmates came by to get a last view of them. Then they were "committed . . . along with the promiscuous multitude, without distinction of either rank or nation, to their wide ocean grave." In the midst of this grim task, one sailor about to be thrown over was found to be still alive and breathing and was later sent to the hospital, where after a week the musket "ball which [had] entered [his] temple came out of his mouth," to the wonder and marvel of the doctors.

The *Belleisle*'s upper deck "presented a confused and dreadful appearance: masts, yards, sails, ropes, and fragments of wreck, were scattered in every direction" and "covered with blood and mangled remains." Although the first task was to clear the decks, the crew also needed to set up some kind of a minimal jury rig, to steady the ship in the storm that was obviously on its way. The *Naiad* sent over her surgeon, plus the carpenter and his crew to assist. Now safely under tow, the Belleisles could pause and face their problems with some optimism, and at "about five o'clock the officers assembled in the Captain's cabin to take some refreshment . . . [and] the parching effects of the [battle] smoke made this a welcome summons."[41]

Towing the *Belleisle* with the light breeze then blowing made for slow progress, and it was dark by the time the two ships reached the area where they expected to find their boats. But nothing was there. At 10:30 P.M. they found one of them carrying ninety-five prisoners, and as the tired boat crew came aboard Captain Dundas and John Maples got the story of what had happened. The *Naiad's* three boats had picked out of the water about 190 men from the French *Achille,* including her surgeon, who told them that nearly 300 wounded men had been left aboard to suffer the fire and explosion. One of the boats also saved a woman whom they found "floating by the assistance of the Ship's Quarter Bill Board." They had transferred all but the ninety-five of the French survivors to the schooner *Pickle* and the cutter *Entreprenante*, and these ships later took the public credit for saving them all, much to the disgust of the Naiads who had actually done the job. Finally, at 1:30 in the morning the other missing boats returned unharmed—"which we were happy to see as we had Despaired of seeing them any more."[42]

During the night the storm arrived, and by noon of the twenty-second the *Naiad* and *Belleisle* were experiencing "fresh gales with rain." The frigate had been towing the *Belleisle* with the relatively lightweight stream anchor cable, 720 feet long. But as the weather worsened it became necessary to strengthen the towline, so it was spliced to the heavier sheet anchor cable, also 720 feet, and veered to the length of the sheet cable, the *Belleisle* taking in most of the lighter line.[43] As night came on the weather increased to strong gales with dense rain, and the swell from the west became very heavy, but somehow the ships got through the night with the towline intact.

By daylight on the twenty-third the weather had moderated, although the swell was still heavy. The rain stopped for a time, and from the masthead of the *Naiad* the lookouts discerned, with some difficulty, Cape Spartel in North Africa about twenty-seven miles to the southeast. Several of the fleet were in sight to the west and north. Cape Trafalgar was about ten miles to the northeast, and with the wind now coming from the southwest it presented all the dangers of a lee shore. At 4 P.M. the weather picked up again, and "it came to blow strong and squally" and started to rain.

Then at 5 P.M. trouble struck: the stream cable parted, and the *Belleisle* was loose from the tow and drifting. The *Naiad* worked her way around to the larboard side of the *Belleisle,* where in the lee of the larger ship the water was a little calmer, and put her boats in the water to try to take her in tow again. But the sea was too rough, and in the attempt the *Belleisle* drifted down on the *Naiad,* smashed her jolly boat, which was hanging in davits at the stern, and carried away her starboard quarter gallery and part of the ship's structure near it. Then the ships parted. The *Naiad* struggled to stay near the *Belleisle* and keep her in sight, but as the storm, rain, and gathering darkness brought the visibility down to near zero, the vessels lost sight of each other. The *Belleisle* was now truly in distress, rolling, mastless, in the trough of heavy seas, the wind carrying her toward the lee shore near Cape Trafalgar less than ten miles away. At about midnight Captain Hargood called all the *Belleisle's* officers to come on deck and told them he thought it was probable that the ship would go ashore soon. As they were digesting this frightening news, a 24-pounder gun in one of the gun-deck stern ports broke loose from its lashings and crashed about, making terribly real the metaphor of the loose cannon. The ship rolled wildly in the trough of the seas, with water coming in at the gunports and over the hammock nettings in the waist. The heavy rolling tipped the shot out of the shot racks, and these six-inch-plus iron balls bowled their way around the gun decks, striking the tired and exhausted men lying there.[44] Throughout the long night the *Belleisle's* officers scanned the sky and horizon, hoping for an early dawn.

The *Naiad,* with Captain Dundas and John Maples, were frantic to find the *Belleisle* and get her in tow again. The frigate made night signals but got no reply. In her night search she carried more sail than she should have, and the wind carried away the main-topsail and one of the staysails. Early twilight finally came, and at 5:40 A.M. the lookouts sighted the *Belleisle,* close in to the shore east of Cape Trafalgar, "seemingly in a perilous situation."[45]

The *Naiad* made all the sail she could carry and bore down on the *Belleisle.* The weather was now moderating, and at 7:10 A.M. the frigate was close enough to put a boat in the water to carry a line to the *Belleisle* and get her in tow again. Dundas was just in time: the two ships were so close to going ashore that a Spanish battery on the cliffs was tempted to fire several shot at them, but all missed.

From now on all went well. The wind had moderated to a fresh breeze from the west, just right for the two British ships. They saw a battleship ahead and at first thought it might be French, one of Dumanoir's squadron. But a British "private signal dispersed [their] hasty fears"—she was one of Admiral Louis's ships returning from watering at Tetuan, too late for the battle. At one in the afternoon of that day, 24 October, the *Naiad* arrived in Gibraltar Bay and cast off the *Belleisle's* towline. By 1:30 both ships were safely anchored, and the adventure was over. They were the first of the veterans to arrive in Gibraltar after the Battle of Trafalgar, although a market boat had come in earlier with the first news. They were greeted with a *"feu-de-joy,"* a clamorous salute from all of Gibraltar's guns, "and cheers all around the Garrison and that night a Lumination took place in Consequence of the Glorious action and Victory."[46]

It was truly a glorious and significant victory. Eighteen of the French and Spanish ships had been captured or destroyed, and never again during the long war did Napoleon challenge the British at sea or threaten invasion. The British home islands remained inviolable, and this ensured Napoleon's final defeat: the British Navy blockaded his coasts, and British wealth subsidized the armies of his enemies.

In the larger frame, the Battle of Trafalgar was the cornerstone of the worldwide British naval supremacy that lasted for well over a century. This sea power was the key instrument of British policy during that long period of relatively peaceful relations among the great powers, nostalgically remembered today as the *Pax Britannica*.

In Gibraltar on 24 and 25 October the *Naiad* got aboard boatswain's stores and fresh beef and retrieved the cables of her towline from the *Belleisle*. The surgeon and the carpenter's crew came back aboard after their wild night ride on the drifting *Belleisle*. At three in the afternoon on the twenty-fifth the *Naiad* got under way to return to her duty in the area of the late battle. But the favorable wind that she sailed with soon turned into strong gales and heavy rain from the west, and with that and the current the frigate was driven eastward, twenty-seven miles into the Mediterranean. The weather continued squally and from the west for the next several days, and although Dundas tried his best, the *Naiad* was not a good sailer, and he was unable to get past Gibraltar until the thirtieth and was not back in the battle area until 31 October.[47] The *Naiad*'s squadron mates were still cleaning up the mess, destroying prizes that couldn't be taken home, and taking and exchanging prisoners. This work was almost over, and on 1 November the *Naiad* headed for England to get her quarter gallery repaired, and John Maples's involvement with the Battle of Trafalgar was over.

In the aftermath of the battle came rewards and honors. Nelson's body was brought home aboard the *Victory,* and after lying in state in the Painted Hall at Greenwich, he was given a state funeral on 9 January 1806 and buried in St. Paul's Cathedral, under the dome, "with all the pomp and solemnity befitting the occasion."[48] Nelson's other rewards from a grateful government took the strange form of creating his older brother, William Nelson, a self-seeking Church of England clergyman, an earl with a grant of £6,000 a year and £100,000 to purchase an estate. Lady Nelson received a pension of £2,000 per year, and Nelson's sisters were each given £10,000.

Lady Hamilton and Horatia, whom Nelson in his dying agony had left as a legacy to his country, received nothing from the government. Although Lady Hamilton received the Merton estate from Nelson, and some other property from Sir William Hamilton, she was overgenerous, entertained lavishly, and finally died in poverty in Calais, France, in early 1815. She was followed to her grave by the many captains of British merchant ships then in the harbor as a mark of respect to her relationship with Nelson.[49] Nelson's daughter, Horatia, grew up to marry a clergyman, the Reverend Philip Ward, and bear five children, four of whom survived to have children of their own. Horatia lived to be eighty-one, dying in 1881. Her numerous descendants today carry the genes of the Admiral of Admirals.

Villeneuve was taken to England as a prisoner of war and for a few months was placed on parole there. In April of 1806 he was released and returned to

France. He took rooms in a hotel at Rennes to await Napoleon's pleasure. Then one morning he was found dead, five stab wounds in his body. A letter was found with him, implying suicide, but in the judgment of many he was put to death by agents of Bonaparte. The matter has never been resolved.

The lieutenants serving at Trafalgar received a variety of rewards. The prize-money share for lieutenants was £65 plus a government grant of £161, and John Maples received this. But the really important rewards of promotion were reserved for the first lieutenants of ships actually engaged muzzle-to-muzzle in the battle: First lieutenants who had commanded their ships during the action, because of the death or absence of the captains, were promoted to the all-important rank of post-captain. Other first lieutenants of engaged ships were made commanders. The first lieutenants of the frigates, including John Maples, were not promoted.[50]

So John Maples, now thirty-five, continued on as first lieutenant of the *Naiad*. These post-Trafalgar times were relatively uneventful, although the *Naiad* took a number of prizes, including a valuable Spanish ship.[51] In his autobiographical note John Maples passed over this period, and his brief service in 1809 and 1810 as first lieutenant of the *Mars* and *Atlas,* in a sentence.[52]

Then in 1810 his luck turned: in commemoration of the fifth anniversary of Trafalgar, the Lords of the Admiralty promoted twenty senior lieutenants "who were actually first lieutenants of effective ships of the line, or had particularly distinguished themselves in the command of small vessels," to be commanders.[53] John Maples's name was the second on the list.

The same day, 21 October 1810, that he was promoted to commander, John Maples was assigned as captain of the *Ætna,* a bomb vessel, and he commanded her for two years, mostly off Cadiz, a period that he described as "service of a very harassing nature."[54] Then in November 1812, soon after the start of the war with the United States, he was assigned to command a new brig, still under construction, H.M. Brig *Pelican.*

CHAPTER SIXTEEN

H.M. Brig *Pelican* and Her Company

THE NAME "PELICAN" has always been popular for small ships in the British Navy. There have been twenty-one of them, the first, the *Pelycan,* in 1577. John Maples's *Pelican* was the thirteenth. Number twelve had been wrecked in a "tremendous gale" in November 1800, leaving the name available again.[1]

John Maples's *Pelican* was built as one of a class of ship known as the "Cruizer" or "Childers" Class, a very successful design. The British eventually built about eighty of them. A set of the standard class plans was sent on 22 October 1811 to Robert Davy, who owned a small shipyard at Topsham in Devon, about six miles up the Exe River from the sea, a few miles below Exeter, and about fifty-five miles east around the coast from Plymouth. Mr. Davy was told to build two identical hulls, one to be the *Wasp,* the other the *Pelican.*[2]

Work started on the *Pelican* in January 1812, she was launched in August, and Mr. Davy received £5,928 for his work on her. After her launching she was towed around to Plymouth, where she was taken in the graving slip and her bottom coppered. Then her masts were put in and yards installed, her rigging fitted, and her basic suit of stores loaded.[3]

The *Pelican* was masted and rigged as a brig, that is, with foremast and mainmast, with square sails on both masts, and with a gaff-headed fore-and-aft mainsail carried on the after side of the mainmast. In general appearance and arrangement she was much like the *Argus,* although she was actually a more formidable warship. She was larger than the *Argus* in nearly every dimension. She was one hundred feet long on her gun deck as compared to ninety-six feet for the *Argus.* She was a little wider, 30 feet and 6 inches in extreme breadth; had a deeper hold, 12 feet and 10 inches; and was rated at 385 tons, compared with 315 tons for the *Argus.* She was also more strongly built, with a structurally significant berth deck supported by heavy beams that were attached to the framing on the ship with oak knees and iron brackets—making her sides stronger and more able to resist damage. The *Argus* had a light-weight, nonstructural berth deck, held up by small beams and no knees, that provided very little strength to her sides. Seen from a distance, the *Pelican,* like others of her class, had a rather raffish appearance because her masts were not parallel—her mainmast had about ten degrees more rake than her foremast.

The *Pelican's* armament was somewhat heavier: she carried sixteen 32-pound carronades on slides, each firing a shot six inches in diameter, plus two 6-pounder iron guns normally kept in the bow gunports, and a 12-pounder boat carronade.[4] She also had two nice 6-pounder brass guns, usually pointed through her stern ports. John Maples bought these two expensive brass guns in Jamaica, with his own money, sometime during his first months in command. They may have been the same two pesky field pieces that the *Magicienne* had captured after so much annoyance at Carcasse Bay in 1797. As described earlier, the *Argus* mounted eighteen 24-pound carronades, each firing a 5-inch ball, plus two 12-pound long guns in the bow ports. In addition, the *Pelican* was a tight, brand-new ship, whereas the *Argus* was ten years old.

The one area in which the *Argus* had it over the *Pelican* was in speed. The *Argus* was taller in mast, spread more sail in proportion to her size, and had a long-standing reputation as an excellent sailer. The *Pelican,* like all Cruizer-class brigs, was conservatively masted. While not slow, the Cruizer brigs did not have a reputation for speed and dash. The *Argus* and *Pelican* were never tested in a race or a chase, but on the available evidence the *Argus* would probably have to be rated considerably faster and more weatherly as well.

During the building of the *Pelican* at Topsham and most of her fitting out at Plymouth, the only member of her future crew present was William Ingram, the purser, who was there to follow the performance of the contract and keep track of the costs.[5] But about a month before she was ready for sea the officers and crew began to arrive.

John Maples was detached from the *Ætna* on 1 November in Portsmouth and arrived in Plymouth in time to put the *Pelican* in commission on 5 November.[6] Most of the officers but none of the crew had reported aboard by the date of the commissioning ceremony. Present with John Maples to hear James McGhie, the first lieutenant, "read the ship in" were the other lieutenant,

William Weiss; the surgeon, Richard Coniby; plus five of the warrant officers—Peter Stewart, the gunner; Richard Hobbs, the carpenter; Thomas Robinson, the boatswain; Thomas Gough, the cook; and William Ingram, the purser.[7]

The Admiralty had two weeks earlier asked Maples whether there was any particular officer that he wished to have as his first lieutenant. Apparently, no one that he wanted was available, and he reluctantly told this to the Admiralty, knowing that it would be an invitation for them to send him a difficult-to-place "problem" officer.[8] So it turned out: they sent Lieutenant James McGhie, he and John Maples had trouble almost from the beginning, and Maples was apparently eager to get rid of him. John Maples may well have been a difficult skipper to work for. He had been a first lieutenant himself for about nine years and undoubtedly knew just how he wanted the job handled, and McGhie was very likely given little leeway to do things in his own way.

In addition to McGhie, John Maples also wanted to get rid of Thomas Robinson, the boatswain, whose reputation for poor conduct had preceded him aboard. Maples asked him to exchange jobs with Richard Scott, the boatswain of the fire ship *Otter,* whom John Maples knew from their service together after the Battle of Copenhagen. When Robinson refused to make the swap, Maples asked the Admiralty to order him off and send Scott in his place. The Admiralty turned down Maples's request, telling him to discipline Robinson if his conduct was bad.[9]

The *Pelican's* allowed complement was 121 total officers, men, boys, and marines, and in the days following the commissioning the rest of the initial ship's company came aboard, a few at a time. Three midshipmen were assigned: Henry Cox, James Morland, and William Pearce. On 11 November four men from the *Ætna* arrived, chosen by John Maples to follow him to the *Pelican:* Thomas Palmer, Maples's coxswain; George Parker, to be the ship's corporal or master-at-arms; and William Baker and John Emery, able seamen. The first three of these were English, born in southern England, but thirty-year-old John Emery was an American from New York.

Nine other Americans reported aboard as part of the initial crew: Martin Wilsey, thirty-four, from New York, a sailmaker's mate, a stocky man with scarred lips; Richard Thornhill, twenty-nine, a tall man from Philadelphia, who was given the key job of captain of the foretop; John Mainwaring, thirty-one, from Newport, Rhode Island, a gunner's mate; Peter Davis, thirty, from Salem, a quartermaster; John Smith, twenty-five, from New York, Dan Marshall, thirty-four, from Albany, New York, and John Warbreck, twenty-one, all three able seamen; James Jackson, thirty-four, an ordinary seaman from Cape Elizabeth, in the District of Maine, described as having a crooked mouth; and Benjamin Jackson, a tall black man from Alexandria, Virginia, a seaman, thirty-five years old, with several badly crippled fingers. All but one of them were no strangers to the British Navy and had been sent to the *Pelican* from other ships. The exception was Dan Marshall, who had recently been impressed out of a merchant ship, the *Rosa*.[10]

Although there were many Americans serving in the British Navy, either voluntarily or under duress, this is an exceptionally large number for a small ship like the *Pelican*—more than 10 percent of the ship's company, excluding the marines. A more typical number would be 5 percent.

There were five others on board who were not British: two Germans from Hamburg, a Swede from Stockholm, a Portuguese from Lisbon, and a Greek from the Island of Corfu.

The rest of the initial ship's company that came aboard during November and December of 1812 were British-born. Twenty-seven came from the southern coast or from inland southern England, eleven were from the north of England, six were Scots, seventeen were Irish, two were from the colonies Halifax and Bermuda, and one came from Guernsey in the Channel Islands. All in all, except for the number of Americans, this was a fairly typical crew for the time. On 31 December 1812, at the time of the first muster at sea, Maples counted eighty-four men in the crew, plus seventeen boys, plus twenty marines.

Five of the "boys" were really men, two eighteen and three nineteen years old. But the rest were young, ten to fourteen years old, with one fifteen and one sixteen.

The *Pelican* sailed from Plymouth on 11 December 1812 and spent a few days in shaking down her new crew and equipage. John Maples, like Henry Allen, placed great importance on gunnery training, and nearly every day found the crew "exercising the great guns" and frequently actually shooting at a cask or some other mark that Maples would have set afloat as a target. The Pelicans also spent many of their hours in small-arms and boarding drills. All of this, when taken together with the normal work of handling sails, splicing rope, tarring rigging, scraping and painting, and other ship's duties, kept the men going nearly all day, every day.

The drills and ship's work were overlaid on the duties assigned to Maples and the ship by the Admiralty and his own admiral. During the months after her commissioning the *Pelican* was employed principally in carrying the "West India Mails"—dispatches, letters, and light freight—back and forth between Plymouth or Falmouth and the admirals commanding in Barbados and Jamaica, with a way stop in Bermuda on the return leg.[11]

John Maples also faced the manpower problems common in the British Navy during those days: there were always some men on board who were looking for an opportunity to desert. Over the months between December 1812 and early August 1813, ten men managed to "run" in Plymouth, five in Falmouth, and two each in Bermuda and Jamaica. John Maples made up for this in the way he was expected to: he stopped merchant ships, usually British ones, and impressed one or two or three men for service with His Majesty in the *Pelican*.

The hazards of seafaring also made for changes in the *Pelican's* crew. Tragedy solved John Maples's problems with Thomas Robinson, the boatswain: Robinson was drowned at sea in January. Whether pressure on him from Captain Maples had anything to do with this accident is unknown. Richard Scott came aboard as the new boatswain a week after Robinson's death. John Vane and John Sullivan, seamen, also lost their lives by drowning, and John Cooper, an able seaman, was killed in a fall from the masthead.

Other changes took place as well: after some kind of a blow up with John Maples, James McGhie, the first lieutenant, was transferred off in early February at his own request. His letter to the Admiralty, written in large, hasty, toppling letters, was clearly the product of an angry man. Maples forwarded the letter and asked the Admiralty to appoint Lieutenant Thomas Taplen, then on half-pay in Plymouth, to replace him.[12] John Maples was hard on his first lieutenants: Thomas Taplen lasted only until 18 June 1813 and was then replaced in his turn by Lieutenant Thomas Welsh, who kept the job until after the battle with the *Argus*.

In early July, in the days just before the *Argus* was arriving at L'Orient, the *Pelican* returned from a trip to the West Indies and reported to the Irish Station, under the command of Vice-Admiral Edward Thornbrough, John Maples's old skipper from the *Hebe* of many years before.

PART THREE

RAMPAGE, CHASE, AND BATTLE

CHAPTER SEVENTEEN

Rampaging around Ireland and Stalking the Raider

ON 8 JULY, A RAINY IRISH DAY, the *Pelican* got a pilot aboard and came into the Cove of Cork. John Maples came to an anchor, fired a fifteen-gun salute to Thornbrough's flag flying in H.M.S. *Trent,* then hoisted out the boats and moored the ship.[1] The *Pelican* had hardly settled into her moorings and been taken into Thornbrough's command when she was ordered to sea again, to chase the rumors of American privateers in the north of Ireland, rumors that were coming in from all directions—from the Admiralty, from private citizens, and from the powerful herring barons of Rothesay.

Maples was ordered to put himself under the command of Captain Montressor of the *Helena,* a ship-sloop somewhat larger than the *Pelican,* and the two ships were ordered to range the western Irish coast from Cape Clear at the southwestern corner to Tory Island in the north. They were occasionally to stretch across to the Firth of Clyde on the coast of Scotland, checking for orders every three weeks at the fishing village of Killybegs on Donegal Bay or at the town of Buncrana in Lough Swilly.[2]

The *Helena* and *Pelican* got under way midmorning the next day, 9 July. As soon as they were out of the harbor, John Maples assembled the officers and crew and told them that the *Helena* had proposed the usual arrangement whereby the two ships would split any prize money coming from captures made by either of them during the cruise. The Pelicans agreed to the arrangement, but only for the time that they were under the *Helena*'s orders, and

Maples went over to the *Helena* in a boat to accede to the agreement and clinch the deal. As things turned out, this limit on the contract was a wise move by the Pelicans.

The *Pelican* traveled in company with the *Helena* around Cape Clear and up the west coast, chasing several strange sail but not meeting any Americans or even rumors of them. On 12 July the two ships ran into a thick fog, and when it lifted several hours later, the *Pelican* was alone and the *Helena* was nowhere to be seen. Maples made a brief search the next day but soon gave up on it—he was probably just as happy to be out from under Captain Montressor's control—and continued north, clockwise around Ireland.

Farther north Maples chased and stopped passing ships but found nothing except some three-week-old rumors of an American privateer, told by a Portuguese ship that had recently left Londonderry. On 17 July the *Pelican* stopped a ship homeward bound from Bermuda to Liverpool and impressed William Cowle, a seaman, out of her. The next day Maples stopped and boarded a Danish ship that was making a passage under British license from Norway to Limerick with a load of timber. By now the brig was off Tory Island, at the northern end of her range, and Maples headed for Lough Swilly, about thirty-five miles to the east to check for orders and to see if the *Helena* by some chance happened to be there. He entered around noon on the nineteenth and anchored off Dunree Head, some seven miles up the Lough, in midafternoon. The *Helena* was nowhere to be seen. Maples sent a boat ashore for information, but the boat returned at 11 P.M. with no orders, messages, or other information, and without two of her crew, who had managed to desert.[3]

Taking advantage of the long summer twilight, John Maples got under way again at three the next morning. But the winds were light and variable, and by midmorning he had made good only five miles and was still well inside the Lough, so he ordered the sweeps manned and rowed out until the brig picked up a better wind. She cruised to the west, John Maples planning to put into Killybegs to look for orders there and to get water. The *Pelican* arrived on the twenty-sixth and was taken by a pilot into the tiny, narrow, south-facing pocket of Killybegs Harbor.

John Maples sent the boats for water, but for some reason they returned empty-handed. However, there were two letters from Admiral Thornbrough addressed to Montressor of the *Helena,* which had been sent by the overland mail. Maples opened them and found that the *Pelican* was ordered to return immediately to Cork.

This was not John Maples's lucky week. By evening, when the boats had returned with the information but without the water, the wind was shifting around from the northwest toward the southwest and picking up. By midnight it was blowing strongly and was coming directly into the harbor. There was no way the ship could work her way out. Maples wrote to Thornbrough by the land mail, explaining his predicament and saying he would get out and start for Cork as soon as possible. But the wind continued foul for eleven days and was so strong one day that he had to let go another anchor and point the yards into the wind to reduce the drag on them.

To add to John Maples's problems, two men deserted from the shore party that finally got the water, and one swam ashore from the ship. Then the boats went aground on an ebb tide while away from the ship, and during the night that they were stuck three men deserted from them, and one from another boat later in the day. Then another man swam ashore in the night from the ship. All in all, including the two that escaped in Lough Swilly, Maples lost 10 men of the roughly 110 in the crew—all in addition to those he had lost earlier in England and the West Indies.

Of course, the Royal Navy was full of men watching for an opportunity to desert, and the situation at Killybegs was tailor-made for escape. The harbor was small enough that even a fair swimmer could make it ashore, and the people in this part of Ireland had no love for the English or their navy and were not likely to betray deserters and turn them in. But this was a feral and lawless corner of northwestern Ireland, dangerous to a stranger, and it took some degree of desperation to desert there.

By 5 August, when the *Pelican* was finally able to get out, John Maples was probably wondering, with some apprehension, what Admiral Thornbrough was going to say to him when he eventually did make it back to Cork. Then he got one last blow: just as he got out of Killybegs Harbor into Donegal Bay, a thick fog set in, and he had to anchor again.[4] But John Maples's luck was soon to change.

The *Argus* had arrived in L'Orient on 11 July and remained there, moored in the stream, for a little more than a week, the crew busy with the small tasks of getting cleaned up after the trip across and making the ship ready for sea again. They brought provisions aboard, plus a boatload of wood for the galley stove, and they watered ship.

Surgeon Inderwick remained busy: Minister Crawford became ill. He was staying in the house of the American consul, about a mile up the river, and Dr. Jackson sent a note asking Inderwick to attend him. Inderwick diagnosed catarrh and administered a purge. Richard Groves was still laid up with the arm bruised by the anchor cable and continued to need attention, Midshipman Temple was still in pain with his bruised testicle, and two other men came down with "rheumatismus."[5]

On the sixteenth an American, a marine deserter named Frederick Hyatt, came on board and asked to join the *Argus*. He had been a marine on board the frigate *United States* and was apparently known to Henry Allen, at least by sight. He was added to the crew. Another man, calling himself Henry Jeffers and claiming to be an American deserter, came aboard and was signed up, but then rejected the same day and sent ashore.[6]

In the meantime, Captain Row of the *Salamanca* and his crew had remained aboard as prisoners of war. That they were still on board at all at this time was the result of an excess of kindness on Henry Allen's part. British prisoners of war were supposed to be turned over to the custody of an agent for prisoners for exchange, or to an American consul if no regular prisoner agent was available. In the case of the *Argus* in L'Orient, the *Salamanca's* crew (less, of course, the two that had signed on with the *Argus*) should have been given over to Mr. Vail, the consul, who would have turned them over to the French authorities after getting a receipt for them. The men would then, or eventually, have been sent back to England in exchange for the release of an equivalent number of American prisoners of war in England. However, this would have put the *Salamanca's* crew into French prisoner-of-war depots for an indefinite period—a hard thing indeed, as these depots had a notorious reputation for harsh treatment and rampant disease.

That this was not done shows that Henry Allen had generous instincts and was probably a soft touch for the pleadings of Captain Row and his men, who were no doubt urging that they be allowed to stay aboard until the next capture, then sent directly to England on a captured ship designated as a cartel to carry prisoners. Given the close quarters of the berth deck, by the time the *Argus* arrived in L'Orient the captives were probably viewed more as shipmates than as prisoners. However, this bit of kindness meant that an equal number of American seafarers being held in the British prison depots and hulks would not be released—the British-dictated rules did not permit exchanges of American prisoners for British prisoners sent in from ships at sea, insisting rather that all exchanges must come through the official prisoner agents.[7] In any event, the *Salamanca's* sailors remained on board, eating American rations and contributing to the always crowded conditions in the berth deck.

When the *Argus* was nearly ready to go to sea again, Henry Allen assembled the officers in the wardroom and read to them from the secretary of the navy's orders the part sending them on their commerce-destroying mission. This was red meat to them. They cheered, and toasts were drunk.

On 20 July, a rainy, squally day with low visibility, the wind was fresh from the northeast, favorable for the *Argus* to get to sea. Allen ran up the signal for a pilot and fired a gun to call attention to it. Later he fired another gun to recall any officers who were ashore, and a second gun for the pilot, who hadn't responded to the first. He got under way at 7 P.M. and, after dropping the pilot near the Ile de Groix, headed west, out to sea far enough to clear Ushant and the Brest peninsula, then headed north toward the mouth of the English Chan-

nel and St. George's Channel, between England and Ireland—toward his
hunting ground. On the twenty-second Henry Allen ordered the crew to quarters and for the first time fired the guns in broadsides—one broadside of round
shot, then one of grape. He probably put a cask or some other kind of marker in
the water to shoot at, but he may have just gone through this firing to get the
crew used to actually working the guns together.[8]

The *Argus* was now approaching the mouth of the English Channel, in an
excellent position to create havoc among the crowd of British merchant vessels
funneling into the ports of the home islands. On 23 July, the day that Admiral
Thornbrough sent word by mail to the north to recall the *Pelican,* the *Argus*
was just beginning her rampage.

Late that afternoon Henry Allen detected a sail on the *Argus*'s weather quarter. After chasing her for an hour he made her out to be a schooner headed east,
up the Channel. By 7:30 in the evening the brig caught up with her, and after
Allen had fired a couple of guns at her, she stopped and surrendered. Lieutenant
Howard Allen was sent over in a boat and soon returned with her master. She
proved to be the *Matilda,* formerly an American privateer schooner. She had
been captured by the British and was now on a voyage from Pernambuco, Brazil,
to London. Henry Allen decided that she was valuable enough that he could
stretch his orders and risk manning as a prize, so he sent Richard Groves, the
master's mate, as prize master, plus thirteen men, including Peter Neho and
Peter Hansen, the two Salamancas who had joined the *Argus,* and sent her to try
to make a close port in France. At the same time, Allen took ten of the *Matilda*'s
crew out of her and brought them aboard the *Argus* as prisoners.[9]

The *Matilda* stayed with the *Argus* during the night but broke away at 4:15
A.M. when, in the growing daylight, just off the Scilly Islands, the *Argus* spotted a sail on her weather quarter and went in chase. The brig came up with her
at about seven. She was a large English brig and, when boarded, turned out to
be the *Susannah,* from Madeira, bound for London with a partial cargo of wine.
Some of the wine was intended for the countess of Shaftesbury and was apparently of very good quality. The *Argus* took aboard "a few half-pipes of the
best"—a half-pipe was a sixty-gallon barrel used especially for wine—and
stove in the heads of nearly all the rest, all that could be reached. In the ship's
strongbox was a bag containing $600, the property of one Nathaniel Cogswell,
a merchant who was sending the money from Madeira to his wife in London.[10]
The *Argus* gratefully took it aboard.

But the *Susannah* presented a complication: she had two women passengers
on board. So Henry Allen ordered Captain Row and his Salamancas and the
skipper of the *Matilda* and his men aboard the *Susannah,* declared her to be a
cartel for prisoners, and turned her back over to George Porratt, her captain,
to take in to England.

The *Matilda* was less fortunate. After breaking away from the *Argus* early on the twenty-fourth, Richard Groves and his prize crew headed for France. The next day the *Matilda* was stopped and retaken by H.M. Frigate *Revolutionnaire*. The *Matilda* was later brought into Plymouth, but Groves and his crew were taken aboard the *Revolutionnaire* as prisoners of war, then put aboard H.M.S. *Thames* and taken into Chatham, on the Medway River, on 9 August. There they were put into a prison ship. Richard Groves, because of his rank as master's mate, was released on 13 September from the prison hulk and allowed to live on parole at Ashburton in Devon.[11]

Back aboard the *Argus,* 25 July was squally and rainy. Allen started to chase a strange ship, but as he got closer found that she was one of a fleet of eleven sail, one of which was a frigate, so he hauled off and stayed clear. The wind increased to a gale with heavy rain, and the seas picked up—making it impossible to sight any prospective victims, let alone chase them. On the morning of the twenty-seventh the weather moderated a bit, although there were still squalls around and the seas were still heavy. At 4:15 A.M. the brig sighted a stranger and within a couple of hours had caught up with her. Allen had to fire three guns before the stranger hove to, then Howard Allen went across in the cutter to board her. She was the English brig *Richard,* of Whitby, on a passage from Gibraltar to London in ballast. The *Argus* crew spent a couple of hours in bringing over some stores that Allen wanted from the prize and ferrying across the prisoners: Captain Biggs, the master; Henry Saunderson, the mate; nine crewmen; and a woman passenger, whose name was not recorded. Henry Allen couldn't afford to be chivalrous this time—he took the woman on board the *Argus* with the others, then torched the *Richard.*[12]

The *Argus*'s activities of the last few days had made this area between Scilly and Ushant a risky place for her to be, and Henry Allen was sure that as soon as the *Susannah* made port the cat would be out of the bag and the British Navy would be swarming out after him. So he headed the *Argus* to the northwest, toward Cape Clear and around the southwestern corner of Ireland, to a different hunting ground. His crew needed a couple of days rest and a chance to get ready for the next actions. Surgeon Inderwick had his hands full too: John Bladin, a seaman, had come down with fever; Alex Brown, a marine and one of the older men aboard, had chest pains; Isaac Allister had rheumatismus; and Frederick Hyatt, the marine deserter picked up in L'Orient, turned up with a case of syphilis, as did one of the prisoners from the *Richard,* Andrew Mourens.[13]

The *Susannah* arrived in Penzance on 25 July, and the news soon reached Plymouth, London, and the Admiralty that what was out there was not a privateer but something much more dangerous with bigger teeth, an American brig-of-war.[14] It was an Admiralty nightmare made real: a heavily armed, nimble, fast-sailing warship, like the *Argus,* loose in the short-sea traffic lanes around the home islands could destroy a lot of shipping. Unless caught soon, the raider would make the Admiralty look clumsy and cause all manner of political problems.

Henry Allen, now heading northwestward toward Cape Clear, apparently decided at this point that the *Argus's* American-style paint job made her stand out too much and that a disguise would be useful. On the afternoon of the twenty-seventh, taking advantage of a couple of hours of calm weather, he had the *Argus's* sides repainted in the British style, black hull with a broad yellow stripe along the gunports on each side, *à la Nelson*—a very canny move.[15]

Early the next day Allen sighted a sail to the south and gave chase. Then the lookouts saw a second stranger, and a bit later a third. As the brig got closer Allen realized that what he had in view were three British warships—a man-of-war brig, a cutter, and a schooner. This was more than the *Argus* could handle, and Henry Allen headed north and west, away from them. But by this time the British had become suspicious and began to chase the *Argus.* By noon she had outrun the cutter and schooner, but the brig was more tenacious and remained in sight all afternoon. The *Argus* finally lost her as night came on.

By the thirtieth the *Argus* was off the west coast of Ireland, off the Blaskets, just north of Dingle Bay, with Inishtooskert Island in sight. She continued to work her way north. Daybreak the next morning revealed a ship in sight, which Allen chased and brought to after firing a couple of guns. Howard Allen went in a boat to board her and returned to report that she was a Dane coming from Arendal, Norway, loaded with timber for Limerick, and had been boarded several days earlier off the north of Ireland by a British warship, H.M. Brig *Pelican.*[16]

The next adventure was more productive. On 1 August Henry Allen headed in toward the coast, and by noon on a pleasant, breezy day the *Argus* was just a mile and a half off the lighthouse at Loop Head, on the northern side of the entrance to the Shannon River. The Shannon leads to Limerick, after about sixty mostly narrow miles, but at the ocean end the entrance is roomy, about eight miles wide. The *Argus* came in under easy sail, showing British colors, with an English Union flag flying at her fore-topgallant masthead. Lieutenant Fricker, R.N., manning the signal station on Kerry Head, on the southern side of the entrance to the Shannon, mistook her for "one of His Majesty's Brigs on the largest scale with a bright yellow side and nine ports . . . beside the bridle port."

Lieutenant Fricker watched the ensuing events with helpless fascination. A smaller English merchant brig came down the river, and as the two vessels neared each other, the *Argus* fired a gun, then brought down her British flag and hoisted American colors. The merchantman knew what that meant and hove to. Henry Allen sent two boats to board the capture, which turned out to be the *Fowey,* of Dartmouth, loaded with about eighty-five thousand pounds of pork consigned to the British government in Portsmouth. Her crew of four—Captain Stuart McDonald, Robert Rowe, his son Robert junior, and William Rowe—were brought aboard the *Argus* as prisoners, and then Henry Allen ordered the *Fowey* set afire.

All this was taking place quite close to the northern bank of the Shannon, and the shore was lined with spectators, local inhabitants experiencing the most exciting event to have taken place in some time. As the *Fowey* burned down to her waterline, she drifted into the breakers in Kilbaha Bay and finally went ashore. The local Irish, always hungry, swarmed over this welcome bounty from the sea, which was probably no less sweet to them for its coming at the expense of the British crown. The *Argus* stayed in the mouth of the Shannon until the *Fowey* was nearly aground, then toward evening stood out to sea.[17]

Admiral Thornbrough received word from Lieutenant Fricker of these events in the River Shannon late the next day and immediately ordered H.M. Sloop *Jalouse* to sea, to cruise from the Shannon north to Achill Head "in quest of [the] privateer."[18] She carried twenty-two guns, 32-pounders—plenty of power to handle the *Argus*. However, there was a strong flood tide and a gale of wind blowing directly into Cork Harbor, and the *Jalouse* couldn't get out for three days.

Thornbrough still didn't realize what was out there: he had been hunting all the month of July for an American privateer, and his assumption apparently was that he had located one, in spite of Lieutenant Fricker's clear description of a man-of-war brig. The knowledge that the raider was the U.S. Brig *Argus,* already available in England, would not reach Ireland for some time, so Thornbrough had no expectation that she was other than a privateer. There was certainly no precedent for an American warship operating alone in British home waters—the *Argus* was the first and by far the most successful.

Meanwhile, the *Argus* stayed off the Shannon estuary and on the afternoon of 2 August captured the cutter-rigged sloop *Lady Frances* loaded with butter, flour, and hides and bound from Limerick to Liverpool. Henry Allen had her four-man crew taken aboard the *Argus* as prisoners, took out some of the butter for the use of his crew, and put Howard Allen and some *Argus* men aboard her. The two ships stayed together during the night. It is unclear what Henry Allen's plans for her were: she doesn't seem valuable enough to have qualified under his orders as a prize to be sent in; besides, the ships were so far from France as to make unrealistic any hope of getting her safely there.

By the next morning the weather had turned bad. It was blowing a gale from the southwest, a high sea was running, and it was too rough to board the prize, so Howard Allen and his men were stuck on board her. He found that there was no navigational gear on board the *Lady Frances* and became afraid of getting separated from the *Argus* and lost. He signaled the *Argus,* perhaps a little frantically, to wait for him to come within hail. After hearing what the problem was, Henry Allen had a quadrant, a navigation book, and other useful items sealed in a cask, slung it on a rope, and veered it out astern of the *Argus.* After "some difficulty" Howard Allen and his men got the cask aboard the *Lady Frances.* The two ships stayed together during the night.

The gale blew all night and all the next day, 4 August, carrying them as far north as Galway Bay. The seas were so heavy that the men were unable to board the prize. In the late afternoon the storm abated briefly, and Henry Allen was able to send Uriah Levy across in the gig with some men to relieve Howard Allen and his exhausted crew.[19] The weather provided work for Surgeon Inderwick: Seaman John Bladin received a hernia from falling against a gun. Inderwick treated it by using his finger to push the hernia back up inside the abdominal wall.

In spite of the problems that it caused, this gale, like most of the ill winds experienced by the *Argus,* was blowing them some good: the same storm kept the *Jalouse* from getting out of Cork Harbor until late on 4 August and kept the *Pelican* locked in Killybegs until the sixth.[20]

The weather finally moderated on the fifth, and although the sea was still heavy, it was subsiding. However, the storm looked as though it would soon pick up again, and Henry Allen decided to cut his losses. The *Argus* put her boats in the water, took provisions and water out of the prize, and with the wind increasing to a heavy gale brought Uriah Levy and his men back on board. Their last act before leaving the *Lady Frances* was to put the torch to her.[21]

The wind had shifted around to the northwest, so the *Argus* now began to make her way to the southeast along the coast, past the Blaskets and toward Cape Clear. At daybreak on Saturday, 7 August, the brig was close off the Skellig Rocks, south of Dingle Bay. By Sunday morning she had rounded Cape Clear and headed east when soon after daylight the lookouts sighted a large ship. As soon as Henry Allen had closed enough to make her out more clearly he saw that she was a frigate. He broke off the chase, headed in the other direction, and soon lost sight of her. He continued eastward all of Sunday without sighting anything. By that night the *Argus* was off the entrance to Cork Harbor but then turned back toward the west, Allen probably hoping for better hunting in that direction.[22]

At first light the next morning he was off Kinsale, and there were four sail in sight. He brought to the largest and closest one and boarded her. She proved to be a Russian ship, the *Jason,* and was one of a group of several ships that had left Cork on 7 August in ballast, bound for Limerick to load grain to be taken to Santander in Spain to feed Wellington's army. Some of the group had gone into Kinsale, but the four now in sight had stayed at sea and proceeded on their way. The *Jason* also gave Henry Allen the first information that H.M. Sloop *Jalouse* had left Cork five days earlier to hunt for the *Argus*.

Henry Allen allowed the *Jason* to proceed on her way and started after the other three vessels. One was well to leeward of the *Argus,* immediately stood away from her, and got clean away. The winds were very light, and there appeared to be little chance of catching the others, but Henry Allen had the boats manned with the *Argus*'s boarding parties and captured both vessels a considerable distance to the west of Kinsale after chasing them all day. They turned out to be the ship *Barbadoes* and the brig *Alliance,* both British and engaged in government service and, like the *Jason,* in ballast for Limerick for grain. Allen brought the captains and crews of both vessels aboard the *Argus,* where two of the sailors from the *Barbadoes,* George Bernard, "a stout-built man [with] a cast in his eyes," and George Browne immediately volunteered into the *Argus*'s crew. As soon as the prisoners were aboard, at about 10 P.M. in the late twilight, Henry Allen ordered the prizes burned. The fires were seen from the signal station on Clear Island.[23]

By now the *Argus* had forty-nine prisoners aboard, including the woman from the *Richard,* and they were becoming a serious inconvenience for Henry Allen and his crew. Fortunately, a solution to the problem soon came along. The following morning, 10 August, found the brig about twenty miles southwest of Cape Clear in foggy weather. At about 2 A.M. Henry Allen suddenly found four large vessels close by to windward. At daybreak he saw that the *Argus* was in the middle of a large fleet of ships. It was part of the Leeward Islands convoy, about ninety sail, fully and richly loaded with the products of the West Indies, homeward bound for Bristol, Liverpool, and the Clyde.

The fog opened briefly, and Henry Allen saw that one of the ships very close to them, "within musket shot," was a frigate. He ordered the crew to their quarters, but quietly by passing the word, not by the usual beating of the drum. The frigate was so close that the *Argus*'s crew, at their guns, watched with dreadful fascination as the frigate's crew stowed their hammocks in the nettings on her bulwarks. Henry Allen maneuvered the *Argus* as quickly as possible to get the weather gauge so that he could use the *Argus*'s nimble sailing ability to get away. Luck was with him: the brig had already weathered the frigate before she was noticed. The frigate made sail to come after but was unable to come up with the American. The first frigate then made signals to another one, but she was even farther downwind, and both of them were soon closed off by the fog.

This excitement was still going on when the *Argus* nearly ran over H.M. Brig *Frolick,* which was lying to sharp on the larboard bow. The *Argus* ran silently by her, close aboard, the crew at their battle stations concealed behind the bulwarks. No one on the *Frolick* made a move to molest the *Argus*, which soon passed on into the fog.[24]

Leaving the *Frolick* astern, Henry Allen and the *Argus*, with the greatest sangfroid, dropped back to the tail end of the convoy and at about 8 A.M. of the same morning picked off the schooner *Cordelia*, a former-American vessel that had been condemned by the British prize court in Antigua. She was loaded with sugar and molasses, which the *Argus*'s crew destroyed. During this capture another frigate broke through a clearing in the fog. The Americans could see only her hull and gunports—her masts and rigging were hidden in the fog. She took no notice of the *Argus*, perhaps mistaking her for the *Frolick*.

Then Henry Allen ordered all the prisoners into the *Cordelia*, including the probably highly relieved woman from the *Richard*, who had spent fifteen rough-and-ready days aboard the *Argus*. She had experienced enough excitement to enable her to extort rapt attention from her children and grandchildren for ever and ever. Her name was not recorded. Somewhere in an attic in England there may be a manuscript of her memoirs.

The *Cordelia*, designated a cartel for prisoners and now back in the hands of John Avery, her skipper, headed for her original destination of Bristol with her cargo of spoiled sugar and her bilges full of molasses. As she passed Cork Harbor the captains of the *Barbadoes, Alliance,* and *Lady Frances* embarked in one of the *Cordelia*'s boats and headed into Cork to report on all these events to Admiral Thornbrough. They arrived the next morning, 11 August, and provided Thornbrough with his first real, solid information about what was going on.

All of this raiding was happening practically in Admiral Thornbrough's front yard, none of it more than sixty miles from his headquarters, and he was highly embarrassed. His letter reporting to the Admiralty, written later that day, has a flavor of resentful respect as he chronicled the exploits of the *Argus*, not failing to note that Henry Allen was the first lieutenant of the *United States* at the capture of the *Macedonian*. But when he described the failure of the three frigate captains and the skipper of the *Frolick* to seize their opportunities to capture the *Argus*, his tone moved to sarcasm. It was clear that in the days ahead those officers would be faced with some career-threatening questions.[25]

Before writing this steaming letter, Thornbrough ordered the frigate *Leonidas* to sea to hunt for the *Argus* to the east, in the track of the convoy, which by then was passing Cork Harbor. This order delayed the departure of a convoy to Lisbon that was forming at Cork, which the *Leonidas* was assigned to escort—Thornbrough was simply out of ships. He had sent the *Jalouse* off to hunt in the wrong place, and the *Pelican,* although by now only about fifty miles away to the west, had not yet returned to Cork from Killybegs, and Thornbrough didn't know when to expect her.

On the eleventh the *Pelican* was in water where the *Argus* had been the day before. The weather had cleared somewhat, but the area was still partly covered with patchy fog. At first light John Maples saw and chased a strange sail to the south, which turned out to be a brig from Demerara bound for Liverpool. From her John Maples learned that "an American brig privateer" had been in the area and boarded a Russian ship, no doubt the *Jason*. Maples ran in toward Cape Clear and, after exchanging identification codes with the signal station there, sent an officer ashore in a boat to get more information concerning the American. The officer returned in the late afternoon with some rather garbled information about the *Argus*'s activities of the day before and the burning of the *Barbadoes* and *Alliance* on the night of the ninth. As the *Pelican* sailed up the coast toward Cork she passed, off Galley Head on Dundeady Island, a cutter trying to salvage one of the burned hulks.[26]

Early the next morning, 12 August, the *Pelican* entered Cork harbor and at 6:30 A.M. anchored off Spike Island. Maples put the boats in the water to pick up "a few necessary stores" and to carry him immediately ashore to Admiral Thornbrough's headquarters, where Thornbrough revealed the identity of the *Argus* and what she had done and told Maples to hunt for her in St. George's Channel, between Ireland and Wales, and to provide some additional protection for the Leeward Islands convoy, which was now well to the east of Cork.[27]

Maples was back on board the *Pelican* by 8:20. The crew hoisted in the boats, got the anchor up, and made sail out of the harbor. As of the time the *Pelican* had anchored in Cork Harbor, the prize money–sharing agreement with H.M.S. *Helena* was terminated, and anything that the Pelicans captured from now on was all theirs.

By noon the brig was thirty miles east, well out to sea off Helvick Head, and by evening on 12 August was south of Hook Head. At this time the *Argus* was near the Saltees Islands, only about twenty miles east of the *Pelican*.[28]

After the capture of the *Cordelia* on the tenth, Henry Allen decided to stay on the heels of the convoy and try to pick off some more stray lambs. The weather was still foggy, just right for this tactic, and the next two days were the busiest of the entire cruise. Early on the eleventh the *Argus* caught up again with the Bristol-bound part of the convoy off the entrance to Bristol Channel and after a four-hour chase captured the *Mariner,* a large ship, loaded with sugar and other tropical products from St. Croix. Her crew was taken aboard the *Argus,* and Howard Allen and some men were put aboard with orders to follow the *Argus.*

There were twelve sail in sight to leeward and a brig and a cutter to windward. Henry Allen selected as his next victim one of the vessels to leeward and with the *Argus* flying British colors "crowded all sail after [her]." He captured her at about 8 P.M. after a long chase and found her to be the *Betsey,* loaded with sugar and rum from St. Vincent, bound for Bristol. Allen took the Britishers in her crew into the *Argus,* leaving some Swedes and other sailors of neutral nationality on board, then he ordered Sailing Master Uriah Levy with nine men on board her as a prize crew, telling Levy to try to make a port in France. Close by as they were manning the *Betsey* came the pilot-boat cutter *Jane,* Allen's next quarry. Quickly after that he captured the brig *Eleanor* and the cutter-sloop *John and Thomas* traveling with her from Poole to Liverpool, both vessels loaded with pipe clay. Henry Allen put all the prisoners into the *Eleanor* and sent her into Bristol. Then he got Howard Allen and his men back aboard the *Argus,* set fire to the *Mariner,* and sank the *John and Thomas.*[29] He apparently released the pilot boat *Jane.*

At this point he found another vessel close by, the cutter-sloop *Dinah and Betty,* and after taking her found she was loaded with cattle, having thirty head on board. The *Argus* crew killed two of the cattle and brought the beef aboard the *Argus,* then set fire to the prize. The *Dinah and Betty* seems to have burned with twenty-eight live cattle aboard.[30] It is possible that the cattle were killed before the vessel was fired, but the evidence points the other way. This is a real blot on Henry Allen's otherwise estimable record.

By now it was about 1:30 A.M. on the twelfth. Perhaps thinking that the fires had attracted the attention of some British warships, Henry Allen decided to move to another area and took the *Argus* northwest across St. George's Channel, heading toward the Saltees Islands just off the southeastern corner of Ireland.

After leaving the scene of her capture in company with the *Argus,* the *Betsey* broke off and went her own way, heading south to round the tip of Cornwall on her risky course to France. Uriah Levy had some wooden plugs made up, then had several holes augered through the bottom of the vessel and put the plugs firmly in the holes. The idea was to enable the prize crew to scuttle the ship if recapture appeared imminent.

Under the unwritten rules of warfare at sea in those days, this was not playing fair. The biggest part of the income of all wartime officers of whatever navy was prize money, and prizes were highly cherished. It was fair game to capture a prize and even to burn or sink it on the spot if your government had ordered you to, and it was fair game to recapture a prize, but destroying a prize that was about to be recaptured was considered an affront to all right-thinking naval officers.

Less than twenty-four hours after leaving the *Argus,* the *Betsey* was intercepted by H.M. Frigate *Leonidas,* Captain Seymour, and recaptured. As Uriah Levy and his prize crew were being taken aboard the *Leonidas* as prisoners of war, a Swedish seaman, one of the *Betsey's* original crew that had been left on board her, told Captain Seymour about the plugs and said that they had been pulled to scuttle the ship. Seymour immediately sent the *Leonidas's* carpenter's crew aboard the prize, and they were able to stop the leaks and save her. Seymour, in a high state of indignation, then had Uriah Levy brought up and questioned. Levy said that he was acting under Henry Allen's orders. However, by the time there was an opportunity to check this statement, it was too late. The question of whether Levy's action was legal was put to the law officers at the Admiralty, whose opinion was that while it was "irregular and attended with inconvenience," it was not a breach of any law, and that Levy couldn't be punished for it, whether or not he was acting under orders.[31]

The *Argus* was now, on 12 August, off the southeastern corner of Ireland, near the Saltees Islands. In spite of all the action, life aboard the *Argus* went on with some semblance of normality, and Surgeon Inderwick had patients to treat. The sick list had been running at about six to eight men, with a continual turnover as newly ill men replaced the ones cured. Amidst all the capturing and burning of prizes Boatswain's Mate Joseph Jordan sought treatment for secondary syphilis; Robert Jamison, a fifty-four-year-old seaman, turned up with erysipelas; and Quarter Gunner John Freeman cut himself badly across the instep near the ankle joint with an adz and lost a lot of blood. Inderwick sutured the wound and used adhesive plaster and a roller bandage to help keep it closed.

That day the *Argus* captured a new brig named the *Ann* loaded with slate and Welsh woolens, bound from Cardigan to London. Henry Allen ordered her sunk. Next he stopped a Portuguese brig bound for Cork and put the prisoners from the *Dinah and Betty* and the *Ann* on board her. He sighted two large ships and a brig to leeward, all showing English colors, and chased them. Henry Allen let the brig get away, continuing to chase the other two.

These two were beginning to look as if they might be a handful: one of them had eighteen gun ports, the other sixteen, and they gave every appearance of preparing to fight. The *Argus* brought them to and sent Howard Allen across in a boat to board the largest of the two. Her captain refused Howard Allen's orders to come aboard the *Argus,* and even before Allen and the boat could return with this information, both of the vessels made sail and took off, keeping close to each other for mutual protection. The *Argus* went after them and, coming alongside, began firing into them. The larger vessel hauled down her flag and stopped after receiving two broadsides, but the other kept running, with the *Argus* in chase. The quarry ran in among the rocks off the Saltees Islands, her skipper probably having local knowledge and experience of where he could safely go. Henry Allen was reluctant to risk following the vessel into such tight quarters and let her go, returning to the larger ship. She proved to be the *Defiance,* a Scotch ship bound from Greenock to Newfoundland. She was well armed—fourteen long 9-pounder guns—but no match for a brig-of-war like the *Argus.* Henry Allen apparently had her crew of twenty-one men brought aboard the *Argus* and put a small, temporary prize crew aboard her.

This day stretched into night and into the early morning of the thirteenth. At 2 A.M. Allen captured a large brig, one of the convoy that the *Argus* had been dogging for several days. She was the *Baltic* and was loaded with sugar from Barbados for Dublin. Three hours later the *Argus* caught a sloop loaded with lumber, and after throwing her cargo of deal boards over the side, Henry Allen put aboard her the prisoners from the *Defiance* and the *Baltic* and sent her away. Then at about 6 A.M. Henry Allen ordered the torch to be put to the *Baltic* and *Defiance.*

Nothing else came his way until evening, when at 9 P.M. on 13 August a large brig nearly ran over the *Argus.* Henry Allen fired a gun and brought her to. She was the *Belford,* bound from Dublin to London, and was the most valuable vessel that he had captured, loaded with wine and 16,500 pieces of fine linen and worth £100,000 sterling. Allen took out of her a box of silver articles and at around midnight had her set afire.

At this point the *Argus* had taken twenty vessels, twelve of them in the last three days, and had burned, sunk, or destroyed the cargo of all but two of them. This was more than any other single American warship of any size had done or was to do.[32]

H.M. Brig *Pelican* with John Maples had spent 13 August somewhat to the west in the same general area, stopping ships to see if they were perhaps prizes of the *Argus* or had any information about her. Maples impressed one unlucky man, Barney Murry, from a brig bound from Greenock to Cork. That night, at 10 P.M., the *Pelican* stopped the *Mary,* a small coaster bound from Wexford to Milford, in Wales, and got the information that Maples had been seeking. Earlier in the day the *Mary*'s crew had watched the *Argus* set two ships on fire, and the *Argus* had remained in sight until 8 P.M., just two hours before. Showing a singular lack of gratitude for this useful information, Maples impressed one of the *Mary*'s men, Phillip Miller.

Then at midnight John Maples saw a vessel on fire to the north and east. It was the *Belford.* He headed in that direction and in the dark came across a brig, brought her to, and boarded her. She was a British merchantman bound from Liverpool to Falmouth and was not a prize of the *Argus.* The *Pelican* was still shorthanded, and Maples coolly took the time to impress a seaman, James Hatton, out of her, then recovered his boat and continued heading toward the fire. At 3:45 A.M., in the early twilight of 14 August, Maples saw a brig to the northeast.[33] This time it was the *Argus.*

CHAPTER EIGHTEEN

The Battle off
St. David's Head

THAT MORNING, 14 AUGUST 1813, Henry Allen had planned to inter-
rupt his rampage and stop making captures for perhaps a day to give the crew
a rest. All hands had spent the hours since 9 P.M. the night before in capturing
the *Belford,* getting the valuables out of her cargo, and then burning her. When
the *Pelican* was sighted in the early morning twilight at about 4 A.M., most of
the crew, dead tired, had been turned in to their hammocks for only about ten
minutes.[1]

Henry Allen was familiar enough with ships of the British Navy to realize
that the brig-of-war closing on him with all sail set was somewhat larger and
more heavily armed than the *Argus.* Common sense and wise judgment should
have led him to avoid battle: not only was his crew much in need of rest and
his potential antagonist more powerful, but even if he emerged the victor it was
very likely that he would have received enough damage to leave him vulnerable to capture by any ship of the Royal Navy that found him. Since Henry
Allen had kicked the hornets' nest with his captures and burnings, the area was
beginning to swarm with British warships.

His orders emphasized the value of destroying British merchant ships and
disrupting commerce right in British home waters, and up to the present
Henry Allen had done a great job of this. But even if he won the fight with the
Pelican, capturing one small warship out of the hundred or so in the British
Navy would contribute very little to what the secretary of the navy wanted the

Argus to accomplish. The *Argus* was faster and a better sailer, and there is little doubt that Henry Allen could have gotten clean away from the *Pelican* had he chosen to, and that is what he should have done.

But Henry Allen's personal values apparently entered the equation and distorted his judgment. His orders told him to "proceed upon a cruize against the commerce, and light cruizers of the enemy, which you will capture and destroy in all cases. . . ."[2] Here was clear permission to take on the *Pelican;* indeed, he was told to "capture and destroy in all cases."

These were poorly written orders, given the commerce-destroying objectives of the cruise of the *Argus,* but commanders of detached ships were, in those days, expected to use wisdom and initiative and to disregard parts of their orders if such disregard better served their mission. But Henry Allen's highly developed sense of personal honor plus all of the experiences of his professional life had pointed him toward just this moment, when he would command a ship in action against a roughly equal British ship of war. He would finally erase in his mind all the little humiliations handed to the infant U.S. Navy by the British during his service in the Mediterranean, expunge the disgrace of the *Chesapeake* and *Leopard* encounter, and wipe clean the memory of the arrogance of the British first lieutenant after the victory of the frigate *United States* over the *Macedonian.* There was probably never any real doubt in his mind that he should fight the *Pelican,* and he was fully confident—indeed, overconfident—of winning. He had "made up his mind not to run away from any two-masted enemy ship" and had told his crew that the *Argus* could "whip any English . . . sloop-of-war in ten minutes."[3]

On board the *Pelican,* John Maples's thoughts on the upcoming battle were probably less complex and can be reconstructed with some confidence: The long wars were winding down, and there were fewer and fewer opportunities for the commander of one of His Majesty's brigs to distinguish himself in a single-ship engagement with an enemy, particularly a notorious and destructive enemy like the *Argus.* If Maples could bring the *Argus* to battle and capture her, he might well be rewarded with that all-important promotion to post-captain. This promotion would open up pleasant vistas of commanding larger ships, then later on bring him a fairly comfortable retirement on a captain's half-pay and certain eventual promotion to rear-admiral, if he lived long enough. The alternative was a stultified career ending up as commander, followed by a gritty, impoverished retirement. To John Maples the *Argus* was the lucky break of a lifetime, the ticket to everything he had waited for and worked toward for thirty-one years. He would do everything in his power to keep her from slipping through his fingers.

When the captains could first see each other clearly, shortly after first light at about 4 A.M. that Saturday morning, John Maples with the *Pelican* was per-

haps six miles to the southwest of the *Argus* and headed toward her with every
sail set. The wind was from the southwest, giving the *Pelican* the favored,
upwind, weather-gauge position. The *Argus* was headed a little south of east
under easy sail, and Henry Allen could see the *Pelican* on his starboard quarter, coming down on him "under a press of sail." Allen first tried to get to
windward of the *Pelican,* to seize the weather gauge, but John Maples changed
course and cut him off. At that point, at about 4:30 A.M., Henry Allen had the
Argus shorten sail to her topsails, topgallant sails, jib, and fore and aft driver
mainsail and waited for the *Pelican* to catch up.

Both ships had plenty of time to clear for action and get ready for the fight.
Both stowed the hammocks in the nettings on top of the main-deck bulwarks to
protect against musketry and grapeshot, sent their crews to quarters, and carefully loaded full charges in all of the guns. The surgeons made ready to cope
with the wounded: Richard Coniby in the *Pelican* and James Inderwick in the
Argus. Only Inderwick would be busy today.

By a few minutes before 6 A.M. the *Pelican* had closed to within just a few
hundred yards, and John Maples ordered his British colors raised. Henry Allen
hoisted the Stars and Stripes to the gaff peak of the *Argus,* then immediately
wore ship to the west—a sharp turn to the left. The *Pelican* wore round to stay
with the American brig, and the two ships came parallel less than two hundred
yards apart. Henry Allen and the *Argus'*s crew gave three cheers and fired their
larboard broadside, the *Pelican* came back with three cheers and her starboard
broadside, and the fight was on. Both ships fired as fast as they could load and
aim, but much of the *Argus'*s fire went high, some shots going through the royal
sails on the *Pelican.* The noise of the battle was heard ashore twenty miles away
at Milford, where the inhabitants were "alarmed by a tremendous firing."[4]

The *Pelican'*s fire was deadly and effective. A few short minutes after the
battle opened disaster struck the *Argus:* a 32-pound shot hit Henry Allen just
above his left knee, knocking him across the deck and shattering his leg. He
held himself up on an elbow and tried to continue in command, but he was
quickly unconscious from the loss of blood. Lieutenant William Watson took
over, and Henry Allen was carried below. Then in quick succession the hail of
shot from the *Pelican* carried away the main braces and much of the other rigging needed to handle the mainmast and tore away the larboard shrouds supporting the foremast. Midshipman Edwards had his head taken off by a shot,
and Seaman Joshua Jones was killed by another. Lieutenant William Watson
was hit a grazing blow by a grapeshot, an iron ball the size of a plum. His scalp
was torn open to the skull, and he was knocked unconscious. The remaining
lieutenant, Howard Allen, took command of the deck, and Watson was carried below to the surgeon.

Now John Maples turned the *Pelican* to the right to pass under the stern of the *Argus* and give her a raking broadside. Howard Allen neatly thwarted this move by backing his main-topsail, slowing the *Argus* and putting her across the *Pelican*'s bow, in position to rake her. This could have been the turning point of the battle: single-ship actions were often decided by one, hugely destructive raking broadside. But the *Argus*'s broadside was ineffectual and left the *Pelican* almost undamaged.

It was now all downhill for the *Argus*. The *Pelican* ranged up alongside, and the next few broadsides tore away the *Argus*'s main preventer braces, the tyes holding the main-topsail yard to the mast, and the wheel ropes controlling the rudder. With this, the *Argus* lost the ability to maneuver. John Maples then put the *Pelican* off the American brig's starboard quarter, then under her stern, and poured in his fire without the *Argus*'s being able to bring but a few guns to bear. Many of the *Argus*'s guns were knocked out of their slides, and her deck was becoming a shambles. Midshipman Delphey was hit in the knees with a 32-pound shot that almost severed both legs. He died within a few hours. William Moulton, a seaman, was killed outright. Seaman George Gardiner had his leg taken off close to the body by a shot and lived for about half an hour. Ten others were wounded, not counting Henry Allen and William Watson, and several of these men died during the following hours or days.

Lieutenant Watson regained consciousness and, after Surgeon Inderwick tacked his scalp down with a few stitches, returned to again take command of the deck. By this time the *Pelican* was moving around the *Argus* at will, firing as she went. Watson tried to find an opportunity to carry the *Pelican* by boarding, but the *Argus* was shattered and the crew demoralized by the damage and the loss of their captain, and boarding was out of the question. The *Pelican* sat close off the starboard bow of the *Argus,* raking her, and it was clear to Lieutenant Watson that surrender was inevitable and imminent. Just as the battle was ending Seaman John Finlay's head was taken off at the neck by a shot. Then the *Argus* drifted down against the *Pelican* and was promptly boarded. Most of the *Argus*'s crew ran below as the Pelicans swarmed aboard. Lieutenant Watson and a few others remained on deck to bring down the colors, which fell in a tumbled heap of broad stripes and bright stars on the *Argus*'s quarterdeck. It had all happened in just forty-five minutes.

The *Pelican* suffered very little. William Young, a master's mate, was killed by a musket ball from the *Argus*'s foretop as he led the boarders. The only other man killed on the *Pelican* was John Emery, a seaman from New York, one of the Americans serving aboard. Five others were wounded, but all recovered. John Maples was struck by a spent canister shot, a musket ball, which hit a button on his coat and fell to the deck. He was uninjured. One of the *Argus*'s shot went through the side of the berth deck and demolished Boatswain Richard Scott's cabin, and another went through the carpenter's cabin. There was considerable damage to the *Pelican's* rigging, but nothing crippling. Two of her guns were dismounted, and her sides were full of grapeshot, but that was all.

What caused the ineffective fire of the *Argus* and led her to make such a poor showing? Lieutenant Watson, in his postwar report, and the court of enquiry, blamed it on the fatigue of the crew. The *Argus's* company all acted bravely right up until the end, although one seaman, Isaac Allister, apparently became nervous and rolled a shot into his gun before loading the powder, disabling the gun for the duration of the battle. And John Hendricks, a sixteen-year-old boy assigned to carry powder, got scared and went below, but Midshipman Jamesson went after him and brought him back, after which he served his gun for the rest of the battle.[5]

James Fenimore Cooper wrote a history of the navy early in the nineteenth century at a time when he could have talked to some of the survivors of the battle. He quoted an "authority [apparently] entitled to credit" as stating that on the night before the battle the *Argus* captured a ship "from Oporto" loaded with wine, and that the crew smuggled some of the wine aboard. According to this account, some of the crew got drunk and were still drunk or badly hung over during the battle, as well as tired. Of course, there was no ship "from Oporto," but the *Belford,* captured the night of the thirteenth, was carrying some wine in her cargo, and it could have gotten aboard. However, if the crew did get into some liquor, a more likely source was the *Betsey,* which was carrying rum and sugar from St. Vincent in the West Indies. The *Argus* captured her on the eleventh, and she was alongside for some time while Uriah Levy and his prize crew were fitted out and put aboard. Sailors of that day were extremely ingenious when it came to getting clandestine liquor on board, so it is possible that there is some truth to the story.

Probably the most accurate source of information about the *Argus's* defeat, however, is the general opinion held in the U.S. Navy right after the war, that the loss of her captain and other officers, plus crew fatigue, caused her inaccurate, ineffective fire.[6] No excuses ever needed to be made for her defeat: she was up against a bigger, heavier opponent, fully as well-trained and as competently commanded, officered, and manned as she was. But the loss of the *Argus* changed the way the Navy Department viewed single-ship actions between American and British warships: President Madison, after hearing of her loss, asked Secretary of the Navy Jones, "Would it be amiss to instruct such crews positively never to fight where they can avoid it, and employ themselves entirely in destroying the commerce of the Enemy. . . ." In orders sending Lewis Warrington, captain of the U.S.S. *Peacock,* on a cruise similar to that of the *Argus,* Jones clearly told him not to repeat Allen's mistake.[7]

The *Pelican's* boarding party ran wild for a short time, looting whatever they could get their hands on. They trampled on the wounded men of the

Argus, who were lying in agony on the berth deck, and this led to later problems with their treatment and recovery. But John Maples sent Lieutenant Welsh and most of the starboard watch of the *Pelican* on board as the prize crew to bring the *Argus* into port and recalled the boarders. Most of the *Argus*'s officers and crew were boated over to the *Pelican,* including William Watson and Howard Allen, leaving about thirty of the *Argus*'s men on board, including the wounded. Defeated, and with their officers gone, the remaining crew of the *Argus* apparently were beyond discipline and almost out of control.[8]

John Maples came over to the *Argus* to see his prize firsthand and visited Henry Allen, who was being tended in his cabin by Surgeon Inderwick. Allen was by this time drifting in and out of consciousness and lucidity. Visualizing this moment, one can hope that John Maples had the grace to be compassionate.

John Maples promised Inderwick that the ships would lie to until the amputation of Henry Allen's leg had been accomplished. Surgeon Inderwick took the leg off at midthigh, and it seemed at first that Henry Allen would recover. Midshipman Delphey, both legs shattered at the knee, was beyond hope and bled to death within three hours after the battle.[9] Mercifully, he died before Inderwick could get around to amputating his legs, but he lived long enough after the battle that custom dictated that he be taken ashore for burial—those that were killed outright in the action had been thrown overboard.

Then Inderwick, working by lantern in the semidarkness of the berth deck, turned his attention to the other wounded. Seaman Charles Baxter had received a gunshot wound in his right thigh and a compound fracture of his lower left leg, which was hemorrhaging. He would not allow Surgeon Inderwick to amputate his left leg, but the doctor did apply some emergency compression dressings. Baxter's death was inevitable after fever and shock set in the next day, but he lived painfully on for eighteen days. Francis Eggert, a seaman, was apparently hit by a large splinter, which caused a severe contusion of his lower right leg. He would not consent to amputation, but there was nothing in any event that the medicine of that day could have done for him. He developed fever and gangrene, which he suffered for sixteen terrible days before he died. Joseph Jordan, a boatswain's mate, received a compound fracture of his left thigh—which shattered the bone—and was hideously wounded in the other thigh and buttocks, much of the skin and muscles having been torn away. His case was hopeless, although Dr. Inderwick applied compression dressings until death came two days later. Carpenter James White had a fractured left thigh and a scalp cut. He developed a high fever and was gone two days later. Seaman Joshua Jones died two days after the battle, but Inderwick left no details of his wounds or treatment.

Seven wounded men survived. Lieutenant Watson's scalp gash healed well, probably because of the quick repair by Inderwick during the battle. Seaman

James Hall was cut over the eye by a splinter. Inderwick dressed the wound, which was healing well two days later. William Harrington, who received a large contusion on his back, was cured in two days by liniment and an analgesic. Seaman James Kellam was wounded in the right calf and hamstring. Dr. Inderwick applied simple dressings, and in spite of a fever Kellam pulled through. Boatswain Colin McLeod received several wounds: he was hit by a grapeshot or piece of langrage, which cut deeply into the muscles on the front of his right thigh; his shoulder was dislocated by a flying splinter; his face was cut up; and he was hurt less badly in several other places, including "one too immodest to mention."[10] All of his wounds healed eventually, although he was left disabled. Quartermaster John Young was shot in both the chest and the hand, and his recovery was a close call. He was probably saved by Surgeon Inderwick's keeping his wounds clean. Seaman John Nugent was the luckiest of the surviving wounded: he received a compound fracture of his left thigh—which left the bone much splintered—a wound that should have been fatal. The standard treatment for an open fracture was amputation, but for some unrecorded reason, possibly because it was too close to the groin, Inderwick instead explored the wound, removed several pieces of bone, and cleaned it as best he could. Fever ensued two days later, and although Inderwick's standard treatment of opiates and mild laxatives could not have brought it down, Nugent apparently had a strong immune system and did recover.

Inderwick's most difficult case was Henry Allen. Before and after the amputation Inderwick gave Allen strong opiate analgesics. John Hudson, the sailing master; Henry Denison, the purser; and Inderwick took turns sitting with Allen around the clock. Two days later Allen seemed to be recovering. Then that night serum began to ooze from the stump of his leg, and he vomited constantly. Inderwick treated him for fever, but Henry Allen was slowly slipping away. His final days were coming.

So six men died during or within a few hours after the battle, and six died later of their wounds, including Henry Allen. Seven wounded men recovered. This was the highest per capita battle-casualty rate of any American navy ship during the War of 1812. None of the killed or wounded were marines.

At 10 A.M., a little more than three hours after the battle, the *Pelican* got under way and headed southwest.[11] The *Argus* followed in company, now commanded by Lieutenant Welsh, R.N., as prize master and manned by a British prize crew, with the British Red Ensign flying above the Stars and Stripes. At 5:45 that afternoon the *Pelican* buried her dead from the battle: William Young, the master's mate, and Seaman John Emery, the American from the city of New York. Emery had come with John Maples from the *Ætna* as one of his chosen best men, and now he was dead, killed fighting against his own countrymen, perhaps willingly, perhaps unwillingly—there is no way to know.

He went to his grave in the cold waters of St. George's Channel, no doubt sewed in his hammock with two 32-pound shot at his feet, slipping out from under the Union Jack off a tilted plank.

The two ships stayed together until 9 A.M. the next morning, the fifteenth, then they parted company, and the *Argus* headed for Plymouth. John Maples set the *Pelican* on a course for Cork to report the victory to his boss, Vice-Admiral Thornbrough. Maples's feelings must have been pride, satisfaction, and pleasant anticipation. All his experience and training had finally paid off for him in a brief forty-five minutes, and now there would certainly be some rewards.

The frigate *Leonidas*, Captain Seymour, after recapturing the *Betsey* with Uriah Levy and his prize crew, was still looking for the *Argus*. By early on the fifteenth the *Leonidas* was near the Smalls Islands, when at 8:30 A.M. she sighted a "suspicious" brig. No doubt thinking he had found the *Argus*, and savoring the prize money almost in his grasp, Captain Seymour made all sail in chase.

After several hours of chasing and the exchange of some signals it turned out that his quarry was instead H.M. Brig *Pelican*. The two ships were soon hove to near each other, and John Maples came over to the *Leonidas* in a boat, bearing his good news. Although probably disappointed not to have found the *Argus* himself, Captain Seymour was generous enough to be willing to take some of the American prisoners aboard and carry them into Cork. John Maples was probably happy to get this help: the *Pelican* had about ninety-seven prisoners on board, along with only about half, roughly fifty, of her own crew, and was not only overcrowded but was also in some possible danger of being taken over by her captives. The *Leonidas* sent over two boats and took aboard forty of the Americans, and then in the late afternoon both ships got under way again and headed for Cork.[12]

Among the Americans taken to the *Leonidas* was Lieutenant William Watson. Captain Seymour questioned Watson as to whether Captain Allen had ordered Levy to scuttle his prize if recapture was imminent. Levy was still on board the *Leonidas*, and Seymour may have had the two American officers confront each other on the question, although there is nothing in the surviving record to show this. Watson said that he was "persuaded that no such orders were given by the Captain" and went on to be critical of Levy's conduct.[13] This statement caused strained feelings between Watson and Levy and apparently also led to some conflict between Howard Allen, Watson's close friend, and Levy.[14]

Watson was probably right. The scuttling idea was totally out of character for Henry Allen, whose sensitivity to matters of honor between naval officers was enormous. On the other hand, Uriah Levy was quite pragmatic when it came to solving problems, and the idea of scuttling the prize might well have occurred to him. It was certainly consistent with the *Argus*'s orders, if not her captain's intention, to destroy all the vessels except those that could be carried for certain into a French port.

The *Leonidas* was a faster sailer and arrived in Cork Harbor at 10 A.M. on the seventeenth, several hours ahead of the *Pelican*. Captain Seymour immediately went ashore and reported to Admiral Thornbrough the capture of the *Argus* and the recapture of the *Betsey*. Thornbrough was delighted with the news: his in-box was full of letters from important merchants and mayors crying rumors and alarms that the *Argus* had been seen off their ports and wanting protection. Now he could answer them all with the announcement of her capture. Viewing this result from the perspective of the United States shows in one small way what was lost to the American strategic position when Henry Allen decided to fight instead of run: the *Argus*'s operations had greatly stressed Thornbrough's ability to cope with his problems, but her early—and avoidable—capture had now solved them for him.

The *Pelican* arrived in the early evening and at 8:15 P.M. anchored near the *Leonidas*. John Maples was rowed ashore for the pleasant duty of describing his victory to Admiral Thornbrough and handing in his official report of the action. Thornbrough sent the report on to the Admiralty the next morning with a covering memo commending Maples "to the attention of their Lordships"—meaning that Thornbrough endorsed Maples for the kinds of rewards that only the Admiralty itself could give.[15] One can see Thornbrough saying to his friends, "Good man, Maples. Trained him myself. He was one of my mids in the old *Hebe* frigate." The Admiralty considered the action important enough to be "gazetted," and John Maples's report appeared in the *London Gazette* on 24 August 1813.

The mood changed abruptly on the morning of 18 August. John Robinson, ordinary seaman, one of the prisoners from the *Argus* now on board the *Leonidas,* asked to see the captain to impart some important information. When brought before Captain Seymour he stated that he was a British subject, born in Dundee, Scotland, not New York City, and that his name was really James Hunter. He told Seymour that there were seven more Britishers among the *Argus*'s prisoners now aboard the *Leonidas* and about ten others on the *Pelican* or back on the *Argus*. Robinson named seven, but when the prisoners were lined up and mustered for him to identify, he pointed out eight men: Judson Gilbert, James Beens, William Shaw, William Smith, Thomas Hill, Richard Kennedy, George Andrews, and George Starbuck. The suppressed fury of the American prisoners toward this traitorous act can scarcely be imagined. This was no small matter: British subjects "taken in arms against His Majesty" were court-martialed and, if found guilty, hanged or even "hanged, drawn and quartered."[16]

Admiral Thornbrough had the eight men brought on board his flagship, H.M.S. *Trent,* and put in irons, to be separately sent to Plymouth for investigation by Mr. Bicknell from the Admiralty—Thornbrough felt it wouldn't be safe to send them on the *Pelican* with so many other Americans on board. Robinson, however, was put aboard the *Pelican,* and John Maples was told to "take particular care" of him.[17] Here was a hot potato indeed, and John Maples came back to ask Thornbrough "in what manner he should dispose of John Robinson alias [James] Hunter." Admiral Thornbrough quickly took a Pilate-like stance, telling Maples to dispose of Robinson upon arrival in Plymouth in whatever way the admiral there might direct. Nobody likes a traitor, as John Robinson was to learn over the next several months.

Robinson's evidence against his shipmates was flimsy. For example, James Beens, a quartermaster, was pointed out because he appeared to be "perfectly acquainted with the Irish Coast and St. George's Channel."[18] But a good quartermaster should make himself familiar with the area his ship is operating in. Richard Kennedy, captain of the foretop, was accused because he said he was born in Brooklyn but didn't seem to know that Brooklyn was on Long Island. Of course, the world has always been amused by numbers of true Brooklynites who are without the faintest notion as to the location of Long Island. And Starbuck's family had lived on Nantucket Island for many generations.

Robinson asserted that the men had told him that they were English, although the men denied this and all the records were to the contrary. In any event, all those accused by Robinson were securely ironed on board the *Trent* and were sent on to Plymouth some days later on a separate ship.

The *Pelican* was ordered to Plymouth to repair her battle damage and to have an extensive refit. Captain Seymour transferred back to the *Pelican* the forty American prisoners he had brought into Cork, including Uriah Levy and the *Betsey's* prize crew, less those now in irons in the *Trent,* bringing the number of prisoners aboard the *Pelican* up to eighty something. Admiral Thornbrough ordered a couple of officers from his flagship, navy Lieutenant Harty and marine Lieutenant Hancock, to report aboard the *Pelican* for the trip to help Maples, who had only one lieutenant and two midshipmen at this time. Then at daylight on 20 August the *Pelican* sailed for Plymouth. She arrived two days later, anchoring in Plymouth Sound at 7:30 A.M. on the twenty-second.

The trip over from Cork was John Maples's last voyage in the *Pelican*. On 25 August he received word that he had been rewarded with that vital, all-important promotion and that as of 23 August 1813 he was a post-captain. He was now secure. The honor and position of a captaincy were his, and the significant jump in pay would make his life much more pleasant. He now had his feet firmly on that ladder from which only death could displace him, the inexorable ladder of seniority that would bring him to be an admiral if he managed to outlive those ahead of him.

But it was a bittersweet reward: brigs like the *Pelican* were commanded by commanders, and on 3 September 1813 John Maples was relieved and put on half-pay to await another appointment. He knew from past experience that this might be some time in coming and that he had to act to get further employment while the memory of his victory over the *Argus* was fresh in the minds of those in power. To his great credit, most of his letters to the Admiralty during this trying time were requests that the men who had come with him to the *Pelican* be promoted and taken care of: Thomas Palmer, his coxswain, and Richard Scott, boatswain of the *Pelican,* whom Maples had requested from the *Otter.* Only after this was done did John Maples, now living in London at 34, Canterbury Place, Lambeth, write on 7 November 1813 to ask their lordships for an appointment. The secretary of the Admiralty replied to him with good news, that he was on the list of candidates for an appointment.[19]

The *Argus* arrived in Plymouth Sound on the afternoon of Monday, 16 August. The able-bodied of the *Argus*'s crew who were still on board were boated over to the prison ship *Hector,* an old battleship fitted out to house prisoners of war, which was lying in the Hamoaze, west of the sound. The next morning the wounded and sick, except for Captain Allen, were taken ashore to the hospital at Mill Prison, off Mill Bay, on the southwestern side of Plymouth. John Hudson, the sailing master, accompanied them to help handle any problems that might develop.

In the afternoon Surgeon Inderwick got permission from his British captors to go into Plymouth to look for clean, quiet, private lodgings to which he could take Henry Allen—the ship was becoming overrun with surveyors and sightseers, and "the noise and tumult . . . [was] very disagreeable." Henry Allen was experiencing some fever, nausea, and vomiting when Inderwick left on his search, and Inderwick returned to find him worse. That night Allen was restless, and his vomiting continued unchecked. In the morning, 18 August, the surgeon of the *Salvador del Mundo,* a captured Spanish battleship that served as the receiving ship at Plymouth, came aboard and helped Inderwick dress the stump of Allen's leg. The wound was not healing well, and the tissue at the site was septic and probably on the edge of becoming gangrenous. Dr. Magrath, the head surgeon at Mill Prison Hospital, had also come aboard, and the three doctors decided to move Allen to the Mill Prison Hospital, where he could receive the best care that those times had to offer. These were Henry Allen's last moments aboard his ship. Weak but lucid, surrounded for a farewell by the last of the *Argus*'s men to remain aboard, he is quoted to have said, "God bless you, my lads; we shall never meet again."[20]

At 11 A.M. the captain of the *Salvador* sent his launch, fitted with a large cot, to receive Henry Allen and take him to the boat landing in Mill Bay, close to the hospital. A large, separate room was prepared and female attendants brought in to care for him. Inderwick, John Hudson, Henry Denison, and an unnamed midshipman—plus Allen's personal servants; Appene, his Chinese steward; and his coxswain—were allowed to stay by him. Dr. Magrath, older and more experienced than Inderwick, took over direction of the case but seems to have continued the same treatment started by Inderwick. But the medical knowledge of that day had nothing to offer to anyone as seriously injured as Henry Allen. He went into severe septic shock, then became more restless and delirious, and sank into a coma. At 11 P.M. that night, 18 August 1813, he died.[21]

What shall we say of this young man, now that his life is finished and can be summed up? He was a naval officer of great promise—courageous, skilled, eager to learn his profession and advance in it. He was generous to his adversaries in war. He was loyal to those who led him and to those below him entrusted to his leadership. In turn, he inspired loyalty, and both salt-matured sailors and young officers followed him from ship to ship to serve with him. He was a gentleman in that early-nineteenth-century pattern that called for uncompromising integrity and for kindness and sympathy to the weak and vulnerable. He had that excessive sense of personal honor often found in officers of that day, and it was this that brought him to his death.

He was shy in the presence of women and apparently never expressed his interest or intentions to the girl at home in Providence who might have enlarged his life. To the end of his short life he was intensely close to his family and waited impatiently for their letters, and they for his. He was the darling of his older sister, a strong staff for his weak younger brother to lean on, the concern of his stepmother, who worried for his safety; and he was the pride, the immense pride of his father. This old gentleman, an officer of the Revolutionary War, was broken by his son's death and himself died two years later to the day.[22]

William Henry Allen's funeral was arranged by John Hawker, the American ex–vice consul, and the officers of the *Argus*. Rear-Admiral Thomas Byam Martin, commanding at Plymouth, ordered that the ceremonies be done with military honors and be attended by British officers of rank, and that a lieutenant-colonel's guard of Royal Marines take part. Hawker and the *Argus*'s officers bought a fine "wainscot coffin" for Allen and had the breastplate of it inscribed with his name, rank, age, and a brief eulogy.[23]

The funeral procession assembled at the Mill Prison Hospital at 11 A.M. on Saturday, 21 August. The coffin was brought down and covered with a black velvet pall, over which was spread the American ensign of the *Argus,* those Stars and Stripes under which the battle had been fought. On top of the flag were laid Henry Allen's hat and sword. As the coffin was placed in the hearse the marine guard saluted, and the procession began to move out into Millbay

Road. The guard of honor was first, led by the lieutenant-colonel of Royal Marines, followed by two companies of marines with their captains, subalterns, and field adjutant, the officers wearing black hatbands and scarves. Behind them came the marine band, playing the "Dead March" from Handel's *Saul,* and the vicar, curate, and clerk of St. Andrew's Church.

Then came "THE HEARSE, With the corpse of the deceased captain," attended by eight seamen from the *Argus* with black crape arm bands tied with white crape ribbons. With the hearse were eight captains of the Royal Navy, acting as pallbearers, with black hatbands and scarves. Following the hearse came Henry Allen's servants, his steward, Appene, and his coxswain, in mourning; then the officers of the *Argus,* two by two, wearing black crape sashes and hatbands; John Hawker and his clerks; Captain Pellowe, R.N., the commissioner for prisoners of war at Plymouth; and Dr. Magrath. Behind them were all the captains of the Royal Navy that were in port, marine and army officers, and the servants of the officers of the *Argus,* all walking two by two. Last came "a very numerous and respectable retinue of inhabitants."[24] Henry Allen would have been pleased to know that such a great event was organized to honor him.

The procession moved east, up Millbay Road and into George Street, then right into Bedford Street and on to St. Andrew's Church. There the marine guard halted and formed lines in single file, with arms reversed, and the procession passed through them into the church, where the coffin was set down in the center aisle. The vicar read the first part of *The Order for the Burial of the Dead,* then the coffin was taken out into the south yard of the church for burial, and the reading of the *Order* completed *at the grave.* Midshipman Delphey had been put to rest there just the night before, although with less ceremony, and the vault was still open. Henry Allen was let down into the vault to a place on Richard Delphey's left, the vault was sealed, and the grave filled. There they still sleep.

No detail survives about how their headstone was designed and the epitaph written, but this scenario fits the available facts: Perhaps John Hawker and the *Argus*'s officers met with the monument maker to draw up the inscription to be cut in the stone. The officers asked that an American eagle be carved at the top, and when the stonecutter asked what an American eagle looked like, one of the officers pulled a gilt-brass button off his uniform jacket and left it as a model. For what appears at the top of the stone is the representation of an American naval officer's uniform button of the pattern that had been in use some years before and was still worn: a circle of thirteen stars, and inside the circle an eagle, its wings half open, its head turned to the right, standing on its right foot with the left talons holding up an oval shield with a foul anchor shown on it.[25]

The inscription below the eagle says,

SACRED
to the MEMORY of
WILLIAM HENRY ALLEN, Esq.
Aged 27 Years
Late Commander of the
United States BRIG ARGUS
who died August 18th 1813
In Consequence of a Wound
Received in Action
with H.B.M.BRIG PELICAN
August 14th 1813

ALSO in Remembrance of
RICHARD DELPHEY, *Midshipman*
Aged 18 Years
U.S. NAVY, Killed in the *same action*
Whose remains are Deposited
on the Left

———

HERE SLEEP THE BRAVE

———

The morning after the funeral, Sunday, 22 August, the *Pelican* arrived from Cork and anchored in Plymouth Sound. The *Argus*'s men aboard her were taken to the prison ship *Hector,* and some of those already aboard the *Hector,* who had been accused by the traitor Robinson, were taken to the *Salvador* and put in close confinement. Robinson himself was taken aboard the *Salvador* and held there for his own safety. One of the men he accused was Colin McLeod, the boatswain, who was still recovering from his wounds at the Mill Prison Hospital. Apparently, the case against McLeod was felt to be very strong, and as soon as he was well enough to leave the hospital he was sent with a guard to travel to a village in Scotland where it was thought he could be identified. Either the information was wrong or, just as likely, the Scots villagers perceived Colin McLeod's predicament and decided to protect him. In any event, they did not identify him, and the case against him collapsed.

None of the *Argus*'s men accused by Robinson were proved to be British subjects, even after a thorough investigation by Mr. Bicknell. All seventeen of these men were eventually released from their "close confinement" on board the *Salvador* and rejoined their prisoner-of-war shipmates.[26] Robinson apparently continued to be a problem for the British: nothing he had told them had proved out, and Robinson himself was actually the only member of the *Argus*'s crew "taken in arms against His Majesty" who admitted to being a British sub-ject. In late April of 1814 he was sent from the *Salvador* to Mill Prison, and on 6 June escaped from there and disappeared.[27] It would be satisfying to think that one day, on some dockside street, he ran into some of his ex-shipmates from the *Argus*.

CHAPTER NINETEEN

Prisoners of War

A FEW DAYS AFTER HENRY ALLEN'S FUNERAL the *Argus*'s officers were sent to live as prisoners of war on parole at Ashburton, a village about twenty-five miles northeast of Plymouth. Warrant officers like the boatswain and the gunner were denied parole and were sent to the huge prison depot at Dartmoor, about sixteen miles north of Plymouth. The fourteen men in the recaptured *Matilda*'s prize crew had earlier been taken to the floating prison hulks at Chatham, but Richard Groves was judged eligible for parole, released from the hulks, and sent to Ashburton.[1]

The *Argus*'s officers were not alone at Ashburton: perhaps a hundred French officers, army and navy, were on parole there, plus some Americans who had been captains and first lieutenants of large privateers of more than fourteen guns, or masters and first mates of major-size merchant ships.[2]

The crew of the *Argus,* except for the *Matilda*'s prize crew, arrived at Plymouth, some on 17 August in the *Argus,* and the rest in the *Pelican* on the twenty-third. They were all taken under guard and put aboard the prison ship *Hector,* which was lying in the Hamoaze along with several other hulks. The seventeen men pointed out by the traitor Robinson were taken to the *Salvador del Mundo,* the receiving ship, and closely held in irons.[3] On 8 September the *Argus*'s men, plus about 170 other new prisoners of war, were marched up to the Dartmoor prison depot. At this time there were about six hundred American prisoners already there, merchant ship and privateer crews, and ex–Royal

Navy men who had refused to serve further now that the war was with America. There were also about seven or eight thousand French prisoners—soldiers of Napoleon's Grand Army and sailors from the French Navy and merchant marine.

Dartmoor prison, officially styled in those days as "The Depot for Prisoners of War at Dartmoor," was new, having just been finished in 1809. It had been built specifically to hold prisoners of war and could have held nearly ten thousand, although during the long wars it rarely had more than about eight thousand at one time. The prison was built to last of granite quarried nearby: it is used today as a convict prison.

In late 1813 most of the American prisoners at Dartmoor and elsewhere faced a gloomy future. The exchange of prisoners had been stopped for an indefinite period because the British held many times the number of Americans than the American government had British prisoners. This situation was not likely to change, and the war looked as though it might go on forever.

The only prisoners who had the right to hope for better conditions or an early release were the crew of the *Argus*. As the only U.S. Navy crew in Dartmoor at that time, they expected that the American government would put a high priority on their exchange. Also, some powerful domestic American political pressure had been applied for their release—their ex-shipmate Minister William H. Crawford had written to prisoner agent Reuben Beasley to ask that the *Argus*'s men be given preference—and they knew that they were to be the first ones exchanged or released.[4]

Late in October Lieutenant William Watson wrote to the Transport Office from Ashburton and obtained permission for Henry Denison, the purser, and himself to visit the *Argus*'s crew in Dartmoor to find out what winter clothing they needed. The two officers held a muster of the *Argus*'s men, and Denison worked up a payroll list claiming pay for everyone from their dates of capture onward.[5]

Warm clothing would be needed: the winter of 1813–14 was one of the coldest in history. On New Year's night of 1814 the temperature plummeted, and water buckets in the prison froze solid in four hours. Within a day or so the stream that ran through the prison and supplied all the water for everything— drinking, cooking, washing, and waste removal—turned to solid ice. The prisoners tried to quench their thirst with snow, but with little success. Inside the unheated prison buildings they clustered together like bees, but the intense cold even overcame the body heat of the hundreds of men, and the moisture from their breath condensed on the chilled granite walls in sheets of ice. Then the snow began to fall, and by 19 January it was four feet deep on the open ground, and drifts reached to the tops of the walls. The guards all stayed inside—it was too bitter cold to stand sentry duty outside.

The situation was rapidly heading for disaster: the roughly 9,000 prisoners and 1,500 soldiers and civilian staff were all dependent on food and fuel carted in over the wagon road from Plymouth, now blocked by the snow. There were ten days' worth of salt provisions, but even those were inaccessible until Captain Shortland, the prison commander, mobilized two hundred of the French prisoners and much of the guard to dig a path to the storehouse.[6]

The really deep cold lasted for about three weeks, and by late January of 1814 the snow and ice were thawing, and in February it was all gone. Also in February came some good news for the American prisoners: they began to receive a small allowance from the U.S. government for soap and tobacco.[7]

With some money coming in, the American prisoners, including the *Argus's* men, began to view life with more optimism. By this time, in the midwinter of 1813–14, the long war was clearly nearing its end. Leipzig had been fought, Napoleon was in retreat, and the armies of his enemies—Russia, Austria, Prussia, Sweden, and England—were on the edge of invading France itself. As a gesture to their allies the British decided to release prisoners of war who were citizens of the allied nations but who had been captured under the American flag. When this was announced at Dartmoor, prisoners who could speak some German, Swedish, or Russian came forward to present themselves as loyal subjects of those sovereigns. Three of the *Argus's* men took this path: Isaac Allester became a Swede. Henry Groger was a German from Lubeck. John Barlow, born in Amsterdam, was "released as a neutral national." The *Argus's* crew lost two others to death during the spring—not the last to die. James Coombes, a twenty-two-year-old seaman from Wiscasset, died from diarrhea, and William Dillon, a marine private, fifty years old, from New Jersey, was struck down by dysentery.[8]

Then in April came truly momentous news: Paris had fallen to the allied armies. "After a brilliant victory, God has placed the capital of the French Empire in the hands of the Allied Sovereigns, a just retribution for the miseries inflicted . . . by the Desolator of Europe." This was followed on 9 April by the news in an *"Extraordinary"* issue of the *London Gazette* ". . . announcing the abdication of the Crowns of France and Italy, by Napoleon Buonaparte. . . ."[9] Elba was now just ahead, and the twenty-one years of war with France were over, except for the final convulsion of the Hundred Days and Waterloo.

At Dartmoor these events meant that the French prisoners would soon be released, and the excitement in the prisons was electric. Now Americans who could speak some French made plans to try to be released along with the French prisoners. Several *Argus* men took this route out: Peter Noney, alias Neho, alias Honey, had been captured in the *Salamanca* and had joined the *Argus's* crew. He was a bona fide Frenchman from Bordeaux. Less certain were Oliver Givel from New Orleans, John Carbenett of New York, Francis Couret, James Smith, and Joseph Curtis.[10]

From departure or death, the *Argus*'s crew had now been diminished by twenty-eight men, about a quarter of the total, and there were a few more losses to come, one by violence. Two of the *Argus*'s men, Thomas Hill and James Henry, got into a serious argument and at 9 A.M. on 3 July met to settle their differences. It was a short and violent battle. Hill attacked Henry with fists and feet and after a short time managed to get hold of him and throw him to the floor. While Henry lay there, Hill beat him on the head, shoulders, and breast and finally struck him violently and repeatedly in the stomach with both fists. James Henry died without getting up. A coroner's inquest, held literally over James Henry's body, indicted Thomas Hill for manslaughter, and he was taken to Exeter Gaol and locked up to await his trial. He was later acquitted and returned to the prison, but there was to be more violence in his future.[11]

On 24 October 1814 eight *Argus* men, those that were left of the thirteen originally in the *Matilda*'s prize crew, arrived in a draft from Chatham. Two of the other five had joined the Royal Navy, and two had been released as Frenchmen. One was dead: Able Seaman Hans Handerson, thirty-five years old, born in Norway, died of "debility" in early September on board one of the prison hulks at Chatham.[12]

Another able seaman, twenty-three-year-old William Shaw, from Philadelphia, died in the hospital at Dartmoor prison from "dropsy."[13] This made a total of thirty-three of the crew that were now dead or gone to foreign lands. All of the rest of the *Argus*'s crew were now at Dartmoor.

The joyful news, long awaited, that the *Argus*'s crew was to be released and sent home reached Dartmoor in the same week that William Shaw died and the *Matilda*'s men arrived. Now events came swiftly, one after another. An American merchant ship, the *Jenny,* arrived in England as a flag of truce, and Reuben Beasley, the American agent for prisoners, chartered her as a cartel to take home some American citizens stranded in England and also sixty-seven prisoners of war, including nineteen of the crew of the *Argus*.[14]

Among this first nineteen to go were John Sniffen, the carpenter's mate; John Young, a quartermaster; and Thomas Hill, the violent seaman. None of the *Argus*'s officers went in the *Jenny*. No reason is given for this. Perhaps her accommodations were considered too spartan, or perhaps the officers felt it their duty to go last.

The *Jenny* had been brought into Dartmouth, and on 19 October the homebound prisoners marched out of the gate at Dartmoor, east along the road passing just south of Ashburton, then through Totnes and on to Dartmouth—twenty-six miles, made short by the exhilaration of their freedom. They boarded the *Jenny* on the twentieth, and after waiting a couple of days for mail from London that she was to carry, she sailed on about 23 October.

Reuben Beasley had already engaged another cartel to take home the rest of the *Argus*'s officers and crew, plus a few other navy sailors and about 150 U.S. soldiers that had been captured in the fighting around the Great Lakes and had lately arrived at Dartmoor. This cartel was a Spanish ship, the *St. Philip*.[15] She arrived in Dartmouth on 31 October, and on 2 November the rest of the *Argus*'s crew, now fifty-nine in number, left the prison to board her. They were joined by ten of the *Argus*'s officers from Ashburton—all of the officers except Midshipman Pottenger, who was being detained by the local magistrate.[16]

The *St. Philip* sailed on about 8 November 1814, and the officers and crew of the *Argus* were finally homeward bound.

The exact nature of Midshipman Pottenger's problem with the British civil authority is not clear, but it seems to have been a result of his relationship with a young woman of Ashburton, Frances Broom. The parish marriage register at Ashburton shows that on 21 November 1814, about two weeks after the *St. Philip* sailed, "William Pottenger an American Prisoner on Parole and a Bachelor, married Frances Broom a Spinster. . . ." There is no record of a child's being born or baptized. He was finally liberated in the early summer and arrived in Philadelphia on 1 August 1815.[17] A few months later he came back to Ashburton to fetch his English bride and took her home with him to America.

Two months after the last of the *Argus*'s crew sailed for home, there was an echo at Dartmoor of the *Argus-Pelican* battle. Six of the Americans who were serving aboard the *Pelican* had decided in September 1814 to give themselves up and be prisoners of war. It was a strange decision, given that these men had been serving in the British Navy for several years, long before coming to the *Pelican,* had served during the entire war against America, and except for one had all been in the battle with the *Argus* and had made no previous objection to fighting against the land of their birth. They arrived in Dartmoor on 26 December 1814: Richard Thornhill, Martin Wolsey, John Mainwaring, James Jackson, Peter Davis, and Benjamin Jackson, who was the only black in the group.[18]

They might have escaped notice, but some of the prisoners apparently knew one or two of them, and also one night a couple of them became drunk and bragged that they had bought the liquor with prize money that they got from taking the *Argus*. One, probably Thornhill, boasted that he had been the first from the *Pelican* to board the *Argus* and had "killed the Carpenter with his own sword."[19] This was too much for the American prisoners. They seized the six of them, tied them up, and proceeded to hold a court on them. Two, probably Thornhill and Peter Davis, were sentenced to be hanged. The other four were acquitted, although two of them were crudely tattooed on the cheeks with "U.S." on one side and "T" on the other, meaning "United States Traitor."

Before the hangings could take place, someone got word out to Captain Shortland about what was happening. He sent in a strong guard, and after a considerable fight the six ex-Pelicans were rescued. They were sent to Plymouth, where they revolunteered for the Royal Navy and were sent on board H.M.S. *Impregnable* as part of her company. John Mainwaring was transferred from the *Impregnable* to Plymouth Hospital and died there on 25 January 1815, very possibly from an infection brought on by the primitive tattooing. The other five were later transferred to H.M.S. *St. George* and in September 1815 were still serving in the Royal Navy when the ship ended her current commission.[20] They disappear at that point.

The *Jenny* cartel arrived in New York after an uneventful journey, and the *Argus's* men aboard her scattered to resume their lives. Some of them still had time to run in their enlistments and went right back to the navy, but others no doubt took berths on merchant ships. The shipping industry was prosperous at that time as trade resumed with England.

The *St. Philip* had a more troubled voyage. Something, probably storm damage, caused her to put into Tenerife, in the Canary Islands, "in distress," and she was there for some weeks while making repairs. She finally arrived in Hampton Roads on 25 February 1815 and entered Norfolk the next day.[21]

The officers all reported their return to the secretary of the navy and then waited for new orders. Those of the petty officers and seamen whose terms of service had not expired were sent by boat to Baltimore to join the ship-sloop *Ontario,* and the rest simply scattered.[22]

The Great Adventure was over. Few of them would ever again have the experience of battle or the tight comradeship among shipmates that service in war provides. They had fought, and they had tasted the bitterness of defeat and captivity. Now peace stretched out ahead of them into the future. The officers and crew of the *Argus* now parted and went their separate ways, and only a few of them ever served together again.

CHAPTER TWENTY

Afterwards

MANY YEARS WERE TO PASS before the last of the actors in the *Argus-Pelican* drama left the stage, but only a few could be traced through the years following 1815. Nearly all of them simply disappear. Here is all that I could find about them, the ships and the men.

The Ships Themselves, the *Argus* and the *Pelican*

After her crew and officers were taken off to their imprisonment, the *Argus,* forlorn in defeat, was left at a pier in the Plymouth dockyard, guarded by a small watch section of men from the *Pelican*. Her sides were pocked with shot holes, and some of the spars and much of her rigging, damaged by the *Pelican's* fire, had been repaired just enough to get her into port. Her appearance was a far thing from what it had been during those halcyon days in New York, just after Henry Allen took command, and it was a merciful thing that Henry didn't have to see her as she finally was.

The task now for John Maples and the *Pelican's* crew was to keep the *Argus* reasonably clean and to fix up some of the obvious damage while the prize agents, a firm named Standart and Marsh, tried to get a buyer for her at the best possible price.

She was offered to the Admiralty in the last days of August, two weeks after the battle. The Admiralty Lords ordered the Navy Board to have the *Argus* surveyed and to come back to them with a recommendation about whether or not to purchase her.[1]

The survey, done by officers of the Plymouth dockyard, with John Maples looking over their shoulders, was a very thorough workup and was not completed until 16 September. The dockyard officers found her to be "a sound vessel" and gave as their opinion that she was "a fit vessel to be purchased for His Majesty's Service." They valued her at £2,721 11s, plus whatever value might later be put on her furnishings and stores.[2]

This was great news for John Maples and the Pelicans, and they began to have pleasant thoughts about how they would spend the money, but Commissioner Robert Fanshawe of the Plymouth Dockyard decided that "it will not be advisable to purchase her for H.M. Service."[3] He said that at ten years she was too old, and that she had received major repairs a few months previously, referring to the work done on her after her bruising voyage under Sinclair. Unsaid, but probably most important—the war was winding down, and the Royal Navy's need for more ships of any kind was rapidly diminishing.

The prize agents then turned their energies elsewhere and after some lapse of time found a buyer. Who bought the *Argus,* and for what purpose, is unknown. She may have been broken up for her copper sheathing and fittings. The last trace of her is the announcement that the Pelicans were paid their shares of her sale price on 2 March 1814 at No. 3 Clifford's Inn, Fleet Street.

Back in the United States in late 1813 the navy took the now-honored name and gave it to a 117-foot ship-sloop then under construction at the Washington Navy Yard. This new *Argus* was to have been a beautiful, sleek 22-gun ship of the most modern design. But when the British attacked Washington in 1814, the commandant of the navy yard, Captain Tingey, on 24 August ordered the yard torched to avoid its surrender. The new *Argus,* still on her stocks, went up in flames, along with the new frigate *Columbia* and all of the yard facilities. Captain Tingey watched the fire from his gig as he was being rowed down to Alexandria.[4] Two losses were apparently enough, and the U.S. Navy never gave another ship the name "Argus."

The *Pelican* remained in active service through the rest of the Napoleonic War and then on 7 December 1818 was taken out of commission and laid up "in ordinary."

In the early 1820s there was a sudden increase in piracy in the Eastern Mediterranean, and the British reactivated some small ships to cope with the marauders. The *Pelican* was fitted out and recommissioned in August 1826 and spent the next year and a half in active service around Greece, breaking up nests of pirates.[5]

She was still in active service in 1839, at the start of "The First China War," best known as the war in which the British received Hong Kong. The *Pelican* was involved in the action in China until 1842 and was later a customs vessel. She was finally sold out of government service in 1865.[6] There would be other *Pelicans* in the Royal Navy, but they would be iron built and steam powered.

THE MEMORY OF WILLIAM HENRY ALLEN

When word of the capture of the *Argus* and Henry's death reached Providence, Rhode Island, the Reverend Mr. Crocker gave a eulogy in St. John's Church on Sunday, 17 October 1813. No doubt the Allen family members then living in Providence—Henry's father, the old general; his stepmother, Mary Allen; Henry's eight-year-old half-brother, George; and Henry's older sister, Sarah Rhodes, her husband, Peleg, and their children—were present, although the newspaper report doesn't say so. As Mr. Crocker spoke, minute guns were fired from the frigate *President,* then in Providence Harbor.[7]

The preservation of Henry Allen's memory began shortly thereafter. In 1814 a seventy-five–foot gunboat built on Lake Champlain was named the *Allen.* Then the city of New York named a street after him. A fashionable address in those early days, Allen Street in 1817 ran between Division Street and North Street in the old Ninth Ward on the Lower East Side.[8] Now it runs from Division Street to East Houston Street and is crossed by Delancey Street on the way to the Williamsburg Bridge.

After the news of Allen's death arrived in Washington, Secretary of the Navy Jones had Commodore Rodgers carry Henry's formal, parchment commission as master commandant, together with a letter of condolence, to his father.[9] The old gentleman was not only Henry's pride-filled father but had also been his closest correspondent. With his oldest and favorite son gone he began to languish and died on 18 August 1815.

Henry's death devastated the Allen family, and with the father also dead, the strength left in the family was centered in Sarah, the sister, and her husband, Peleg Rhodes, a successful merchant and shipowner. Henry's younger brother Thomas relocated to Baltimore in late 1813, then later to New Orleans, where he died, probably in 1819. Somewhere along the way he had married, and after his death family letters note that Thomas's "two little sons are with their mother at Natchez."[10] Nothing more about these two children survives in the available Allen family papers. There may well be persons alive today related to William Henry Allen, the descendants of Thomas's sons, or of Sarah and Peleg Rhodes.

In the fall of 1857 the U.S. ships *Niagara* and *Susquehanna* made a goodwill visit to Plymouth, England. While there, the wardroom officers of the *Niagara* received an anonymous letter telling them that the tombstone of William Henry Allen and Richard Delphey in St. Andrew's churchyard was badly in need of repair, time and weather having nearly effaced the inscription. The officers of the two ships provided the money to repair the tombstone, apparently having the inscription reincised and filled in with black paint.[11] In 1932 the tombstone was again in need of repair. By now it had considerable historical interest, and the National Society, United States Daughters of 1812, provided funds to remove the stone from the site of the grave and furnish it with a permanent mounting close by, on the wall of an adjacent building, the medieval Prysten House. It was there in May 1945 when I visited St. Andrew's Church, then a bombed-out shell, and became interested in the story of the *Argus*. It is still there today and provides the focus for occasional ceremonies of British-American friendship.

Other mementos of Henry Allen survive into modern times. In 1846 Nathaniel Currier published a lithograph displaying six oval portraits of "Naval Heroes of the United States" surrounding a battle scene. One of the heroes portrayed was Henry Allen, shown in the right-side profile that is the only surviving likeness of him.[12] The lithograph itself is now rare, but a textile manufacturer in the 1960s used it in an upholstery fabric. A chair in my home is covered in this fabric, which shows the profile of William Henry Allen repeated together with five of his colleagues.

Some time in the mid–nineteenth century a whaleman-scrimshander engraved Henry Allen's portrait on a large sperm-whale tooth. Was this perhaps an old *Argus* sailor, a veteran of the cruise and the battle? The tooth is in the collection of scrimshawed articles assembled by the late President Kennedy.[13]

Earlier in this century American destroyers were always named after bona fide naval heroes. In 1916 the navy gave the name *Allen* to a four-stack destroyer of the old raised-forecastle "broken-deck" type, then building in Bath, Maine. She was DD 66 and had a long and distinguished career. There is a beautiful and lively oil painting at the U.S. Naval Academy showing the U.S.S. *Allen* knifing through heavy seas, her forefoot clear out of the water, while escorting the giant troop transport *Leviathan* across the Atlantic in World War I.[14]

Two of the midshipmen of the *Argus,* killed in the battle, also had ships named after them. Richard Delphey was honored by the World War I four-stack, flush-deck destroyer U.S.S. *Delphy,* DD 261, of later design than the *Allen,* built in 1918. A sister ship of the *Delphy* was named after William Edwards, the U.S.S. *Edwards,* DD 265.

JOHN MAPLES

The capture of the *Argus* gave John Maples a good reputation with the Admiralty and consequently some, if only a little, credit with them upon which he could draw. He realized that his moment of fame would be brief, and after losing the command of the *Pelican,* he urgently requested other employment. The reply was very heartening: he was told that he was "on the list of candidates for an appointment." But ten months later he was still waiting and on 25 August 1814 again wrote to the secretary, asking him to please "state to my Lords Commissioners of the Admiralty how extremely anxious I have been to be employed."[15]

This letter was sent from Woodbridge, in Suffolk. John Maples had earlier that year, on 27 April, married a lady of Woodbridge, the widow of John Carthew, a solicitor. His new wife's maiden name had been Mary Jeaffreson, and she had married solicitor Carthew in 1797, so she was now a lady of some maturity. Her portrait, apparently done about 1815, shows her as a pleasant, handsome, but not beautiful woman of perhaps thirty-nine or forty years, with dark hair, dark eyes, and a slightly aquiline nose. She is dressed in the Regency fashion, with a small spray of ostrich feathers in her hair.[16]

John Maples's letter asking for employment got action more quickly than he had expected. A 1 September letter from the Admiralty told him that he was to be appointed to command H.M.S. *Favourite,* a twenty-gun ship-sloop.[17] Maples began his preparations for resuming active service, but a brief interval of ill health prevented him from taking the command. An Admiralty note of 17 September simply states that he was "unable."[18] This was unfortunate. Had John Maples taken the *Favourite,* he would have left yet another thumbprint on history: H.M.S. *Favourite* was the ship chosen in January 1815 to carry the Treaty of Ghent, ending the war between America and Great Britain, to the United States for ratification.

John Maples's credit with the Admiralty was now almost used up. But the Lords Commissioners gave him another opportunity and on 13 December 1814 appointed him to the command of H.M.S. *Larne,* another twenty-gun ship-sloop. He joined the *Larne* in Sheerness Harbor on 19 December 1814, a cloudy, windy day. He apparently was still suffering from ill health, possibly from malaria, which he may have had since his days in the West Indies. The *Larne* remained moored at Sheerness until 9 January 1815, when at 2:30 in the afternoon she "slipped her hawser and made sail," moving out to the Little Nore, a distance of about three miles. There she anchored, and there too, John Maples's career at sea ended. As much as he wanted to continue his sea life, his health was fragile, and he could not go on. He was "superseded" from the command of the *Larne* six days later, on Sunday, 15 January. In a brief letter, painful in its austere intensity, he asked the Admiralty to place his name on the half-pay list.[19] Thirty years of service at sea—those long, hard years, twenty-two of them in war, in battles great and small—were now behind him.

Although his active career was over, life would not be too bad for Captain

John Maples. The half-pay of a post-captain, which amounted to about £189 per year, or 15 guineas per month, was an adequate, if not ample, amount for a couple to live on. Then too he had apparently been frugal and saved much of his prize money over the years and invested it conservatively and wisely. And his new wife belonged to a prosperous, although not wealthy, family with roots in the gentry. Her oldest brother, the Reverend Christopher Jeaffreson, was a prominent and well-to-do churchman, and her other surviving brother, John, was a surgeon and a member of the Royal College of Surgeons.[20] Beyond all of this John Maples knew that if he lived long enough, the inexorable processes of seniority would see him promoted to rear-admiral, with a consequent increase in half-pay.

As John Maples was beginning to adjust to his new life ashore, another bit of good fortune and honor came his way. On 2 January 1815 the Prince Regent announced that the Most Honourable Military Order of the Bath was to be expanded to encompass three classes of members, the Knights Grand Crosses of the Bath, or K.G.B.s, the Knights Commanders of the Bath, or K.C.B.s, and the Companions of the Bath, or C.B.s. The first two classes conferred knighthood and were restricted to the upper ranks of society and the military. The Companions of the Bath were to be commissioned officers of the navy or army who had received a medal for a battle or who had been mentioned by name in dispatches published in the *London Gazette*. They were not to be knights but were to "take place and precedence of all Esquires of the United Kingdom of Great Britain and Ireland." Each C.B. was to receive a "very handsome gold enameled medal . . . worth between 30 and 40 guineas," which was to be suspended from a narrow red ribbon and worn on the left coat lapel.

In late September of 1815 John Maples was informed that the Prince Regent had nominated him as a Companion of the Bath.[21] He eminently filled the qualifications: he had been "gazetted" in his own right for the capture of the *Argus* and had been "mentioned in dispatches" in two *Gazette* issues describing the *Magicienne*'s exploits at Cape Roxo and at Irois.

Sometime in 1815 or shortly thereafter, John Maples and his wife sat for their portraits. The artist is unknown, but the paintings are in the style of Lawrence.

Whoever the artist, John Maples's portrait is a beautiful piece of work. It shows him in the uniform of a Royal Navy captain of the period at the end of the long wars, dark blue, with a high, stand-up collar outlined in gold braid, gold epaulets, and gold-braided buff lapels. On the left lapel is pinned the red ribbon and "handsome gold enameled medal" of a Companion of the Most Honourable Military Order of the Bath.[22]

John Maples, the man, is skillfully portrayed in the picture. He is bald, with a long, straight nose, level blue eyes, and dark hair graying around his ears. He looks out at the world with a slightly quizzical aspect—perhaps, as he sat for the portrait, contemplating the erratic twists of fortune that had brought him to this unexpected but not unpleasant situation.

As time went on, John Maples became more and more involved with the Jeaffreson family, and he seems to have been especially close to his wife's two brothers and the children of one of them, the Reverend Christopher Jeaffreson. John and Mary Maples did not have any children of their own. After Mary died, sometime before 1840, John Maples remained close to the Jeaffreson family.

He bought a house in a newly opening part of northwest London, No. 3 in a road named Kilburn Priory, two miles out the Edgeware Road and Maida Vale from what is now Marble Arch, and there he lived for the rest of his life. The prospect in that vicinity at the time was described as a scene of "fields and hedges," with "rustic[s] in smock-frock[s]," far removed from any view of the sea.[23]

In about 1835 John Maples's health began to fail, and among other infirmities he became blind. He was cared for by a woman named Sarah Coolbear, who had been a servant with him since about 1830. The Jeaffreson family members seem to have been his main outside contacts during these years, and when on 2 December 1841 he made the will that was to be his last will and testament, his late wife's brothers the Reverend Christopher Jeaffreson and John Jeaffreson, plus the Reverend Christopher's son, William Jeaffreson, also a surgeon, became the executors.[24]

The will bequeathed John Maples's house, with its "bath house, stable, yard, garden and appurtenances," plus all his ready money and personal effects, to the three executors. The rest of his estate, which amounted to something less than £8,000, not a great fortune but a snug little sum, was to be converted to cash, with which good British securities were to be purchased. These securities were to be put in trust to provide an income of £50 per year to Eliza Mary Kemball, née Jeaffreson, Christopher's daughter, niece of John Maples's "late dear wife."

The rest of the income from the trust, which should have amounted to perhaps £160 per year, was to be divided between the children of Christopher and John Jeaffreson.[25] A relatively small amount, £30, was left to Sarah Coolbear, and £20 to another servant, but £1,000 was left to William Jeaffreson. The executors were charged to pay into his estate any monies that they owed to him at the time of his death. The implication seems to be that the Jeaffresons occasionally borrowed from John Maples.

A will made by a blind widower, naming his brothers-in-law as executors, and leaving to them and their children all of his property, should have raised a red flag for the consistory court handling the probate. There is no indication that this happened. There may have been no others who could possibly contend for the estate; the Jeaffresons seem to have been all the family that John Maples had in his last years. So it may have all been completely straightforward. But there was one other matter that tends to reinforce the tiny suspicion that maybe John Maples, old, sick, and blind, was mulcted by his brothers-in-law:

After John Maples's death, when the will came to probate, William Jeaffreson brought forth a codicil that he had kept, written on a half sheet of note paper and witnessed by himself and Frances Wilkins, an illiterate servant who made her mark with an "X." The codicil said that "any money that Mr. Jeaffreson has in his hands on my account at the time of my death may be considered as his own."[26] The brief writing then goes on to leave £200 more to Sarah Coolbear.

This codicil was made on 5 December 1846, just five months before John Maples's death, a time when he was probably quite ill. Did John Maples decide that he wanted to leave more money to Sarah Coolbear and ask William Jeaffreson to prepare a codicil to that effect, and then William, seeing an opportunity, add in the part benefiting himself? If so, just the part relating to Sarah Coolbear could have been read to the blind old man, and the illiterate servant would not have been able to detect the fraud and warn John Maples. Did this in fact happen? There is no way to know.

In 1846 the Admiralty, to remove the blockage in the seniority system caused by the group of wartime post-captains who were now much too old to serve actively, offered them promotion to rear-admiral on the retired list, with half-pay in the higher rank. So on 1 October 1846 John Maples accepted the new rank and became Retired Rear-Admiral John Fordyce Maples, C.B. It had been a long road since he had entered as a captain's servant on board the battleship *Triumph* almost exactly sixty-four years before. What were his thoughts, lying blind in his bed in these last times of his life? Did he reflect on that morning in 1813 when the *Argus* shortened sail to let him come up, and he knew that everything he had worked for was finally in his grasp? Or did he think of Captain William Henry Ricketts, now long dead, and the excitement of those prize-taking years around Saint-Domingue?

John Maples died on 12 May 1847 in his home at No. 3 Kilburn Priory. His death certificate listed him as seventy-eight years old and showed the cause of death as "Gradual Decay."[27] Sarah Ann Coolbear was with him at his death. The Jeaffresons were not present.

SURGEON JAMES INDERWICK

Surgeon Inderwick was released as a noncombatant from his confinement on parole at Ashburton on 5 July 1814 and returned to the United States as a passenger in the *Saratoga,* a cartel vessel. He arrived in Boston on 3 September and on the fifth wrote to the secretary of the navy, reporting his return and providing a list of the men who were killed and wounded on board the *Argus*. He was eager to get another assignment and told the secretary that he would go to New York and await orders.

But he waited, and no orders came, so on 31 January 1815 he again wrote to the secretary, who was by now Benjamin Crowninshield. This letter probably crossed in the mail with the orders he had been hoping for, which were issued on 9 February. He was told to report aboard the U.S.S. *Epervier* at Savannah as her surgeon.[28] The *Epervier* was an eighteen-gun, 32-pounder brig, captured from the British late in the war, and was a carbon-copy of the *Pelican*.

In the spring of 1815 Commodore Decatur was taking an American squadron to the Mediterranean to fight a brief, victorious war with the Algerines. This largest of the postwar squadrons sent out by the U.S. Navy was headed up by Decatur's flagship, the new heavy frigate *Guerrière*, and included the frigates *Macedonian* and *Constellation*, plus the ship-sloop *Ontario*, the *Epervier*, and five smaller brigs and schooners. The squadron left New York on 20 May 1815 and by early July had brought the Algerines to terms. Although the *Epervier* was involved in the brief skirmishes of this miniwar, she apparently suffered no killed or wounded, so Surgeon Inderwick's employment was probably restricted to treating hurts from shipboard accidents, plus the usual rheumatismus and syphilis.

The squadron memorialized its success over the Algerines with a huge Fourth of July celebration, and later that week the *Epervier* was detached to return to the United States, carrying a copy of the Treaty with Algiers for ratification. She had been assigned a new skipper to bring her home, William Lewis of the *Guerrière*, who had left a new bride when the squadron had sailed for the Mediterranean and was now anxious to return.

The *Epervier* left the squadron a few days after the Fourth of July, and on 14 July was seen west of Gibraltar. But that was the last of her. She never reached home and was lost at sea with all hands. All that remains of Surgeon James Inderwick are a few letters and his journal from the cruise of the *Argus*, which he left at the New York Hospital before joining the *Epervier*.

Lieutenants William Henry Watson and William Howard Allen

Henry Watson and Howard Allen had been shipmates and friends for several years before their time together on the *Argus*. They had been appointed as midshipmen on the same day, 1 January 1808, and had been sent to the same ship, the *Chesapeake*, where they first met William Henry Allen, then a lieutenant. Henry Watson was the senior of the two, becoming a lieutenant in March of

1813, while Howard Allen was not promoted until July.

Late in February of 1815 the Spanish cartel vessel *St. Philip* arrived in Hampton Roads after her long and difficult voyage.[29] Henry Watson now had the painful task of reporting the details of the loss of the *Argus* to the secretary of the navy.[30]

A court of enquiry was inevitable, and Watson and some of the other surviving officers were ordered to Baltimore where it was to be held. The court heard testimony from Watson and Allen, plus Midshipmen Jamesson and Snelson, then came to the conclusion that the *Pelican* was "decidedly superior" to the *Argus,* whose crew had been subjected to "extraordinary fatigue and exposure," and that all the *Argus*'s crew except Allister and Hendricks had made "every practical exertion" to take the *Pelican.*[31] So they were all honorably acquitted.

After the court of enquiry was over, Henry Watson and Howard Allen went their separate ways. Howard Allen was ordered to the fourteen-gun brig *Flambeau* and went to the Mediterranean and the Algerine fracas with Commodore Decatur. Henry Watson went home for a brief leave with his parents in Virginia. In the fall he was ordered to the frigate *John Adams,* bound for the Mediterranean.

The paths of the two friends didn't cross again until 1822, when they were both ordered into the fight against a new breed of brutal pirates just then creating havoc in the West Indies.

Henry Watson was ordered to command a new vessel designed for pirate hunting, the eighty-six–foot, twelve-gun schooner *Alligator,* but just at that time he had some urgent personal business to take care of and asked to have his sea assignment delayed for a few months. So it turned out that on 11 June 1822 Howard Allen was told to take command of the *Alligator.*[32]

The late fall of 1822 found Howard Allen and the *Alligator* cruising on the northern coasts of Cuba and Porto Rico. In a small bay, forty miles east of Matanzas, Cuba, he saw several vessels at anchor. There were three pirate schooners, well armed, each one nearly the size of the *Alligator,* and five captured merchant vessels. There were shoals and rocks between the *Alligator* and the pirates, and no one knew the way through them, so Howard Allen anchored the *Alligator* and manned the boats to do some boarding and cutting out.

Howard Allen himself took command of the lead boat, the largest boat, the launch, and with him were Captain Freeman, a marine officer, and thirteen men. Lieutenant Dale, the *Alligator*'s first lieutenant, followed in the cutter with eleven men, and behind him came the gig with Midshipman Henly and four men. It was a long row in, several miles, and the pirates had ample time to get ready.

As Howard Allen and the launch pulled toward the closest one, the pirate schooner broke a red flag at her masthead and opened fire with round shot, grape, and musketry. In spite of some casualties, Allen and the launch crew got on board her and carried the deck. The pirates then abandoned the schooner, took to their boats, and went aboard the second schooner, which was close by, about a "pistol shot" away.

Howard Allen led the launch and cutter to attack this second pirate. But her fire was too heavy. Howard Allen was struck full in the chest with a musket ball, and the attack had to be abandoned. The killed and wounded were taken back to the prize schooner and then out to the *Alligator*. The two other pirate schooners "made all sail and run off," leaving their five merchant-vessel prizes to be retaken by the *Alligator's* boats.

Howard Allen was conscious for about three hours after the attack, talking with his men and giving orders on what to do with the prizes. Then at about 1 P.M. on the afternoon of 9 November 1822, in his thirty-second year, he died. He was buried ashore in Matanzas two days later. His family in Hudson, New York, was desolate. Not only was he the beloved son and brother, but he was the main financial support of his mother and unmarried sisters.[33]

Nothing survives to describe Henry Watson's feelings at hearing the news of his friend's death, but it must have been a difficult shock for him to accept: had he taken command of the *Alligator,* as was originally ordered, Howard Allen might still be alive and Henry Watson possibly dead.

Then at about this moment the American government finally lost patience with the piratical depredations and moved to end them once and for all. Congress appropriated $500,000 for the purpose, a very large sum for that time, and Commodore David Porter, a capable, aggressive, and hot-tempered man, was given carte blanche to solve the problem. On 22 December 1822 Henry Watson was ordered to report to Porter, "to command a schooner."[34] In early 1823 Commodore Porter led his squadron south from Norfolk and began to sweep the western Caribbean. Henry Watson, probably with much satisfaction, "revenged the loss of his old comrade by a successful slaughter of pirates."[35]

The cruise under Porter was the last tour for William Henry Watson. By early fall he was back in Key West, Florida. There was an outbreak of yellow fever there at that time, and he was taken by the disease on 13 September 1823.

Colin McLeod

After arriving back in the United States aboard the cartel *St. Philip,* Colin McLeod was ordered to report to the sloop-of-war *Ontario,* then laying in Baltimore. This should have been his embarkation upon a successful and fulfilling career in the new, peacetime U.S. Navy. He was a war hero, a capable warrant boatswain—the most prestigious, mainstream rank that a warrant officer could have—and he was exceptional in another way: he was thoroughly literate, writing his own letters in complete sentences, coherently and legibly. With a touch of luck he would soon have become a sailing master and perhaps even a lieutenant.

But although his wounds from the battle had healed, his right thigh was mutilated, and he had only a limited use of that leg. Within a month of joining the *Ontario* he wrote to the secretary of the navy that he was "not fitt for service afloat" as a boatswain and asked for a shore assignment or harbor duty, or to be discharged from the navy. But his requests were denied, and he continued to serve at sea. By December of 1815 he was unable "to do his duty" and "rendered his warrant," resigning his hard-won boatswain's rank.[36]

Just as he was now incapable of being an active boatswain at sea, he was also unable to handle the kind of physical work ashore that his sea experience fitted him for. He now tried to get a navy pension, but to apply for a pension he needed a certificate to prove that he was disabled and that his disability came from his naval service. For some reason, Colin McLeod was unable to get a letter from Lieutenant Watson to prove his service until January 1818, two years later.

The bureaucracy of 1818 was even more impenetrable than that of today, and another year had passed before Colin, even with the help of a lawyer, got together the needed paperwork, including a current examination by a naval surgeon. Then on 4 March 1819 he was issued a certificate allowing him a pension of $10 per month, half of his active duty "base" pay. This was just barely enough to live on.

In his last letter to the Navy Department he wrote, "The R[ight] H[onourable] Mr. Crawford, Secretary of the Treasury . . . I dare say remembers the Boatswain of the *Argus*. . . ," and expressed his intention to try to get in touch with Crawford. Colin McLeod's file ends with this letter of 12 August 1819. Did he get in touch with William Crawford, one-time shipmate, now a cabinet officer? Is it possible that Crawford brought him to the Treasury Department for a sinecure as a gatekeeper or watchman? There is no record of this. The likelihood is that Boatswain Colin McLeod died sometime in 1819 or 1820.

THOMAS HILL

A little more than two years after Seaman Thomas Hill beat James Henry to death in Dartmoor prison, Hill appeared again at the center of a violent, murderous event. At that time, in 1816, serving in the ship's company of the U.S. Brig *Boxer,* and well known to her crew as "a very desperate fellow," Thomas Hill was a member of a working party sent ashore in mid-September at Bay Saint Louis, Mississippi.

Hill and another man named John Smith had managed to bring some rum ashore and, "fired with its fumes," got into an argument. Words led to blows, but this time, unlike in his brutal fistfight in Dartmoor with James Henry, Thomas Hill soon found himself losing to Smith. So Hill broke off from the battle and ran back to the launch, anchored just off the shore. There were several pistols in the boat, and Thomas Hill carefully loaded one of them, then jumped ashore again, pistol in hand. He went back to where Smith was standing, unarmed except for his fists, and threatened to shoot him. Smith asked for a pistol to make it a more even match, but at that point Thomas Hill fired, hitting Smith in the middle of the chest.

Smith fell to the ground and lay bleeding profusely and in much pain. The rest of the working party seized Thomas Hill and rowed him and Smith back to the *Boxer*. Hill was put in irons, and Smith was taken to a hospital ashore, where he died a few days later, on 17 September.

Thomas Hill was sent to the naval station at New Orleans to be tried for murder and was probably turned over to the civil authorities for trial. In any event, Thomas Hill disappears from sight at this point.[37]

JOHN NUGENT

John Nugent was a true Jack Tar. He was twenty-seven years old at the time of the battle, a stocky five-foot-three-inch man with blue eyes and light brown hair. He was an able seaman, one of the seventy salty-dog sailors that made the *Argus* go, handling her sails and manning her guns. But he was the least likely of all the *Argus*'s crew to survive for long after the war. He had been badly wounded in the battle, receiving a compound fracture of his right thigh that was apparently so high up that Surgeon Inderwick was afraid to amputate the leg.

After the *Argus* arrived in Plymouth, John Nugent was taken to the hospital at Mill Prison, where he was kept for nearly a year. He was released from the hospital and sent to Dartmoor prison in July 1814. Even though badly crippled, he somehow managed to survive the next four months in Dartmoor and the voyage home in the cartel vessel. He returned to Philadelphia, his hometown, and as soon as Lieutenant Watson arrived in Norfolk, Nugent asked him for a certificate attesting to the fact that he had been wounded in the battle, to enable him to apply for a pension.[38] He was granted a pension of $6 per month, half of his pay as a seaman.

How and where John Nugent lived in Philadelphia is not clear. But he apparently received good care and ate a diet ample enough in protein to sustain his immune system in its terrible struggle against the infections in his wound. This grisly hole in his thigh never healed. He was, without a doubt, in continuous, hardly bearable pain and needed loving support to get through each day. A likely scenario is that he went home and was cared for by relatives, perhaps his mother.

A modern orthopedist would give John Nugent little chance to survive for long without antibiotics and effective, modern treatment. His condition would probably be described today as a "draining osteomyelitis." But he was a tough customer with a strong constitution, and in January 1822, more than eight years after the battle, he was examined by two naval surgeons at the time his pension was up for renewal. They found that "the wound . . . has produced a carious ulcer [i.e., a lesion of the bone] which still freely discharges, accompanied occasionally by small pieces of bone." In 1824 he was again examined, and "there is now an extensive caries of the *os femoris,* accompanied with a profuse discharge of foetid matter."

But he was still alive and fighting it in 1826.

And 1828.

And 1832.

Here the record ends. John Nugent's pension was renewed in March of 1832, but he apparently died before 1834, when he would have needed to go through the process again.[39] But he reached about forty-seven years of age, well over the life expectancy for someone born when he was.

GEORGE STARBUCK

George Starbuck was a member of the prominent seafaring and whaling family of Nantucket Island. He was a twenty-five-year-old volunteer seaman and one of the last men to join the *Argus* before her last cruise. His name is the last one on her muster list, added in pencil at the end. Although not listed as one of Surgeon Inderwick's patients, he was listed in news accounts of the action as one of the wounded and told his family that he "was wounded at the close of the action." But he didn't apply for a pension for over forty years and in the meantime had moved to San Francisco, getting there as a sailor should, by sea.

It is not clear whether he went out for the Gold Rush in '49. If so, he did not strike it rich. In 1857 he was in "low circumstances" and at age sixty-nine "far advanced in years." He had a family, which he supported by working as a wharfinger, a general factotum and watchman on a pier on the waterfront. He had applied for and received a veteran's "Land Warrant" giving him 150 acres, the location of which is not decipherable.

His brother Frederick, back in Nantucket, hired a Washington lawyer in late 1857 to try to get a navy pension for George. The Pension Office, true to its bureaucratic tradition, sent back a sheaf of forms to be filled out. It was no use. George Starbuck was refused a pension, and the trail ends in January 1859.

Even so, George Starbuck lived longer than any of the other traceable sailors of the *Argus* and was only outlived by two of the officers, Uriah Levy and William Jamesson.[40]

URIAH PHILLIPS LEVY AND WILLIAM JAMESSON

Uriah Levy is in many ways the most interesting of the characters involved in the cruise of the *Argus*. He was the only *Argus* officer to become wealthy, and he left two significant marks on the American scene: he purchased Monticello, Jefferson's home, and saved it from early neglect and probable destruction, and he commissioned and presented to the country the magnificent statue of Jefferson that now stands in the U.S. Capitol. But he has his own biographers and will not be further chronicled here.

Midshipman, later Commodore, William Jamesson turned out to be the longest living, the last traceable survivor, of all of those connected with the cruise of the *Argus*. He had a long and active career in the post-1815 navy, a career cut short near its end by blindness, the delayed result of a wound received during the Mexican War. His biography has not yet been written, but his life is a metaphor for the navy during those mostly somnolent years between 1815 and the Civil War.

Commodore William Jamesson died in Alexandria, Virginia, on Monday, 6 October 1873, at eighty-two years of age, the relict of a navy that had vanished long before. It was his wish to be buried in Norfolk alongside his wife and their youngest daughter, who had died in 1855.

His casket, flag-draped, was taken from the steamer wharf at Norfolk's Town Point to Christ Church, where the Reverend O. S. Barten, D.D., read *The Order for the Burial of the Dead* of the Protestant Episcopal Church. The flags of the city were at half mast, and the warships present fired minute guns. After the service in the church, eight sailors carried the casket out to the hearse, and a procession formed, moving north along Cumberland Street, first the hearse and seven naval officers as pallbearers, then the U.S.S. *Worcester*'s brass band playing the "Dead March," followed by two companies of marines with arms reversed, then the carriages of mourners, first the old commodore's family, then many friends of former times.[41]

The procession moved north about one-half mile to Cedar Grove Cemetery, where William Jamesson had long owned a burial plot.[42] He was buried there alongside his wife and daughter, and the marines fired three volleys over the open grave.

The grave site is marked by a red granite monument listing all of their names. In the surrounding area at Cedar Grove are many of William Jamesson's old naval contemporaries: Commodore Arthur Sinclair, who recruited for the *Chesapeake* and commanded the *Argus,* Commodore Samuel Barron, Captain Benjamin Bissell, Commodore William Skinner, Captain Lewis Warrington, and others. One is left with the feeling that an active cemetery-lot salesman must have visited the wardrooms of the navy in Norfolk in the early nineteenth century.

With the death of William Jamesson, commodore and *quondam* midshipman, there was no one left alive to remember that long-ago cruise in 1813, no one who knew what the *Argus* looked like, or who could recall the appearance of Henry Allen as he stood on her quarterdeck, or remember that August morning when the *Argus* ran gun to gun with the *Pelican.*

Notes

RGB	Reuben G. Beasley
RS	Robert Smith
SAR	Sarah Allen Rhodes
SBA	Sarah Bowen Allen
SD	Stephen Decatur
SecNav	Secretary of the Navy
SecState	Secretary of State
TB	Transport Board
TO	Transport Office
TRL	Metropolitan Toronto Reference Library
UPL	Uriah Phillips Levy
WA	William Allen
WHA	William Henry Allen
WHC	William Harris Crawford
WHR	William Henry Ricketts
WJ	William Jones
WLC	William L. Clements Library, University of Michigan

CHAPTER 1

1. Arnold, *Vital Record,* 3, 208, 260.

2. *Port Folio,* 3:2; Walker, *So Few The Brave,* 155, 157.

3. SAR to J. L. Tillinghast, Pawtuxet, 20 Dec. 1841, *Allen Family Letters,* LC.

4. *Providence Gazette,* 19 Aug. 1815.

5. Arnold, *Vital Record,* 3, 208.

6. Bailey, *American Naval Biography,* 206.

7. See WHA, *George Washington* and *Chesapeake* journals, Huntington, and *John Adams* journal in GWBW. For evidence that WHA did his own portrait, see WHA to SBA, 15 Apr. 1804, and WHA to WA, 24 and 30 Apr. 1804, all Huntington. This right-side profile portrait, probably done by WHA as a pencil or pen-and-ink sketch, was put into a stipple engraving by David Edwin, and this is the usually seen portrait of WHA. Edwin probably did this right after Allen's death, as it appears in the *Port Folio* for 1814. FDR Library, Hyde Park, New York, Accession 505, negative R-1949.

8. Hoppin, "Jones Memoir," 21–4.

9. *Port Folio,* 3:2; DeConde, *Quasi-War,* 117, 128.

10. *Abstracts of Service,* entries for WHA, 28 Apr. 1800–Apr. 1807, Roll M-330, NA; Sen. Ray Greene to WA, Philadelphia, 20 Mar. 1800, Huntington.

11. There are fifty-two of WHA's letters plus a number between other members of the Allen family from the years after Henry's death in Huntington. There are also about ten Allen family letters in the LC Manuscript Collection at AC 4815.

12. WHA to WA, *Washington,* 30 May 1800, Huntington.

13. Chapelle, *American Sailing Navy,* 142–3, 536, 541.

14. *Muster Roll of George Washington,* June 1800–May 1801, NA.

15. WHA to WA, Frigate *Washington,* 30 May 1800, Huntington.

16. DeConde, *Quasi-War,* 223 and passim.
17. WHA to WA, Philadelphia, 26 June 1800; Whipple, *Journal,* 16 June 1800, both Huntington.
18. *Muster Roll of Washington,* 20 June 1800, NA.
19. Long, *Ready to Hazard,* 58.
20. Rea, *Letter to Bainbridge,* paragraph 3.
21. *Muster Roll of Washington,* 20 June–9 July 1800, NA.
22. McKee, *Honorable Profession,* 480–1, table 10.
23. WHA to WA, Philadelphia, 26 June 1800, Huntington.
24. Ibid.
25. Rea, *Bainbridge Letter,* paragraph 6.
26. WHA to WA, Philadelphia, 26 June 1800, Huntington.
27. *Treaties, &c.,* 2:343.
28. Ibid., 352–68.
29. Whipple, *Journal,* 23 and 24 June 1800, Huntington.
30. Dunne, *George Washington,* 03-07-1800 and 04-05-1801.
31. Dunne, *George Washington,* 12-07-1800.
32. WHA, *Journal,* 19 Sept.–1 Oct. 1800, Huntington.
33. WHA to WA, Frigate *Washington,* 3 Aug. 1800, LC.
34. WHA to WA, Philadelphia, 16 May 1801, Huntington.
35. The *Nautical Almanac and Astronomical Ephemeris* and its companion volume, the *Tables Requisite to be used with the Nautical Almanac for finding the Latitude and Longitude at Sea,* were tabulations of astronomical data giving positions of the sun, the moon, and a small group of the brighter stars that were used for navigation. Cotter, *History of Nautical Astronomy,* passim.
36. WHA, *Journal,* Sunday, 10 Aug. 1800, Huntington.
37. Inside cover and flyleaf of WHA, *Journal,* Huntington.
38. WHA, *Journal,* 8–15 Aug. 1800, Huntington.
39. Ibid., 21–8 Aug. 1800.
40. Rea, *Bainbridge Letter,* paragraph 6.
41. DeConde, *Quasi-War,* 120.
42. Laird Clowes, *Royal Navy,* 6:11–2.
43. *Port Folio,* 3:6; Paullin, "Dueling in the Old Navy," 1,159, 1,164–5, 1,170–1.
44. WHA, *Journal,* 5–7 Sept. 1800, Huntington.
45. Ibid., 6–13 Sept. 1800.
46. Ibid., 4 Oct. 1800.
47. Ibid., 18 Sept. 1800.
48. Fowler, *Jack Tars and Commodores,* 63; Guttridge and Smith, *Commodores,* 57–8; Cooper, *History of the Navy,* 1:214, says that the dey's request came about 7 Oct. 1800. The sequence of events used here comes from Dunne, *George Washington,* 18-09-1800, 20-09-1800, 26-09-1800, and 09-10-1800.
49. Oman, *Nelson,* 177, 528, 549–53.
50. Cooper, *History of the Navy,* 1:214.
51. Rea, *Bainbridge Letter,* paragraph 18.
52. Thursfield, *Five Naval Journals,* 139–40; Cooper, *History of the Navy,* 1:214, 215, 215f, 216.

53. *Treaties, &c.,* 2:364.

54. Dunne, *George Washington,* 18-09-1800, 20-09-1800, 26-09-1800, and 09-10-1800; Rea, *Bainbridge Letter,* paragraph 18.

55. WHA, *Journal,* 9 Oct. 1800.

56. Ibid., 10–3 Oct. 1800, Huntington; Cooper, *History of the Navy,* 1:218.

57. WHA, *Journal,* 11–2 Nov. 1800; Dunne, *George Washington,* 14-10-1800 and 19-10-1800.

58. Fowler, *Jack Tars and Commodores,* 63.

59. WHA, *Journal,* 20 Oct. 1800.

60. Ibid., 25–6, 28 Oct. 1800.

61. Ibid., 6–9 Nov. 1800.

62. Ibid., 9–10 Nov. 1800.

63. Ibid; Cooper, *History of the Navy,* 1:217.

64. Newton, "Pictures of Turkey," 77. The Turkish oarsmen were saying, "Istanbul, beautiful and great!"

65. WHA, *Journal,* 10–2 Nov. 1800.

66. Rea, *Bainbridge Letter,* paragraphs 11, 13, 14.

67. WHA, *Journal,* 12–6 Nov. 1800.

68. Thursfield, *Five Naval Journals,* 140.

69. Cooper, *History of the Navy,* 1:218.

70. Rea, *Bainbridge Letter,* paragraphs 13 and 17.

71. WHA, *Journal,* 30 Dec. 1800, 4, 11, and 22 Jan. 1801.

72. Ibid., 17 Jan. 1801; Rea, *Bainbridge Letter,* paragraph 16.

73. WHA, *Journal,* 21 Jan. 1801.

74. Cooper, *History of the Navy,* 1:218.

75. WHA, *Journal,* 26 Jan. 1801.

76. Ibid., 31 Jan. 1801.

77. Rea, *Bainbridge Letter,* paragraph 20; Henningsen, *Crossing the Equator,* 57–8, 60–2, 65, 66, 74, 92; Barker, *The Old Sailor's Jolly Boat,* 452–6.

78. WHA, *Journal,* 19 Apr. 1801.

79. McKee, *Honorable Profession,* 185–6.

80. WHA to WA, Frigate *Philadelphia,* 27 June 1802, Huntington.

81. Fowler, *Jack Tars and Commodores,* 113–4; Guttridge and Smith, *Commodores,* 103–7.

82. Noadiah Morris, quoted in McKee, *Edward Preble,* 309–10.

83. Painter to President Jefferson, 11 Feb. 1806, *Letters from Officers,* M-148, Roll 1(2), no. 47, RG 45, NA.

84. WHA to WA, Frigate *John Adams,* 6 Oct. 1802, Huntington.

85. Ibid.

86. WHA, Frigate *John Adams* Journal (Log 227), GWBW, hereinafter cited as *JA Journal,* 22 and 27 Oct., 14 Nov. 1802.

87. WHA to WA, Malaga, 23 Nov. 1802, Huntington.

88. WHA, *JA Journal,* 4 Jan. 1803.

89. WHA to WA, Malaga, 23 Nov., 13 Dec. 1802, Huntington.

90. Guttridge and Smith, *Commodores,* 68; Fowler, *Jack Tars and Commodores,* 75; Dunne, *Chesapeake,* 1–10 Mar. 1803; WHA, *JA Journal,* 23 Feb. and 10 Mar. 1803.

91. WHA, *JA Journal*, 8 and 9 May 1803.

92. Dunne, *John Adams*, 07-06-1803.

93. Cooper, *History of the Navy*, 1:245; WHA, *JA Journal*, 13–20 May 1803.

94. WHA, *JA Journal*, 5–9 June 1803; Dunne, *John Adams*, 05-06-1803 to 09-06-1803.

95. Fowler, *Jack Tars and Commodores*, 80.

96. Guttridge and Smith, *Commodores*, 69–70; Cooper, *History of the Navy*, 1:249–50; WHA, *JA Journal*, 21 and 22 June 1803.

97. St. Medard to Rodgers, *New York*, 11 Nov. 1803, Rodgers Papers, WLC; WHA to WA, Washington Navy Yard, 12 Dec. 1803, Huntington; McKee, *Honorable Profession*, 123.

98. WHA to WA, Washington Navy Yard, 12 Dec. 1803 and 24 Apr. 1804; WHA to SBA, Washington, 15 Apr. 1804, both Huntington.

99. WHA to SBA, Washington, 15 Apr. 1804, Huntington.

100. WHA to WA, New York, 6 Apr. 1804, and Washington, 24 Apr. 1804, Huntington.

101. WHA to SBA, Washington, 15 Apr. 1804, Huntington.

102. WHA to WA, Washington, 29 and 30 Apr. 1804, Huntington.

103. WHA to WA, Washington, 15 May 1804, Huntington.

104. *Port Folio*, 3:4.

105. WHA to WA, Gibraltar Bay, 1 Sept. 1804, Huntington.

106. Cooper, *History of the Navy*, 2:1–42; Fowler, *Jack Tars and Commodores*, 90–112; Guttridge and Smith, *Commodores*, 63–98.

107. McKee, *Edward Preble*, 297–9, 303–6, 336–7.

108. WHA to WA, Syracuse, 14 Nov. 1804, Huntington.

109. Cooper, *History of the Navy*, 2:42–53.

110. WHA to WA, Syracuse, 14 Nov. 1804, Huntington. The sketch of the *Intrepid* is on the second page; Roscoe, *Picture History*, plate 282.

111. Cooper, *History of the Navy*, 2:52.

112. McKee, *Edward Preble*, 309.

113. Note from Dr. Christopher McKee, Preble's biographer.

114. Guttridge and Smith, *Commodores*, 189.

115. Paullin, *John Rodgers*, 123–4.

116. *Port Folio*, 3:4, 5; Bailey, *Naval Biography*, 208–9.

117. Fowler, *Jack Tars and Commodores*, 115–9.

118. Paullin, *John Rodgers*, 77–82, 137.

119. *Treaties, &c.*, 2:388–90.

120. WHA to WA, Tunis Bay, 31 Aug. 1805, Huntington.

121. WHA to SBA, off Malta, 23 July 1805, LC.

122. WHA to WA, Tunis Bay, 31 Aug. 1805, Huntington.

123. Fowler, *Jack Tars and Commodores*, 121; Paullin, *John Rodgers*, 146–59.

124. *Norfolk Gazette and Publick Ledger*, 6, 8, and 13 Nov. 1805; *National Intelligencer*, 13 and 18 Nov. 1805.

125. WHA to WA, *Constitution*, Tunis Bay, 31 Aug. 1805.

126. *Treaties, &c.*, 2:344; James, *Naval History*, 6:397–410.

127. *Port Folio*, 3:5, 6.

CHAPTER 2

1. Cross, *Chesapeake Biography,* 17.
2. *Norfolk Herald,* 3 Dec. 1799.
3. Chapelle, *American Sailing Navy,* 135.
4. Cross, *Chesapeake Biography,* 40, 41, 43; WHA to RS, Providence, 5 Feb. 1807, *Letters from Officers,* M-148, Roll 3(1), no. 57, RG 45, NA.
5. WHA to WA, Philadelphia, 9 Mar. 1807, Huntington; WHA to RS, 9–12 Mar. 1807, *Letters from Officers,* M-148, Roll 3(1), nos. 116, 118, 121, 123, RG 45, NA.
6. RS to JB, Navy Department, 23 Feb. 1807, *Barron Papers,* I, Folder 40, in EGS.
7. WHA to WA, Philadelphia, 30 Mar. 1807, Huntington; 23 letters WHA to RS, 10 Mar.–7 Apr. 1807, *Letters from Officers,* M-148, Roll 3(1), nos. 118–71, and 23 Mar. 1807, no. 153, RG 45, NA; WHA to Gordon, Philadelphia, 27 Mar. 1807, *Barron Papers,* I, 43.
8. Lt. Sidney Smith to RS, Norfolk, 13 Mar. and 24 May 1807, *Letters from Officers,* M-148, Roll 3(1), no. 124, and Roll 3(2), no. 28, RG 45, NA.
9. B. Cocke to JB, Washington, 29 July 1806, *Barron Papers,* I, Folder 35; Printed document, J. Stricker to JR, Havre de Grace, 31 Jan. 1807, *Barron Papers,* I, Folder 36, EGS; Paullin, "Dueling in Old Navy," 1,156; John Rodgers's bark seems to have exceeded his bite: in all his long life he never once fought a duel. Paullin, *John Rodgers,* 174–83.
10. JB to Bullus, Back River, near Hampton, 3 July [1807], *Barron Papers,* I, Folder 63, EGS.
11. Nine letters Gordon to Bullus, 1811 to 1813, *Personal Miscellaneous,* Manuscripts Division, NYPL.
12. Calderhead, "Strange Career," 373–86.
13. Notes by James Barron on matters that came up during his court-martial (hereafter CM Notes), *Barron Papers,* I, Folder 73b, EGS.
14. James, *Naval History,* 4:211; William Wood to Anthony Merry, Baltimore, 3 Sept. 1806. *Berkeley Papers,* TRL, Toronto, Ontario, Canada; Merry to GCB, Lancaster, Pennsylvania, 4 Sept. 1806, *Berkeley Papers*, TRL; Thomas Barclay to GCB, New York, 30 Sept. 1806, and Barclay to Charles James Fox, New York, 4 Sept. 1806, Rives, *Correspondence of Barclay,* 243–5.
15. James, *Naval History,* 4:210, 211; Barclay to Fox, New York, 29 Sept. 1806, Rives, *Correspondence of Barclay,* 247–8.
16. Peterson, *Defence of Norfolk,* 15, note 3.
17. Captain A. P. Hollis to GCB, H.M.S. *Mermaid,* 4 Aug. 1806; Erskine to GCB, Washington, 11 Dec. 1806, both *Berkeley Papers,* 269, 405, TRL; *Trial of Ratford,* Remarks, pp. i–ix.
18. *Publick Ledger,* Norfolk, Virginia, 26 June 1807.
19. Cooper, *History of the Navy,* 1:179–89; Erskine to GCB, Philadelphia, 16 Aug. 1807, *Berkeley Papers,* 437, TRL.
20. Laird Clowes, *Royal Navy,* 4:165.
21. Guttridge and Smith, *Commodores,* 117.
22. McKee, "Foreign Seamen in US Navy," passim.
23. Lewis, *Social History of the Navy,* 129.

24. Barron, Report to Mr. Madison, *Berkeley Papers,* 388, 389, TRL.

25. RS to JB, Navy Department, 23 Feb. 1807, *Barron Papers,* I, Folder 40, EGS; Lt. Arthur Sinclair to JB, Norfolk, 12 Mar. 1807, *Barron Papers,* I, Folder 42, EGS; Lt. Sidney Smith to RS, Norfolk, 24 May 1807, *Letters from Officers,* M-148, Roll 3(2), no. 28, RG 45, NA.

26. Barron, Report to Mr. Madison, *Berkeley Papers,* 388, 389, TRL; *Public Ledger,* Norfolk, 3 July 1807; *Argument Against War,* 16; Barclay to GCB, New York, 11 Aug. 1807 and [Aug. 1807], and Barclay to George Canning, New York, 2 Sept. 1807, Rives, *Correspondence of Barclay,* 267, 268.

27. *Trial of Ratford,* 9, 15, Remarks, vi, vii; NC, 18:337; James, *Naval History,* 4:327.

28. *Trial of Ratford,* 8–10; NC, 18:337.

29. James, *Naval History,* 4:328; *Trial of Ratford,* 9, 11.

30. *Trial of Ratford,* 7–10; NC, 18:337.

31. Guttridge and Smith, *Commodores,* 118; NC, 18:339.

32. Sinclair to RS, Mathews County [Virginia], 14 Oct. 1807, and Norfolk, 22 Oct. 1807, *Letters from Officers,* M-148, Roll 4(1), nos. 103 and 134, RG 45, NA.

33. *Trial of Ratford,* 4–8; Perkins, *Prologue to War,* 142.

34. JB, Report to Mr. Madison, *Berkeley Papers,* 388–9, TRL; JB, rough notes in defense of his actions, no date, hereinafter Barron's Notes, *Barron Papers,* I, Folder 73b, EGS.

35. Erskine to John Hamilton, British Consul at Norfolk, Washington, 11 July 1807, *Berkeley Papers,* 381–3, TRL.

36. JB, Barron's Notes, *Barron Papers,* I, Folder 73b, EGS; *Trial of Ratford,* Remarks, pp. viii–ix.

37. *Trial of Barron,* 45, 115, 263; *Trial of Ratford,* Remarks, pp. vi, vii, ix.

38. RS to JB, Navy Department, 28 Mar. 1807, and note by JB, *Barron Papers,* I, Folder 40, EGS.

39. Document, undated, a chronology of events aboard the *Chesapeake* between 9 May and 19 June 1807, hereinafter cited as Chronology, *Barron Papers,* I, Folder 72, EGS.

40. *Trial of Barron,* 415; WHA to WA, 24 June 1807, LC.

41. Chronology, *Barron Papers,* I, Folder 72, EGS.

42. *Trial of Barron,* 262.

43. Ibid., 368, 380; WHA to WA, *Chesapeake,* Norfolk, 17 July 1807, LC.

44. *Trial of Barron,* 90, 193, 210.

45. Chronology, 25 May 1807, *Barron Papers,* I, Folder 72, EGS.

46. *Trial of Barron,* 434; Chronology, 28 May 1807, *Barron Papers,* I, Folder 72, EGS.

47. Chronology, 3–15 June 1807, *Barron Papers,* I, Folder 72, EGS.

48. WHA to WA, 17 July 1807, LC; *Barron Papers,* I, Folder 72, EGS.

49. *Trial of Barron,* 154, 398, 400.

50. Ibid., 369, 399, 424; Chronology, 15 June 1807, *Barron Papers,* I, Folder 72, EGS.

51. *Trial of Barron,* 210, 420; Barron's Notes, *Barron Papers,* I, Folder 81, EGS.

52. WHA to WA, 17 July 1807, LC; *Trial of Barron,* 368.

53. WHA to WA, 17 July 1807, LC; *Trial of Barron,* 265.

54. He was reputed to have spent £100,000 to get himself elected member for Gloucestershire. Pope, *Nelson's Navy,* 255.

55. NC, 12:88–113; Perkins, *Prologue to War,* 140.

56. *Berkeley Papers,* 111–9, TRL; *Boston Repertory,* summer of 1807.

57. Letter in cipher, *Berkeley Papers,* 116, TRL.

58. Undated document, *Berkeley Papers,* 120, TRL.

59. NC, 28:117–8, 354.

60. NC, 28:353–69.

61. NC, 18:117–8.

62. NC, 28:353–69; Undated newsclip (ca. 1851), quoting Humphreys (Davenport), *Barron Papers,* I, Folder 82, EGS. Nothing in the Berkeley Papers gives any indication that Humphreys had any specific orders to do the job himself.

63. Erskine to GCB, Philadelphia, 16 Aug. 1807, *Berkeley Papers,* 437, TRL.

64. James, *Naval History,* 4:329; *Trial of Ratford,* 12.

65. WHA to WA, 17 July 1807, LC.

66. Chronology, 17 June 1807, *Barron Papers,* I, Folder 72, EGS; *Trial of Barron,* 113.

67. Allen, *Chesapeake Journal,* 21–22 June 1807, Huntington; *Trial of Barron,* 401; WHA to WA, 17 July 1807, LC.

68. *Trial of Barron,* 44, 56, 265.

69. James, *Naval History,* 4:329; NC, 28:355.

70. *Trial of Barron,* 44, 45, 196–7, 245, 249.

71. Rough draft MS testimony, Lt. S. Smith and Slg. Mstr. Brooke, both *Chesapeake-Leopard* Archives, EGS.

72. *Trial of Barron,* 44–5, 62, 67.

73. WHA, *Chesapeake Journal,* 23 June 1807, Huntington.

74. *Trial of Barron,* 138; Humphreys (Davenport) is quoted, ca. 1851, "No person could regret more than myself that the admiral should have issued such a circular to the different ships under his command," *Barron Papers,* I, Folder 82, EGS.

75. *Trial of Barron,* 102, 138, 143, 193, 250, 251; Laird Clowes, *Royal Navy,* 4:165.

76. RS to JB, 15 May 1807, in *Trial of Barron,* 132–5.

77. *Trial of Barron,* 166.

78. Ibid., 31, 232–3, and 253.

79. Ibid., 48, 90, 102–3, 121, 193.

80. WHA, *Chesapeake Journal,* 23 June 1807, Huntington.

81. *Trial of Barron,* 48–50; WHA to WA, 17 July 1807, LC; Rough draft MS testimony, Lt. Crane, *Chesapeake-Leopard* Archives, EGS.

82. *Trial of Barron,* 253.

83. Rough draft MS testimony, Midn. Shubrick, *Chesapeake-Leopard* Archives, EGS.

84. WHA, *Chesapeake Journal,* 23 June 1807, Huntington; *Trial of Barron,* 51, 60, 86; *Port Folio,* 3:7.

85. *Port Folio,* 3:7.

86. *Trial of Barron,* 140.

87. JB to Bullus, Back River, near Hampton, 3 July [1807], *Barron Papers,* I, Folder 63; Document, undated, headed "for page 162," *Barron Papers,* I, Folder 73b, EGS.

88. *Publick Ledger,* Norfolk, 29 June 1807.

89. *Trial of Barron,* 146, 257; Rough draft MS testimony, Midn. Shubrick, *Chesapeake-Leopard* Archives, EGS.

90. NC, 18:117; *Trial of Barron,* 141.

91. NC, 18:116–7, 128–30.
92. James, *Naval History,* 4:329, 331.
93. NC, 18:116.
94. They didn't notice the small-arms fire during the action but found numerous musket balls later. Rough draft MS testimony, Peter Muhlenberg, *Chesapeake-Leopard* Archives, EGS.
95. *Port Folio,* 3:7.
96. *Trial of Ratford,* 12; NC, 18:338.
97. *Trial of Barron,* 225.
98. Ibid., 226; WHA, *Chesapeake Journal,* 23 June 1807, Huntington.
99. WHA, *Chesapeake Journal,* 23 June 1807, Huntington; *Trial of Barron,* 226.
100. *Trial of Ratford,* 5, 18; NC, 28:356–7; Lt. Tazewell to Humphreys, 26 July 1807, *Berkeley Papers,* 384, TRL.
101. NC, 28:357.
102. JB to RS, *Chesapeake,* 23 June 1807, *Barron Papers,* I, Folder 54, EGS.
103. Lt. Sidney Smith to RS, *Chesapeake,* 21 Feb. 1808, *Letters from Officers,* M-148, Roll 4(2), no. 60, RG 45, NA; *Trial of Barron,* 202–8, passim; JB to Bullus, Back River, 3 July [1807], *Barron Papers,* I, Folder 63, EGS.
104. *Port Folio,* 3:8; Lt. Benjamin Smith, et al., to RS, late U.S.S. *Chesapeake,* Hampton Roads, 23 June 1807, *Letters from Officers,* M-148, Roll 3(2), letter 67, RG 45, NA.
105. Anonymous to JB, Washington, 5 Mar. 1808, *Barron Papers,* I, Folder 76, EGS.
106. JB to Bullus, 3 July 1807, *Barron Papers,* I Folder 63; Document, undated, *Barron Papers,* I, Folder 73b, EGS.
107. NC, 28:362; Document, undated and untitled, GCB's rationalization of the affair, hereafter cited as Berkeley's Rationale, Douglas to GCB, *Bellona,* 27 June 1807, both *Berkeley Papers,* 130, 336, TRL; MS testimony, Lt. Crane, *Chesapeake-Leopard* Archives, EGS.
108. *Publick Ledger,* 6 July 1807; Berkeley's Rationale, *Berkeley Papers,* 131, TRL; Barclay to Canning, New York, 2 July 1807, Rives, *Correspondence of Barclay,* 264.
109. Robert Saunders to JB, Williamsburg, [Virginia,] 30 June 1808, *Barron Papers,* I, Folder 80, EGS.
110. NC, 28:364.
111. Pole to GCB, Admiralty Office, 24 Aug. 1807, *Berkeley Papers,* 527, TRL.
112. NC, 28:363–9; Newsclip (ca. 1851), *Barron Papers,* I, Folder 82, EGS; O'Byrne, *Naval Biographical Dictionary,* 265.
113. NC, 18:119–22.
114. Peterson, *Defence of Norfolk,* 17–8.
115. Ibid., 44–5, 53–5.
116. Hardy to Hamilton, *Triumph,* 15 and 28 July 1807, *Berkeley Papers,* 380 and 387, TRL.
117. *Trial of Ratford,* 23 and passim.
118. WHA to WA, [off] Newport Light, [Aug. 1808,] Huntington; Guttridge and Smith, *Commodores,* 144, 170–1; WHA mentions seven by mid-1808, plus Gordon's last plus the Decatur-Barron affair gives nine; Calderhead, *Strange Career,* 381; Gordon to Bullus, Baltimore, 4 May 1812, *Personal Miscellaneous,* NYPL.

Chapter 3

1. Erskine to GCB, Washington, 24 Apr. 1807, and Philadelphia, 2 July 1807, *Berkeley Papers,* 413, 423, TRL.
2. WHA to WA, [Norfolk, 15 Aug. 1807,] Huntington.
3. WHA, *Chesapeake Journal,* 28–30 June 1807, Huntington.
4. RS to JB, 26 June 1807, *Barron Papers,* I, Folder 56, EGS.
5. *Publick Ledger,* Norfolk, 3 July 1807.
6. WHA, *Chesapeake Journal,* 23 June, 2–6 July 1807, Huntington.
7. Ibid., 3, 4, 7–11 July 1807.
8. Douglas to GCB, *Bellona,* 23 and 27 June 1807, *Berkeley Papers,* 334, 336, TRL.
9. Gore, *Nelson's Hardy,* quoted in Dunne, *Data File, Chesapeake,* 00-12-1807.
10. WHA to WA, *Chesapeake,* 1 Sept. 1807, Huntington.
11. WHA, *Chesapeake Journal,* 1 and 3 Sept. 1807, Huntington.
12. Ibid., 6 Sept. 1807.
13. WHA to WA, *Chesapeake,* Norfolk, 17 July 1807, LC.
14. *Trial of Barron,* 91, 202–8; S. Smith to RS, *Chesapeake,* 21 Feb. 1808, *Letters from Officers,* M-148, Roll 4(2), no. 60, RG 45, NA.
15. WHA to WA, *Chesapeake,* 14 Oct., 10 and 14 Nov. 1807, Huntington.
16. Brighton, *P.B.V. Broke Memoir,* 442–3.
17. WHA to WA, *Chesapeake,* 15 Jan., 19 May 1808, Huntington.
18. WHA to WA, *Chesapeake,* 14 Nov. 1807, Huntington.
19. WHA to WA, *Chesapeake,* 19 May 1808, Huntington.
20. WHA to WA, *Chesapeake,* 30 Sept. 1808, Huntington.
21. WHA to RS, 2 Feb. 1809, *Letters from Officers,* M-148, Roll 5(1), no. 32, RG 45, NA.
22. Brown, *American Naval Heroes,* 298; Bailey, *American Naval Biography,* 215; *Port Folio,* 3:12; WHA to SAR, Frigate *United States,* Washington, [Mar. 1809,] Huntington.
23. WHA to SAR, *United States,* [Mar. 1809,] Huntington.
24. WHA to Goldsborough, 11 Mar. 1809, enclosing letter from Midn. William Howard Allen, US Brig *Argus,* 2 Feb. 1809, *Letters from Officers,* M-148, Roll 5(1), 112, 113, RG 45, NA.
25. WHA to WA, *United States,* 19 Dec. [1809], Huntington.
26. WHA to SAR, *United States,* [Mar. 1809,] 9 May [1810]; WHA to WA, Norfolk, 19 Dec. [1809], all Huntington.
27. *Log of the United States,* 21 Feb. 1811–19 Feb. 1812, passim, RG 24, NA.
28. *Quarter Bill, U.S. Frigate United States,* LC.
29. *Log of the United States,* 5 Mar. 1811, NA.
30. Ibid., 10 June 1811.
31. Ibid., 11 Feb. 1812.
32. Littleton Waller Tazewell to SecState James Monroe, Norfolk, 27 Feb. 1812, copy furnished by Dr. W. M. P. Dunne. These funds were part of a secret British campaign of economic warfare, to be exchanged for U.S. gold and silver coin at a temporary artificially high rate of exchange created by British agents, tending to drain the United States of hard money.
33. Leech, *A Voice From the Main Deck,* 103; L. W. Tazewell to Monroe, Norfolk, 27 Feb. 1812.
34. Leech, *A Voice from the Main Deck,* 103.

CHAPTER 4

1. Parkinson, *Trade Winds,* 168, 181, 183.

2. Ibid., 180, 183, 187, 190.

3. *Muster List of the United States,* 192, 193; *Log of the United States,* 17 Aug. 1812, NA.

4. *Muster List of the United States,* 196; Ott, *Haitian Revolution,* 9.

5. *Muster List of the United States,* 74, 79, 80, 84, 85, 86, 196, entries for John Evrit, Martin Hine, John Vantoovner, Robert Duplex, Edward Rowe, and Osmin Nichols.

6. Eckert, *Navy Department in 1812,* 14–5; Laird Clowes, *Royal Navy,* 6:31.

7. Laird Clowes, *Royal Navy,* 6:29–30.

8. Mahan, *Sea Power in 1812,* 1:298–9.

9. WHA to SAR, *United States,* [20 Sept. 1812,] Huntington.

10. *Log of the United States,* 7 Aug.–3 Sept. 1812, NA.

11. Dudley, *Documentary History,* 1:471.

12. Cooper, *History of the Navy,* 2:127.

13. *Port Folio,* 3:13.

14. *Port Folio,* 3:15; Leech, *Voice from the Main Deck,* 123; James, *Naval Occurrences,* 154.

15. Leech, *Voice from the Main Deck,* 124.

16. Ibid., 115, 148; Laird Clowes, *Royal Navy,* 6:41–2; James, *Naval Occurrences,* 159, 161.

17. Laird Clowes, *Royal Navy,* 6:29, 37; James, *Naval Occurrences,* 97.

18. O'Byrne, *Naval Biographical Dictionary,* 167, 168.

19. Leech, *Voice from the Main Deck,* 87–9; Pope, *Life in Nelson's Navy,* 226; Durand, *Able Seaman of 1812,* 64–5; Langley, *Social Reform in Navy,* 142.

20. Leech, *Voice from the Main Deck,* 99.

21. Ibid., 90–1; James, *Naval Occurrences,* 159.

22. O'Byrne, *Naval Biographical Dictionary,* 537; Leech, *Voice from the Main Deck,* 110, 136; *Port Folio,* 3:14.

23. Leech, *Voice from the Main Deck,* 125–6; Cooper, *History of the Navy,* 2:127.

24. Mahan, *Sea Power in 1812,* 1:416–7; Leech, *Voice from the Main Deck,* 149; NC, 30:159.

25. *Port Folio,* 3:13; *Newport Mercury,* 13 Dec. 1812; *The War,* 194.

26. Laird Clowes, *Royal Navy,* 6:45, 46; Leech, *Voice from the Main Deck,* 129–39; Cooper, *History of the Navy,* 2:126–8; Mahan, *Sea Power in 1812,* 1:417–9.

27. *The War,* 1:115, 119, 171; NC, 28:507.

28. Cooper, *History of the Navy,* 2:128; *Log of the United States,* 7 and 26 Oct. 1812; *Argus Muster List,* 213.

29. James, *Naval Occurrences,* 156; Douglas, *Naval Gunnery,* 260-1; Laird Clowes, *Royal Navy,* 6:46–7.

30. *Intelligence Report to ADM Warren,* [late 1812]; Leech, *Voice from the Main Deck,* 142–5; *Port Folio,* 3:14.

31. *Port Folio,* 3:15.

32. Mahan, *Sea Power in 1812,* 1:421.

33. *Port Folio,* 3:13–4.

34. *The War,* 1:115.

35. *Muster List of the United States,* 111–9; Leech, *Voice from the Main Deck,* 144, 146–7; Laird Clowes, *Royal Navy,* 6:43–4, 44n, 46; James, *Naval Occurrences,* 161.

36. Leech, *Voice from the Main Deck,* 144, 146–7.

37. *Connecticut Gazette,* 16 Dec. 1812; *The War,* 1:115.

38. Eckert, *Navy Department in 1812,* 14.

39. Leech, *Voice from the Main Deck,* 147.

40. Cooper, *History of the Navy,* 2:128.

41. *Log of the United States,* 25–30 Oct. 1812.

42. Leech, *Voice from the Main Deck,* 148.

43. James, *Naval Occurrences,* 156–7, comments on this.

44. *Log of the United States,* 16 Nov. 1812.

45. Ibid., 18–21 Nov. 1812; *Port Folio,* 3:15.

46. Dudley, *Documentary History,* 1:616; *Newport Mercury,* 12 Dec. 1812; Leech, *Voice from the Main Deck,* 152; *The War,* 1:118. The French *L'Insurgente,* captured by the *Constellation* in 1799, was taken into the navy but was later lost at sea.

47. *Newport Mercury,* 12 Dec. 1812; O. H. Perry to SecNav Hamilton, 12 Dec. 1812, Dudley, *Documentary History,* 1:616.

48. Mrs. B. H. Latrobe to Mrs. Juliana Miller, Washington, 14 Dec. 1812, tipped into *Biographical Sketch, and Services of Commodore Charles Stewart of the Navy of the United States,* Philadelphia: Printed for J. Harding, 1838, the New-York Historical Society: Y-q. 1838 Bio.

49. *Connecticut Gazette,* 9 Dec. 1812; *Rhode Island American,* 15 Dec. 1812; Leech, *Voice from the Main Deck,* 159; *Intelligence Report to ADM Warren,* "British Seamen."

50. Guernsey, *New York in the War of 1812,* 1:143–5.

51. Leech, *Voice from the Main Deck,* 153, 161; *Columbian Phenix,* 19 Dec. 1812; *Log of the United States,* 13–14 Dec. 1812.

52. Leech, *Voice from the Main Deck,* 153, 154; Guernsey, *New York in the War of 1812,* 1:passim; *Log of the United States,* 15–30 Dec. 1812.

53. WHA to SAR, off New York, 9 Jan. 1813, Huntington.

54. Decatur's gold box is in the Naval Academy Museum.

55. Guernsey, *New York in the War of 1812,* 1:143–4; James, *Naval Occurrences,* appendix 20, p. xxxi; Decatur's medal is shown in USNI *Proceedings,* Oct. 1967, p. 58.

56. *Calendar of Virginia State Papers,* 10:188–9; *Newport Mercury,* 26 Dec. 1812; *Port Folio,* 3:14.

57. *Connecticut Gazette,* 6 Jan. 1813; *Rise of the American Navy,* 154–6.

58. Guernsey, *New York in the War of 1812,* 1:150–6.

59. Ibid., 158–9.

60. *Log of the United States,* 1 Jan., 3 Mar. 1813; Guernsey, *New York in the War of 1812,* 1:160; Leech, *Voice from the Main Deck,* 159.

61. *Rhode Island American,* 8 Jan. 1813.

62. Dudley, *Documentary History,* 1:547; *New York Gazette,* 4, 12 Oct. 1812.

63. *Muster List of the United States,* note on page 119; Leech, *Voice from the Main Deck,* 159.

64. TO to Admty, 20 Mar. 1813, ADM 98/120; ADM 98/292, 16, entry of 2 June 1813, PRO.

65. O'Byrne, *Naval Biographical Dictionary,* 167–8, 537; Lloyd, *Keith Papers,* 3:241.

66. *Log of the United States,* 7 Jan. 1813; Guernsey, *New York in the War of 1812,* 1:160–4; Leech, *Voice from the Main Deck,* 160–1.

67. Leech, *Voice from the Main Deck,* 160–1.

68. NC, 29:190–2.

69. Guernsey, *New York in the War of 1812,* 1:160–2; Leech, *Voice from the Main Deck,* 160; *Rise of the American Navy,* 154–5.

70. Leech, *Voice from the Main Deck,* 160–1.

71. PH to SD, 29 Dec. 1812; James, *Naval Occurrences,* 165.

72. McKee, *Honorable Profession,* 341, table 33, 494.

73. Ibid., 297; WHA to SAR, 9 Jan. 1813, Huntington; SD to PH, 30 Oct. 1812, in Dudley, *Documentary History,* 1:552–3.

74. Dudley, *Documentary History,* 1:516–23; McKee, *Honorable Profession,* 299.

75. McKee, *Honorable Profession,* 294–5; Gordon to Bullus, Baltimore, 14 Mar. 1813, *Personal Miscellaneous,* NYPL.

76. T. I. Allen to Peleg Rhodes, 2 Dec. 1813, Huntington; SD to WJ, Frigate *United States,* 25 Jan. 1813, NA; WHA to SAR, *Argus,* [16 Apr. 1813,] Huntington.

77. WHA to SAR, mailed 9 Jan. 1813, Huntington.

78. *Argus Muster List,* 17 Jan., 17 Feb. 1813, PRO.

79. Dudley, *Documentary History,* 1:354.

CHAPTER 5

1. Chapelle, *History of American Sailing Navy,* 388–9; Gill, *Steel's Mastmaking, Sailmaking and Rigging,* 36.

2. Chapelle, *History of American Sailing Navy,* 181–2, 532; *Argus, Surveyed and Valued,* 16 Sept. 1813, ADM 106/1942, PRO; *American State Papers, Naval Affairs,* 1:149.

3. *London Times,* 24 Aug. 1813; James, *Naval History,* 6:221.

4. James, *Naval Occurrences,* 280; James, *Naval History,* 6:222.

5. *Log of the Argus,* 6 and 7 June 1811; Dunne, "Naval Architectural Study of *Argus,*" 130.

6. Journals in 1813 refer to a launch, a cutter, and a gig.

7. Article 22, Standing Orders, *Log of the Argus,* 1811, NA.

8. Gardner, *Recollections,* 159; Rediker, *Devil and Sea,* 160.

9. Thursfield, *Five Naval Journals,* 10.

10. Water tanks were in wide use by 1813.

11. Who often used French brandy even during the war with France.

12. Langley, *Social Reform in the Navy,* 210–1.

13. Rorabaugh, *Alcoholic Republic,* 8, chart 1.1, passim.

14. Mstr.-Cmdnt. Wederstrand to RS, *Argus,* 29 Dec. 1808, M-147, Reel 2, no. 124, RG 45, NA.

15. Stephen Decatur, in 1803, during her maiden voyage.

CHAPTER 6

1. Sinclair to WJ, New York, 2 Jan. 1813, *Master Commandants' Letters,* no. 5, 1813, RG 45, NA.

2. *The War,* 1:124, 130.

3. *Columbian Phenix,* 23 Jan. 1813.

4. SD to WJ, *United States,* 25 Jan. 1813, *Captains' Letters,* no. 35, 1813, RG 45, NA.

5. WJ to WHA, Navy Department, 28 May 1813, *Letters to Officers,* RG 45, NA.

6. *The War,* 1:172; WHA to SAR, *Argus,* [16 Apr. 1813,] Huntington; WJ to WHA, Navy Department, 5 June 1813, *Letters to Officers,* RG 45, NA.

7. *Muster Roll of Argus,* Apr. 1812–Apr. 1813, 191, NA.

8. NC, 30:181; *Argus* crew heights from *General Entry Book(s) of American Prisoners of War,* ADM 103 series, PRO.

9. WHA to SAR, *Argus,* Friday 15th [16 Apr. 1813], Huntington.

10. Eckert, *Navy Department in 1812,* 50–1; *Muster Roll of Argus,* 221–3, lines 49–96; SD to WJ, 18 Feb. 1813, *Captains' Letters,* RG 45, NA.

11. Strong, *Eulogium,* 14; WHA to WA, *Chesapeake,* [27 Aug. 1808,] Huntington; Sailing Master Howard Allen to WJ, Navy Yard, New York, 25 Sept. 1813, *Letters from Officers,* Roll 12(1), no. 183, RG 45, NA.

12. Dudley, *Documentary History,* 1:628; *Muster Roll of Argus,* April 1812, NA.

13. *General Entry Book,* Plymouth, ADM 103/269, record 1930.

14. Private communication from Mrs. Evelyne E. Boose of Westminster, Maryland, a descendant of Richard Delphey's brother; Robert Thompson to PH, Hampton, 19 Sept. 1810, *Letters from Officers,* M-148, Roll 7(1), no. 39, NA; McKee, *Honorable Profession,* 205, 547 note 12.

15. SD to WJ, 25 Feb. 1813, *Captains' Letters Received,* 1813, M-125, no. 114, RG 45, NA.

16. Medical information prior to 23 Apr. 1813 is from Clarke, *Journal,* NYPL; "Wounded by Venus" from Thursfield, *Five Naval Journals,* 240; Surgeon Clarke's journal was interpreted by Dr. J. Worth Estes, M.D., Boston University School of Medicine.

17. Bailey, *American Naval Biography,* 218; C. Ellis, et al., to JR, Norwich, [Connecticut,] 2 Apr. 1813, letter in the author's possession.

18. *The War,* 1:180, 184.

19. *Muster Roll of Argus,* 203–6, 14–17 Apr. 1813, NA; Clarke, *Journal,* 8 Apr. 1813; *Officer's Journal,* 8 Apr. 1813, NYPL.

20. *Officer's Journal,* 10 Apr. 1813.

21. WHA to SAR, *Argus,* Friday 15th [16 Apr. 1813], Huntington.

22. *Officer's Journal,* 18 Apr.–18 June 1813, passim, NYPL.

23. Clarke to WJ, *John Adams,* 7 Oct. 1813, *Letters from Officers,* M-148, Roll 12(2), no. 17, RG 45, NA; Clarke, *Journal,* 23 Apr. 1813; *Muster Roll of Argus,* 190.

24. WJ to SD, Washington, 3 May 1813, *Confidential Letters,* Entry 7, RG 45, NA.

25. Estes and Dye, "Death on the *Argus,*" 6; SD to WJ, New York, 16 Feb. 1813, *Captains' Letters Received,* M-125, no. 39, RG 45, NA.

26. *The War,* 1:203.

27. After the war, Uriah Levy said he had been appointed "acting Lieutenant" by WHA. Butler, *Defense at Court of Inquiry,* 7.

28. UPL to BWC, 22 Mar. 1816, *Letters from Officers,* M-125, Roll 17, no. 152, RG 45, NA.

29. WJ to SD, 10 May 1813, *Letters to Captains,* RG 45, NA.

30. *The War,* 1:210.

31. Ibid., 1:216.

32. WJ to WHA, Navy Department, 28 May 1813, *Letters to Officers,* RG 45, NA.

CHAPTER 7

1. These were the Berlin decree of 1806, the Milan decree of 1807, the Bayonne decree of 1808, and the 1810 decree of Rambouillet.
2. Woodress, *Yankee's Odyssey,* 286, 287, 304.
3. Ibid., 289–90.
4. Bassano to Barlow, 10 May 1812, *The War,* 1:169, 2:21–7.
5. Herold, *Age of Napoleon,* 324–8; Riehn, *Russian Campaign,* 37, 41–2, 50.
6. Riehn, *Russian Campaign,* 162, 164.
7. Ibid., 178, 179, 185.
8. Ibid., 229–30.
9. De Segur, *Russian Campaign,* 52–89; Minard, *Carte Figurative;* Riasanovsky, *History of Russia,* 346; Riehn, *Russian Campaign,* 255.
10. De Segur, *Russian Campaign,* 90–8; Riehn, *Russian Campaign,* 263–7.
11. Minard, *Carte Figurative.*
12. Riehn, *Russian Campaign,* 302–3.
13. Woodress, *Yankee's Odyssey,* 298.
14. Bassano to Barlow, Wilna, 11 Oct. 1812, *The War,* 1:169–70.
15. Barlow to Monroe, Paris, 25 Oct. 1812; Barlow to Bassano, Paris, 26 Oct. 1812; both in *The War,* 1:169–70.
16. De Segur, *Russian Campaign,* 140–60.
17. Woodress, *Yankee's Odyssey,* 299–301; Howard, "Joel Barlow and Napoleon," 44.
18. Minard, *Carte Figurative.*
19. Howard, "Joel Barlow and Napoleon," 49–50.
20. De Segur, *Russian Campaign,* 262–70; Woodress, *Yankee's Odyssey,* 302–5; Minard, *Carte Figurative;* Riehn, *Russian Campaign,* 387–90.
21. Todd, *Letters of Joel Barlow,* 280–1.
22. Woodress, *Yankee's Odyssey,* 303. Italics in the original.
23. Woodress, *Yankee's Odyssey,* 23, 305.

CHAPTER 8

1. Barlow to Monroe, Paris, 25 Oct. 1812, *The War,* 1:169.
2. Serurier to Bassano, Washington, 6 Mar. 1813, quoted in Brant, *Madison, Commander in Chief,* 151.
3. Mooney, *William H. Crawford,* 27–8; Shipp, *Giant Days,* 174n.
4. Shipp, *Giant Days,* 126, 129–30.
5. Mooney, *William H. Crawford,* 50.
6. *The War,* 1:192.
7. *Officer's Journal,* 17–8 May 1813, NYPL; Crawford, *Journal,* 11 June 1813, LC.
8. WJ to WHA, Navy Department, 5 June 1813, *Letters to Officers,* RG 45, NA.
9. WJ to WHA, Navy Department, 5 June 1813, *Letters to Officers,* RG 45, NA; P. W. Bannatyne, president of the Herring Fisheries of Greenock, to Vice-Admiral Thornbrough, Greenock, 6 Aug. 1813, ADM 1/625, PRO.
10. *Officer's Journal,* 13 June 1813, NYPL.
11. *Muster Table of Argus,* entry 882, PRO.

12. Ibid., 12 June 1813, PRO; *General Entry Book, Dartmoor,* ADM 103/87, entry 1,043; *Officer's Journal,* 10 June 1813, NYPL.
13. *Officer's Journal,* 12–18 June 1813, NYPL.
14. Crawford, *Journal,* 18 June 1813, LC.

CHAPTER 9

1. Crew size and makeup at the time of departure is from *Muster Table of Argus,* PRO.
2. Birthplaces and physical appearances of crew members from the *General Entry Books,* ADM 103 series, PRO.
3. Estes and Dye, "Death on the Argus," 179–95.
4. *Log of the Argus,* Ship's Orders, Articles 22, 34, RG 24, NA.
5. Estes and Dye, "Death on the Argus," passim.
6. Estes, "Drug usage in Colonial America," passim.

CHAPTER 10

1. Crawford, *Journal,* 19 June 1813, LC; *Officer's Journal,* 19 June 1813, NYPL; Personal communication from Dr. W. M. P. Dunne.
2. Crawford, *Journal,* 19 June 1813, LC.
3. Ibid., 20 and 21 June 1813; *Officer's Journal,* 21 June 1813, NYPL.
4. *Officer's Journal,* 24–8 June 1813, NYPL; Crawford, *Journal,* 23 and 24 June 1813, LC.
5. Shipp, *Giant Days,* 116; Crawford to WJ, Paris, 2 Sept. 1813, LC.
6. Shipp, *Giant Days,* 127–8.
7. Crawford to WJ, Paris, 2 Sept. 1813, LC; Shipp, *Giant Days,* 116.
8. Crawford, *Journal,* 28 June–2 July 1813, LC.
9. *Officer's Journal,* 28 June–2 July 1813, NYPL.
10. Crawford, *Journal,* 4 July 1813, LC.
11. Ibid., 6 July 1813; *Officer's Journal,* 7 July 1813; Inderwick, *Journal,* 7 July 1813, NYPL.
12. *Muster Table of Argus,* Supernumerary List, numbers 215–30, 6 July 1813, PRO; *Officer's Journal,* 7 July 1813, NYPL.
13. Inderwick, *Journal,* 5, 7, and 8 July 1813, NYPL.
14. *Muster Table of Argus,* records 5 & 10, Prisoners of War, PRO.
15. Longford, *Years of the Sword,* 302–25.
16. Delderfield, *Imperial Sunset,* 29–84.
17. *Officer's Journal,* 10 and 11 July 1813, NYPL; Crawford, *Journal,* 10 July 1813, LC; Shipp, *Giant Days,* 127–8.
18. Crawford, *Journal,* 11 July 1813, LC; *Officer's Journal,* 11 and 12 July 1813; Inderwick, *Journal,* 11–3 July 1813, NYPL.
19. *Officer's Journal,* 12 July 1813, NYPL; Crawford, *Journal,* 12 July 1813, LC.

CHAPTER 11

1. ET, *Journal,* 3–23 July 1813; ET to Admty, nos. 617, 619, *Trent,* Cork Harbor, 8 and 9 July 1813, both ADM 1/625.
2. ET, *Journal,* 19 July 1813; Capt. Burgogne to ET, Loch of Belfast, 6 July 1813; ET to Admty, no. 641, Cork Harbour, 19 July 1813, ADM 1/625, PRO.
3. Parish Registry, Parish of the Holy Trinity, Colchester, Essex, Baptisms in the Year 1770.
4. Marshall, *Royal Naval Biography;* O'Byrne, *Naval Biographical Dictionary;* Lewis, *Social History of the Navy,* 27–59.
5. *Log of Triumph,* 5 Oct.–21 Dec. 1782, passim.
6. For an example, see Maples, *Memo of Services.*
7. Portrait and biosketch in NC, 31:445–53.
8. *Log of Triumph,* 1782–1784, passim; Maples, *Memo of Services.*
9. *Log of Triumph,* 3 and 4 Sept. 1784.
10. O'Byrne, *Naval Biographical Dictionary,* 1,176–7.
11. Marshall, *Royal Naval Biography,* 1:1 et seq.
12. W. E. May to author, London, 23 Aug. 1969. Lt. Lock's sword is in the NMM. JFM's dirk is in the author's possession.
13. Maples, *Memo of Services,* Apr. 1789; *Lieutenants' Passing Certificates,* vol. 16, no. 80.
14. Ott, *Haitian Revolution,* 6.
15. Ibid., 6, 9.
16. Scott, *Tropical Medicine,* 2:987.
17. Ott, *Haitian Revolution,* 10, 16–7.
18. DeConde, *Quasi-War,* 131.
19. Lloyd and Coulter, *Medicine and the Navy,* 3:343; Ott, *Haitian Revolution,* 176–82; Cole, *Christophe,* 281–6.
20. Scott, *Tropical Medicine,* 2:987.
21. Ott, *Haitian Revolution,* 78.
22. Charlton, *Journal,* 26 Dec. 1791; NC, 31:448.
23. *Lieutenants' Passing Certificates,* 16: no. 80, NMM.
24. O'Byrne, *Naval Biographical Dictionary,* 1,011–3.
25. Laird Clowes, *Royal Navy,* 4:197, note.
26. *Log of Penelope,* 16 and 17 Apr. 1793; O'Byrne, *Naval Biographical Dictionary,* 723; Laird Clowes, *Royal Navy,* 475, has the war's first naval action on 13 May 1793 in the Bay of Biscay. The *Penelope–Le Goelan* action predates that.
27. *Log of Penelope,* 4 and 5 June 1793; Ott, *Haitian Revolution,* 14; Cole, *Christophe,* says 2,000 Livres = £83; Richardson, *Mariner of England,* 65, says the price of a new slave in Jamaica in 1790 was £44; Lewis, *Social History of the Navy,* 294–6.
28. Phillimore, *Life of Parker,* 91; Cole, *Christophe,* 41.
29. Dunn, *Sugar and Slaves,* 259; Ott, *Haitian Revolution,* 76.
30. Phillimore, *Life of Parker,* 91–3; O'Byrne, *Naval Biographical Dictionary,* 723; Laird Clowes, *Royal Navy,* 4:214; Ott, *Haitian Revolution,* 77, 78; Cole, *Christophe,* 41, 42.
31. O'Byrne, *Naval Biographical Dictionary,* 723.
32. Ibid.

33. Ott, *Haitian Revolution,* 78; Laird Clowes, *Royal Navy,* 4:250; O'Byrne, *Naval Biographical Dictionary,* 723.

34. For example, Pocock, *Engraved Ships of War,* plate 6.

35. Laird Clowes, *Royal Navy,* 4:74, 114; Phillimore, *Life of Parker,* 99; Boudriot, *History of the French Frigate,* 135.

36. Anon. (Mr. "B") to Melville, dated 5 Jan. 1813, PRO. See also Boudriot, *History of the French Frigate,* 135, 136.

37. Sheer Draught and Other Plans of *La Magicienne,* NMM.

38. Boudriot, *History of the French Frigate,* 136.

39. O'Byrne, *Naval Biographical Dictionary,* 723.

40. Ott, *Haitian Revolution,* 80.

41. Laird Clowes, *Royal Navy,* 4:251; JFM, *Journal,* 1:18–23 May 1794.

42. JFM, *Journal,* 1:22 May 1794; Cole, *Christophe,* 45.

43. Ott, *Haitian Revolution,* 82–3.

44. JFM, *Journal,* 1:12, 23, 26–9 June 1794.

45. Ott, *Haitian Revolution,* 80–2.

46. Scott, *Tropical Medicine,* 1:317.

47. McNeill, *Plagues and People,* 188–9; *Virginian-Pilot,* Norfolk, Virginia, 10 Apr. 1989, page A1; Scott, *Tropical Medicine,* 1:294–5, 309, 314.

48. Scott, *Tropical Medicine,* 1:355–6.

49. Ott, *Haitian Revolution,* 81; Scott, *Tropical Medicine,* 1:316-9.

50. Scott, *Tropical Medicine,* 1:317–9.

51. *Log of HMS Penelope,* several entries in 1793 and early 1794.

52. JFM, *Journal,* 1:1 July–2 Aug. 1794.

53. Marshall, *Royal Naval Biography,* 150.

54. JFM, *Journal,* 1:15 July, 10 Sept. 1794.

55. Ibid., 1:5 and 7 Dec. 1794; Ott, *Haitian Revolution,* 85; Laird Clowes, *Royal Navy,* 4:251.

56. JFM, *Journal,* 1:13 and 14 Apr. 1795.

57. Scott, *Tropical Medicine,* 1:334. Monument to Major T. Drinkwater in Trinity Church, Salford, England.

58. O'Byrne, *Naval Biographical Dictionary,* 723.

CHAPTER 12

1. JFM, *Journal,* 1:5–26 May 1795.

2. Ibid., 1:26–30 May 1795.

3. Ibid., 1:6–24 June, 27 and 28 July, 6, 7, and 13 Aug. 1795.

4. Ibid., 1:9 Aug.–16 Sept. 1795.

5. Thomson, *Journal,* 15 Sept.–4 Nov. 1795, passim.

6. Ibid., 11–14 Nov. 1795; Richmond, *Spencer Papers,* 3:374–5; Ott, *Haitian Revolution,* 86; Cole, *Christophe,* 282.

7. Thomson, *Journal,* 18–26 Nov. 1795, gives this vivid and detailed account of the storm and near loss of the ship.

8. Thomson, *Journal,* 10 Feb. 1796.

9. *Gentleman's Magazine,* 1757, p. 88; 1789, p. 177; 1798, p. 1,152; 1799, p. 78; 1801, p. 66; 1811, p. 396. Berckman, *Portrait of St. Vincent,* 58, 218–20.

10. NC 13:165–6; NC, 20:1, 13; Phillimore, *Life of Parker,* 119, 152; JFM, *Journal,* 2:19 Oct. 1796.
11. T. Ricketts, *Journal,* 1 June 1796.
12. See JFM, *Journal,* 2:30 Mar. 1797, and 3:1 July 1797.
13. T. Ricketts, *Journal,* 16–7 July 1796.
14. JFM and T. Ricketts, *Journals,* 8–9 Aug. 1796; NC, 20:4.
15. JFM and T. Ricketts, *Journals,* 15 Oct. 1796.

Chapter 13

1. Gardner, *Recollections,* 278.
2. Pope, *Black Ship,* 72.
3. O'Byrne, *Naval Biographical Dictionary,* 841, 843; Otway's portrait is in Laird Clowes, *Royal Navy,* 6:250; NC, 20:1.
4. T. Ricketts, *Journal,* 16, 18, 27, 30, and 31 Aug. 1796.
5. JFM, *Journal,* 2:19 Oct. 1796.
6. Phillimore, *Life of Parker,* 118.
7. JFM, *Journal,* 2:2 and 3 Nov. 1796; Phillimore, *Life of Parker,* 100, 101; Marshall, *Royal Naval Biography,* 150; WHR to HP, *Magicienne,* off Altavela, 2 Nov. 1796, published in *London Gazette.*
8. JFM, *Journal,* 2:2 Nov. 1796; WHR to HP, 2 Nov. 1796; T. Ricketts, *Journal,* 2 Nov. 1796; Richmond, *Spencer Papers,* 3:245–6. Prize money for the *Cerf Volant* was not paid until 1826! Phillimore, *Life of Parker,* 115.
9. JFM, *Journal,* 2:3 Nov. 1796.
10. T. Ricketts, *Journal,* 8–9 Nov. 1796; Phillimore, *Life of Parker,* 101.
11. Phillimore, *Life of Parker,* 101, 127; T. Ricketts, *Journal,* 14–5 Nov. 1796.
12. T. Ricketts, *Journal,* 10, 14, and 15 Nov. 1796.
13. Ibid., 17 Nov. 1796.
14. JFM and T. Ricketts, *Journals,* 18 Nov. 1796
15. T. Ricketts, *Journal,* 18 and 23–9 Nov. 1796; JFM, *Journal,* 2:18 and 28 Nov. 1796.
16. JFM, *Journal,* 2:30 Nov., 2–3 Dec. 1796; Phillimore, *Life of Parker,* 101.
17. JFM, *Journal,* 2:30 Nov., 4 Dec. 1796; Phillimore, *Life of Parker,* 101, 118.
18. JFM, *Journal,* 2:5–10 Dec. 1796.
19. Ibid., 2:10–3 and 24 Dec. 1796; Phillimore, *Life of Parker,* 117.
20. JFM, *Journal,* 2:31 Aug., 26 Oct., 30 Dec. 1796, 5–6 Jan. 1797, and 3:31 May 1797.
21. Ibid., 2:9–11 Jan. 1797.
22. Ibid., 2:11 and 12 Jan. 1797; Phillimore, *Life of Parker,* 102.
23. JFM, *Journal,* 2:12 and 13 Jan. 1797.
24. Ibid., 2:13–5 Jan. 1797.
25. Ibid., 2:28 Mar. 1797 refers to her as their tender.
26. Ibid., 2:17–20 Jan. 1797.
27. Ibid., 2:21 and 26 Jan. and 2 Feb. 1797; Phillimore, *Life of Parker,* 102.
28. JFM, *Journal,* 2:7–10 Feb. 1797.
29. Ibid., 2:10–1 Feb. 1797.
30. Correlation of JFM, *Journal,* 2, with a modern chart indicates that they were probably attacking Mayaguez Bay. U.S. Defense Mapping Agency Chart 25700, *Mona Passage.*

31. JFM, *Journal,* 2:13–4 Feb. 1797; WHR to HP, 5 Apr. 1797; Phillimore, *Life of Parker,* 103.

32. JFM, *Journal,* 2:14 Feb. 1797; Phillimore, *Life of Parker,* 103 and note.

33. Laird Clowes, *Royal Navy,* 6:541; Phillimore, *Life of Parker,* 121–2. He later became Admiral of the Fleet Sir William Parker.

34. JFM, *Journal,* 2:14–5 Feb. 1797.

35. Ibid., 2:16 Feb. 1797.

36. Ibid., 2:20–6 Feb. 1797.

37. Ibid., 2:27 Feb., 3, 8, 9, 12, 13, 14, and 17 Mar. 1797.

38. Ibid., 2:28, 29, and 31 Mar. 1797; Phillimore, *Life of Parker,* 103.

39. JFM, *Journal,* 2:30–1 Mar. 1797.

40. The quote is from WHR to HP, 5 Apr. 1797, *London Gazette.*

41. Pope, *Black Ship,* 84–8.

42. JFM, *Journal,* 2:5 Apr. 1797.

43. Ibid., 2:6 Apr. 1797; Phillimore, *Life of Parker,* 104; James, *Naval History,* 2:101; Laird Clowes, *Royal Navy,* 4:335. James and Laird Clowes place the action at Cape Roxo in Saint-Domingue. JFM, *Journal,* 2, clearly places it on Porto Rico, as does NC, 20:4–5.

44. JFM, *Journal,* 2:7 Apr. 1797; Phillimore, *Life of Parker,* 104.

45. WHR to HP, Calabash Bay, 5 Apr. 1797; Admty, 22 July 1797, quoting HP's letter of 11 June 1797 and WHR's letter, Carcasse Bay, 24 Apr. [1797], all *London Gazette;* NC, 20:1–14.

46. Phillimore, *Life of Parker,* 106–7; JFM, *Journal,* 2:1 May 1797.

47. Ott, *Haitian Revolution,* 92–3.

48. JFM, *Journal,* 2:24 Apr. 1797.

49. Ibid., 2:24–5 Apr. 1797; Phillimore, *Life of Parker,* 104–7; James, *Naval History,* 2:102; Laird Clowes, *Royal Navy,* 4:335.

50. JFM, *Journal,* 2:29 Apr. 1797; Pope, *Black Ship,* 95–113.

51. JFM, *Journal,* 2:30 Apr.–6 May 1797; NC, 20:6–7.

52. JFM, *Journal,* 2:15 May 1797.

53. Ibid., 3:16–25 Aug. 1797; Pope, *Nelson's Navy,* 140.

54. James, *Naval History,* 2:103.

55. Pope, *Black Ship,* gives the full story of the mutiny.

56. Ibid., 214.

57. Ibid., 330–1.

58. JFM, *Journal,* 3:7 May 1798.

59. Berckman, *Portrait of St. Vincent,* 218–20; *Gentleman's Magazine,* 1801, p. 66.

60. NC, 13:166; *Gentleman's Magazine,* 1830, p. 91.

61. NC, 13:166; NC, 20:12–3; *Gentleman's Magazine,* 1805, p. 282.

62. Berckman, *Portrait of St. Vincent,* 220; She was the Honorable Cassandra Twistleton. *Gentleman's Magazine,* 1799, p. 78.

63. Berckman, *Portrait of St. Vincent,* 165, 220; British Library, Additional Manuscript 30012, folio 185, verso; NC, 17:415.

64. He was Mrs. Ricketts's nephew, Midn. Lord George Rosehill, eldest son of Admiral the Earl of Northesk, and Rev. Halloran, Northesk's chaplain, wrote the lines on the monument. NC, 17:415; Midn. Rosehill was lost in HMS *Blenheim* along with Adm. Troubridge and other notables. Also see Laird Clowes, *Royal Navy,* 5:395.

Chapter 14

1. Marshall, *Royal Naval Biography,* 152.
2. Richmond, *Spencer Papers,* 3:284–6, Spencer to HP, 10 Apr. and 11 May 1800; Pope, *Great Gamble,* 6.
3. Richmond, *Spencer Papers,* 3:261–83, passim.
4. Warner, *Nelson's Battles,* 109; Batter Pudding was a dish for the poor, often "a stout pale pudding, heavy and flabby," Pool, *Austen and Dickens,* 208.
5. Richmond, *Spencer Papers,* 3:373–4, 378.
6. Ibid., 3:376–7.
7. Ibid., 3:377; Smith, *Letters of St. Vincent,* 1:165.
8. *Journal, HMS Captain,* 14 Feb. 1797.
9. Herold, *The Age of Napoleon,* p. 182.
10. DeConde, *Quasi-War,* 296.
11. DeConde, *Quasi-War,* 303, 304.
12. Pope, *Great Gamble,* 67, 210 (note); Oman, *Nelson,* 433–69, passim.
13. Laird Clowes, *Royal Navy,* 4:191–5 (table), 291–2 (note). Cornwallis was available up to Feb. 1801. See also Smith, *Letters of St. Vincent,* 1:238–9.
14. Richmond, *Spencer Papers,* 3:18–9, 274, 378; Laird Clowes, *Royal Navy,* 4:108.
15. Smith, *Letters of St. Vincent,* 1:59.
16. Pope, *Great Gamble,* 159.
17. Maples, *Memo of Services.*
18. Pope, *Great Gamble,* 181 and note.
19. Smith, *Letters of St. Vincent,* 1:86–7.
20. Ibid., 1:60.
21. Ibid., 1:61–2; Pope, *Great Gamble,* 241.
22. Pope, *Great Gamble,* 312, 433.
23. There are other versions of this incident. This is taken from Pope, *Great Gamble,* 411.
24. Lewis, *Social History of the Navy,* 362 (table XI), 363, 365, 412, provides estimates by various authorities. Pope, *Great Gamble,* 446–7, is the expert on Copenhagen.
25. Maples, *Memo of Services.*
26. Vernadsky, *History of Russia,* 194–5.
27. Pope, *Great Gamble,* 493.
28. Smith, *Letters of St. Vincent,* 1:69.
29. O'Byrne, *Naval Biographical Dictionary,* 841–4.
30. Maples, *Memo of Services.*

Chapter 15

1. Keegan, *Price of Admiralty,* 13–4; Herold, *Age of Napoleon,* 195–7, 217–9.
2. Keegan, *Price of Admiralty,* 13–4.
3. NC, 14:481, plate opposite.
4. Warner, *Nelson's Battles,* 152.
5. James, *Naval History,* 3:280–3.
6. Laird Clowes, *Royal Navy,* 5:84–5.
7. Herold, *Age of Napoleon,* 144.

8. Laird Clowes, *Royal Navy,* 5:85 and note, 86; James, *Naval History,* 3:298.

9. Laird Clowes, *Royal Navy,* 5:92–3, 182–3.

10. Ibid., 5:89, 95–6.

11. Rear Adm. Murray to Capt. Sotheron, *Victory,* 7 Apr. 1805 (letter in author's collection).

12. Laird Clowes, *Royal Navy,* 5:97.

13. Ibid., 5:96.

14. James, *Naval History,* 3:337.

15. NC, 14:64; Laird Clowes, *Royal Navy,* 5:108–10.

16. Laughton, *Papers of Lord Barham,* 3:258–9.

17. Laird Clowes, *Royal Navy,* 5:111–8.

18. James, *Naval History,* 3:334–5.

19. Laird Clowes, *Royal Navy,* 5:121; James, *Naval History,* 4:17.

20. Herold, *Age of Napoleon,* 143–5.

21. Howarth, *Trafalgar,* 91–3; Pope, *England Expects,* 141–3.

22. James, *Naval History,* 4:21–2.

23. Oman, *Nelson,* 596–608.

24. Keegan, *Price of Admiralty,* 35, 51.

25. NC, 14:503–4 quotes Nelson's memorandum in full.

26. NC, 14:469.

27. James, *Naval History,* 4:25.

28. Captain's Log, *Naiad;* Master's Log, *Naiad;* Andrews, *Remarks, Naiad;* Jackson, *Logs of Sea Fights,* 2:139–327.

29. Captain's Log, *Naiad;* Master's Log, *Naiad,* 15–9 Oct. 1805; Jackson, *Logs of Sea Fights,* 2:146, "*Euryalus* Log," 18 Oct. 1805.

30. Captain's Log, *Naiad,* 19 Oct. 1805.

31. Jackson, *Logs of Sea Fights,* 2:145–7, "*Euryalus* Log," 18–9 Oct. 1805.

32. Master's Log, *Naiad,* 19 Oct. 1805; Andrews, *Remarks, Naiad,* 19 Oct. 1805.

33. Master's Log, *Naiad,* 20 Oct. 1805; Jackson, *Logs of Sea Fights,* 2:"*Euryalus* Log," 20 Oct. 1805; Andrews, *Remarks, Naiad;* Bridge, *Tactics at Trafalgar,* 2, 63, 96, 97.

34. Jackson, *Logs of Sea Fights,* 2:"*Euryalus* Log," 20 Oct. 1805; Bridge, *Tactics at Trafalgar,* 2, 24.

35. Bridge, *Tactics at Trafalgar,* 1; Taylor, *Battle of Trafalgar,* 288.

36. Bridge, *Tactics at Trafalgar,* ix, 24, 98, 99; Taylor, *Battle of Trafalgar,* 292.

37. NC, 14:469.

38. Allen, *Memoir of Hargood,* 283, 285; Laird Clowes, *Royal Navy,* 5:150–1; Howarth, *Trafalgar,* 194–5 (illustration).

39. Andrews, *Remarks, Naiad,* 22 Oct. 1805.

40. Beatty, *Death of Nelson,* passim; Oman, *Nelson,* 638.

41. Allen, *Memoir of Hargood,* 285, 287; Keegan, *Price of Admiralty,* 81; Andrews, *Remarks, Naiad,* 22 Oct. 1805.

42. Andrews, *Remarks, Naiad,* 22 Oct. 1805.

43. Captain's Log, *Naiad,* Master's Log, *Naiad,* 23 Oct. 1805.

44. Allen, *Memoir of Hargood,* 288–9.

45. Captain's Log, *Naiad,* Master's Log, *Naiad,* Andrews, *Remarks, Naiad,* all 24 Oct. 1805.

46. Allen, *Memoir of Hargood,* 290–1; Captain's Log, *Naiad,* Master's Log, *Naiad,* Andrews, *Remarks, Naiad,* all 25 Oct. 1805; Howarth, *Trafalgar,* 232.

47. Captain's Log, *Naiad,* Master's Log, *Naiad,* 24–31 Oct. 1805; Phillimore, *Life of Parker,* 153.

48. James, *Naval History,* 4:96–7.

49. Gerin, *Horatia Nelson,* 326.

50. James, *Naval History,* 4:96–7; Laird Clowes, *Royal Navy,* 5:166-8.

51. Steel, *List of the Royal Navy, 1806,* Aug. 1806; ADM 68/315, PRO.

52. O'Byrne, *Naval Biographical Dictionary,* 723.

53. NC, 24:349–50.

54. O'Byrne, *Naval Biographical Dictionary,* 723.

CHAPTER 16

1. Gosset, *Lost Ships of the Royal Navy,* 29; she may possibly have recovered and lasted until 1810—the record is unclear.

2. Notes on *Sheer Draught of the Childers,* NMM.

3. *Progress Books of the Admiralty,* 7:202.

4. James, *Naval History,* 6:221.

5. Steel, *List of the Royal Navy, 1812.*

6. JFM to JWC, 7 Nov. 1812, ADM 1/2171, PRO.

7. Crew data from *Muster Table of HMS Pelican,* ADM 37/4732, PRO.

8. JFM to Admty, *Ætna,* 22 Oct. 1812, ADM 1/2171, PRO.

9. JFM to JWC, *Pelican,* Hamoaze, 10 Nov. 1812, and JWC's note on reverse side, ADM 1/2171, PRO.

10. Physical data from *General Entry Book, Dartmoor,* ADM 103/90, records 5,725–9, 5,792, PRO.

11. JFM to JWC, *Pelican,* 26 Feb. 1813, ADM 1/2172, PRO.

12. Lt. James McGhie to JWC, Plymouth Sound, 5 Feb. 1813; JFM to JWC, 5 Feb. 1813, ADM 1/2172, PRO.

CHAPTER 17

1. Captain's Log, *Pelican,* 8 July 1813.

2. ET, *Journal,* 8 July 1813.

3. Captain's Log, *Pelican,* 9, 12, 19–20 July 1813; Master's Log, *Pelican,* 19–20 July 1813.

4. ET, *Journal,* 4 and 8 Aug. 1813; Captain's Log, *Pelican,* Master's Log, *Pelican,* 26 July–6 Aug. 1813.

5. *Officer's Journal,* 13–20 July 1813; Inderwick, *Journal,* 13–20 July 1813, NYPL; Crawford, *Journal,* 12–5 July 1813, LC.

6. *Muster Table of Argus,* "Supernumeraries for Victuals Only," no. 232, PRO.

7. RGB to Monroe, 30 Nov. 1812, *Consular Letters,* NA.

8. *Officer's Journal,* 21–2 July 1813; Inderwick, *Journal,* 20–2 July 1813, NYPL.

9. *Officer's Journal,* 22–4 July 1813; Inderwick, *Journal,* 22–4 July 1813, NYPL; *General Entry Book, Chatham,* 2,136–49.

10. *Prize Court Papers, Argus,* HCA 32/1793, PRO.

11. *Officer's Journal,* Inderwick, *Journal,* both 24 July 1813, NYPL; *General Entry Book, Chatham,* 2,136-49.

12. *Officer's Journal,* 27 July 1813; Inderwick, *Journal,* 27 July 1813, NYPL; *Muster Table of Argus,* Prisoners of War, 17-27, PRO.

13. Inderwick, *Journal,* 25, 27, and 28 July 1813, NYPL.

14. *London Times,* 29 July 1813.

15. *Officer's Journal,* 27 July 1813, says "painted ship's sides"; Lt. J. Fricker to ET, Kerry Head Signal Station, 1 Aug. 1813, says the *Argus* had "a bright yellow side"; also see Laird Clowes, *Royal Navy,* 6:86 (illustration).

16. *Officer's Journal,* Inderwick, *Journal,* both 28 and 31 July 1813, NYPL.

17. Fricker to ET, Kerry Head, 1 Aug. 1813, ADM 1/625, PRO; *Bell's Weekly Messenger,* 1813:263; *Muster Table of Argus,* Prisoners of War, 28-31, PRO; Inderwick, *Journal,* 1 Aug. 1813, NYPL.

18. ET to JWC, no. 673, Cork Harbor, 3 Aug. 1813, ADM 1/625, PRO.

19. ET to JWC, no. 702, Cork Harbor, 3 Aug. 1813, ADM 1/625, PRO; Inderwick, *Journal,* 3 and 4 Aug. 1813, NYPL.

20. ET, *Journal,* 4 Aug. 1813; Master's Log, *Pelican,* 5 and 6 Aug. 1813.

21. Inderwick, *Journal,* 5 Aug. 1813, NYPL.

22. ET to JWC, no. 702, Cork Harbor, 11 Aug. 1813, ADM 1/625, PRO; Inderwick, *Journal,* 6, 7, and 8 Aug. 1813, NYPL.

23. ET to JWC, no. 702, 11 Aug. 1813, ADM 1/625, PRO; Inderwick, *Journal,* 9 Aug. 1813, NYPL; *London Times,* 18 Aug. 1813; Master's Log, *Pelican,* 11 Aug. 1813.

24. Inderwick, *Journal,* 10 Aug. 1813, NYPL; ET to JWC, no. 702, 11 Aug. 1813, ADM 1/625, PRO.

25. ET to JWC, no. 702, 11 Aug. 1813, ADM 1/625, PRO.

26. Master's Log, *Pelican,* 11 Aug. 1813.

27. James, *Naval History,* 6:220; ET, *Journal,* 12 Aug. 1813.

28. Master's Log, *Pelican,* 12 Aug. 1813; Inderwick, *Journal,* 12 Aug. 1813.

29. Inderwick, *Journal,* 11 Aug. 1813; *London Times,* 16 Aug. 1813; *General Entry Book, Plymouth,* records 1894, 1878, 1919, 1923, 1888, 1897, 1875, 1905 and 1883, ADM 103/268.

30. Inderwick, *Journal,* 11 Aug. 1813, NYPL; *Niles Weekly Register,* 20 Nov. 1813, 206.

31. Seymour to ET, *Leonidas,* 18 Aug. 1813, enclosure to ET to JWC, no. 728, Cork Harbor, 19 Aug. 1813, ADM 1/625, PRO; LCA to ET, 7 Sept. 1813, ADM 2/996, PRO.

32. Inderwick, *Journal,* 9, 11, 12, and 13 Aug. 1813, NYPL; Paullin, *John Rodgers,* 275-6.

33. *London Times,* 18 Aug. 1813; Master's Log, *Pelican,* 13 and 14 Aug. 1813.

CHAPTER 18

1. Ridgely, *Court of Enquiry, Argus.*

2. WJ to WHA, 5 June 1813, *Letters to Officers,* RG 45, NA.

3. Paltsits, "Cruise of the *Argus,*" 389; James, *Naval History,* 6:221; *Port Folio,* 3:17.

4. Captain's Log, *Pelican,* Master's Log, *Pelican,* 14 Aug. 1813; W. H. Watson to BWC, 2 Mar. 1815, *Letters from Officers,* M-148, Roll 14, NA; Ridgely, *Court of Enquiry, Argus;* Mahan, *Sea Power in 1812,* 2:217–9; *Naval Temple,* 102; *London Times,* 18 Aug. 1813.

5. Ridgely, *Court of Enquiry, Argus,* Jamesson's testimony.

6. Cooper, *History of the Navy,* 2:190–1.

7. Eckert, *Navy Department in 1812,* 21; WJ to Mstr.-Cmdnt. Warrington, 26 Feb. 1814, RG 45, NA.

8. Dudley, *Documentary History,* 2:274–6; ET to JWC, 17 Aug. 1813, ADM 1/625, PRO.

9. Estes and Dye, "Death on the Argus," 179–95.

10. *Pension Application File, War of 1812, Navy Invalid,* no. 1,024.

11. Master's Log, *Pelican,* 14–7 Aug. 1813.

12. ET, *Journal,* 11 Aug. 1813; Master's Log, *Leonidas,* 15 Aug. 1813; *General Entry Book, Plymouth,* ADM 103/269, PRO.

13. ET to JWC, no. 728, 19 Aug. 1813, enclosing Capt. Seymour to ET, 18 Aug. 1813, ADM 1/625, PRO.

14. UPL to BWC, 22 Mar. 1816, *Letters from Officers,* M-148, Roll 17, no. 152, RG 45, NA.

15. ET, *Journal,* 18 Aug. 1813; NC, 30:246–7.

16. Anon. (Andrews), *Prisoners' Memoirs,* 50–1; ET to JWC, no. 727, enclosing Seymour to ET, 18 Aug. 1813, Admty to ET, order 675, ET to Admty, 30 July 1813, ADM 1/625, PRO; NC, 27:152–61.

17. ET to Admty, no. 727, 19 Aug. 1813, ADM 1/625, PRO.

18. Enclosure in Seymour to ET, 18 Aug. 1813, ADM 1/625, PRO.

19. JFM to Admty, 26 and 28 Aug., 14 Sept., 7 Nov. 1813, ADM 1/2174 and ADM 1/2175, PRO; JWC to JFM, 12 Nov. 1813, ADM 2/880, PRO.

20. Inderwick, *Journal,* 17–8 Aug. 1813, NYPL; *Port Folio,* 3:19.

21. Inderwick, *Journal,* 18 Aug. 1813, NYPL; John Hawker to WA, 19 Aug. 1813, in *Naval Temple,* 104–6; Estes and Dye, "Death on the *Argus,*" 192–3.

22. Obituary of WA, *Providence Gazette,* 19 Aug. 1815.

23. *Naval Temple,* Hawker to WA, 19 Aug. 1813.

24. NC, 30:180–2.

25. Tily, *Uniforms of the Navy,* 64, 74. The 1813 button had fifteen stars, but the earlier, still-worn button had thirteen.

26. *General Entry Book, Dartmoor,* records around 1,028, ADM 103/87, PRO; Anon. (Andrews), *Prisoners' Memoirs,* 82.

27. *General Entry Book, Plymouth,* record 2,563, ADM 103/270, PRO.

CHAPTER 19

1. TO to RGB, 4 Nov. 1813, ADM 98/291; *General Entry Book, Chatham,* records 2,136–49, ADM 103/58, PRO; *List of Officers of Argus on parole at Ashburton,* 18 May 1814, NA.

2. B. Thomson, *Dartmoor Prison,* 30.

3. *General Entry Book, Hector,* records 1,815–927, ADM 103/177, PRO.

4. WHC to RGB, Paris, 21 Sept. 1813, in Fay and Faulkner, "Journal of Crawford," 57–8.

5. *Muster Roll of Argus,* 233–9, NA.

6. B. Thomson, *Dartmoor Prison,* 108, 111–2; Anon. (Andrews), *Prisoners' Memoirs,* 51, 57, 63–7.

7. Anon. (Andrews), *Prisoners' Memoirs,* 67, 76.

8. *TO Out Letters,* ADM 98/291, 100, 101; *General Entry Book, Dartmoor,* ADM 103/87, records 570, 574, 602; *American Prisoners who have Died at Dartmoor,* 25 Mar.–13 May 1814, ADM 103/640, all PRO.

9. *The London Gazette Extraordinary,* 754, 785, 5 and 9 Apr. 1814, nos. 16,879, 16,882.

10. *General Entry Book, Dartmoor,* ADM 103/87, records 581, 567, 573, 638, 582, PRO.

11. *Inquest on James Henry,* ASSIZES 25/11/2, [5 July 1814]; *Exeter Assizes, Trial of Hill,* ASSIZES 23/10, 2 Aug. 1814, PRO.

12. *General Entry Book, Chatham,* records 2,136–49, ADM 103/58; *General Entry Book, Dartmoor,* records 2,923–30, ADM 103/89, all PRO.

13. *American Prisoner Deaths at Dartmoor,* 14–21 Oct. 1814, ADM 103/640, PRO.

14. *General Entry Book, Dartmoor,* ADM 103/87, entries with release date of 19 Oct. 1814, PRO.

15. *TO Out Letters,* 21 Sept., 31 Oct., 3 Nov. 1814, ADM 98/135; *TO Out Letters,* 9, 27, 28 Sept. 1814, ADM 98/291, PRO; *Norfolk Gazette,* 25 Feb. 1815.

16. TO to J. Gribble, 9 Nov. 1814, ADM 98/211, PRO.

17. J. T. Charnley to author, Ashburton, 18 May 1964; Pottenger to BWC, 2 Aug. 1815, *Letters from Officers,* RG 45, NA.

18. *General Entry Book, Dartmoor,* ADM 103/90, records 5,725–9, 5,792, PRO.

19. Palmer, *Diary,* 127.

20. Anon. (Cobb), *Green Hand's First Cruise,* 2:250–1; Anon. (Andrews), *Prisoners' Memoirs,* 138–9; Hawthorne, *Papers of an Old Dartmoor Prisoner,* 462–3; *Minutes of the Transport Board* (TB), 22, 6 Jan. 1815, ADM 99/259; TB to Admty, 4 Jan. 1815, 178, ADM 98/123; Rear Adm. T. B. Martin to JWC, 3 Jan. 1815, ADM 1/836, all PRO; W. E. May to author, 26 Oct. 1974; *Muster Books,* HMS *Impregnable* and HMS *St. George* for 1815, PRO.

21. *Norfolk Gazette and Ledger,* 25 Feb. 1815.

22. BWC to Gordon, 5 Mar. 1815; BWC to J. Elliott, 23 Mar. 1815, both in *Letters from the Secretary of the Navy to Officers, 1798–1868,* Record Group 45, M-149, Roll 12, NA.

Chapter 20

1. JWC to Navy Board, 1 Sept. 1813, ADM 2/677, PRO.

2. *Argus surveyed and valued,* 16 Sept. 1813, ADM 106/1942, PRO.

3. Navy Board to JWC, 25 Sept. 1813, ADM 106/2261; JWC to Navy Board, 28 Sept. 1813, ADM 2/678, PRO; Laird Clowes, *Royal Navy,* 6:187.

4. Chapelle, *History of American Sailing Navy,* 258; Lord, *Dawn's Early Light,* 118–9.

5. Laird Clowes, *Royal Navy,* 6:251, 252, 260; O'Byrne, *Naval Biographical Dictionary,* 567, 568, entry for C. L. Irby.

6. Laird Clowes, *Royal Navy,* 6:279–88; *The Progress Books of the Admiralty,* 7, entries for HMS *Pelican.*

7. *Columbian-Phenix,* 23 Oct. 1813.

8. Chapelle, *History of American Sailing Navy,* 298; Hooker, *Plan of New York,* NYPL.

9. Bailey, *American Naval Biography,* 218 note.

10. Mary Allen to SAR, 23 Jan. 1822, Huntington.

11. *National Intelligencer,* Washington, D.C., 26 Nov. 1857.

12. Smith, *American Naval Broadsides,* 177, 178.

13. Barnes, *JFK, Scrimshaw Collector,* 93–7.

14. Reilly, *US Navy Destroyers of World War II,* 6, 10; Koch to editor, USNI *Proceedings,* 95, Nov. 1971; Cover, USNI *Proceedings,* July 1971.

15. JFM to JWC, Lambeth, 7 Nov. 1813, ADM 1/2175; Admty to JFM, 12 Nov. 1813, ADM 2/880; JFM to JWC, Woodbridge, 25 Aug. 1814, ADM 1/2177, all PRO.

16. Her portrait, and a matching one of John Maples, are the property of Signor Godwin Spani, of Veroli, Italy, and the Seychelles Islands, her descendant.

17. Admty to JFM, 1 Sept. 1814, ADM 3/183, PRO; NC, 32:259-60.

18. Entry in IND 4918, 17 Sept. 1814, referring to ADM 3/183, PRO.

19. Admty minutes of 13 Dec. 1814, ADM 3/183, IND 4918; *Log of HMS Larne,* 19 Dec. 1814, ADM 51/2494; JFM to JWC, 17 Jan. 1815, all PRO.

20. Mr. Clifford P. Jeaffreson to author, 27 Dec. 1963; Mrs. Ida M. Williams to author, 10 Jan. 1964.

21. NC, 33:80–4; NC, 34:297–8; JFM to Admty, 27 Sept. 1815, ADM 1/2180, PRO.

22. Count Godwin Spani very kindly provided photographs of the portraits of John Maples and his wife.

23. Leslie, *Sea Wings,* xiii.

24. JFM, *Last Will and Testament.*

25. Ibid.

26. Ibid., codicil.

27. *Certified Copy of an Entry of Death,* District of St. John's, Middlesex, 1847, GRO, Somerset House, Application no. 410393.

28. Inderwick to WJ, 5 Sept. 1814, M-148, Roll 14, no. 106, Inderwick to BWC, 31 Jan. 1815, M-148, Roll 15, no. 76, *Letters from Officers,* RG 45, *Abstracts of Service Records,* RG 24, NA.

29. *Norfolk Gazette and Ledger,* 25 Feb. 1815.

30. Watson to BWC, 2 Mar. 1815, M-148, Roll 14, NA.

31. BWC to Ridgely, and BWC to Watson, 24 Mar. 1815, *Letters to Officers,* M-149, Roll 12, RG 45, NA; Ridgely, *Court of Enquiry,* 19 Apr. 1815.

32. Chapelle, *History of American Sailing Navy,* 324, 326, 330; SecNav to Howard Allen, 11 June 1822, M-149, nos. 323 and 325, RG 45, NA.

33. Strong, *Eulogium,* 11–4.

34. *Records of Officers,* William Henry Watson, RG 24, NA.

35. Paltsits, *Cruise of the Argus,* 386, note 22.

36. McLeod to BWC, 27 Mar. 1815, M-148, Roll 14, no. 113, RG 45, NA; *Pension Application File, War of 1812, Navy Invalid,* no. 1,024, RG 15, NA.

37. Leech, *Voice from the Main Deck,* 243–5, places the incident on 4 July 1816, but the Muster List says 17 Sept. 1816.

38. Affidavit by Watson, 20 Mar. 1815, in *Pension Application File, War of 1812, Navy Invalid,* no. 1,141, RG 15, NA.
39. *Pension Application File, War of 1812, Navy Invalid,* no. 1,141, RG 15, NA.
40. Pension Application file No. 887, RG 15.
41. *Norfolk Virginian,* 9, 10, and 11 Oct. 1873.
42. The card indicates that he bought the lot while a lieutenant; Jamesson was promoted to lieutenant in 1817 and became a commander in 1837.

Bibliography

It is certain beyond a reasonable doubt that the document called the "Log of the Frigate *George Washington*" in the Huntington Library (HM 250, entries from 14 August 1800 on) and the document called the "John Rodgers Logbook" (Log 227) in the G. W. Blunt White Library at the Mystic Seaport Museum are both journals kept by William Henry Allen. This conclusion is based on spelling anomalies that are identical in both journals and in Allen's letters of the same period; the formatting of the two documents; and a handwriting examination of the two journals and Allen's letters by a court-certified handwriting expert, who stated with a high degree of certainty that the same person wrote the journals and the letters.

Manuscript and Archival Sources

Abstracts of Service Records of Naval Officers, 1795–1893. Records of the Bureau of Naval Personnel. Record Group 24. Microfilm Roll M-330. National Archives.

Admirals' Letters to Admiralty. VADM Edward Thornbrough, ADM 1/625; RADM T. B. Martin, ADM 1/836. Public Record Office. London, England.

Allen Family Letters. Accession 4815. Library of Congress Manuscript Collection.

Allen, William Henry, *Journal kept on board the U.S. Frigate Chesapeake.* Huntington Library Manuscript HM 564. Henry E. Huntington Library and Art Gallery, San Marino, California.

[Allen, William Henry]. Journal kept on board the U.S. Frigate *George Washington,*
    (Log Book of the Frigate George Washington). Huntington Library Manuscript HM
    250. Henry E. Huntington Library and Art Gallery, San Marino, California.

[Allen, William Henry]. *Journal of the U.S. Frigate John Adams.* Log 227. G. W. Blunt
    White Library. Mystic Seaport Museum, Mystic, Connecticut.

Allen, William Henry. *Letters of William Henry Allen, and other Allen Family Letters.*
    Henry E. Huntington Library and Art Gallery, San Marino, California.

[Allen, William Henry?]. Portrait, *William Henry Allen, Esq., Late of the United States Navy.*
    David Edwin, sculpt. FDR Library, Hyde Park, New York. Accession 505, negative
    R-1949. Roosevelt-Vanderbilt National Historic Sites. National Park Service.

[Allen, William Henry?]. *"Quarter Bill, U.S.F.U.S., Stephen Decatur, Esq., Commander,*
    Lieut. Wm. H. Allen." Accession 4815. Manuscript Collection. Library of Congress.

[Andrews, Master Henry?]. An officer's journal kept on board H.M. Frigate *Naiad,* 19–25
    October 1805, headed *Remarks, etc., H.M.S. Naiad, off Cadiz,* then later, . . . *off Cape*
    Trafalgar. Four closely written folio sheets. Manuscript in the author's possession.

Argus, prize to the Pelican, Surveyed and Valued, etc. Plymouth Yard. 16 September 1813.
    ADM 106/1942. Public Record Office, London, England.

Baptisms in the year 1770. Parish of the Holy Trinity, Colchester, Essex, England.

Barron, Commodore James, et al. *The James Barron Papers I.* The Earl Gregg Swem
    Library, College of William and Mary, Williamsburg, Virginia.

Berkeley, Vice-Admiral George C., et al. *The Papers and Letters of Admiral George Cran-*
    field Berkeley. Metropolitan Toronto Reference Library, Toronto, Ontario,
    Canada.

Charlton, Lieutenant William. *Journal of the Proceedings of H.M.S. Blonde, 24 January*
    1791–31 December 1791, William Affleck, Esq., Commanding. Also another lieu-
    tenant's journal from the *Blonde,* author unknown. ADM/L/B/116. The Trustees of
    the National Maritime Museum, Greenwich, England.

Chesapeake-Leopard Archives. The Earl Gregg Swem Library, College of William and
    Mary, Williamsburg, Virginia.

Clarke, William M. *Journal of Surgeon William M. Clarke, 1812–1813.* Rare Books and
    Manuscripts Division. The New York Public Library. Astor, Lenox and Tilden
    Foundations.

Confidential Letters from the Secretary of the Navy. Record Group 45. National Archives.

Crawford, William Harris. *Journal Commencing on June 4th, 1813.* Manuscript Divi-
    sion. Library of Congress.

Croker, J. W. *Secretary's Common Letters to Captains and Lieutenants, R.N., from 7 Octo-*
    ber–25 December 1813. ADM 2/880. Public Record Office, London, England.

The General Entry Books for American Prisoners of War at Plymouth (ADM 103/268,269,270),
    Chatham (ADM 103/56,57,58,59) and Dartmoor (ADM 103/87,88,89,90,91). Public
    Record Office, London, England.

General Muster-Book. Muster Table of the United States Vessel of War the Argus between
    the 18th day of April 1813 and the [blank]. HCA 32/1793. Public Record Office, Lon-
    don, England.

Gordon, Charles. "Letters to John Bullus" in *Charles Gordon Personal Miscellaneous*
    Papers. Nine letters dated from 1811 to 1813. Rare Books and Manuscripts Divi-
    sion. New York Public Library. Astor, Lenox and Tilden Foundations.

Inderwick, James. *James Inderwick, Journal Kept on Board U.S. Brig Argus, May 11–August 21, 1813.* Rare Books and Manuscripts Division. New York Public Library. Astor, Lenox and Tilden Foundations.

An Intelligence Report to Admiral Sir J. B. Warren. 1812–1813. Manuscript in the author's possession.

Letters from the Secretary of the Navy to Officers, 1798–1868. M-149, Record Group 45. National Archives.

Letters Received by the Secretary of the Navy from Masters Commandant. M-147, Record Group 45. National Archives.

Letters Received by the Secretary of the Navy from Officers below the Rank of Commander, 1802–1884. M-148, Record Group 45. National Archives.

Lieutenants' Passing Certificates. Trustees of the National Maritime Museum, Greenwich, England.

List of the Officers of the late United States Brig Argus, Prisoners of War on parole at Ashburton. Document dated 18 May 1814 and marked "RA." Record Group 45. National Archives.

Log of H.M.S. Larne. 1814–1815 captain's log, ADM 51/2494. Public Record Office, London, England.

Log of H.M.S. Leonidas. Master's log, ADM 53/786 13880. Public Record Office, London, England.

Logs of H.M.S. Naiad. Captain's log, ADM 51/1518 2646; master's log, ADM 52/3659 2701. Public Record Office, London, England.

Log of H.M.S. Penelope (32). 1792–1794 captain's log, ADM 51/680. Public Record Office, London, England.

Log of H.M.S. Triumph. 1782–1784 captain's log, ADM 51/1015. Public Record Office, London, England.

Log of the Proceedings of H.M. Sloop Pelican between the 1st July and the 5th September 1813. Captain's log, ADM 51/2660, and master's log, ADM 53/1003. Public Record Office, London, England.

Log of the U.S. Brig Argus 1811–1813, and ship's orders at end of log for 1811. Records of the Bureau of Naval Personnel. RG 24. Microfilm Roll NNO-34(359). National Archives.

Log of the U.S. Frigate United States. 1812 and 1813. Records of the Bureau of Naval Personnel. Record Group 24. Microfilm Roll NNO-742 (213). National Archives.

Maples, John F. *A Journal of the Proceedings of H.M. Ship Magicienne, George Martin Esq, Commander, Beginning ye 18th of May 1794 and Ending the 20th of September 1795, Jno. Maples, Lieut.* (JFM, Journal 1). ADM/L/L/291. Trustees of the National Maritime Museum, Greenwich, England.

———. *Journal Kept by Lieut. Jno. Maples of His Majesty's Ship the Magicienne . . . of the Proceedings of Said Ship between 18 May 1796 and 17 May 1797.* (JFM, Journal 2). ADM/L/L/291. Trustees of the National Maritime Museum, Greenwich, England.

———. *A Journal of the Proceedings of His Majesty's Ship Magicienne, Wm. Hy. Ricketts, Esq., Commander, Commencing 18th May 1797 & Ending 17 May 1798.—Kept by John Maples, Lieut.* (JFM, Journal 3). ADM/L/L/291. Trustees of the National Maritime Museum, Greenwich, England.

————. *Last Will and Testament.* Somerset House, *Wills, 1847,* volume 2, Middlesex, July. Folio 596. London, England.

————. *Memorandum of the Services of Jno Fordyce Maples.* ADM 9/3. Public Record Office, London, England.

Minutes of the Transport Board. ADM 99/259. Public Record Office, London, England.

Muster Books of H.M.S. Impregnable and H.M.S. St. George. 1815. Public Record Office, London, England.

Muster List of the U.S. Frigate United States, 1812. Record Group 45. National Archives.

Muster Roll, No. 154 Ship George Washington, 1800. Misc. vol., Record Group 45. National Archives.

Muster Table of His Majesty's Ship the Pelican Between 5 November 1812 and the 31st day of December 1812. ADM 37/4732. Public Record Office, London, England.

Muster Tables of the U.S. Brig Argus. April 1812–April 1813. Microfilm NNO-34(359). National Archives.

An Officer's Journal, kept on board H.M.S. Agamemnon, May 15 to June 11, 1796, and H.M.S. Captain, June 11, 1796 to February 14, 1797. Manuscript formerly possessed by the author.

Officer's Journal. Log of the *Argus.* U.S. Brig, William H. Allen, Commander. April 7–August 1, 1813. Rare Books and Manuscripts Division. New York Public Library. Astor, Lenox and Tilden Foundations.

Pension Application Files, War of 1812. Record Group 15. National Archives.

Prize Court Documents relating to the Argus. HCA 32/1793. Public Record Office, London, England.

The Progress Books of the Admiralty. Volume 7. Admiralty Library, Ministry of Defence (Navy), London, England.

Ricketts, Lieutenant Tristram Robert. *Journal of the Proceedings on Board His Majesty's Ship La Magicienne, Commanded by William Henry Ricketts, Esq., From the Eleventh of May 1796 to the Twenty-third of December 1796, Kept by Tristram R. Ricketts.* ADM/L/L/291. Trustees of the National Maritime Museum, Greenwich, England.

Ridgely, Captain Charles G., U.S.N. *Proceedings of a Court of Enquiry Held at Baltimore to Investigate the Causes of the Capture of the U.S. Brig Argus, W.H. Allen, Master-Commandant, April 18, 1815.* Item 203. Record Group 125. National Archives.

Rodgers, John. *The John Rodgers Papers.* William L. Clements Library, University of Michigan, Ann Arbor.

Sheer Draught [and five other views] of the Childers, (and *Pelican,* et al.). Ships Plans Section, NMM. Trustees of the National Maritime Museum, Greenwich, London, England. Registered Numbers 3537, 3538A, 3539–3541, 3542A, Box 51, Admiralty, Whitehall.

Sheer Draught and Other Plans of La Magicienne. Ships Plans Section, NMM. Trustees of the National Maritime Museum, Greenwich, London, England.

Thomson, Lieutenant Andrew. *A Journal of the Proceedings of His Majesty's Ship Magicienne, George Martin, Esq., Captain, Commencing September 15th, 1795 and Ending May 10th, 1796, Andrew Thomson, 1st Lieutenant.* ADM/L/L/291. Trustees of the National Maritime Museum, Greenwich, England.

Thornbrough, Vice-Admiral Edward. *Journal of the Proceedings of Vice Admiral Edward Thornbrough, Commander-in-Chief of the Irish Station, Commencing the 24th day of*

June 1813 and Ending the 2nd of October 1813. ADM 50/70. Public Record Office, London, England.

Transport Board. *Out Letters of the Transport Board.* ADM 98. Public Record Office, London, England.

Whipple, Arnold. *Journal of Midshipman Arnold Whipple.* 16–24 June 1800. In the front section of Manuscript HM250. Huntington Library and Art Gallery, San Marino, California.

Whiteford, Joseph, et al. Coroner and jury for the County of Devon. *An Inquisition . . . on view of the body of James Henry then and here lying dead . . . etc.* 5 July 1813. ASSIZES 25/11/2. And *Trial of Thomas Hill.* 2 August 1813. ASSIZES 23/10. Public Record Office, London, England.

Willson, William. *A Journal of the Proceedings of HMS Magicienne from 8th July 1798 to 6th July 1799, Lieut. William Willson.* ADM/L/L/291. Trustees of the National Maritime Museum, Greenwich, England.

Books, Journal Articles, and Newspapers

Abell, Francis. *Prisoners of War in Britain, 1756 to 1815.* London: Oxford University Press. 1914.

Allen, Joseph, Esq. *Memoir of the Life and Services of Admiral Sir William Hargood, G.C.B., G.C.H., Compiled from Authentic Documents under the direction of Lady Hargood.* Printed for private circulation only. Greenwich, England: Henry S. Richardson, 1841.

[Andrews, Charles]. *The Prisoners' Memoirs.* New York: printed for the author, 1815.

An Argument Against War With Great Britain, Recently Published at Boston, by an American Farmer. London: J. Butterworth, 1807.

Arnold, James N. *Vital Record of Rhode Island, 1630–1850.* Vol. 2. Providence County. Providence, Rhode Island: Narragansett Historical Publishing Company, 1892.

Bailey, Isaac. *American Naval Biography.* Providence, Rhode Island: Published by Isaac Bailey, H. Mann and Co., Printers, 1815.

Barclay, Thomas. *Selections from the Coorrespondence of Thomas Barclay, Former British Consul-General at New York.* Ed. by George Lockhart Rives. New York: Harper and Brothers, Publishers, 1894.

Barham, Charles Lord. *Letters and Papers of Charles, Lord Barham, Admiral of the Red Squadron, 1758–1813.* Ed. by Sir John Knox Laughton. Three volumes. London: Printed for the Navy Records Society, 1911.

Barker, M. H. *The Old Sailor's Jolly Boat.* London: W. Strange, 1844.

Barnes, Clare, Jr. *John F. Kennedy, Scrimshaw Collector.* Boston: Little, Brown and Company, 1964.

Beatty, William, M.D. *Authentic Narrative of the Death of Lord Nelson.* London: Cadell and W. Davies, 1807.

Berckman, Evelyn. *Nelson's Dear Lord, A Portrait of St. Vincent.* London: Macmillan and Co., Ltd., 1962.

The Boston Repertory. Boston, Massachusetts, 1807.

Boudriot, Jean. *The History of the French Frigate, 1650–1850.* Rotherfield, United Kingdom: Jean Boudriot Publications, 1993.

Bridge, Admiral Sir Cyprian A. G., Admiral Sir Reginald N. Custance, and Professor Charles H. Firth. *Report of a Committee Appointed by the Admiralty to Examine and Consider the Evidence Relating to the Tactics Employed by Nelson at the Battle of Trafalgar.* HMSO Cd. 7120. London: Eyre and Spottiswoode, Ltd., 1913.

Brighton, The Reverend J. G., M.D. *Admiral Sir P.B.V. Broke, Bart., K.C.B., etc.: A Memoir.* London: Sampson Low, Son, and Marston, 1866.

Brown, John Howard. *American Naval Heroes.* Boston: Brown and Company, 1899.

Butler, B. F. *Defence of Uriah P. Levy, Before the Court of Inquiry, Held at Washington City, November and December, 1857.* New York: Wm. C. Bryant and Co., Printers, 1858.

Calderhead, William L. "A Strange Career in a Young Navy: Captain Charles Gordon, 1778–1816." *Maryland Historical Magazine.* Vol. 72, no. 3 (Fall 1977).

Calendar of Virginia State Papers. Richmond, Virginia.

Chapelle, Howard I. *The History of the American Sailing Navy.* New York: W. W. Norton and Company, Inc., 1949.

[Cobb, Josiah]. *A Green Hand's First Cruise.* Two volumes. Baltimore: Cushing and Brother, 1841.

Cole, Hubert. *Christophe, King of Haiti.* New York: The Viking Press, 1967.

Columbian Phenix, or, Providence Patriot. Providence, Rhode Island.

The Connecticut Gazette. New London, Connecticut.

Cooper, J. Fenimore. *The History of the Navy of the United States of America.* Two volumes. Paris: Baudry's European Library, 1839.

Cotter, Charles H. *A History of Nautical Astronomy.* New York: American Elsevier Publishing Company, Inc., 1968.

Crawford, William Harris. "The Journal of William H. Crawford." Ed. by S. B. Fay and H. U. Faulkner. *Smith College Studies in History.* Vol. XI, no. 1 (October 1925).

Cross, Charles B., Jr. *Chesapeake, A Biography of a Ship.* Chesapeake, Virginia: Published by the Norfolk County Historical Society, 1968.

DeConde, Alexander. *The Quasi-War: The Politics and Diplomacy of the Undeclared War with France, 1797–1801.* New York: Charles Scribner and Sons, 1966.

Delderfield, R. F. *Imperial Sunset, The Fall of Napoleon, 1813–14.* New York: Stein and Day, 1984.

De Segur, Count Philippe-Paul. *Napoleon's Russian Campaign.* Trans. from the French by J. David Townsend. Boston: Houghton Mifflin Company, 1958.

Douglas, Sir Howard. *A Treatise on Naval Gunnery.* Second edition. London: John Murray, 1829.

Dudley, William S., ed. *The Naval War of 1812, A Documentary History.* Two volumes. Washington: Naval Historical Center, 1985 and 1992.

Dunn, Richard S. *Sugar and Slaves: The Rise of the Planter Class in the English West Indies, 1624–1713.* New York: W. W. Norton & Company, 1972.

Dunne, W. M. P. "A Naval Architectural Study of the U.S. Brig Argus." *Nautical Research Journal.* Vol. 34, no. 3 (September 1989). Gloucester, Massachusetts: Nautical Research Guild. 126–36.

―――. *Resource Data File, Operational History, United States Frigate Chesapeake 1794–1820.* Unpublished manuscript. 1993.

―――. *Resource Data File, Operational History, United States Frigate John Adams, 1798–1867.* Unpublished manuscript. 1989.

————. *Resource Data File, Operational History, United States Ship George Washington, 1798–1802*. Unpublished manuscript. 1987.

Durand, James. George S. Brooks, editor. *James Durand An Able Seaman of 1812*. New Haven: Yale University Press, 1926.

Eckert, Edward K. *The Navy Department in the War of 1812*. Gainesville: University of Florida Press, 1973.

Estes, J. Worth, M.D. "Patterns of drug usage in Colonial America." *New York State Journal of Medicine*. Vol. 87 (January 1987).

Estes, J. Worth, M.D., and Ira Dye. "Death on the *Argus:* American Malpractise versus British Chauvinism in the War of 1812." *Journal of the History of Medicine and Allied Sciences*. Vol. 44, no. 2 (April 1989).

Five Naval Journals. Ed. by Rear-Admiral H. G. Thursfield. London: Printed for the Navy Records Society, 1951.

Fowler, William M., Jr. *Jack Tars and Commodores*. Boston: Houghton Mifflin Company, 1984.

Gardner, James Anthony. *The Recollections of James Anthony Gardner, Commander R.N. (1775–1814)*. Ed. by Admiral Sir R. Vesey Hamilton, G.C.B., and John Knox Laughton. London: Printed for the Navy Records Society, 1906.

A General View of the Rise, Progress, and Achievements of the American Navy. Brooklyn, New York: 1828.

Gentleman's Magazine. London. Issues of 1757, 1789, 1798, 1799, 1801, 1805, 1811, 1830.

Gerin, Winifred. *Horatia Nelson*. Oxford: Clarendon Press, 1970.

Gill, Claude S., arranger. *Steel's Elements of Mastmaking, Sailmaking and Rigging* (from the 1794 edition). London: W. & G. Foyle, Ltd., 1932.

Gore, John. *Nelson's Hardy and His Wife*. London: John Murray, 1935.

Gosset, W. P. *The Lost Ships of the Royal Navy, 1793–1900*. London: Mansell Publishing, Ltd., 1986.

Guernsey, R. S. *New York City and Vicinity During the War of 1812–'15*. Two volumes. New York: Charles L. Woodward, 1889.

Guttridge, Leonard F., and Jay D. Smith. *The Commodores*. New York: Harper and Row, 1969.

Hamersly, Lewis. *List of Officers of the Navy of the United States and Marine Corps from 1775 to 1900*. New York: L. R. Hamersly and Co., 1901.

Hawthorne, Nathaniel, ed. *Papers of an old Dartmoor Prisoner*. New York: Published in seven parts in the *U.S. Democratic Review*. January through September 1846.

Henningsen, Henning. *Crossing the Equator, Sailors' Baptism and Other Initiation Rites*. Copenhagen: Munksgaard, 1961.

Herold, J. Christopher, and Marshall B. Davidson, editor in charge. *The Horizon Book of the Age of Napoleon*. New York: American Heritage Publishing Company, 1963.

Hooker, W. *Plan of the City of New York*. Engraved by W. Hooker. New York: Blunt's Strangers Guide, October 1817. The Map Division, New York Public Library. Astor, Lenox and Tilden Foundation.

Hoppin, Hon. William W. "Memoir of Governor William Jones." *Proceedings of the Rhode Island Historical Society, 1875–76*. Providence (1876).

Howard, Leon. "Joel Barlow and Napoleon." *Huntington Library Quarterly*. Vol. II, no. 1 (October 1938).

Howarth, David. *Trafalgar, The Nelson Touch.* New York: Atheneum, 1969.

James, William. *A Full and Correct Account of the Chief Naval Occurrences of the Late War between Great Britain and the United States of America.* London: T. Egerton, 1817.

————. *The Naval History of Great Britain.* Six volumes. London: Richard Bentley, 1837.

Jervis, Admiral John. *Letters of Admiral of the Fleet The Earl of St. Vincent.* Ed. by David Bonner Smith. Two volumes. London: Printed for the Navy Records Society, 1922.

Keegan, John. *The Price of Admiralty.* New York: Viking Penguin, Inc., 1989.

Keith, Admiral Lord. *The Keith Papers.* Ed. by Christopher Lloyd. London: Printed for the Navy Records Society, 1955.

Laird Clowes, William, et al. *The Royal Navy, A History from the Earliest Times to the Present.* Seven volumes. London: Sampson Low, Marston and Company, 1897 to 1903.

Langley, Harold D. *Social Reform in the United States Navy, 1798–1862.* Urbana: University of Illinois Press, 1967.

Leech, Samuel. *Thirty Years From Home, or, A Voice From the Main Deck.* Fifteenth edition. Boston: Tappan, Whittemore and Mason, 1843.

Leslie, R. C. *Old Sea Wings Ways and Words.* London: Chapman and Hall, Ltd., 1930.

Lewis, Michael. *A Social History of the Navy, 1793–1815.* London: George Allen & Unwin Ltd., 1960.

Lloyd, Christopher, and Jack L. S. Coulter. *Medicine and the Navy, 1200–1900.* Edinburgh and London: E. & S. Livingstone, Ltd., 1961.

Logs of the Great Sea Fights, 1794–1805, Ed. by Rear-Admiral T. Sturges Jackson. Two volumes. London: Printed for the Navy Records Society, 1900.

The London Gazette (and Gazette Extraordinary). London: various dates between 1792 and 1815.

The London Times. London, England.

Long, David F. *Ready to Hazard, A Biography of Commodore William Bainbridge, 1774–1833.* Hanover, New Hampshire: University Press of New England, 1981.

Longford, Elizabeth. *Wellington, The Years of the Sword.* New York and Evanston: Harper & Row, 1969.

Lord, Walter. *The Dawn's Early Light.* New York: Dell Publishing Co., Inc., 1972.

Mahan, Captain A. T. *Sea Power in its Relations to the War of 1812.* Two volumes. London: Sampson Low, Marston and Company, Ltd., 1903 and 1904.

Marshall, John. *Royal Naval Biography,* London: Printed for Longmans, Rees, Orme, Brown, and Green, 1829.

McKee, Christopher. *A Gentlemanly and Honorable Profession, The Creation of the U.S. Naval Officer Corps, 1794–1815.* Annapolis: Naval Institute Press, 1991.

————. *Edward Preble, A Naval Biography, 1761–1807.* Annapolis: Naval Institute Press, 1972.

————. "Foreign Seamen in the United States Navy: A Census of 1808." *The William and Mary Quarterly.* 3rd series, vol. 42 (July 1985).

McNeill, William H. *Plagues and People.* Garden City, New York: Anchor Books, Anchor Press/Doubleday, 1976.

Minard, Charles Joseph. *Carte Figurative des pertes successives en hommes de l'Armée Française dans la campagne de Russie 1812–1813,* (Paris, le 20 Novembre 1869). Reprint. Cheshire, Connecticut: Graphics Press, 1987.

Mona Passage. West Indies. Chart 25700. Washington: U.S. Defense Mapping Agency, 1992.

Mooney, Chase C. *William H. Crawford, 1772–1834*. Lexington, Kentucky: The University of Kentucky Press, 1974.

The National Intelligencer and Washington Advocate. Washington, D.C. 13–18 November 1805; 26 November 1857.

The Naval Chronicle. Ed. by Joyce Gold. Thirty-six volumes. London: Bunney and Gold (later by Joyce Gold), 1797–1816.

Naval Regulations. 25 January 1802. Facsimile reprint. Annapolis: U.S. Naval Institute, 1970.

The Naval Temple. Boston: Barber Badger, 1816.

The Newport Mercury. Newport, Rhode Island. December 12, 26, 1812.

Newton, Charles. "Stratford Canning's Pictures of Turkey." In *The V & A Album 3*. London: DeMontfort Publishing, Inc., 1977.

The New York Gazette & General Advertiser. New York, New York. 12 October 1813.

The Norfolk Gazette and Publick Ledger. Norfolk, Virginia. Various dates in November 1805, June and July 1807, February 1815.

The Norfolk Herald. Norfolk, Virginia. 3 December 1799.

The Norfolk Virginian. Norfolk, Virginia. 9–11 October 1873.

O'Byrne, William R. *A Naval Biographical Dictionary*. London: John Murray, 1849.

Oman, Carola. *Nelson*. Garden City, New York: Doubleday and Company, Inc., 1946.

Ott, Thomas O. *The Haitian Revolution, 1789–1804*. Knoxville: The University of Tennessee Press, 1973.

Palmer, Benjamin F. *The Diary of Benjamin F. Palmer, Privateersman*. New Haven: Privately printed for The Acorn Club by The Tuttle, Morehouse and Taylor Press, 1914.

Paltsits, Victor Hugo. "Cruise of the U.S. Brig *Argus* in 1813." *Bulletin of the New York Public Library*. Vol. 21, no. 6 (June 1917).

Parkinson, C. Northcote, ed. *The Trade Winds*. London: George Allen and Unwin Ltd., 1948.

Paullin, Charles Oscar. "Dueling in the Old Navy." U.S. Naval Institute *Proceedings*. Vol. 35, part 2, whole numbers 131, 132. Annapolis (1909).

———. *Commodore John Rodgers, 1773–1838*. Annapolis: Naval Institute Press, 1967.

Perkins, Bradford. *Prologue to War*. Berkeley: University of California Press, 1974.

Phillimore, A. *The Life of Admiral of the Fleet Sir William Parker, 1781–1876*. London: 1876. Library of Congress copy.

Pocock, Nicholas. *Six Engraved Outlines of Ships of War, From a First-rate to a Cutter*, London: R. Martin, 1815.

Pool, Daniel. *What Jane Austen Ate and Charles Dickens Knew*. New York: Simon and Schuster, 1993.

Pope, Dudley. *The Black Ship*. London: Weidenfeld and Nicolson, 1963.

———. *England Expects*. London: Weidenfeld and Nicolson, 1959.

———. *The Great Gamble*. New York: Simon and Schuster, 1972.

———. *Life in Nelson's Navy*. Annapolis: Naval Institute Press, 1981.

Popham, Sir Home. *Telegraphic Signals or Marine Vocabulary*. London: T. Egerton, 1803.

The Port Folio, Third Series, Conducted by Oliver Oldschool, Esq. Vol. III, no. 1. 1814.

Proceedings of the General Court Martial Convened for the Trial of Commodore James Barron, Captain Charles Gordon, Mr. William Hook, and Captain John Hall, of the United States' Ship Chesapeake, in the Month of January, 1808. Washington?: By order of the Navy Department. Printed by Jacob Gideon, Junior, 1822.

The Providence Gazette and Country Journal, Providence, Rhode Island. 19 August 1815.

Rea, John. *A Letter to William Bainbridge, Esqr., Formerly Commander of the United States Ship George Washington; Relative to some transactions on board said ship, during a voyage to Algiers, Constantinople, &c. By John Rea, at that time, an ordinary seaman on board.* Philadelphia: Printed for the author, 1802.

Rediker, Marcus. *Between the Devil and the Deep Blue Sea.* Cambridge: Cambridge University Press, 1987.

Reilly, John C., Jr. *United States Navy Destroyers of World War II.* Poole, United Kingdom: Blandford Press, 1983.

The Rhode Island American and General Advertiser. Providence, Rhode Island. 15 December 1812 and 8 January 1813.

Riasanovsky, Nicholas V. *A History of Russia.* Second edition. New York: Oxford University Press, 1969.

Richardson, William, Colonel Spencer Childers, C.B., R.E., ed. *A Mariner of England.* London: Conway Maritime Press, first published 1908, new impression 1970.

Riehn, Richard K. *1812: Napoleon's Russian Campaign.* New York: John Wiley and Sons, Inc., 1991.

Rorabaugh, W. J. *The Alcoholic Republic, An American Tradition.* New York: Oxford University Press, 1979.

Roscoe, Theodore, and Fred Freeman. *Picture History of the U.S. Navy.* New York: Charles Scribner's Sons, 1956.

Scott, H. Harold. *A History of Tropical Medicine.* Two volumes. Baltimore: The Williams and Wilkins Company, 1939.

Seybert, Adam. *Statistical Annals of the United States.* Philadelphia: Thomas Dobson & Son, 1818.

Shipp, J. E. D. *Giant Days, or, The Life and Times of William H. Crawford.* Americus, Georgia: Southern Printers, 1909.

Signal Book for the Ships of War. London: Published by the Admiralty, London, England, circa 1794.

Smith, Edgar Newbold. *American Naval Broadsides.* New York: Philadelphia Maritime Museum and Clarkson N. Potter, Inc., 1974.

Spencer, George, 2nd Earl. *Private Papers of George, second Earl Spencer, First Lord of the Admiralty, 1794–1801.* Ed. by Julian S. Corbett. Two volumes. London: Printed for the Navy Records Society, 1913 and 1914.

———. *Private Papers of George, Second Earl Spencer, First Lord of the Admiralty, 1794–1801.* Ed. by Rear-Admiral H. W. Richmond. Two volumes. London: Printed for the Navy Records Society, 1924.

Steel, David. *List of the Royal Navy,* for 1806, 1812, 1813. London.

Strong, Hon. James. *An Eulogium, Pronounced by the Hon. James Strong at Hudson, N.Y., Upon the Late Lieut. Com. Allen, of the U.S. Navy, who was killed in an Engagement between the U.S. Schooner Alligator, and Three Piratical Vessels, off Matanzas.* New York: W. Grattan and T. Longworth, 1822.

Tatham, William. *The Defence of Norfolk in 1807, as told by William Tatham To Thomas Jefferson*. Ed. by Norma Lois Peterson. Chesapeake, Virginia: Published by the Norfolk County Historical Society of Chesapeake, Virginia, 1970.

Taylor, Rear-Admiral A. H. *The Battle of Trafalgar*. Reprinted from *The Mariner's Mirror*. Vol. 36, no. 4 (October 1950).

Thomson, Basil. *The Story of Dartmoor Prison*. London: William Heineman, 1907.

Tily, James C. *The Uniforms of the United States Navy*. New York: Thomas Yoseloff, 1964.

Todd, Charles Burr. *Life and Letters of Joel Barlow, LL.D.* New York and London: G. P. Putnam's Sons, 1886.

Treaties, &c., [no date, title page missing], circa 1830. In author's collection.

The Trial of John Wilson, alias Jenkin Ratford, for Mutiny, Desertion and Contempt, to which are subjoined a Few Cursory Remarks. Halifax: John Howe and Son, 1807.

Vernadsky, George. *A History of Russia*. Sixth edition. New Haven: Yale University Press, 1969.

Walker, Anthony. *So Few The Brave (Rhode Island Continentals, 1775–1783)*. Newport: Seafield Press, 1981.

The War, being a faithful record of the transactions of the war between the United States . . . and . . . Great Britain. New York: S. Woodworth and Co., 1812–1814. A weekly newspaper devoted to events of the war.

War in Disguise; or, The Fraud of the Neutral Flags. Fifth Edition. London: J. Hatchard and J. Butterworth, 1807.

Warner, Oliver. *Nelson's Battles*. New York: The Macmillan Company, 1965.

Woodress, James. *A Yankee's Odyssey, The Life of Joel Barlow*. Philadelphia/New York: J. B. Lippincott Company, 1958.

Index

About the Author

Ira Dye served in the U.S. Navy as a submarine officer during World War II and the Korean War and until retiring as a captain in 1967. He has navigated most of the areas where the actions in this book took place, and as an ex-skipper himself is thoroughly familiar with how the captain of a small ship thinks and acts. He has researched deeply into the story of the *Argus* and *Pelican* and into the details of the lives of the men who sailed the two ships and has published sixteen articles about how the sailors of the early nineteenth century lived and worked. He lives in Virginia Beach about three miles from the place offshore where the *Leopard* attacked the *Chesapeake*.

NAVAL INSTITUTE PRESS

THE FATAL CRUISE OF THE *ARGUS*
Two Captains in the War of 1812

Set in Granjon and Weiss on the Macintosh Quadra 610
Printed on 50-lb. Glatfelter eggshell cream
and bound in ICG Arrestox
by The Maple-Vail Book Manufacturing Group
York, Pennsylvannia